THEORETICAL ISSUES IN PSYCHOLOGY

Proceedings of the International Society for Theoretical Psychology 1999 Conference

edited by

John R. Morss
Dunedin, New Zealand

Niamh Stephenson
University of Western Sydney

Hans van Rappard
Free University, Amsterdam

KLUWER ACADEMIC PUBLISHERS
Boston / Dordrecht / London

D1206218

Distributors for North, Central and South America:
Kluwer Academic Publishers
101 Philip Drive
Assinippi Park
Norwell, Massachusetts 02061 USA
Telephone (781) 871-6600
Fax (781) 681-9045
E-Mail <kluwer@wkap.com>

Distributors for all other countries:
Kluwer Academic Publishers Group
Distribution Centre
Post Office Box 322
3300 AH Dordrecht, THE NETHERLANDS
Telephone 31 78 6392 392
Fax 31 78 6546 474
E-Mail <services@wkap.nl>

 Electronic Services <http://www.wkap.nl>

Library of Congress Cataloging-in-Publication Data
International Society for Theoretical Psychology. Conference (8th : 1999 : Sydney, Australia)
  Theoretical issues in psychology: proceedings of the International Society for
Theoretical Psychology 1999 conference / edited by John R. Morss, Niamh Stephenson,
Hans van Rappard.
    p. cm.
  Includes bibliographical references and index.
  ISBN 0-7923-7337-5 (alk. paper)
  1. Psychology—Congresses. I. Morss, John R. II. Stephenson, Niahm. III. Rappard,
Hans V. IV. Title.

BF20 .I64 2001
150—dc21   2001022506

Printed on acid-free paper.

Printed in the United States of America

*The Publisher offers discounts on this book for course use and bulk purchases.
For further information, send email to <michael.williams@wkap.com>.*

CONTENTS

I EMBODIED EXPERIENCE

II SOCIAL AND CULTURAL PROCESSES

vi

III PERCEPTION, COGNITION AND REASONING

IV SOCIAL CONSTRUCTIONISM AND METATHEORETICAL ISSUES

viii

VI THERAPY AND THE UNCONSCIOUS

CONTRIBUTORS

Michael Andrews Psychology Department, University of Guelph, Guelph, ON N1G 2W1, Canada

Cor Baerveldt NCPG, Department of Cultural Psychology, University of Nijmegen, PO Box 9104, 6500 HE Nijmegen, The Netherlands baerveldt@psych.kun.nl

Natasha Bauer Department of Psychology, York University, North York, ON M3J 1P3, Canada

Angelina Baydala Department of Psychology, University of Calgary, 2500 University Drive N.W., Calgary, Alberta T2N 1N4, Canada ambaydala@ucalgary.ca

Betty Bayer Department of Psychology, Hobart and William Smith Colleges Geneva, New York 14456-3397, USA

Ciarán Benson Department of Psychology, University College, Belfield, Dublin 4, Ireland

Steven D. Brown Department of Human Sciences, Loughborough University, Leics, LE11 3TU, UK   s.d.brown@lboro.ac.uk

Ailsa Burns Department of Psychology, Macquarie University, NSW 2109, Australia

Sue Edmonds Psychology Department, University of Guelph, Guelph, ON N1G 2W1, Canada

Rachel Joffe Falmagne Department of Psychology, Clark University, 950 Main Street, Worcester, MA 01610-1477, USA   rfalmagne@clarku.edu

Angela Febbraro Department of Psychology, Wilfrid Laurier University, Waterloo, ON, N2L, Canada

Mark Ferris Department of Psychology, University of Western Ontario, Canada

Ann Game School of Sociology, University of New South Wales, Sydney 2052, Australia

Fiona J. Hibberd Department of Psychology, University of Sydney, NSW 2006, Australia

Martin Hildebrand-Nilshon Institute for Critical Psychology, Free University of Berlin, Marienburger Allee 13, 14055 Berlin, Germany
hildenil@zedat.fu-berlin.de

Ian Hodges Department of Psychology, University of Westminster, 309 Regent Street London W1R 8AL, UK   I.Hodges@wmin.ac.uk

Arnd Hofmeister Centre for Critical Psychology, University of Western Sydney, Nepean, PO Box 10, Kingswood, NSW 2747, Australia   arnd-h@gmx-de

Rosemary Leonard School of Social, Community and Organisational Studies, University of Western Sydney, Nepean, PO Box 10, Kingswood, NSW 2747, Australia   r.leonard@uws.edu.au

Ian Lubek Psychology Department, University of Guelph, Guelph, ON N1G 2W1, Canada

Peter Lunt Department of Psychology, University College, London, UK

Doris McIlwain Department of Psychology, Macquarie University, NSW 2109, Australia   dcmcilwai@bunyip.psy.mq.edu.au

Terence McMullen Department of Psychology, University of Sydney, NSW 2006, Australia   terrym@psych.usyd.edu.au

Wolfgang Maiers Institute for Critical Psychology, Free University of Berlin Marienburger Allee 13, 14055 Berlin, Germany   maiers@zedat.fu-berlin.de

John R. Morss 107 Wickliffe Terrace, Port Chalmers, Dunedin, New Zealand
morjo483@student.otago.ac.nz

Johanna Motzkau Institute for Critical Psychology, Free University of Berlin, Marienburger Allee 13, 14055 Berlin, Germany   jomo@zedat.fu-berlin.de

Lars Näcke Institute for Critical Psychology, Free University of Berlin, Marienburger Allee 13, 14055 Berlin, Germany   naecke@psychologie.de

Claudia Orthmann Centre for Media Research, Malteser Str 74-100, 12249 Berlin, Germany   orthmann@cmr.fu-berlin.de

Ute Osterkamp Institute for Critical Psychology, Free University of Berlin, Marienburger Allee 13, 14055 Berlin, Germany   oster@zedat.fu-berlin.de

Dimitris Papadopoulos Institute for Critical Psychology, Free University of Berlin, Marienburger Allee 13, 14055 Berlin, Germany papado@zedat.fu-berlin.de

David Paré Faculty of Education, Room 231 Lamoreux Hall, University of Ottawa, 445 Jean Jacques Lussier, PO Box 450 Stn A, Ottawa Ont K1N 6N5, Canada   dpare@uottowa.ca

Eri Park Institute for Critical Psychology, Free University of Berlin, Marienburger Allee 13, 14055 Berlin, Germany   park@zedat.fu-berlin.de

Christopher Peet P-220, Biological Sciences Building, Psychology Department, University of Alberta, Edmonton, Alberta, T6G 2E9 Canada chris.peet@ualberta.ca

Agnes Petocz Department of Psychology, University of Western Sydney Macarthur, PO Box 555, Campbelltown NSW 2560, Australia a.petocz@uws.edu.au

Hans van Rappard Department of Psychology, Vrije Universiteit Amsterdam, Van der Boechorststraat 1, 1081 BT Amsterdam, The Netherlands jfh.van.rappard@psy.vu.nl

Katrina Roen 40 Tamar Street, Island Bay, Wellington, New Zealand katravels@yahoo.com

Brian Ross Department of Psychology, York University, North York, ON M3J 1P3, Canada

Donald L. Rowe Brain Dynamics Centre, Psychological Medicine, Westmead Hospital, NSW 2145, Australia   drowe@physics.usyd.edu.au

Inna Semetsky Teachers College, Columbia University, New York NY, USA
irs5@columbia.edu

Lee Spark Jones Department of Psychology, University of Wollongong, NSW,
Australia   leesparkj@aol.com

Henderikus J. Stam Department of Psychology, University of Calgary, 2500
University Drive N.W., Calgary Alberta T2N 1N4 Canada
stam@ucalgary.ca

Niamh Stephenson Centre for Critical Psychology, University of Western Sydney,
Nepean, PO Box 10, Kingswood, NSW 2747, Australia
n.stephenson@uws.edu.au

Gavin B. Sullivan School of Health & Nursing ,University of Western Sydney,
Nepean, Cumberland Hospital, PO Box 10, Kingswood, NSW 2747, Australia
g.sullivan@uws.edu.au

Heather Thoms-Chesley Psychology Department, University of Guelph, Guelph,
ON N1G 2W1, Canada

Theo Verheggen NCPG, Department of Cultural Psychology, University of
Nijmegen, PO Box 9104, 6500 HE Nijmegen, The Netherlands
verheggen@psych.kun.nl

Paul Voestermans NCPG, Department of Cultural Psychology, University of
Nijmegen, PO Box 9104, 6500 HE Nijmegen, The Netherlands
voestermans@psych.kun.nl

PREFACE

Theoretical Issues in Psychology is published as the discipline of psychology enters its (at least) third century. The year 2001 brings with it millennial reflections, as well as the strange sense of *déjà vu* that we derive from the Kubrick movie. As to the former, a glance at the contents list of this volume will demonstrate both the maturity and the vigour of theoretical debate within psychology. There is a level of sophistication here that should be the cause of quiet celebration. Recent ideas about discursive practice and subjectivity, chaos theory and autopoiesis, are effortlessly entrained with classical issues. Canonical texts are looked at with fresh eyes. Unresolved social and political questions are doggedly persisted with, and new perspectives on the human experience are pioneered. We are not afraid of long words, even if French in origin, but nor are we afraid to recognise that we are physical beings who touch other beings, who hold, desire, and remember – and who talk, talk, talk.

For surely it is theoretically-sensitive work in psychology – whether "critical" or not – that best represents what the discipline has to offer the wider community. Working with people as they construct memories or re-sex their bodies; working with therapists as they struggle to assimilate new perspectives; challenging, while not off-handedly rejecting, the hugely significant claims of the evolutionary psychologists; struggling to comprehend the fascist extremes of people's treatment of other people; quietly re-examining platitudes about supposedly outmoded approaches; even daring to ask why the mainstream persists in downplaying the significance of theoretical work (publish *and* perish) when theoretical work is its lifeblood… All of these enterprises, and many more, are represented in this millennial collection.

As for *2001: A Space Odyssey*: there are no shortage of connections that one might make between that movie and the topics covered in this volume. Cultural evolution; "man"-machine interaction and "man"-machine interchangeability; mysticism; memory; recapitulation; Nietzsche; fear, hope, and awe. Like theoretical psychology, human, all-too-human.

The papers in this volume have been selected from the programme of the Eighth Biennial Conference of the International Society for Theoretical Psychology (ISTP), held in Sydney in April 1999. The work of the editors has been greatly eased by the diligence of authors in getting submissions submitted and revisions attended to almost always in good time and always cheerfully. Editing has been a collaborative process both among the team and between authors and ourselves. This has been made possible by the magic of electronic communication. Facilities for institution-less JRM to play his part in this process were made available by Maria Nichterlein without whose practical, as well as spiritual contribution, the troika would have been a duo. Thanks are also due to the staff of Kluwer for their patience and encouragement in bringing this project to fruition.

Theoretical psychology is in good heart and it is a genuinely international enterprise. This year the ISTP Conference returns to Canada. It is hoped that this book will help to set the agenda and the tone for the Conference as it carries on the project of the careful thinking and the thoughtful caring about being human, that is surely the task of theoretical psychology.

THE EDITORS

I EMBODIED EXPERIENCE

CREATIVE WAYS OF BEING

Ann Game
University of New South Wales

SUMMARY

This paper considers the idea that creative states of aliveness and openness to newness (in art, in academic knowledge, and in everyday life) involve a relational way of being in which self as subject, agent, author, identity is suspended. Drawing on Winnicott's account of transitional space, the paper develops an understanding of the between state of holding as a precondition for creativity, arguing that holding and openness presuppose each other, thus demonstrating the ways in which betweenness contributes to an understanding of the spiritual character of creative experiences.

HOLDING PARADOX

It sometimes happens that an idea comes to life for us. In these moments we find ourselves living, experiencing that idea; we can feel it. Then that experience- idea goes, and then it comes again. Each time it returns, it does so as new, as if for the first time. These experiences of knowing defy any grasping, and just as well, for with the elusiveness comes the aliveness. Each instance of an idea coming to life is in a sense the first, and yet not: simultaneously we feel we have experienced this idea before and that we are experiencing it as new. In fact I keep having this sort of experience in connection with this idea itself. Looking over old writings, I find I have said it before. Now it has come to me again, anew, and I want to say "I have got it now – the idea, that is, that knowing involves experiencing, and that with experience comes a sense of newness". In this common enough experience, I learn that when, in welcoming the mysterious, we let go of a desire for

4

an end, knowledge becomes a living knowledge, and we are enlivened. Thus it is that in these moments of coming to life and newness, I have glimpses of the possibilities for creativity in knowledge practices.

William James cites this sort of experience as an example of the mystical in everyday life:

> The simplest rudiment of mystical experience would seem to be that deepened sense of the significance of a maxim or formula which occasionally sweeps over one. "I've heard that said all my life," we exclaim, "but I never realized its full meaning until now." (1982, p. 382)

As James says, this sense of deeper significance can sweep over us in connection with countless phenomena: "rational propositions", words, "effects of light on land and sea", smells, music, poetry. It's not in the object, but in our relation with it that the mystical quality lies. Mystical experiences of coming to life are relational or in-between. They require a relational way of being. James says that "we are alive or dead to the eternal inner message of the arts according as we have kept or lost this mystical susceptibility", this capacity to allow ourselves to be "beckoned and invited" by the music of the world (James, 1982, p. 383).

Considering these moments of newness and aliveness, when we say we are really experiencing an idea, the sunset, a piece of music, a poetic image, I want to think about the ways in which they involve an in-between state of holding. I am suggesting that we need to feel held in order to open ourselves to the world, to *live* our relations with the world. But more than this, and countering the asymmetry implied in "feeling held", we need to be able to hold. Opening ourselves to the world involves the doubled state and capacity of holding and being held. It is this reversible intertwining that makes holding an in-between state allowing openness.

In making this connection between creativity and holding, I am drawing on D.W. Winnicott's (1991) notion of transitional space, a space that has both "potential" and "holding" qualities. Transitional space is a space in-between self and other, inside and outside, me and not-me, a connecting space which both connects and separates. And so, in this space we live paradox. We live the paradox of "me and not-me" or separation and connection, without the desire for resolution. Letting go of the search for a self, we hold paradox. In the same way, we *hold* an idea, not by grasping at it in a desire to know, but by allowing its elusive coming and going in a creative gap between. Holding then involves a non-attached way of being, a condition and consequence of living relationally or in-between. The capacity to hold paradox implies a capacity to trust. It is when we lose trust or faith in the world perhaps, that we defensively turn in on our self in a search for certainty and resolution, or we grasp at solutions and truths. In holding on or grasping, we close off a world of possibilities, for we are not in-relation. When we try to control and fix, we are no longer able to listen. Trust then is essential to the potential, creative quality of transitional space: it allows us to be open to the emergent and able to experience aliveness in our relations with the world.

SPATIALITY

> *House, patch of meadow, oh evening light*
> *Suddenly you acquire an almost human face*
> *You are very near us, embracing and embraced.*
> (Rilke, quoted in Bachelard 1969, p. 8)

I want now to consider the *experience* of the betweenness of transitional space, and more specifically, the betweenness of holding. Prevailing forms of selfhood that privilege autonomy and agency can make it difficult to appreciate the particularity of a relational way of being, but these two ways involve qualitatively different experiences of space and time. If we speak relationally of a space between mother and child, for example, the emphasis is on "the between" rather than the terms "mother" and "child" with a space (void) between. Transitional space is a full, living space, vibrating with a sense of potential. It is the space of spirit.

In Michel Serres' (1995) book *Angels* there is an image of transitional space that worked for me immediately, showing how we experience the divine in everyday communications. It is an image of two men leaning towards each other in a gesture of sympathy and care. Their bodies are absorbed in the communication, the listener's face, with its smiling lines, matching the speaker's words. The caption that goes with this image says: "There's nothing to beat a third party between us. The truth is that we will only truly live together through him, with him, and in him. The third person precedes the first two" (Serres, 1995, p. 112). This is an image of the creative gap, the invisible connecting ground which, in holding the men together and apart, makes communication possible. And in this image I can feel the substance of this gap, of religion's binding: the present absence of an angel or God. I can feel the aliveness and spirit of living in-between.

The space involved in holding then, is not empty or fleshless and the holder is not a container that holds others like a bowl holds peas. Indeed, disrupting this Euclidean space of separate identities, holding consists of a simultaneous holding and being held: embracing *and* embraced. Think for example of the reversibility in the experience of holding hands, and the ambiguity about which hand holds and which is held. This brings us back to being in-relation: holding hands is a good image of the connection between relationality and a mutuality in holding. In holding, I am being held, and vice versa. And thus, in experiencing myself in both places at once – holding, being held – I no longer identify as a self,

6

but instead, experience being or living.

The following example from a children's book has allowed me to get something of the quality of this experience of holding. *Sleep Time* (Gleeson & Greder, 1993) is a story about a little girl whose mother put her to bed early. "'Stay and sing to me, and pat me?' 'No,' said her mum". The little girl couldn't go to sleep, wouldn't go to sleep. She addresses, one after the other, all the things in her room, starting with her stuffed kangaroo: "'Will *you* have my sleep for me?'" Kangaroo, the doll on the windowsill, Grandma Josie, puss, the boy in the painting, all stare and say nothing.

> Then slowly she took her teddy bear and held it very close. "Will *you* have my sleep for me?" she said. Teddy stared and said nothing. "I'll sing to you and pat you." She yawned and then squeezed the teddy tightly. "Grrrowl". And the two of them climbed into bed … and fell asleep. (1993)

Something different has worked with Teddy, starting with the phrase "I'll sing to you and pat you", which is what was asked of the girl's mother and refused. The striking feature of this story, that won't allow for simple accounts in terms of identification and projection, is that "grrrowl" and "I'll sing to you and pat you", without "she said", have no source of origin, are not expressive. "Grrrowl" has emerged in the gap between. What has gone on here is not simply a matter of the little girl putting herself in the place of the mother and projecting herself onto teddy – a structure that consists of two separate terms. Rather, through teddy, she simultaneously takes up mother and child in a manner that is between both. (And by extension, if the little girl isn't a little girl in holding the bear, the mother isn't a mother either. When we put children to bed are we not both child and parent at once?) Teddy makes the doubleness of holding possible, an experience of holding and being held: through the relation with the bear I am both here and there, all at once. I experience the spirit, the betweenness of holding.

Here is another story that is suggestive of the same relationality. *Aldo* (Burningham, 1993) is about another little girl who spends a lot of time on her own or, more precisely, in solitude. "I'm lucky though. I'm really very very lucky because I have a special friend." "His name is Aldo." "Aldo is my friend only, and he's secret. I know he will always come to me when things get really bad. Like when they were horrid to me the other day." An image of children being horrid at school is followed by one in which Aldo has his arm around the little girl, holding her securely. "I'm sure they went away because Aldo came." With Aldo, she is not scared of anything. There are some days when she even forgets about him, but she knows that if things get really bad, Aldo will always be there. In the closing image they dance, arms lightly around each other, through a row of pot plants. Their trust in each other makes relations with the world possible: difficult, potentially fearful encounters can be faced with Aldo's presence. And the trust in this holding even makes it possible to forget, momentarily, Aldo's presence: he is just there, he will be there when things are bad. Aldo is a guardian angel, and like all angels, he is invisible and he comes and goes in a flash. Aldo is a double. He, like teddy, is the condition of possibility of the little girl's being.

> Before anything at all is produced, the palette, the invisible spirit or the hidden object here take on a role as that thing through which I pass in order to enter into relation with everything and everyone … a double who accompanies me. … I have to feed it so that it can finally make me live and think … a guardian angel. (Serres, 1995, p. 129)

The guardian angel is a double, not in the sense of a representation of the self, but as the other who is the condition of possibility of our living and being. A guardian angel is one who "lies between us" who "preconditions all our relationships" (Serres, 1995, p. 130). Any creative activity requires a double – a muse, daemon, or genius. And this doubling relation involves a mutual holding: the double has to be fed and housed so that it can make me live and think.

Rilke's image of "embracing and embraced" is also one of a mutual housing or holding. Furthermore it highlights the mutual vitalisation in holding: of the house, it is said, "suddenly you acquire an almost human face". Likewise, teddy, in *Sleep Time*, is no mere inert object. The little girl listens to teddy, brings him to life, as he brings her to life, moves her. Were she to have treated him as an object, holding would not have been possible. And if teddy is not an object, the little girl is not a subject either: the condition of possibility of holding is a letting go of the self as subject. So, in the holding space of creativity, the non-human world, animate or inanimate, comes to life: the ball plays me, the music sings me, the palette or the invisible spirit makes me live. My aliveness is made possible by the aliveness of the world. But, it is a particular way of being that allows this lively experience of the world: a *living* in-between. Creative aliveness happens in transitional space: "grrrowl" is in-between, it comes from neither teddy nor the little girl.

EMBODIMENT

The quality of aliveness draws attention to the embodiment in holding. This reminds me of Gaston Bachelard, who says that when we can experience house images as moving in both directions, as being "in us as much as we are in them", then we can abide *within ourselves* (1969, p. xxxiii). The two-way relation between house and body has the in-between structure of transitional space. This is how it works for Bachelard: I put myself in the position of the house so that I experience, in an embodied way, the house as a body: the house as body and my body as house. The body and house are implicated in each other and are, in a sense, doubled. This is, then, an in-between experience of holding.

Rearranging my study recently brought this spatiality home. Immediately I felt different in that space which, needless to say, was now a different space. Spatial arrangements of furniture, it struck me, don't just make certain rituals and relations possible, they don't simply represent self and social relations. Rather, we are *in* the furniture, and the furniture is in us, just as, Rupert Sheldrake notes, nest and termite are implicated in each other (1994, p. 229). In the very process of moving table and chairs I was moving my relations, and, in a sense, the table and chairs were moving me, facilitating my relationships. The embodiment of our relations with transitional objects allows a relational way of being in the world.

In Bachelard's work, to be in-relation with the world means enacting, living, embodying images, and this vitalisation is the basis of creativity (1969, p. xxix). But the precondition of a creative way of being is a capacity for imagining-embodying the house or some other holding space, which could be the sky, water, a nest, the cosmos or the palm of a hand. That is to say, one needs to feel protected and sheltered in order to imagine, to be open to "the world pulse" which "beats beyond my door" (Bachelard, 1969, p. 3). Thus in living, embodying transitional holding space, we have the capacity to be open, we *are* open.

This way of being, described by Winnicott as the capacity to just BE, is a state of relaxation and unintegration which requires a letting go of an integrated and integrating self (1971, pp. 63-4, pp. 83-4). It is a way of being similar to that involved in the Buddhist meditation practice of bare attention. Mark Epstein (1995) joins the Winnicottian and Buddhist traditions when speaking of bare attention as a transitional phenomenon essential to a "being present"- not grasping at what was or will be, but just being now, in openness. A meditative internalisation of Freud's non-judgemental "evenly suspended attention", bare attention requires an openness to all experiences, sensations and emotions. It involves a capacity for holding, we might say. I can openly experience an emotion, however fearful it might seem, but I experience it without either repression and denial or grasping and attachment. With bare attention, I simultaneously experience and let go of the emotion (Epstein, 1995, pp. 114-125). I hold this paradoxical emotional state.

In the practice of bare attention, holding and openness presuppose each other. For example, think of the way people become either attached to or opposed to ideas in intellectual or political life. Either way, we find ourselves closing down, retreating to the hardened, heavy objective intellectual or political body. By contrast, the holding of bare attention would allow us to retain an open lightness towards ideas and their potential, to remain open in the face of whatever emotional-bodily responses we might have. It would allow us to follow intuitions and take risks in pushing ideas further, to hear and respond to others' ideas when they invite us to rethink our own, to be open to what the world has to tell us. Where attachment and grasping suffocate, non-attached holding allows enlivened flow.

The significance of being present is nicely illustrated by an experience described by Epstein which, while resonating for me with academic experiences, also clearly applies to any everyday communication. Reading his child a bedtime story, he was thinking about his next writing project – he was elsewhere, projecting, not in the reading experience and thus not present. Significantly, as he points out, this way of reading will have implications for the listener, who will experience him as lifeless, for if we're not present, we cannot be in-relation, in an *alive* relation with an other. When teaching and knowledge practices are conducted like this, it is unlikely that they will have creative effects. More probably, an audience will be left with a sense of lifelessness. As Epstein would put it, aliveness depends on an embodied mindfulness (1995, p. 144).

It is not difficult to see, then, why breathing has such significance in meditation and therapeutic practices which value a capacity to just BE. Breathing draws our attention to the connection between embodiment and being in-relation in a being present and holding way of being. In meditative practices of breathing, the focus on breath, each breath, in and out, brings us right into our body in the moment, now. By focussing on breathing, it is possible to let go of purpose, attachments, ego and desire for a separate self. To be in the breathing is to be in transitional space. As Epstein observes, breath has the characteristics of Winnicott's transitional phenomena, coming from neither within nor without, both me and not-me (1995, p. 123). And it reminds us again of the in-betweenness of creative experiences: in inspiration the world breathes, I breathe, I am breathed, I *am* breathing.

Any activity can be conducted with awareness, mindfully or not, in an embodied or disembodied way, with or without a holding way of being. There are very different ways of reading a bedtime story, thinking thoughts, walking a street, cooking, gardening, eating, swimming. Taking one of my favourite examples, horse riding, there is an unmistakable connection between being present, or mindfully embodied, and being *with* your horse, being in-relation. And the reverse isn't simply a matter of being elsewhere, thinking about the next lecture instead of riding. In fact it is sometimes when thinking too much about riding, trying too hard, that I find I am not with my horse. Winnicott makes a distinction which works for me here, between the "deliberate attention" demanded by play and the "deliberateness of trying" (1991, p. 109). In trying too hard with riding I will be turning it into an intellectual operation of controlling bodies as if objects, at a distance. Objectifying riding techniques might produce results, but only at the cost of tension in the horse. My body tenses, movements feel mechanistic, a matter of will and physical effort, and how could a horse feel anything but tension in response? Rather, what is called for is a relaxed, focussed in-betweenness in which, thinking neither of self nor horse, I am present *in* the riding.

Being mindfully present makes it possible for the movement of riding to have the quality of flow, for it to feel like floating, flying, effortlessly in tune. I'm attuned to and can feel the slightest loss in rhythm. Indeed I feel the loss before it happens, I would say, thus experiencing the future in the now. But it takes trust to avoid projective anticipation and to remain present and in-relation. And then, with trust, it is possible to experience creativity as Serres describes it: "every work of art or science ... consists in catching the wave just right, and following it all the way down the line, for as long as possible, riding the crest, surfing" (1995, p. 34).

And so it is with intellectual performances. Being in relation with a text or an audience requires an embodied *feeling*, just as being in-relation with a wave or a horse does. Only if I am living or embodying the ideas I am speaking in a lecture will I be present and in-relation with my audience. My embodiment requires openness, and my openness requires embodiment. Only with both will my speech be alive in its in-betweenness, only then will it fly. Think of what is going on when we try too hard with writing, try to control and manipulate it, become impatient and force words and passages and ideas together. Not listening, we are distanced from the text-object and there is no rhythm, no flow. When we are attached to our self as the creative source we block collaborative flow. The alternative is to be in a living relation with the text-other, a way of being captured perfectly by Serres:

> Look at those children out there, playing ball. The clumsy ones are playing with the ball as if it was an object, while the more skilful ones handle it as if it were playing with them: they move and change position according to how the ball moves and bounces. As we see it, the ball is being manipulated by human subjects; this is a mistake – the ball is creating the relationships between them. It is in following its trajectory that their team is created, knows itself and represents itself. Yes, the ball is active. It is the ball that is playing.
> (1995, pp. 47-8)

And this account of ball playing works just as well for thinking about the reader's relation with a text, the speaker's relation with listeners, the musician's relation with the music, the painter's relation with paint or the cook's relation with food.

PURPOSELESSNESS

In activities like riding and ball playing, we often feel we lose ourselves, absorbed, immersed in the activity, in a form of concentration where self and object are fused (Milner, 1987, pp. 80-81). We lose a self-consciousness. For Winnicott and Marion Milner (an object relations analyst with a particular interest in creativity and spirituality), this is a creative way of being, it is a just BEing. Milner is specifically talking about these states in activities such as painting, but she says that we can experience them in any everyday activity – using a vacuum cleaner, fishing, and so on. For Winnicott, the model of this sort of experience is the child absorbed in play: it is only in playing that a child or adult is able to be creative. What is crucial to these states is the quality of purposelessness, or what Winnicott also refers to as unintegration and formlessness (1991, pp. 54-5).

Why, as so many accounts of creative experiences insist, is a non-purposive state so important to creativity? Letting go of purpose is closely connected with letting go of self, with being in a held state of unintegration. Going about an activity with purpose involves ego: we plan, anticipate, strive for a goal, and ultimately that goal is the self, the self as identity, as one, as "I". As Winnicott puts it:

> If the artist (in whatever medium) is searching for the self, then it can be said that in all probability there is already some failure for that artist in the field of general creative living. The finished creation never heals the underlying lack of sense of self. (1991, pp. 54-55)

We won't find ourselves in the end products – more promotions, books, bullseyes. All we'll find there is lack. But if the self as an end does not have to be clung to, it is possible to be open to change and receptive to the creative possibilities of being in-relation. In his account of a Zen approach to archery, Eugen Herrigal says: "Sunk without purpose in what he is doing, he is brought face to face with that moment when the work, hovering before him in ideal lines, realizes itself as if of its own accord" (1989, pp. 32-45). Once we let go of ego and purpose, stop trying too hard, willing something to happen as if it is all up to us, once we allow ourselves to be in-between, the new emerges, effortlessly.

These creative states of letting go of self and purpose are experienced in a holding transitional space. Emphasising the need for a sense of safety in order to lose oneself, Milner uses the term "the framed gap" to describe this held opening of self. The painter's relation with the painted, for example, can be transformed through an emptiness that is held or framed (1987, pp. 79-80). There is a mystical connection between "subject and object" in the alive fullness of this emptiness. In Milner's formulation, holding is understood as a precondition, as a holding environment or containment which makes an opening possible: we need to feel held to be open to the emergent and to connection. And we find the same logic in Winnicott and Bachelard. What I want to emphasise is the two-way process or reversibility of holding and opening. It is not just a matter of the gap being framed

12

or held; the gap itself holds and connects. In their nothingness, the angelic and the divine bind.

To be open and have a capacity for being in-relation certainly presupposes being held. But we must be open in order to be held: I must *allow* myself to be held by the sea if I'm going to float; I need to let go and receive its support, give myself up to its giving. If we grasp and defensively close in on ourselves, we will sink. The little girls in the children's books were open to being held, open to holding, open. Their opening to teddy, to Aldo, is a holding. In being open, I am being held *and* I am holding, I *am* holding. Holding and openness presuppose each other. In a holding-open state of betweenness we are receptive to the endless possibilities of being in-relation. We have a mystical susceptibility, a creative capacity to be in a living relation with the mysterious in the world.

REFERENCES

Bachelard, G. (1969). *The poetics of space* (M. Jolas, Trans.). Boston: Beacon Press.
Burningham, J. (1993). *Aldo*. London: Red Fox.
Epstein, M. (1995). *Thoughts without a thinker: Psychotherapy from a Buddhist perspective*. New York: Basic Books.
Gleeson, L. & Greder, A. (1993). *Sleep time*. Sydney: Ashton Scholastic.
Herrigel, E. (1989). *Zen in art of archery* (D.T. Suzuki, Intr., and R.F.C. Hull, Trans.). New York: Vintage.
James, W. (1982). *The varieties of religious experience*. Harmondsworth: Penguin.
Milner, M. (1987). *The suppressed madness of sane men*. London: Tavistock.
Serres, M. (1995). *Angels: A modern myth* (F. Cowper, Trans.). Paris: Flammarion.
Sheldrake, R (1994). *The presence of the past*. London: HarperCollins.
Winnicott, D.W. (1991). *Playing and reality*. London: Routledge.

AND THE SUBJECT WAS MADE FLESH:
The Aesthetic and Corporate Dimensions of Psychology's Body

Henderikus J. Stam
University of Calgary

SUMMARY

In the development of the discipline of psychology two very different types of beings have stood in as psychology's subjects of convenience; children and animals. The properties and characteristics attributed to these beings have varied radically over the history of twentieth century psychology with the result that children and animals under one theory looked little like the same beings under another. Despite the difficulties associated with characterizing these "others," early twentieth century psychologists built bridges to animal psychology and developmental psychology not only for practical reasons but on the presumption that these others were capable of providing the raw material of the discipline. Yet animals and children continually defied the techno-wizardry of psychological theories at the same time as they were its most obvious recipients. This paper develops the thesis that the *aesthetic* representations of subjectivity made possible by animals and children on the one hand and their place in the *corporatist* enterprise of the new psychology on the other, made them suitable artefacts for cultivating the new science.

INTRODUCTION

When he had difficulties obtaining permission to conduct experiments with children, Thorndike's substitution of chickens for children in his graduate school research marked not so much a radical break as a shift to an investigatory object of convenience. Thorndike, whose career would be almost entirely consumed with the problems of an Educational Psychology, wrote in his 1898 thesis:

> Comparative psychology has, in the light of this research, two tasks of prime importance. One is to study the passage of the child mind from a life of immediately practical associations to the life of free ideas; the other is to find out how far the anthropoid primates advance to a similar passage, and to ascertain accurately what faint beginnings or preparations for such an advance the early mammalian stock may be supposed to have had. (Thorndike, 1898, p. 151)

In this paper I wish to theorize this remarkable interest in children and animals in early twentieth century psychology and what it conveyed about the nature of *subjectivity*. I will argue that by conceptualizing subjectivity on aesthetic terms, we can see how it takes such a multiplicity of manifestations in psychology. In addition, I will argue that the most dominant or successful representations of subjectivity in psychology were those that were capable of addressing what I have called *corporatism* (Stam, 1996).

CHOOSING THE RIGHT SUBJECT MATTER

Thorndike was of course not alone in this comparative interest of animals and children. Numerous early twentieth century psychologists, such as Watson and Claparède, moved seamlessly from the one to the other. For psychologists, both of these objects of investigation were based on hierarchies of intelligence and adaptivity, concepts readily transferred to the classroom (Danziger, 1990). Furthermore, intelligence as a graded set of abilities that referred back to individual adaptability, would prove to be of prime importance in the new psychology of learning as well as its industrial applications (Stam & Kalmanovitch, 1998).

What is most unusual about this incorporation of animals and children as objects of investigation is the transition that takes place from the so-called "new psychology" of the late nineteenth century to the technically sophisticated experimental psychology of the early twentieth century in the USA. This transition is neither smooth nor dramatic but it made founding figures such as James, Hall, Baldwin, Ladd, and Titchener obsolete within a generation. It represents a shift from a psychology of consciousness, of a science of mind, to a functional, applicable and marketable expertise (e.g., Richards, 1996). The vast disagreements that existed between many of these founding figures are often obscured by their common project of founding a discipline of psychology. Dissatisfaction with the lack of cohesion among the founders contributed to the search for a scientific and above all, applicable alternative. Nonetheless, the eventual rejection of topics that had their origin in nineteenth century moral philosophy would not be complete until the twentieth century, following the Progressive Era.

What characterized the period immediately preceding World War I, that period known as the Progressive Era in the United States, was its emerging corporatism. This is the system of *interest representation* and the institutional arrangement that links the associationally organized interests of civil society with the decisional structures of the state. (The business corporation, successful beyond imagination by 1900, became the model for other forms of corporatism.) As a non-competitive form of interest representation, corporatism consisted of a "hierarchically ordered, functionally differentiated, state licensed, representational monopoly" (Schmitter, 1974, p. 94). Modern societies, such as North American and European societies at the turn of the century, took on this form of regulation largely through the infusion and active cooperation of large numbers of professionals. Indeed, professionalism is an inherent component of corporatism.

Psychologists as Progressive Era professionals invoked their own form of representational monopoly. These were initially the representations of the "mind," remnants of the moral philosophy from which psychology emerged. With the rapid industrialization and emergent corporatism psychologists came to seek representations of human action more generally under the guise of functionalism (broadly conceived, including its evolutionary sense) and eventually behaviorism. Although psychology was ostensibly a scientific enterprise like others in the academy, the context of science served important representational and legitimating roles. What scientific representations of human actions made possible was the rejection of the more austere and defensive conceptions of the faculty psychology that characterized the moral philosophy of late nineteenth century North America in favor of an adaptationist psychology. Although initially finding its place in the curriculum by avowedly supporting this older philosophy, once having attained a home in the institutional life of the university, psychology gradually reformulated its ties to the question of mind altogether. Although this account requires more detail (see for example Richards, 1996; Stam, 1996), I want to argue that what psychologists managed to achieve was the rejection of a romantic as well as devotional representation of human psychological abilities and its replacement with a techno-rational subjectivity that was scientifically respectable.

The "new psychologists" were determined to rescue their psychology from moral philosophy, replacing it with a form of scientific individualism. Furthermore, the new psychology will not be treated here as simply fact or value, science or a form of "moral science" alone (although conceptually and historically it can and has been understood as either). Instead, I will take it as a form of aesthetic, representing mind while simultaneously denying its socio-cultural constitution and its relationship to new forms of production (Stam, 1999). In order to do this the mind and its contents have to be entirely naturalized. It is this point I wish to elaborate here, namely the deployment of an aesthetic of a techno-rational object of investigation, that was made possible in the investigations of psychologists at the turn of the century by turning to such creatures as children and animals. Ultimately this was entwined with the corporatism that this aesthetic served.

With the rejection of consciousness and mind as the center of the human person, the intellectual elites of psychology in the Gilded Age (e.g., James, Dewey, Munsterberg, Cattell, Hall) modified the infant discipline and passed it to their students. A second generation rapidly completed the transition as functionalism and behaviorism were much better suited to a corporatist mentality, and fit the enthusiasms of the age. What the new representations of the object of psychological study allowed was the technological interpenetration of the machine-world into the personal world. What children and animals uniquely provided was an easy source of research objects that allowed the psychologist to "view" processes and problems that were literally *made visible* (or more appropriately, made flesh) by new methodologies. This requires a highly versatile aesthetic that allowed the creation of new representations whose origins as representations were entirely veiled behind the demands of the new science. These representations had to be real nonetheless, tangible and visible to the student of the new discipline and those who watched from afar, such as university administrators.

Non-human animals made available to psychologists a vehicle through which to represent processes announced by evolutionary theory that supported a hierarchical conception of the animal/human world. This codified into scientific language the already prevalent nineteenth century metaphorical understanding of the relationship between animals and humans. Darwinian and Spencerian theory still ranked animals in relation to humans, and the continuity between animals and people that had emerged in evolutionary theory "made it even easier to represent human competition, and the social hierarchies created by those who prevailed, in terms of animals" (Ritvo, 1987, p. 40). In addition, the Progressive Era intellectual considered animals important only in so far as they illuminated so-called "primitive" forms of mind and made it possible to support an evolutionary hierarchy of intelligence.

Having overcome the divisive sectarianism of their profession that characterized the late nineteenth and early twentieth century, post-World War I psychologists began to narrow their subject matter and rationalize their modes of representation. One of the crucial debates of any profession within corporatist structures is to ensure the hegemonic exercise of its representational functions. This was achieved with the gradual separation of methodological rigour from theoretical claims (cf. Danziger, 1990) and the exchange of metaphysical problems for technical problems. The problem of subjectivity was biologized and gradually reinserted into the biological body as a problem of motivation, attitudes, personality and other manageable topics.

If we examine the success that psychology has booked as a publicly recognizable and continually growing discipline in the twentieth century then it is not the unity of its subject matter that stands out at first glance. It is precisely its *flexibility* of representation that has ensured that contenders can be either eliminated or incorporated into the subject matter of the discipline. By adopting a loose functionalism as a theoretical strategy and instrumentalism as a method of research, no psychological phenomenon need be unacknowledged or unexamined. Yet whenever adopted on these terms, the subject matter is incorporated into the lexicon of the discipline.

REPRESENTATION AND AESTHETICS

What seems at first glance like an entirely critical thesis has what I take to be an important alternate dimension, namely, the claim that to understand the history of psychology within its context as a social scientific discipline is also to understand the way in which social sciences break with classical conceptions of science. The strong claim here is that all representations of subjectivity are inherently historical, cultural and aesthetic formulations. That what humans take themselves to be is historical and cultural seems to me a straightforward thesis consequent to post-structuralism, the linguistic turn in the social sciences and more, and it is a thesis I will not defend here. Yet not all representations of subjectivity are equal, and not all demand our attention. Renderings of the subjective world are driven by aesthetics, by the skilled production of accounts whose influence is determined by far more than the scientific account into which it is originally placed. Aesthetic representations create new objects that are as real as the biological bodies they seek to represent. These representations go into circulation as the objects of investigation of the new disciplines and their strength is related to their acceptance by the discipline as well as the end-users (the clientele) of the discipline such as the education system, prisons, hospitals and the like.

An aesthetic account of subjectivity in the history of psychology is an attempt to break out of seemingly fruitless debates that position socio-rational accounts of psychology's subject (such as constructionist accounts) against those created by naturalist accounts. Ankersmit (1996) has argued that western philosophy and science are inherently Stoic in outlook meaning by this claim that Stoicism creates an explicit bond between the human self and the rational order of the universe. Reason rules both the individual and the universe and the two are connected by a common ground, a *tertia comparationis* in "terms of which reality and thought can be compared and the truth and falsity of our beliefs can be established" (Ankersmit, 1996, p. 71). As a way of proceeding, mid-twentieth century western philosophy and science are broadly Stoical in so far as they subscribe to this inherent metaphysical scheme and agree on the rationality of the self and its universe. Aestheticism rejects this *tertia comparationis* and aesthetic accounts reject the rational ground that ties the self to the world. Works of art cannot be reduced to a common background or to reality. Instead they rely on the surprising, the inventive, the "new." "Accuracy" of representation however is not one of the criteria for an aesthetic account. In the same way, ontology and epistemology are answers to the question of what the world is and how we can know it. Aesthetics is simply indifferent to these questions (but does not reject them outright). It assumes that aesthetic representations are not meant to account for how they come to be in a world of things, nor how we come to appreciate something as aesthetic. Whatever scientific rationality originally attributes to a representation of the subjective, once it moves in a world of consumers and producers of such knowledge it takes on the status of an aesthetic object. The questions that replace traditional scientific grounds focus in the aesthetic realm on the nature of the representation, the skill with which it is produced, the masters it serves (implicitly and explicitly) or in whose name it has been produced, the historical characteristics that are quoted in it, and the "price" it fetches in the marketplace of representations.

Theoretical developments in early twentieth century psychology then can be understood on aesthetic grounds especially if we wish to conceptualize the shortcomings and continuing replacement of accounts of subjectivity. In the twentieth century, subjectivity was re-deployed in other terms and vehicles while seemingly curtailed by the new disciplinary formations. In particular this is where animals and children played a new but important role. By gradually replacing the omnibus, human version of consciousness that entailed a will and morality, the new subjectivity was constituted as entirely natural, adaptive, limited, malleable and neutral.

The late nineteenth century conception of parallelism, popular in North American psychology, supported these theoretical developments by removing the necessity that consciousness must be present for the biomechanical body to act. Even James begins to question the problem of consciousness, and gradually consciousness loses its physical, corporeal presence. The sensory and perceptual phenomena of psychology are capable of functioning without consciousness which takes on a maintenance function at best (cf. Deleule, 1992). Anything that cannot be attributed to the body as bio-mechanism is attributed to consciousness as a remainder, eventually requiring no notion of consciousness at all, but simply a conception of function and behavior. Subjectivity is thus minimized and even irrelevant except in so far as one is concerned with the subjective nature of individual operations of the body – touching, seeing, hearing etc (Stam, 1999).

CORPORATISM

Why would psychologists deploy such limited conceptions of subjectivity at a time when so many were open to them? And how is that such conceptions of subjectivity as were available in the early twentieth century were taken up in the nascent discipline? In order to answer these questions it is important to realize the relationship between psychologists' conceptions of subjectivity and their own positions in the new corporate structures.

In defining human subjectivity, psychologists also defined their own: out of the shared representations of psychological work, formalized as the discipline of psychology, collective rules of method were prescribed under corporatism to which each initiate had to submit upon entrance to the community (Kaufman-Osborn, 1986). However, the role of method extends well beyond its service as a principle of internal organization and regulation in the research laboratory or in the work of science. Emile Durkheim's struggle to establish sociology in France included the recognition that the continuous subjection to method's rule engenders a new self (Kaufman-Osborn, 1986). The confrontations between early psychologists exhibit this concern over the "prescientific ego" (Kaufman-Osborn, 1986, p. 642) and its adherence to the vernacular understandings of psychological categories (see also Morawski, 1992). In 1898 Titchener argued that

> there is reasonable agreement, within the experimental camp, as to the postulates of a purely structural psychology, whereas there is pretty radical disagreement among the psychologists of function. Let it not be supposed, now, that this latter state of affairs is anything else than a disadvantage for psychology at large; above all, let it not be thought that the experimentalist rejoices at the lack of unanimity among his colleagues. (Titchener, 1898/1961, p. 241-242)

And G. Stanley Hall wrote in his autobiography that "one answer to those who attempt to criticize is more and more commonly that they do not understand, and this is increasingly true. Psychologists do not quite understand each other" (Hall, 1923, p. 435). Laurel Furumoto's (1988) account of Titchener's club of Experimentalists is revealing precisely for its disciplinary regulation of the new profession, not only through its exclusion of women but in its selection of participants and in its general practices. These are but examples of the problem that was faced by each of the new social sciences in turn at the beginning of this century. As Kaufman-Osborn argued,

> Science, whose initial determination entailed a radical repudiation of common sense, must win public legitimacy if it is to re-form the world in

the image of its own rationality; its truth, as Durkheim says of society, "can exist only if it penetrates the consciousness of individuals and fashions it in its image and resemblance." Accordingly, science must have created for it, out of a people whose common sense presently resists its intrusion into their daily lives, a social body whose members confirm its status as a suprasocial entity and whose authority does not derive from the practice of those who concede its right to rule.
(Kaufman-Osborn, 1986, p. 646)

The corporate structure, which came to be the foundation of the new universities at the turn of the century also, became a mechanism of self-control. Corporatism was the medium through which progressives restrained and moderated the social body while stridently setting out to conquer the common sense that would prevent the application of scientific knowledge. Corporatism suppresses the ideological nature of social problems and simultaneously enhances the status of social scientific knowledge by giving it stable forums from which to announce its findings to the world. This is a political solution (and one foreseen by Durkheim) to the problem of the common sense and the organic opinions of ordinary citizens and social groupings of pluralist societies. The social sciences needed to overcome both common sense and organic opinions and causes if they were to ensure success both internally and externally. It is, at the same time, the solution that was imposed upon the members of the new community of scientists in the early twentieth century; through corporatization a political solution was found to guarantee the adherence of psychologists to a singular method, no matter how divergent their individual theoretical aims.

Depictions of subjectivity for psychologists were highly restricted if one aspired to belong to the intellectual elite in early twentieth century psychology. Strict requirements on the kinds of identities that were required of psychologists fostered limited kinds of aesthetic displays. There is one counterweight to this tradition however. Despite all its rational exercises, early psychologists could not capture subjectivity in any all-encompassing model or formula. Indeed, even their subjects of convenience, animals and children, were highly resistant to easy characterization, their bodies refusing to cooperate with the designs of the corporatists. Despite the improvements in technique, the sophisticated theory and the elaborate construction of apparatus, children and animals proved unable to be the instruments off of which one could "read" a particular kind of subjectivity. As the history of comparative and developmental psychology makes clear, psychologists' representations of animals and children have diverged and are no longer taken to represent exactly the same hierarchical subjectivity they were almost a century ago. But we are far from settling the issue. On the contrary, modern theories continue to recapitulate the problems inherent in the representations of previous generations of psychologists. The trend to biological theories on the one hand and socio-rational ones on the other merely obscures the difficulties encountered in ascribing subjectivities to other kinds.

REFERENCES

Ankersmit, F. R. (1996). *Aesthetic politics: Political philosophy beyond fact and value.* Stanford, CA: Stanford University Press.

Danziger, K. (1990). *Constructing the subject: Historical origins of psychological research.* Cambridge: Cambridge University Press.

Deleule, D. (1992). The living machine: Psychology as organology. In J. Crary & S. Kwinter (Eds) *Incorporations* (pp. 203-233). New York: Zone.

Furumoto, L. (1988). Shared knowledge: The experimentalists, 1904-1929. In J. G. Morawski (Ed.), *The rise of experimentation in American psychology* (pp. 94- 113). New Haven, CT: Yale

Hall, G. S. (1923). *Life and confessions of a psychologist.* New York: Appleton.

Kaufman-Osborn, T. V. (1986). Emile Durkheim and the science of corporatism. *Political Theory, 14,* 638-659.

Morawski, J. G. (1992). Self-regard and other-regard: Reflexive practices in American psychology, 1890-1940. *Science in Context, 5,* 281-308.

Richards, G. (1996). *Putting psychology in its place.* London: Routledge.

Ritvo, H. (1987). *The animal estate: The English and other creatures in the Victorian age.* Cambridge, MA: Harvard.

Schmitter, P. C. (1974). Still the century of corporatism? *Review of Politics, 36,* 85-131.

Stam, H. J. (1996). *A body coporate: Early North American psychology and institutional culture.* Paper presented at the 104th Convention of the American Psychological Association, Toronto, August, 1996.

Stam, H. J. (1999). Technologies 'R' us: Psychology and the production of new bodies. In Maiers, W., Bayer, B., Esgalhado, B. D., Jorna, R., & Schraub, E. (Eds) *Challenges to theoretical psychology* (pp. 332-340). Toronto: Captus Press.

Stam, H. J. & Kalmanovitch, T. (1998). E. L. Thorndike and the origins of animal psychology: On the nature of the animal in psychology. *American Psychologist, 53,* 1135-1144.

Thorndike, E. L. (1898). Animal intelligence: An experimental study of the associative processes in animals. *Psychological Monographs, 2,* (4, Whole No. 8).

Titchener, E. B. (1961). The postulates of a structural psychology. In T. Shipley (Ed.), *Classics in psychology* (pp. 224-243). New York: Philosophical Library. (Original work published in 1898.)

PLUGGED IN:
Psychology, Technology and Popular Culture

Betty M. Bayer
Hobart and William Smith Colleges

SUMMARY

This chapter focuses on different moments in twentieth century history of human-machine pairings in popular culture and psychology. Characterizing these moments as shifts from early twentieth century "bodies as machines-in-motion" to bodies-as-codes and to codes-as-identity, human-machine couplings serve to elucidate how these transformations brought about changes in gender meanings even as they continued to secure a social and psychological order of heterosexuality. These couplings were likewise charged psychologically with marking off normative from pathological configurations and relations, including machines as madness-in-motion and hysterical breakdowns in social and psychological identity. Using these case studies, the chapter argues to place technology at the centre of feminist and critical psychology and to make this work historical.

INTRODUCTION

Y2K – the seemingly simple three letter acronym packing gigabyte influence in the public imagination (not to mention purses), at least in the U.S. and a few other countries, with the count-down to the new millennium.[1] Its power to set astir endist nightmares derived from what appeared initially as a possible insurmountable coding problem in computers' ability to handle the clock over from the year 1999 to 2000. Animating this frenzy were those ways in which Y2K became metonymic for the place of technology within opposing millennialist fears of ultimate (technological) destruction (damnation) and desires for new beginnings (salvation). Capturing our end-time sensibility as one almost overdetermined by "conflicted longings" (Uglow, 1996) in our relations with technology was that highbrow of techno-magazines *Wired*'s glossy black cover exclaiming "Lights Out," and in between in fine print, "Learning to love Y2K." So there it was in bold print – romance and technology, our megabyte, ambivalent love affair of late twentieth century life.

Of course, as David Noble (1997) argues, technology and millennial couplings are neither "new nor odd" for "the religious roots of modern technological enchantment extend a thousand years further back in the formation of Western consciousness, to the time when the useful arts first became implicated in the Christian project of redemption" (p. 6). "Technoscience" projects, to borrow Donna Haraway's (1997) term, can thus be understood as gaining their narrative momentum through a kind of secularizing of sacred salvation histories in which divining nature becomes science's practicing or useful art for deliverance from sin, ignorance, imperfection and the burden of the body. We therefore find in various late twentieth century entanglements of technology, science and religion, ideas of divine creation, intervention, and recovering "man's" fall from grace (Adamic perfection). Projects that readily come to mind include the Human Genome Project ("Book of Life") and Artificial Intelligence research, such as that by Hans Moravec in which dreams of "downloading" our consciousness render flesh, blood and bones immaterial (see Keller, 1996).

If we see the pursuit of bodily transcendence as the cultural symptom of technoscience projects of human-technology minglings, then, following Marjorie Garber (1998), we need to read this cultural symptom as a kind of code, a "way in which a body – or a culture – signals something that lies beneath or within," a "withheld narrative performed by the body" (p. 3). And so "loving the machine/computer" quickly reveals itself to be a rather charged event – politically, socially, culturally, psychologically, religiously – of historical moment in gender stagings. That the whole Y2K fervor admitted of our longings, of the linked projects of technology and life forms, it just as readily awakened anew technologically-laced threats of disaster and end, of powerlessness and disorder, as *Wired* magazine's cover so boldly exposed. According to programmer Ellen Ullman (1999), it was precisely Y2K's exposure of the "myth of order" that most disrupted for without this myth the ground on which rests promises of perfectibility, progress and deliverance simply slips. Entering a note of uncertainty into the narrative of scientific "man's" positioning and re-positioning of scientific agency from, in Noble's terms, "co-explorer" or "steward with God" to man as "co-creator" denaturalizes the "natural" order of knowing just as proclamations of technologies feeding back on themselves to, as Danny Hillis (1998) says, "evolve new computers" beyond our comprehension point up the double discourse of the "unnatural Nature of naturalism" (Seltzer, 1992, p. 14).

Wrought repeatedly through progressive narratives, such as Moravec's "dawn of the superman ... aris[ing] out of the fertile conjunction of augmented humans and intelligent machines" to create, as Dewdney (1999) reports, "'Exes' – posthumans" (p. D15), Jaron Lanier (1998) argues that the "brain, economy, evolution and politics" have of late been overdetermined by computer metaphors (p. 60). As he puts it, "Memes and sociobiology are given a technological imprimatur; this allows them to serve as the preferred metaphors for our culture and our relationships" (p. 60). But technology has also been given an evolving biological imprimatur such that as overdetermined cultural symptoms together they tell us about the powerful place of gender politics, to use an older phrase, in American culture and the terror of the possibility that indeed anatomy may *not* be destiny. This is what makes human-technology longings so conflicted and conflictual as relations between material bodies and identity become reconfigured even as they lay bare the arbitrariness of their relation to power, mastery and control.

What I want to focus on are moments in human-machine couplings where the relation goes awry, ones where neat and tidy stories give way to messy, gender boundary-conflicting instances. In the heat of varying human-machine moments, the gender, race and class terms of identity become more salient, the stakes more visible, and the reworking of "how boundaries are conceived" more perceptible (Hayles, 1999, p. 84). Using three moments in twentieth century popular culture and psychology, human-technology couplings in the locations of the factory, the scientific psychology laboratory, the office of television research, and the spaceship will be examined for how they are instructive on the hinging and re-hinging of outer and inner worlds as on the interchange amongst culture, science and technology in gendering a kind of psychological order. In short, I consider the incessant posing anew of nature, engendering time and again human-machine configurations such that an appreciation forms of what in these reconstructions becomes "suppressed for the sake of the social order, repressed for the sake of the psychological order" (Kahane, 1995, p. 7). For these and many other reasons, the case will be made for feminist critical psychology to place at its centre those ways in which psychology and technoculture are plugged into one another in so many of our ordering myths.

As will become evident, there is much more to human-technology linkings than enhancements to see, to read, or to detect the "essences" of life (Bayer, 1999). Such pairings transform the self-same entities they purport to reveal, reconstituting "human" kinds in ways that reformulate rights and responsibilities along with our relations with and to humans, nonhumans, and the everyday. While all of this is made particularly palpable in films portraying the popular imagination of human-machine relations, they also provide an entry point to the intermingling of psychology and technoculture.

HUMAN-MACHINE AS BODIES-IN-MOTION

Earmarking our early twentieth century machine age anxieties are Charlie Chaplin's (1936) *Modern Times* and Fritz Lang's (1927) *Metropolis*. Both films situate machine age strain in the tension between order and chaos, between a class ordering of men by machines that labour and those that supervise, and the wearing down of men and masculinity by the machines' tirelessness. But, of course, there is more. *Modern Times* takes us to the factory floor via the observation window of the manager's office, coupling the mechanized worker with systems of surveillance, so much so, in fact, that when Chaplin, playing "a factory worker" takes his cigarette break in the men's room, the manager's face and voice are transmitted onto a videoscreen there too, signifying a consciousness of regulation and surveillance – an internal psyche regulated by the demands of a punch-clock working class life in difficult employment times. Chaplin amplifies the man-machine question by performing with his body the measured rhythm and mechanized functions of factory machine lines – stiff, twitchy, automaton, mechanical man. Further instancing the inanity embedded in time and efficiency management is that famous scene where Chaplin is harnessed to an automatic feeding machine, imagined to enable human workers to continue working non-stop so as to increase production, to become as continuous and indefatigable as the machine itself. But the feeding machine runs amok. Pushing the bounds of machine-worker rationality, Chaplin embodies this mad mechanical psychology wholly, running from the feeding machine to oil fellow workers, mistaking the nose of his foreman, the buttons of an officer, the breasts of a large woman as just more sets of screws to be tightened (Giedion, 1948/1969), and finally throwing his body like a cog into the machinery itself, into machinic breakdown.

Surely the none-too-subtle pairing of the electric buzzing light waves with the over-sized videoscreen for manager's surveillance of workers point up the machine as nerve centre of work life. Once joined with other automations such as voices being transmitted only by mechanical devices, as with the mechanical salesman and videophones used by the president, the "life process and the machine process" begin to articulate one another through information as production in what has been called the "control revolution" (Seltzer, 1992, p. 159). But this is precisely what Chaplin makes hysterically funny, for the very symptoms of machinic control are shown to be overdetermined – "out of control." The hystericized feeding machine, Chaplin's "nervous breakdown" and the factory shutting down thus parallel one another such that the "machine" as cultural symptom indexes a symptomatic culture in which man-machine relations, including scientific management, emerge as hysterical (cf. Garber, 1998).

Caricaturing the machine-in-motion as madness-in-motion, Chaplin's posing of "is man no more than a machine?" makes visible an inner psychic dimension to then prevailing views of the body as "human motor" (Rabinbach, 1990). Insofar as endless productivity turned the working body into the sign of modern times, placing the working body at the "juncture of nature and society" (Rabinbach, p. 290), then Chaplin's bodily fits and starts chart the uncanny semblance of madness in "rationalizing measures" of assembly line and scientific management (Giedion, 1948/1969, p. 121). Chaplin's bodily echopraxia of machines-in-motion speaks out the symptoms of abstracted energy principles of involuntary movement typifying an efficiency-driven machine age, making of his human body a parody of measurement devices, such as those created by Etienne Jules Marey and later Frank Gilbreth, but now to track and record machines-in-motion. With this displacement onto machines of "maladies of energy," or of "failures of will," descriptions tied to hysteria and neurasthenia, man-machine pairings likewise assume a psychological profile of the "diseases of the unreliable subject" (Rabinbach, p. 161). Dissociated from its subject, Chaplin's animation of a machine's paroxysms of madness are as revealing of the mobility and mutability of symptoms as tied to shifting sensibilities as they are of the arbitrary associations of male bodies with mastery, power and control. The male factory worker appears before us not as the epitome of the rational working body but as awkward, powerless and seemingly futile – a feminized man-machine? Perhaps. For what functions in the end as the *deus ex machina* to Chaplin's manhood and masculinity difficulties is not machine age desire but rather heterosexual romance. The working body gone awry, then, signals both the threat and promise of modern times in late 1930s U.S. life of high unemployment and union worker unrest, and of a class ordering of men and masculinity through scientific management. "Man-as-machine" served to point up fears around "modern man" being lost, "impotent" before machine, revealing in scientific management, anxieties about the gender of production and agency (Seltzer, p. 160).

Opening on to the futuristic scenes of an underground bevy of workers (below, hell) and aboveground capitalist advantage (up, heaven), the film *Metropolis* elucidates class interests in the Cartesian coupling of body and clock-like mechanism it recalls. Imagined as soulless and heartless mediators between mind (heaven) and hands (hell), machines' capacity for endless motion signifies machine-age strain and wear as the loss of humanity itself. This darker side of technology becomes displaced onto a female robot who created out of the mad collaboration between the heartsick inventor and the mastermind of *Metropolis* is made in the likeness of the good human Maria. This doubling of Marias dramatizes a split femininity of good versus evil (Mary versus Eve) and associations of these generative powers of good and evil with technology. Both technology and women thereby become subjects-to-be-contained in order to control the "fear of technology's power to destroy humanity by running out of control" (Springer, 1996, p. 56). But the need for control in order to secure masculine authority and identity is revealed here as well as overdetermined, and the order to which classes and gender submitted as of such mythic proportions as to have run riot.

FROM BODIES-IN-MOTION TO BODIES-IN-CODES

Both *Modern Times* and *Metropolis* confront us with the place of heterosexual gender arrangements as a mechanism of social order to help to keep at bay anxieties surrounding what amounts to a remarkable coupling of workers and machine sensibilities. But the anxiety aroused by these pairings also derives from an instability in human-machine configurations as technologies of gendered self-invention. Both films rely on women and machines to secure masculine rationality and authority. Both films foreshadow the passing of the "human motor as a 'paradigm' of social modernity" (Rabinbach, p. 293) through changing forms of technology to what would, by Post-WWII America, come to be known as information technologies of the cybernetic age. If the "human motor" metaphor also served analogically to recast disorders of the body from ones of "idleness" of the previous age (an "infirmity of the spirit") to ones of fatigue ("infirmity of the body"), then we might anticipate a sea change as well in the social, political, moral, and psychological underpinnings to body-technology relations. Shifting from human-machine coordinations as bodies-in-motion to human-computer configurations as bodies-in-codes (infirmity of the post-body) also meant transformations in psychological notions of selves and bodies. As Thomas Foster (1996) argues, it is not so much that the body has become obsolete, despite the hype of the disappearing body. Rather, some of our narratives of embodiment seem conceptually anachronistic. Much as neurasthenia's "maladies of energy" arose within the context of machine-age notions of efficiency, energy, and movement, so might one appreciate a displacement in psychoanalytic notions of penis envy and castration anxiety by memory envy and system crash or loss-of-information anxiety (Foster).

E.G. Boring's (1946) hypothetical robot as Alan Turing's (1950) envisioning of a machine comparable to human intelligence signal this sea change in metaphors of man-machine from "the human motor" to "the human computer" – the tireless labourer turns into the "electronic brain," the industrial, machine age enters the informational, digital age (the tireless thinker?). Turing and Boring each restage the "nature" of humans and of masculinity and both restagings are located in post-WWII U.S. life with its militarily invested cybernetic research and sexual politics around public and private worlds.

Turing most assuredly ushered in our turn to the man-machine-intelligence linkages. His question of "can machines think?" was not necessarily of the extraordinary powers of computers but rather of their ordinary ones, their ability to simulate human thinking undetectably, a problem "drawing a fairly sharp line between the physical and the intellectual capacities of man" (Turing, 1950, p. 434). Passing the Turing test, or imitation game, "presents gender as a performance that can either be denaturalizing ('deceptive') or naturalizing ('truthful'), and the artificiality of gender identity provides an analogy for artificial intelligence, or its discursive performance" (Foster, p. 300). Turing coordinates thinking machines with thinking men, and this embodiment of masculinity is itself revealed as dependent on a convincing performance in which "passing" serves to mark masculinity as man-the-rational-actor even as Turing encodes this cultural sign of masculinity as a set of technological effects (cf. Halberstam, 1998).

Boring, on the other hand, fashions his hypothetical robot in part as response to Norbert Weiner's challenge to "describe a capacity of the human brain" which could not be duplicated by electronic analogues. Insofar as Turing's project may find its coherence in what Sedgwick (1990) terms an "epistemology of the closet," Boring's might more aptly be located in Weiner's command-control-communication-information (C^3I) remakings of logical positivism. If Turing's test follows the logic of sciences of detection, then Boring's pursues the line of warranting essences. In Boring's (1946) words, "Certainly a robot whom you could not distinguish from another student would be an extremely convincing demonstration of the mechanical nature of man and of the unity of the sciences" (p. 191). And if Turing's man-computer test opened the uncertainty of bodily codes of masculinity and sexuality, then Boring's homosocial pairing of robot and man reinscribes "nature" with the codes of "rational masculinity" itself. No wonder Boring feels a thrill – a "scientist's thrill" – with his fantasy of he and his robot "squeezing" one another's hands, much like fraternity brothers who in performing a secret handshake bond to keep the code of brotherhood secret.

BODIES-AS-CODES AND CODES-AS-IDENTITY

By the mid-fifties, popular presses, such as *Life* magazine, recognized the place of computers in the gender politics of work. It was the opinion of popular presses, writes Mari Jo Buhle (1998), that the Machine Age had "failed to liberate women," leaving them with the dilemma of choosing "domesticity only to become Moms; or, careers" only to "jeopardiz[e] their femininity" (p. 173). Certainly in this post-war context of Momism, propaganda designed to constitute women's labour as a temporary work force measure, fears of communism and conformity, not to mention a movement across sociology and social psychology of (re)naturalizing a heterosexual social order as complementary "sex roles," there surfaces with the heightened attention to social and sexual order a sense of gender anxiety about what might run amok, about American national and individual identity. Indeed, Erik Erikson's reconfiguration of femininity *as* identity recast, argues Buhle, the familiar sociology of sex roles into psychoanalytic language – identity became the "rhetorical signature of ego psychology and the chief marker of sexual difference" (p. 185). "In sum," says Buhle, Erikson "provided yet another way to fashion a reproductive teleology for woman and a productive teleology for man" (p. 185). Feminists and/or ambitious women could upset this "natural" order by raising children "alienated from their sexual identities" (p. 194). In a curious reversal of events, "the sociology of sex roles redeem[ed] the biology of sex differences" (p. 194), joining both with psychological identity.

While Turing's test and Boring's robotic fantasy are part of this cybernetic refiguring of "man's" identity, role and nature, it was perhaps Robert Bales' union of Parsonian sex role ideas and cybernetic research that aided the remasculinization of the thinking man's desk job. Bales' reconstruction of communication categories turned the Parsonian familial sexual division of labour of instrumental and socio-emotional roles into functionalist, internal processes of information exchange – the "best ideas man" and the "best liked man." Finding an analogue in the "operation of a large-scale communication and control system such as a defense network" (Bales, 1955, p. 32), Bales translated communications into instrumental and expressive information codes which as a "mutually supporting pair" functioned to stablize the social organization and to normalize the "cultural control of behavior." These depictions once transferred onto the "internal experience of the individual" (Edwards, 1996, p. 204) also served to remasculinize corporate culture, turning expressive roles into masculine team-building skills, and ideas into leadership. In an interesting way, cybernetics and a simple interaction recorder intervened to reconfigure relations between external observations and internal states, to reconfigure masculine subjectivity through information codes, and to retain independent "personality" characteristics in a system of group communication. To be able to read the codes of "personality" of individual men in groups, and to show consensus as distinct from conformity must have been quite reassuring given wider American cultural worries over instability, conformity and hidden inner selves.

In the late 1950s popular movie *Desk Set*, there is dramatized just such conflicts around "nature," "identity," "gender," "sex roles," and "sexuality," in the context of human-computer relations in the corporate work place of a big TV network. The opening scene of a computer sitting alone in a well-lit and colourfully tiled room signals its centrality to the staging of our "natures" much as the factory machines' incessant clockwork efficiency pointed up the "human motor." Katherine Hepburn's character, Bunny Watson, upon seeing a demonstration of a new "electronic brain," expressed it this way: "Maybe, just maybe, people are a little bit outmoded." To which, Spencer Tracy's character, Richard Sumner, replies: "Wouldn't surprise me if they stopped making them – people, that is." Having a little fun with our human propensity for self-invention, the joke returns, much like Chaplin's fits and starts, reminding us that what appears as a natural order may, in fact, be artifactual. And so the banter continues between Bunny, manager of research, and Richard Sumner, the efficiency expert who arrives to arrange to install an EMMARC (electromagnetic memory and arithmetic research calculator). What unfolds over the course of the movie is the story of the office love-triangle with a new twist – the computer as the "other woman" (the movie's other title).

EMMARC (aka Emmy) is positioned as much in the stream of the "battle of the (unequally empowered) sexes" as it is in the whole idea of "progress" – man's and computer's (Slane, 1997). Bunny's research skills, for example, are first compared to the computer's in what appears to be a reenactment of the Turing test, by Richard Sumner – is woman a reliable subject as information processor? Analogies are played out between the computer and Bunny being "single-minded," "relentless" or likely to "go off" if frustrated. It is with Emmy and her masculinized woman attendant, however, where the hysteric fits break out. As Emmy appears to go "berserk," mishandling information, her attendant likewise seems to suffer a short circuit. Their symbiotic relation is found in what the assistant refers to as a "cloud of suspicion" around their presence such that one cannot escape the cultural symmetry being granted to fears of human replacement and of women in the workplace. Bunny and Richard appear to avoid this very situation by surrendering themselves to the social order of heterosexual romance as if once again this remains the preserve for (reliable) gender subjects.

The 1960s release of *2001: A Space Odyssey*, however, posits another dimension to the gender tension in the computer-human interchange. Hal 9000, the computer, tells an interviewer that this computer series has "never made a mistake or distorted information," and so appears at first to be the genuine reliable subject. This narrative starts to fall apart when Hal takes Dave into his confidence about his suspicions surrounding the mission, and Dave begins to doubt Hal, confiding to his fellow crew member a sense of "something strange" with Hal. In this moment, we become aware of Hal as a psychological subject, and of their evolving relation as a *folie à deux* emerging from this shared (mis)recognition of who counts as the reliable – rational – subject. Their mutual suspicions culminate in Hal telling Dave to "sit down calmly ... take a stress pill" as he anticipates Dave's intention to disconnect his lifeline of bits and bytes. As Hal reports "feel[ing] his mind going" and begins to sing "Daisy, Daisy, give me your answer true, I'm half crazy over the likes of you...," the affair with computers emerges as a half-mad enterprise which may have at its core, as Ullman says of programming in general, irrationality.

Surely this madness underlies a twenty-first century e-mail play on Hal and Dave on the cover of the New York Times Magazine.[2] Hal's surveillance of every private little electronic blip about Dave reverses early twentieth century film scenes of surveillance by scientific managers, making us subjects of "electronic brains'" endless recording, tracking, and tracing of our "electronic" clicks and surfings to profile who we are and how we live. Our bodies, and our boundaries around self, private and public lives are most assuredly undergoing more than minor disturbances.

CONCLUSION

Contrary to securing "man's" place in the order of things, the computer may indeed give the lie to ordering myths. No matter the extent of their efforts, popular films' and scientists' accounts alike seem unable to sustain the natural history narrative of man the rational actor, man as tool maker and user, or man' s superior place in the great chain of being. Across these different human-machine configurations in popular culture and psychological science, it is in various moments of disruption that we most readily see how these relations operate, as Ullman said of software, "just like any natural system: out of control" (p. 126). Here as things become a little testy, bodies and selves are submitted to reworkings of gender and class meanings of psychological subjects. Reconfigurations of gender, sexuality, production and reproduction are found in each of the cases examined here: Maria as the hystericized robot; the feeding machine gone mad as the hystericized mother; EMMARC'S breakdown as the hystericized – unreliable – career woman; an eroticization of unflagging efficiency in factory line production; Chaplin's worn down – neurasthenic – masculine labourer; Boring's robot as mechanical "nature" of masculine rationality; Bales' informational style as cybernetic codes of masculine individualist identity; and, Hal's and David's mutual surveillance of each other's rational fault lines as masculinity on the technological brink of human transcendence. In not one of these cases is there returned a general, ahistorical, or eternal understanding of gender, sexuality, production or reproduction. Even so, one cannot help but be struck by certain repetitions, especially a pathologizing of suggested homosexual desire between female-denoted EMMARC and her assistant and between Hal and David. Heterosexuality thus intervenes to deliver normativity.

The human motor, the electronic brain, and now increasingly the cyborgian subject are therefore not to be understood as simply restatements of old gender versions in new configurations. This would oversimplify them as apolitical and ahistorical instances of simple multiplicity and fluidity. They are instead specific refigurations shifting bodily sites and body conceptions from muscle and energy to brain power and now to the realm of identity, senses and emotion while, however unwittingly, continuing to serve mainstream gender politics. And they are reconfigurations that draw on psychological notions as much as changing technologies have their say in psychology's collective imagination. For these reasons we need to place technology at the centre of feminist and critical work in psychology and to make this work historical, for to not do so might well indeed be "*folie*." If Y2K tells us anything in its contradictory announcements of "lights out" and "learning to love" it is that in our conflicted longings at the interface there functions a sexual politics to the psychology of desiring bodies.

Notes

1.   Thanks to Susan Henking for her always careful reads and sound suggestions.

2.   I want to acknowledge Liz Lyon who first spotted this story.

REFERENCES

Bales, R. F. (1955). How people interact in conferences. *Scientific American, 192*, (3), 31-35.
Bayer, B. M. (1999). Psychological ethics and cyborg body politics. In A. J. Gordo-López & I. Parker (Eds), *Cyberpsychology* (pp. 113-129). London: MacMillan Press Ltd.
Boring, E. G. (1946). Mind and mechanism. *The American Journal of Psychology, 59*, 173-192.
Buhle, M. J. (1998). *Feminism and its discontents: A century of struggle with psychoanalysis.* Cambridge, MA: Harvard University Press.
Dewdney, C. (1999) We, Robots? *Globe and Mail* (Feb. 27) D15.
Edwards, P. N. (1996). *The closed world: Computers and the politics of discourse in cold war America.* Cambridge, MA: Harvard University Press.
Foster, Thomas (1996). "The sex appeal of the inorganic": Posthuman narratives and the construction of desire. In R. Newman (Ed.), *Centuries' ends, narrative means* (pp. 276-301). Stanford, CA: Stanford University Press.
Garber, M. (1998). *Symptoms of culture.* New York: Routledge.
Giedion, S. (1948/1969). *Mechanization takes command.* New York: W.W. Norton & Company.
Halberstam, J. (1998). *Female masculinity.* Durham: Duke University Press.
Haraway, D.J. (1997). *Modest_Witness@Second_Millenium.FemaleMan_Meets_Onco- Mouse.* New York: Routledge.
Hayles, K. (1999). *How we became posthuman: Virtual bodies in cybernetics, literature, and informatics.* Chicago: The University of Chicago Press.
Hillis, D. (1998). The big picture. *Wired*, January, 38.
Kahane, C. (1995). *Passions of the voice: Hysteria, narrative, and the figure of the speaking woman, 1850-1915.* Baltimore: The Johns Hopkins University Press.

34

Keller, E. F. (1996). The dilemma of scientific subjectivity in postvital culture. In P. Galison & D. J. Stump (Eds), *The disunity of science: Boundaries, contexts, and power* (pp. 417-427). Stanford: Stanford University Press.

Lanier, J. (1998). Taking stock. *Wired*, January, 60-62.

Noble, D. F. (1997). *The religion of technology: The divinity of man and the spirit of invention*. New York: Alfred A. Knopf.

Rabinbach, A. (1990). *The human motor: Energy, fatigue, and the origins of modernity*. Berkeley: University of California Press.

Sedgwick, E. K. (1990). *Epistemology of the closet*. Berkeley, CA: University of California Press.

Seltzer, M. (1992). *Bodies and machines*. New York: Routledge.

Slane, A. (1997). Vulnerabilities. In J. Terry & M. Calvert (Eds), *Processed lives: Gender and technology in everyday life*. London: Routledge.

Springer, C. (1996). *Electronic eros: Bodies and desire in the postindustrial age*. Austin: University of Texas Press.

Turing, A. M. (1950). Computing machinery and intelligence. *Mind: A Quarterly Review of Psychology and Philosophy, 59*, 433-460.

Uglow, J. (1996). Introduction: 'Possibility.' In F. Spufford & J. Uglow (Eds), *Cultural Babbage: Technology, time and invention* (pp. 1-23). London: Faber and Faber.

Ullman, E. (1999). The myth of order. *Wired*, April, 126-129.

TECHNOLOGIES OF TRANS-SEXING:

Discursive Tension and Resistance within Psycho-Medical and Transgendered Theorising of Transsexual Bodies

Katrina Roen
University of Canterbury

SUMMARY

Throughout the twentieth century, there has been speculation about what is technologically possible in terms of transforming sexed bodies. This chapter argues that what can be done is actually less important than how we understand what is being done. As psychologists and psychiatrists are approached more and more often by people wishing to "change their sex", we need to address theoretical issues behind this complex request. In this chapter, I draw from interviews with transsexual and transgendered research participants and discuss the various strands of meaning that get woven together in the process of making "sex change" make sense. Sex change may become more, or less, meaningful, according to the discursive negotiations between transpeople and clinicians. It is vital for theoretical psychology to engage with these issues, offering an understanding of transsexuality that challenges simplistic approaches.

INTRODUCTION

In December 1993 "Orlan: Omnipresence" brought to the Sandra Gering Gallery in New York the latest work of the French surgical performance artist, Orlan. This consisted in the surgical reconstruction of her face to resemble a computer composite of five canonical representations of beautiful women ... At the exhibition a video of the operation ... showed a surgical team fitted out in black robes and conical hats performing on Orlan's laid-out body. The video of the surgery and its live broadcast, as Julia Epstein observes, "literaliz[ed] the term 'operating theatre.'" Underlining this theatricality, a surgeon's bloody robe stretched and pinned to the wall at Gering's bore the legend, "The body is but a costume." To be sure, by her own account, Orlan seems to divest herself of her lineaments with an ease in keeping with this figure: "Skin is a mask of strangeness, and by refiguring my face, I feel I'm actually taking off a mask." Yet like the robe's disavowal of the body's materiality, Orlan's image for the superficiality of her face only raises anxious questions about the meaning of bodily matter for identity. If skin is a mask, where is the self in relation to the body's surface? (Prosser, 1998, pp. 61-62)

In the theatre that is life, if the skin is a mask, then is our sex part of that mask? Where is our sex relative to the self, and the body's surface? How can certain bodily changes be understood as "sex change"? Prosser's introduction (above) poses questions, not about what can be done, technologically, but about what it means: What does surgical reconfiguration mean for Orlan's identity? Her demonstration may help us question how we understand sex change.

Throughout the twentieth century, there has been speculation, among transpeople,[1] medical professionals, and science fiction writers alike, about what is technologically possible, in terms of transforming sexed bodies. I suggest that what can be done is actually less important than how we understand what is being done. (That is, the material changes involved in sex reassignment may not be as important as the significatory changes.) If we conceptualise sex as hormonal, then do hormonal changes alone constitute sex change? If we conceptualise sex as genital, then does sex reassignment surgery (SRS) provide complete sex change? If sex is chromosomal, what might sex change mean then? I suggest that the meaning we attribute to certain bodily changes is far more important than the material changes which have actually taken place. Sex change has grown to impossible proportions in the public imagination; the fantasy of sex change obscures the very important diversity and fluidity of what sex change can mean.

What sex change currently means hinges largely on legal and medical definitions. While legal definitions vary from one country to another, there is legal precedent for allowing a change in gender identity after surgical and hormonal sex reassignment have taken place. Such medical procedures usually take place upon the recommendation of psychiatrists who assess the candidate in relation to diagnostic criteria that have been developed under the highly contested terms of "gender dysphoria" and "gender identity disorder".

An exploration of what sex change means is crucial for early twenty-first century theoretical psychology. As psychologists and psychiatrists are approached more and more often by people wishing to "change their sex", we need to address theoretical and philosophical issues behind this complex request. Theoretical psychology could pave the way for better understandings between clinicians and their clients by offering an analysis of gender that engages with contemporary critiques of the notion of identity and the fixity of gender. Through critical psychological theorising, sex change may take on different meanings and the overall well-being of those who seek sex change may be better attended to by psycho-medical professionals.

In this chapter, I will draw from interviews with transsexual and transgendered [2] research participants and discuss the various strands of meaning that get woven together in the process of making sex change make sense.[3]

WHAT WE "KNOW" ABOUT TRANSSEXUALITY

I will begin by introducing some of the research participants, and illustrating how they talk about transsexuality generally. I want to highlight the contradictions that impinge on what sex change means for each participant. For some participants, transsexuality is something they wish to pass through, by having a sex change, and becoming men or women. For other participants, transsexuality is a gendered state of being, for which there are no words: it is just a feeling that persists throughout life whether or not one has surgery.

Ami described "transsexual" as "a really limiting label", saying that it "categorized" her. Regarding her sense of her gender, she said, "I've always felt this way, but I don't think it's either 'man' or 'woman'". For Ami, it seemed that male-to-female (MTF) transsexuals can live their lives "as women", but never actually "reach" that place. Rather than trying to assign a label to her sense of her gender, Ami said, "it's just a knowing". She described, "I know how I feel inside and ... growing up as child, I knew how I felt then, really strongly, ... but didn't quite ever talk about it." She also described her sense of "not knowing truly what it was".

The sense of knowing and not knowing, and the sense that language can't express what is felt, are vital in the negotiation of meaning that takes place between psychologists and transpeople. It is the strength of the conviction – the sense of knowing – that drives transsexuals to doctors and psychologists. Yet, once there, they need to find a language; or rather that language is found for them. Suddenly, the sense of knowing, but not knowing what, becomes encapsulated in the very simple terms of transsexuality and sex change.

Another MTF participant told me how, after having been married and become a parent, she "discovered" that she was transsexual. Tania said to me: "my realisation about transsexuality has only been in the last two years. I [had] been to counselling for the last four [years, when] one of the therapists said to me 'have you ever considered being transsexual?'" We can only hope that the therapist did not actually say this. What is important, however, is that this is how Tania remembers it. It is as though transsexuality is one option on a smorgasbord.

Transsexuality may be a sense of "always knowing" (as it is for Ami), or an adulthood "discovery" (as for Tania). Either of these frameworks for understanding transsexuality may be supported by a positivist approach. Both frameworks assume that there is some internal or inherent truth that may be "known" or "discovered".

That the experience of gender is a deep, internal part of the self is reiterated by a number of the participants. Billy, a FTM transsexual, does not like the term "transsexual", but talks about his sense of being a man. He said "I don't like the word transsexual ... if there was no such term as transsexual ... I would just regard myself as a man. I'm not a transsexual because I feel that I'm a man inside". Similarly, for Ami, the feeling of wanting to live as a woman is "a really deep thing" that has to do with "who you are". For her, SRS "doesn't change who I [am] inside ... I always have that feeling inside". Jim made the point that a transsexual can never become a man or a woman, but is inevitably and inherently transsexual. He said, "as much as we'd like to be [men/women], I don't think we can ever be. No matter how much surgery you have it doesn't actually change you. You can change your body around but you don't actually change you."

Anthropological and sociological accounts suggest that transsexuality is only one of many gender-crossing phenomena that have occurred across cultures and across centuries. Alternatively, transsexuality may be understood as a purely twentieth century construction that has come into being due to recent medical technologies which enable sex change (Hausman, 1995).

One anthropologist, Anne Bolin (1988), draws together these understandings in her research. She critiques the role of the medical profession in constructing transsexuality as a psycho-medical phenomenon. She portrays sex change as part of a ritual of becoming which transsexuals are obliged to go through. In this picture, doctors and psychiatrists are masters of ceremony; orchestrating the ritual, and deciding who is allowed to participate, who is eligible for sex change, who is really transsexual. Bolin writes: "The gender dysphoria professionals validate their own position by declaring transsexualism a medical problem" (1988, p. 55). During an exciting era of medical and technological "discovery" it made sense for clinicians to envisage being able to "help" those who felt they did not belong in their gender. The catch-22 situation that results is that too much is assumed to be possible at the hands of surgeons and endocrinologists. As greater medical claims are made, so greater demands are made of medical professionals.

In a recent article, Joanne Meyerowitz (1998) traced the evolution of medical advancement and the increase in transsexuals' demands of medical science. She recounts the experiences of the author, often cited as having coined the term "transsexual", David Cauldwell. As an editor of the journal *Sexology*, Cauldwell tried to respond to readers' questions about making changes to hair growth, or breast growth, or simply being "made into a woman". This took place in the late forties and early fifties as new transsexing technologies began to emerge, and as the possibility of sex change was becoming more and more "real" in the minds of transsexuals. Cauldwell eventually became annoyed with "the persistent requests for surgery. He blamed medicine for creating 'fantastic hopes' and popular magazines for publishing 'tales of magic cures and magical accomplishments of surgeons'" (Meyerowitz, 1998, pp. 169-170).

The situation seemed to escalate. In the 1940s, articles published on sex change procedures claimed that these were only possible in the case of intersexuality (that is, when there has been physical/chromosomal sexual ambiguity since birth). By the 1950s some magazines were claiming that the potential for a complete transition from male to female or vice versa was not far from the horizon of medical advancement (Meyerowitz, 1998). Such claims have fed the fantasy of sex change to this day. In a more recent medical publication, we see Cauldwell's concerns still being raised. Ross writes that "[m]any patients will have grossly unrealistic ideas about what can be achieved by hormone replacement therapy and sex reassignment" (Ross, 1991, p. 90).

If we were to think of transsexuality as an inherent phenomenon which exists across time and across cultures, we could tell a story about early twentieth century transpeople visiting medical professionals for "help". We could tell a story about technological advancement throughout the twentieth century enabling clinicians to better respond to transsexuals' desires for sex change. But where exactly do those "desires" come from? Are we to assume that these desires constitute the very core – the inherent aspect – of transsexuality? If we do understand a desire for sex change as central to transsexuality, then we need to pay attention to the possibility that sex change means completely different things to different transpeople.

SEX CHANGE AND UNCERTAINTY

It became strikingly obvious to me, throughout my research, that what sex change is purported to mean, from a clinical perspective, is very different from what it means to some transpeople. Stating a desire for sex change has become a password among transsexuals, allowing them entry to a smorgasbord of medical treatments, but leaving it up to chance as to what any of those treatments might signify. The positivist drive towards scientific certainty outweighs any attempts to highlight the uncertainty that inheres in all formulations of "gender". The very people involved in negotiating what sex change means do not want, or cannot afford, to admit to uncertainty.

Transsexuals who seek SRS are often not able to discuss feelings of doubt or confusion in a clinical setting for fear of jeopardising their access to the treatments they may want. (However, in the context of my interviews, most research participants talked about the fluidity and uncertainty of gender without hesitation.) Clinicians are similarly at loggerheads with the possibility of uncertainty. The positivist, scientific base of much psycho-medical training and clinical practice makes it enormously difficult for the intensely disruptive uncertainty of gender to be accommodated. Half a century of constructing transsexuality in terms of psychopathology[4] cannot be eroded solely by transgender, queer, and feminist attempts to frame transsexuality politically and discursively.

For psycho-medical theorising to open up to the complexities of gender and of transsexuality, some very fundamental assumptions (about the body, the self, and identity) need to be challenged, at a theoretical level, by psychologists themselves. This may mean developing a psychological theory of gender that interweaves elements of psychoanalytic theory (which is highly concerned with signification and does not rest on positivist assumptions of certainty) (e.g., Millot, 1990; Shepherdson, 1994) and elements of transgender theorising (which specifically challenges traditional medical and psychological understandings of gender and which employs poststructuralist critiques of identity to formulate queered understandings of gender) (e.g., Stryker, 1994 and 1998; Stone, 1991; Prosser, 1998). For future psychological theorising of gender to contribute usefully to the negotiation of meaning around sex change, that theorising must be developed with explicit reference to its socio-political context. That is, psychological theorising of gender cannot afford to marginalise queer, feminist, and transgender theorising, but must engage with the challenges of these approaches, not as "minority group politics" but as valid and academically sound ways of theorising gender.

Sex change may be understood as making the outward physical appearance of the body consistent with the gender. The assumption is that sex is an outward, physical entity, and that gender is inherent, internal, psychological: a part of the self. Sex is the mask that can be transformed through surgery. These assumptions allow us to make sense of claims like: "I am a man trapped in a woman's body".

Sex change is based, therefore, on an assumed split between body and self. The self is what one really is inside. The self has an ontological certainty that is comforting to those used to working within a positivist framework. What is "healthy" is constructed around the assumption that bodily sex and psychological gender ought to be consistent with one another. Sex change is legitimated within the medical institution as helping transsexuals attain that healthy congruity between sex and gender.

This is one very pervasive meaning of sex change. It hinges on the notion of congruity between bodily sex and psychological gender. On this topic, Bolin writes that "Mental health caretakers, like medical professionals, provide symbolic and hence 'real' validation for the transsexual's pursuit of womanhood. They legitimize the societally held beliefs that people who are women should have vaginas" (Bolin, 1988, p. 54).

There are numerous problems with this particular meaning of sex change. It leaves us with no understanding of how the external body and the internal self interrelate. What emotional and psychological processes might a transperson need to go through to cope with SRS? What might surgically constructed genitalia have to signify for a transperson to feel satisfied post-surgically? How do notions of sex change address the multiplicity of ways in which bodies are sexed? Biologically speaking, there are not only two sexes; psychologically speaking, there are not only two gendered ways of being; yet a discourse of sex change only makes sense in a world where there are two discrete sexes, and it is conceivable to make a complete transition from one sex to the other sex.

In order for psychologists to develop a theoretical critique of hegemonic and over-simplistic understandings of sex change, it is useful to look to the recently emerging field of transgender theorising. Contemporary transgender theorist, Jay Prosser, writes:

> sex reassignment surgery is considered the hinge upon which the transsexual's "transsex" turns: the magical moment of "sex change." At the same time conceptions of sex make it difficult to believe that surgery, through the simple excision and restructuring of body parts, can miraculously and wholly alchemize one sex into "the other"... The transsexual would seem to assume a binary difference that doesn't even exist in biology: how, then, can s/he cross a space that is not clearly there? (1998, pp. 63-64)

Here, we see the cracks developing in the positivist facade of certainty. How can transsexuals cross a space that is not clearly there? What is there between the genders?

The "space between genders" is negotiated daily by transpeople and health professionals. Because (the diversity of) what sex change means to transpeople is in tension with what it means according to psycho-medical discourses, the transsexual's body becomes the site of a discursive battle. By taking note of how this battle is articulated by transpeople, and by working with poststructuralist theories of gender and identity, theoretical psychology could play a significant role in renegotiating the terms under debate.

For some people, the physical aspects of sex change are merely "cosmetic" (Ami), for they cannot change "who you are" (Jim). For others, SRS feels absolutely crucial. Billy talked about waiting endlessly for surgery as a process of "dying psychologically because something they've wanted cannot be done". Pat described his desire for surgery as being overwhelmingly strong. He said he is "disappointed that I wasn't born 'proper'". Far from being "cosmetic", in Pat's case sex change is hoped to reshape his body as it ought to have been in the first place.

On the other hand, Myra, who does not anticipate seeking surgery at all, described surgery as completely unimportant. She pointed out the inconvenience of legal identity being based on surgical status: "the law dictates that you must [have surgery] otherwise you can't change your gender. That's ridiculous. That's just an old-fashioned medical dictation. They invented that rule, we didn't". Tania encapsulated this problem succinctly with the words: "To me the law is saying that to be a woman is to be a hole, is to be a vagina. And I don't think that's right ... I know you have to ... draw the line somewhere, it just annoys me that they draw it there."

It is significant that both Tania and Myra feel sex change is deemed important, not by them, but by medical and legal institutions. While Billy and Pat are battling against the medical institution to access surgery, Tania and Myra battle to have their transgendered experience validated, without necessarily having to go through surgery. Here we see the tension between transpeople and the medical institution; this is a battle over meaning: what does it mean to have sex change?[1] Who gets to decide what this change signifies? And what aspects of one's sex must be altered for it to count as sex change?

PSYCHOLOGICAL THEORY AND PRACTICE

If the trans-sexing body is the site of a discursive battle, it comes as no surprise that clinicians' responses to transsexuals' claims generate a great deal of emotion. G.P.s, surgeons, endocrinologists, and psychiatrists can gain lasting (and sometimes very negative) reputations within transsexual communities. The most consistent message coming from the research participants I interviewed was that they did not feel they could ever rely on psycho-medical practitioners. They did not see themselves as seeking the help or support of these "so-called professionals", rather they viewed psycho-medical practitioners purely as service-providers.

Research participants' lack of confidence in psycho-medical practitioners' abilities seemed to stem from three main sources. The first is the realisation that, in this instance, the client often knows more about the "problem" than the clinician. The second is the gauntlet that transpeople have to run to get the services they seek. The third concerns the assumption that transsexuality is a psychological issue. (This assumption is implicit in the requirement that, in order to access SRS, transpeople undergo psychiatric assessment.)

Mimi and Sarah had both been through SRS seven to ten years prior to the interviews and were retrospectively critical of the process they had been required to go through to get the surgery they wanted. Mimi said: "My experience with the [gender clinic team] was that I felt that I needed to satisfy them in order to get what I wanted." This is what I refer to as running the gauntlet. Certain processes (such as psychiatric assessment) have been deemed necessary for transsexuals to go through in order to access surgery, but often those processes do not carry credibility with transsexuals. Sarah said:

> The medical people I dealt with had very little knowledge of what transsexuality was about, and there was quite a clear idea in the medical practitioners' and psychiatrists' views of what a transsexual should be like. In some ways I conformed to their image and in some ways I didn't. But I knew that I wanted surgery ... and if that was the game, then I'd play it.

When clinicians' knowledge and their protocols come into question, the whole process gets reduced to game-playing. Often transsexuals know the rules and play by them to get what they want.

Perhaps the topic which most consistently irritated and angered the participants was the psychiatric classification of transsexuality. It is in this regard that psycho-medical professionals and practices lose credibility most severely. It is in the arena of the psychiatrist's office that transsexuals are most aware that they are "playing games". When I asked Tania how she felt about the terminology of gender dysphoria, or gender identity disorder, she said that the name did not matter, because whatever "they" called it, you still had to play the same game.

Myra emphatically rejected psychiatric procedure, yet she had consulted a psychiatrist. She described her experience of visiting the psychiatrist, then said: "isn't it all a farce? You've got somebody sitting there that wants to interview you for ten minutes when you've been alive for forty years. It's crazy. The whole set-up is crazier than I am!"

In some ways, it is not for health professionals to worry about credibility. Services are tailored for enhancing health, not as part of a marketing campaign to improve the image of health workers. However, in the case where the health "problem" is defined almost entirely through the relationship between the client and the clinician, I think there is room for more careful negotiation of the clinical practices, and it is here that theoretical psychology can play a vital role. Transsexuality, unlike almost any other psycho-medical concern, only becomes a concern in so far as transpeople and clinicians work together to create the possibility of sex change. It is time to carefully reconsider the terms under which clinicians and transsexuals enter into therapeutic relationships, and develop a much greater awareness of the role that psychologists and psychiatrists play in

44

constructing notions of transsexuality and sex change.

For transsexuality to emerge in the twenty-first century, from its shroud of pathology, into a more tolerant and gender-fluid society, it is important that psycho-medical professionals and transpeople work together with greater awareness of how they mutually shape transsexuality and conceptualise sex change. Notions of transsexuality that are now emerging are more fluid than diagnostic categories will ever allow. Transsexuality has been theorised in terms of positivist psychological notions of gender and sex. These theories necessarily become unhinged by the 1990's uncertainty of gender: not just transgender but all gender. If we are to accept poststructuralist challenges to the notions of gender and sex, we must re-think what sex change means. Is it still relevant, at the beginning of the twenty-first century, for "sex change operations" to be compulsory in order for legal gender transition to be possible?

Sex change may become more, or less, meaningful, according to the discursive negotiations between transpeople and clinicians. It is vital for theoretical psychology to engage with these issues, offering a discursive understanding of transsexuality and challenging dangerously simplistic approaches to questions of gender and embodiment. Perhaps if we move beyond the assumption that transsexuality is a medical problem to be treated, or a psychological puzzle to be resolved, we may find a space in which transpeople and clinicians can have meaningful discussions with one another, and thus avoid playing life-threatening "games".

Notes

1. "Transperson" and "transpeople" are terms used to refer broadly to those who question and live outside of the gender identity with which they were raised.

2. I am using the terms "transsexual" and "transgendered" as an acknowledgement of the diverse ways in which transpeople identify. "Transsexual" refers more often to a sex change process that involves surgical alteration. "Transgendered" refers to instances where gender identity may be altered without surgical changes necessarily being sought. However, the discursive investments and political implications of each of these terms is far more complex than any brief definition would allow.

3. In the course of my doctoral research, I conducted interviews with self-identified transsexual and transgendered people during 1996 and 1997. The transcript material from some of these interviews has inspired and formed a base for this chapter. All research participants are referred to using pseudonyms and any possibly identifying features have been omitted or altered. A woman's name signifies a male-to-female (MTF) transperson and a man's name signifies a female-to-male (FTM) transperson.

4.   Whilst I am focusing, in this chapter, on the diversity of perspectives taken up by transpeople, I am not meaning to imply that medical approaches to transsexuality are entirely homogenous. Rather, the conflicting approaches, that exist among psycho-medical professionals, to the contentious issue of sex change tend to be hidden behind the dominant, conservative force of *the Diagnostic and Statistical Manual* (*DSM*) and the criteria it endorses.

REFERENCES

Bolin, A. (1988). *In search of Eve: Transsexual rites of passage*. Westport, CONN: Bergin and Garvey Publishers.

Epstein, J. (1995). *Altered conditions: Disease, medicine, and storytelling*. New York: Routledge.

Hausman, B. (1995). *Changing sex: Transsexualism, technology, and the idea of gender*. London: Duke University Press.

Meyerowitz, J. (1998). *Sex change and the popular press: Historical notes on transsexuality in the United States, 1930-1955. GLQ 4*, 159-187.

Millot, C. (1990). *Horsexe*. (K. Hylton, Trans.). New York: Autonomedia.

Prosser, J. (1998). *Second skins: The body narratives of transsexuality*. New York: Columbia University Press.

Ross, M. W. (1991). Transsexualism and transvestism. *Patient Management*, August, 89-93.

Shepherdson, C. (1994). The role of gender and the imperative of sex. In J. Copjec (Ed.) *Supposing the subject* (pp. 158-184). London: Verso.

Stone, S. (1991). The empire strikes back: A posttranssexual manifesto. In J. Epstein and K. Straub (Eds) *Body guards:The cultural politics of gender ambiguity* (pp. 280-304). New York: Routledge.

Stryker, S. (1994). My words to Victor Frankenstein above the village of Chamounix: Performing transgender rage. *GLQ, 1*, 237-254.

Stryker, S. (1998). The transgender issue. *GLQ, 4,* 145-158.

II SOCIAL AND CULTURAL PROCESSES

HUMAN EXPERIENCE AND THE ENIGMA OF CULTURE:
Toward an Enactive Account of Cultural Practice

Cor Baerveldt, Theo Verheggen and Paul Voestermans
University of Nijmegen

SUMMARY

This paper deals with the way cultural psychology should deal with human experience. The common view about the relation between culture and experience holds that experience becomes "cultural" when people internalize or appropriate ready made cultural meanings. We contend that cultural forms themselves need to be dealt with in experiential terms. To this end we propose an *"enactive"* approach to cultural psychology. A central claim of enactivism is that experience is rooted within the organizational and operational *autonomy* of an acting system. Enactivism considers human experience to be constitutive for social and cultural phenomena. The main question of an enactive cultural psychology relates to the way human action becomes *consensually coordinated*. Both social psychologists who stress "sharedness" as the distinct mark of the social, and evolutionary psychologists who consider culture to derive from a uniform human mind, are criticized for overlooking the ongoing mutual tuning processes that give rise to socially and culturally patterned conduct.

THE PROBLEM: WHY BOTHER ABOUT EXPERIENCE?

In this paper we are concerned with some compelling questions regarding the way cultural psychology should deal with experience. We claim that an adequate view of culturally patterned human action requires a fundamental revision of the way we think about experience. Although cultural psychology has always been concerned with human experience, up to now the common approach has been to consider "culture" as something which is already known and to evoke cultural norms, models, stories and ideologies as an explanation for the observed patterns in human conduct. In our view this approach runs the risk of producing post hoc explanations. One of the main things to be understood by cultural psychology is why human conduct appears to be culturally patterned *especially* when the people in question act on the basis of their own "authentic" experience (Baerveldt & Verheggen, 1999a, 1999b). Apparently there is something about culture itself that has to be explained in experiential terms. Cultural norms, for example, *are* norms *because* of particular configurations of feelings involved, so we have to be careful not to uncritically use those norms as an explanation for the cultural forms of feeling (Voestermans, 1991). Moreover, norms, models, stories, and ideologies cannot explain their own force and persuasiveness. The fact that some stories are more forceful or than other stories, or that they are compelling to some groups, while being meaningless or reprehensible to other groups, demonstrates that they rest on experiences that are already culturally orchestrated (ibid.).

We believe that the idea of culture as a pre-existing symbolic order that needs to be internalized or appropriated by its participants denies both the inherently social character of human psychological processes *and* the psychological or experiential character of cultural entities. The human mind does not become social only after swallowing certain culturally fabricated meanings (Baerveldt, 1997; Baerveldt & Verheggen, 1999a, 1999b). Instead, the mind is always social because it evolves in dialogical relations to other minds right from the beginning. As we have elsewhere claimed, "the basic question of cultural psychology should therefore not concern a presumed dialectical or dialogical relation between personal sense and ready made cultural meanings, *but the issue of how personal sense becomes coordinated in such a way that it gives rise to cultural meanings*" (Baerveldt, 1998, p. 9). So, "culture" in the sense of an already established symbolic order cannot be an explanation of meaningfully patterned actions, because culture itself demands a psychological explanation. We maintain that instead of taking for granted the meaningfulness of already produced cultural entities, cultural psychology should investigate how cultural meanings are actually produced. The notion of "production" brings to our attention the need for an adequate theory of "action" or "agency". What is it that enables human beings to act in meaningful ways? What constitutes their actions as social actions? How is it that people's actions become culturally patterned, while those people nevertheless act on the basis of their own personal experience? Of course these are profound problems, which will not be solved overnight. However, one of the mainsprings of cultural psychology in the past ten or fifteen years has been the perceived need within the social sciences to ask such old questions in renewed ways.

ENACTIVISM AND EXPERIENCE

In order to meet the challenge of accounting for culturally patterned meaningful action, we have tried to sketch the outlines of an "enactive" cultural psychology (Baerveldt, 1998; Baerveldt & Verheggen, 1999a, 1999b). The enactive paradigm has an important part of its roots within the epistemological work of the Chilean biologists Humberto Maturana and Francisco Varela (Maturana, 1978, 1980; Maturana & Varela, 1980; Varela, 1979). The word "enactivism", however, was introduced more recently by Varela, Thompson, and Rosch (1991) in their attempt to apply those epistemological insights to cognitive science.

A central claim of enactivism is that the neural system, like any other architecture embodying some kind of cognition, is "operationally closed". An operationally closed system is a system that is capable of maintaining its own internal coherence, which means that we cannot adequately account for its operations by reference to its environment. The notion of operational closure has often raised confusion, especially among those cognitive theorists who uncritically assume that the brain is some kind of computational machine that operates on the basis of informational input from its environment. Paradoxically, however, it is exactly the notion of closure that brings this environment into focus again, not just as a source of neutral information, but as a life-world charged with significance. According to Maturana a system is operationally closed when its operations are not instructed by its environment, but determined by its own structure and organization (Maturana & Varela, 1980). Although an operationally closed system can be *perturbed* by its environment, its environment cannot *force* the system into a particular course of action. The environment has only a triggering role in the realization of cognitive acts, which means that it cannot be conceived of in terms of pre-existing information. The world in this sense has no prefixed properties. Instead, a cognitive system *enacts* its own domain of significance, or its own domain of distinctions. As such a cognitive system is necessarily an experiencing system.

Within the enactive paradigm "cognition" and "experience" are two sides of the same coin. It should be stressed again that the properties of this experience cannot be derived from what an observer claims to know about a world preceding this experience. Any representational account of cognition and experience falls short, since it confuses the descriptive domain of an outside observer and the phenomenal domain of the acting system. Instead of representing or mapping the informational properties of a pre-given, "out there" world, a cognitive system *enacts* its phenomenal domain on the basis of its own closed organization. Therefore the notion of operational closure has a phenomenological counterpart in what could be called "experiential closure". Each cognitive system is a system that lives in a world of its own experience, a phenomenal world to which an external observer has principally no access. A cognitive agent is a meaning-producer rather than an information processor (Baerveldt & Verheggen, 1999a, b).

The enactive notion of operational and experiential closure has far reaching implications for the way we look upon social interaction. Since the conduct of neither of the interacting systems can be "in-structive" or "in-formative" for the other, enactivism conceives of social interaction as a constant mutual co-adaptation, or a consensual coordination of actions between meaning-producers. When such interactions acquire a recurrent character, the interactors may create a domain of interlocked conduct, or what Maturana and Varela have called a *"consensual domain"*. Contrary to one of the most prevailing intuitions with regard to the social enactivism claims that such consensual domains do not involve a *sharing* of experience. Countering individualistic trends within dominant social psychology some social psychologists have come to use the notion of "sharedness" in order to indicate what is thought of as a central feature of social phenomena. It is assumed that the intrinsically social or cultural dimension of the mind has something to do with mental representations that are *shared* by the members of a certain community. The paper of Verheggen and Baerveldt elsewhere in this volume deals with the epistemological and psychological problems associated with such a notion of "sharedness". It demonstrates that it is not "sharedness" that is the defining property of social phenomena, but the fact that people come to coordinate their own actions with respect to each other. Since each social actor acts on the basis of her or his own personal experience, in a sense all social phenomena can be said to involve a coordination of interpersonal differences rather than correspondences.

ONE BRAIN IS NO BRAIN

Although enactivism is thoroughly rooted within biological insights in the origin of meaning and cognition, it entails in no way a kind of biological reductionism, neither does it comprise a view that is antagonistic with regard to culture. In our view it is exactly the radical opposition of nature and culture that has proved to be rather counterproductive for the scientific study of meaning. As our insight in the biological foundations of the mind advances, the biological and cultural psychological view seem to converge in many respects, for example in their rejection of the essentialism and objectivism contained within present day cognitive functionalism, and in their shared concern with meaning as opposed to a merely formal "syntax of mind" (Bruner, 1990; Edelman, 1992). Now, forty years after the cognitive revolution it is becoming more and more clear that "die hard" cognitivism falls hopelessly short as a theory of meaning, since it passes by both the *embodiment* and the social *embeddedness* of the human mind (Bruner, 1990; Edelman, 1992; Lakoff and Johnson, 1998; Baerveldt, 1997; Baerveldt & Voestermans, 1996; Baerveldt & Verheggen, 1999a, b).

We think that one of the main obstacles for a psychology of meaningful action lies in the persistent inclination to play off biology against culture. After all, even the human brain evolved most dramatically in a period of time that human beings lived in close-knit social communities. This is a point largely overlooked by many self-proclaimed evolutionary psychologists, who trivialize culture in favor of a uniform human mind (see Voestermans & Baerveldt, this volume). Evolutionary psychologists consider the human mind a complex computational machin that was "designed" by natural selection to solve the kind of adaptive problems our ancestors had to face (Cosmides & Tooby, 1994). Voestermans and Baerveldt argue, however, that in its attempt to dispute a rather outdated metaphysics of meaning, evolutionary psychology submits itself to the same limited notions of causality that keeps traditional Turing machine functionalists from dealing with meaning in an adequate way. In our view an enactive approach to psychology inevitably leads to an inherently social or dialogical account of meaningful action. Although a full account of human conduct does indeed involve the biological study of the body and the brain and their evolutionary development by selective pressure, Voestermans and Baerveldt suggest that distinct psychological phenomena which are related to meaning, intentionality, consciousness, and self-awareness can only emerge within consensual domains that comprise the socially coordinated actions occurring within "communities of experiencers".

THE CONSENSUAL CONSTITUTION OF REALITY

A cultural psychology that, radically, starts from experience will have to indicate how a consensual coordination of actions can give rise to certain "frames" of action which *appear* as independent contexts for those actions. Gregory Bateson was probably the first to realize that the framing of social interactions involves a paradox analogous to the kind of paradox that has been bothering logicians for centuries (Bateson, 1972). The best-known paradox is the classical paradox of Epimenides, also known as the "paradox of the liar". In its modern form this paradox is most often represented in the statement "this statement is not true". The problem is of course that if this statement were true, it would be untrue and if it were untrue, it would be true. In their classical work on the logical foundations of mathematics Whitehead and Russell (1910-1913) tried to demonstrate that such paradoxes emerge as a consequence of confusing different logical types. A statement belonging to a certain "class" of statements cannot simultaneously contain a truth about this class. In other words, a statement cannot tell the truth about itself, without creating a paradox, and rendering itself nonsensical.

What Bateson demonstrated is that in spite of this logical prohibition these kinds of paradoxes emerge time and again in the communication between people and even between social animals.[1] The expressive style involved in complex behavioral phenomena like "play", or "threat", or "deceit" seems to violate the Whitehead and Russell prohibition of self reference. A monkey that playfully bites a congener, or two dogs showing off fangs while keeping clear of an actual fight are somehow able to communicate a message of the kind: "the actions I perform do not mean what they mean". In other words, those animals are capable of interacting with their own interactions, thereby setting a "context" or a "frame" in which those actions can be understood as meaningful. This is why Bateson uses the word "framing". Framing is the creation *in* the interaction of a context for that very *same* interaction.

Human communication is characterized by endless possibilities for second and even higher order coordinations of actions. We can signify things like "this is not a joke" or "do you think I'm not serious?" or "stop lying to me" to mention only a few examples. What those higher order consensual coordinations of action have in common is that they are what could be called "reality-constituting practices". By interacting with their own interactions people are able to consensually establish what ought to be taken as real. A central claim of the enactive paradigm is that objective reality, that is, a reality consisting of "objects", does not precede human interaction, since objects can only emerge within a domain of coordinations of coordinations of actions (Maturana, 1978, 1980, 1988; Maturana & Varela, 1980; Baerveldt & Verheggen, 1999a, b). Words are of course the means par excellence to perform such higher order coordinations of actions. The word "table", for example, does not only coordinate the possible ways in which we can interact with an entity in the world, but it also coordinates those possible interactions with respect to other actors. *Calling* something a table presupposes the existence of other actors, of whom we assume that they experience the table in somewhat comparable ways. This implies that the table is already part of a consensual domain, a co-operative domain of interactions which we ourselves help to constitute. The table as an objective entity does not exist apart from our own conduct, neither does it exist apart from the way we coordinate our conduct with respect to other actors.

ENACTIVISM AND THE DISCURSIVE THESIS

Although objective reality is socially constituted it would be a mistake to conceive of all reality as only a matter of free floating discursive construction. Since the consensually coordinated actions that give rise to reality remain firmly rooted within human experience, we should be careful not to derive the whole world from what we claim to know already about discourse. Our argument against such discursive relativism is not that it passes by a real world that precedes human discourse, but rather that it passes by experience. So, far from intending to evoke some naïve realistic argument again, our focus concerns the way in which experiencing human agents coordinate their actions such that it gives rise to objective reality. This becomes particularly important when the "reality" concerned is not that of tables, rocks and trees, but that of cultural entities like "marriage" or "motherhood" or "the constitution". Such entities obviously belong to what Shweder (1991) has called "intentional worlds". Their reality is assembled out of the elements of people's very own experience, as Von Glasersfeld (1991) has phrased it.

According to Shweder, our socio-cultural environment is intentional "because its existence is real, factual, and forceful, but only as long as there exists a community of persons whose beliefs, desires, emotion, purposes, and other mental representations are directed at, and thereby influenced by, it" (Shweder, 1991, p. 74). But in spite of his eloquence, Shweder skirts around the central question rather than elucidating it. After all, we call something "marriage" or "motherhood" *because* of a particular configuration of beliefs, desires, emotion, and purposes that is involved. It therefore hardly makes sense to maintain that such intentional realities influence those same beliefs, desires, emotion, and purposes. As soon as we ask the *empirical* question how those beliefs, desires, emotion, and purposes acquire their particular form, Shweder's assertion appears to be no more than a tautology. The observation that all mothers gave birth to one or more children is not an empirical observation, because the fact of having given birth to children is already included in the word "mother". Likewise, the assertion that people do certain things *because* they are influenced by, for example, the institution of marriage or motherhood is not an empirical assertion, because "marriage" and "motherhood" are themselves no more than words for what people do in apparently patterned ways. As such, cultural entities like "marriage" and "motherhood" cannot function as explanations of patterned conduct. They are realities that have themselves to be understood in terms of cultural psychology. An empirical account of meaningful human actions asks for an explication of the principles that are involved in the coordination of those actions, that does not already include the outcome of those very same actions.

Elsewhere we have argued that a consensual coordination of actions is not necessarily discursive in nature (Baerveldt & Verheggen 1999a, 1999b). Although discourse is certainly most conspicuous in this respect, discursive patterns are themselves to be understood in terms of the mutual tuning processes by which "personal" experience becomes consensually validated. Most discursive psychologists are mainly concerned with the way people account for their own and other people's actions, but remain neutral with respect to the experiential basis of such accounts. An enactive cultural psychology tries to do justice to experience while avoiding the pitfalls of essentialism. Its main focus is the way in which experiencing persons coordinate their actions with respect to other experiencing persons. Neither "true" experience nor a pre-established cultural world can provide us with a substantial ground for understanding patterned conduct. As for culture, our aim is to study how persistent patterns in human action are brought about in a dynamical process that involves nothing else than action itself.

Note

1.   In fact, the Whitehead and Russell theory of logical types is a prohibition of self-referential statements. This is particularly interesting because self-reference is a core concept in the theory of autopoiesis. However, rather than proving their theory, Whitehead and Russell posed it as a rule. As such, it was later contested by several mathematicians and philosophers of mathematics, among who were eminent thinkers like Wittgenstein and — less well known — G. Spencer Brown. Spencer Brown developed a calculus of distinctions (Spencer Brown, 1969) which is the basis for a calculus of self-reference further developed by Varela in his "principles of biological autonomy" (Varela, 1979).

REFERENCES

Baerveldt, C. (1997). Cultural psychology as the study of meaning. Paper presented at the symposium "*Unidades de Análisis en la Psigología Cultural*" at the XVII "Coloquio de Investigación", 14-17 october, 1997, Universidad Nacional Autónoma de México, Escuela Nacional de Estudios Profesionales Iztacala,

Baerveldt, C (1998). Culture and the consensual coordination of actions. Unpublished doctoral dissertation, University of Nijmegen.

Baerveldt, C., & Verheggen, T. (1999a). Enactivism and the experiential reality of culture: Rethinking the epistemological basis of cultural psychology. *Culture & Psychology, 5*, 183-206.

Baerveldt, C., & Verheggen, T. (1999b). Towards a psychological study of culture: Epistemological considerations. In W. Maiers, B. Bayer, B. Duarte Esgalhado, R. Jorna, & E. Schraube (Eds), *Challenges to theoretical psychology*. North York,Canada: Captus.

Baerveldt, C., & Voestermans, P. (1996). The body as a selfing device: The case of anorexia nervosa. *Theory & Psychology, 6*, 693-713.

Bateson, G. (1972). *Steps to an ecology of mind*. New York, NY: Ballantine.

Bruner, J. (1990). *Acts of meaning*. Cambridge, MA: Harvard University Press.

Cosmides, L., & Tooby, J. (1994). Beyond intuition and instinct blindness: Toward an evolutionary rigorous cognitive science. *Cognition, 50*, 41-77.

Edelman, G. (1992). *Bright air, brilliant fire: On the matter of the mind*. London: Penguin.

Lakoff, G., & Johnson, M.(1998). *Philosophy in the flesh: The embodied mind and its challenge to western thought*. New York: Basic Books.

Maturana, H. (1978). Biology of language: The epistemology of reality. In G. A. Miller & E. Lenneberg (Eds.), *Psychology and biology of language and thought: Essays in honour of Eric Lenneberg* (pp. 27-63). New York: Academic Press.

Maturana, H. (1980). Man and society. In F. Benseler, P.M. Hejl, & W.K. Köck (Eds), *Autopoiesis, communication and society: The theory of autopoietic systems in the social sciences* (pp. 11-32). Frankfurt: Campus Verlag.

Maturana, H. (1988). Reality: The search for objectivity or the quest for a compelling argument. *The Irish Journal of Psychology, 9*, 25-82.

Maturana, H., & Varela, F. (1980). *Autopoiesis and cognition: The realization of the living*. Dordrecht: Reidel Publishing Company.

Shweder, R.A. (1991). *Thinking through cultures: Expeditions in cultural psychology*. Cambridge, MA: Harvard University Press.

Spencer Brown, G. (1969). *Laws of form*. London: Allen and Unwin.

Varela, F. (1979). *Principles of biological autonomy*. New York: Elsevier North Holland.

Varela, F.J., Thompson, F., & Rosch, E. (1991). *The Embodied mind: Cognitive science and human experience*. Cambridge, MA: MIT Press.

Voestermans, P. (1991). Alterity/Identity: A deficient image of culture. In J. Leerssen & R. Corbey (Eds), *Alterity, identity, image: Selves and others in society and scholarship* (pp. 219-250). Amsterdam: Rodopi.

Von Glasersfeld, E. (1991). Knowing without metaphysics: Aspects of the radical constructivist position. In F. Steier (Ed.), *Research and reflexivity*. London: Sage.

FROM SHARED REPRESENTATIONS TO CONSENSUALLY COORDINATED ACTIONS:
Toward an Intrinsically Social Psychology

Theo Verheggen and Cor Baerveldt
University of Nijmegen

SUMMARY

A concern in contemporary social psychological theory is to reestablish its intrinsically social or cultural dimension, since psychology (even social psychology) has been too much a science of self contained individuals. We argue that current approaches to this "restoration" – focussing either on social cognitions or on aggregate features people appear to have in common – cannot present an intrinsically social psychology either. A different approach can be found in social representation theory. We address Wolfgang Wagner's approach and his notions of social representations as processes of concerted interaction and as world constituting "enactions". It, however, also holds a problematic notion of social representations as shared representations. As a promising alternative, we present the enactivism framework. While preserving the notion of concerted interaction, it can avoid the epistemological and conceptual pitfalls of "sharedness". In addition, it can offer a criterion for identifying intrinsically social phenomena.

INTRODUCTION

In the last few years of the twentieth century, there have been a number of attempts to "reclaim" (Greenwood, 1994) or "restore" (Farr, 1998) the social dimension within social psychology. Apparently, and despite its explicit label, the discipline has been too much of an individualist science, as Carl Graumann argued (1986; see also Smith, 1997); at least since Floyd H. Allport's book *Social Psychology* (1924), which marks a remarkable but influential choice within the field. From then on, the behavior of *individual* persons would dominate social psychology's (research) agenda. As a consequence, the social became radically individualized. The properties, actions and cognitions of single individuals were identified as the sole source from which we can – even must – gain understanding of all forms of human behavior. Nowadays, within theory and research, the awareness that there is hardly any act, emotion, belief, cognition, or other mental state that is *not* socially affected or culturally modeled, has gained sufficient ground. When thinking about human behavior, the social dimension of that conduct needs to be accounted for from the outset. Not surprisingly, then, several attempts have been made to design an "intrinsically social psychology" in which the inherently social nature of people's behavioral repertoire is the object of study. In a gross outline, it is possible to identify two directions by which social scientist pursue the intrinsically social nature of psychological processes. On the one hand, certain cognitions are believed to hold the key to the social dimension of behavior. On the other hand, the social is searched for in a shared palette of ideas, models, scripts, representations, and so forth.[1]

SOCIAL COGNITIONS AS COGNITIONS OF THE SOCIAL

According to Graumann (1986), psychological social psychology[2] searches for the social dimension of human behavior in the mental states, cognitions and emotions of individual people "insofar as they have been affected by stimulation from other individuals" (p. 100). In the cognitive age, this has been translated in the tendency to search for "the social" in the cognitions an individual person has of others, of the group he or she belongs to, of the "outgroup"; or it is sought for in the cognitions several others have of a certain person. The social is discounted as a function of the reactions or stimuli related to other people. As Graumann rightfully argues, such a psychology studies intra-personal rather than interpersonal processes. As a sub-discipline of psychology, then, social psychology is *not* a *social* science. It remains the study of socially sterile persons as the true unit of analysis. Consequently, the social production of these cognitions is hardly addressed at all. "There is virtually no consideration of the possibility that cognition itself has social dimensions … and it is simply assumed that the same individual psychological explanations that apply to our cognition of non-social objects will apply to the social domain", as John Greenwood (1994, p. 95) put it.

The Social as an Observer-Independent Category

John Greenwood (1994) focuses attention on the difference between aggregate (or derivatively social) and intrinsically social phenomena. His point is that we often confuse "the social" with a feature people may happen to have in common. For instance, as he would argue (p. 87), all the people present in Central Park at 4 p.m. on Sunday afternoon do not for that matter – of sharing a place and time – also constitute a social group. For a group to be truly (intrinsically) social, it is necessary that the members of the group conform to a set of arrangements, conventions and agreements to which they are parties. It is in terms of these arrangements, conventions and agreements that people can be observed to engage in patterns of interactions by which they can be distinguished *as a group* from people that are not parties to these interaction patterns. The important point for our discussion is that social scientists themselves often "construct" social groups by categorizing people on the basis of a feature they are observed to possess, as in the example. It is thus that scholars produce and compare such aggregate groups (e.g. women, Catholics, students, Danes, people wearing blue caps) while assuming that the salient variables that they in fact have introduced themselves (a) actually represent an existing dimension or force that makes a difference in everyday (social) life and (b) that these variables/features can explain behavioral differences between the members of the "groups". But again, the group is only an aggregate here. It is the constructive act of, and a category made by, the scientist/observer. As such, these observer-dependent categories have been often mistaken for the beacons of "the social".

The Social Representation Approach of Wolfgang Wagner

Quite a different approach in the "restoration" of the social dimension comes from social representation theory (SRT). To be sure, there are many variants of SRT, but we single out Wofgang Wagner's approach (1996; 1998) because he poses and tackles the type of questions that we pursue also. Wagner looks for the production principles of social cognitions or representations. What, then, is a social representation about?

To begin with, Wagner observes – in line with Serge Moscovici – that the term "social" must not be understood as a property of objects. Instead, the adjective "becomes a relational attribute characterizing the relationship between a person and an object, event or phenomenon which constitutes his or her group's world" (p. 301). So it is the relationship between the person and the object that constitutes the world, more precisely, that constitutes the world for a person or an observer. An object is, in the words of Wagner (p. 306), any material, imaginary or symbolic entity that people name, assign properties and values to, talk about, in short: that they relate to. The key point is that all these actions we direct towards objects are *social* actions, since naming, assigning value, and so forth imply discourse, elaboration, orientation and coordination of our actions towards these "objects". By this, we make them social, according to Wagner. He continues by claiming that this assigning process has to be carried out in a coordinated or tuned fashion with respect to other members of the community. There has to be some sort of consensus among these members in order to communicate, to understand what they are doing and talking about, and so on. We agree with Wagner (1998, p. 307) that "concerted interaction is the cornerstone of the social construction of the world". Let us tip our hand early: the important question is *how* interaction becomes concerted. Within SRT this remains a question, however.

The social, world-constituting relationship we identified is constituted precisely in the concerted manner in which we elaborate on the undomesticated "somethings" (cf. Searle's "brute facts", 1995). According to Wagner, this practice "may be bodily or verbal or both, and [it is] the expression of and inseparable from the representation" (p. 307). It is "discursive elaboration of a meaning system" on the one hand, and "acting as if the object had those characteristics which it is thought to possess" on the other (ibid.). Wagner's next move is to identify the representation with the social object it seems to represent. He writes: "[a] representation and its object are coexistent as a consequence of people's concerted discourse and conduct and ... this discourse and conduct realizes the object in the social world" (p. 314); and "the world of domesticated objects *is* the local universe of representations" (p. 308).

To briefly summarize Wagner's argument: first, in the concerted manner in which we elaborate on a "something", we create the social object; second, that creative, coordinated praxis is the social representation itself; third, the something is elaborated upon by means of a verbal, discursive and/or bodily act.

THE PROBLEM OF "SHAREDNESS"

So far, so good... According to Wagner, it is through discursive processes that people come to produce and *share* a similar set of representations – apparently by means of some sort of internalization and externalization processes that SRT refers to but does not further specify, such that people in groups come to "calibrate their minds" (p. 304). Wagner claims that the social representation exists on the intersection of personal experience and the "collectively *shared* experience of culturally similar others" (p. 301; our emphasis). An object becomes "a social object within the group's system of common sense and in the course of interactions in which actors *sharing* a representation engage" (p. 307; our emphasis). Likewise, Rob Farr (1998, p. 279) contends that what lends a social representation its "inherently social nature" is the fact that it is shared by a number of people. More precisely, he gives what he calls a minimal definition of a social representation: "A representation is social if it is, or has been, in two or more minds" (p. 291). A social representation is thus an idea, image, belief and so forth that is somehow shared by a number of people.

It may indeed appear *for an observer* that people belong to a group because they share a distinctive feature. This assumption underlies many social psychological theories and most experimental research. See, for instance, theories of cultural models (D'Andrade, 1995), scripts (Fischer, 1991), scenarios, and cultural schemas (Strauss & Quinn, 1998). To give an example, people are held to belong to a group because they share the same or at least very similar representations. Or, people are believed to be members of the same culture because they seem to adhere to the same cultural models or scenarios. It is then assumed that "the social" is somehow locked into the shared nature of such models, scripts, or representations. Unfortunately, it is not at all clear what the term "shared" means in different arguments. It sometimes refers to an idea that exists in a number of minds, but this is problematic: how can we be sure that I have exactly the same idea(s) as my colleague has about the contents of this paper, for instance? In other cases, "shared idea" may indicate that a number of people have very *similar* – instead of identical – notions. This, however, is merely asking the same question in a different manner. Confusion only increases when different connotations are applied within one and the same argument, for instance when people not only are believed to have experiences and representations in common, but also to "collectively share" them (as in one of the above quotations from Wagner). Is this a pleonasm, then? Or is it precisely *not* that? In either case, "shared" does not explain much: if we all wear "the same" uniform, do we then "share" a collective uniform? Certainly not! as Voestermans (1998, personal communication) would say. Many decades ago, the fuzziness of the term "shared" already led Gordon Allport to claim that we should radically avoid it when describing ideas, norms, and the like (Greenwood, p. 97). But even if we would have a clear notion of the term, we, as analysts, must still avoid the pitfall of ourselves constructing the sharedness of the phenomena we observe. We cannot explain intrinsically social behavior by merely saying that the interaction partners have the same representations, for instance, because this is an account in terms of observer-dependent categories. We then confuse the social with what people have in common.

To sum up our argument so far: Neither cognitions *about* social phenomena nor aggregate features can count as social markers since they have no intrinsically social value. If we want to make a statement about inherently social psychological phenomena, then we must not search for the social in a shared property (independent variable) but instead direct our attention toward the consensually coordinated interactions people engage in. The challenge is to understand how these interactions are produced and how they take shape. Wagner's ideas about social representations as processes of concerted interaction and as world constituting "enactions" appear a promising approach. However, he still adheres to a problematic notion of social representations as shared representations. Where to find an alternative then?

ENACTIVISM: CONSENSUS INSTEAD OF SHAREDNESS

Let us start by repeating SRT's claim that all the actions we direct towards objects are *social* actions since they imply coordination of our behavior towards other members of our community: what we recognize as, call, think of, do with, and communicate about an object has somehow become concerted with respect to others.

The enactive paradigm (see Varela, Thompson & Rosch, 1991; Baerveldt & Verheggen, 1999a, b) also focuses on the mutual coordination of actions. One of its starting points is the observation that experiencing agents fundamentally have no direct access to the experiences of others. This inaccessibility does not exclude these actors from having social interactions. Quite on the contrary, it is *because* we cannot immediately know the feelings and cognitions of our fellow men that we need to mutually adjust our actions with respect to others. Put differently: it is because of their experiential closure that people, as well as other experiencing systems, have to communicate in order to operate in a world populated by other experiencers.[3] Enactivism states that the interactions we have with others – other experiencing systems that is – are almost always of the form of second, or higher, order coordinations. This means that experiencers can again (consensually) interact with the product of their concerted interactions. To give a simple example: a history of coordinated interactions with respect to a "fair" division of resources among a couple of people, may lead to a formalization of these patterns of interactions. The competitors could make a division rule that they all support. In effect, they can also relate their actions to this second or maybe even higher order product of their interactions: they can obey or ignore or change the established patterns of conduct (more formally, the rule). The important point is that a history of interactions has gained a particular meaning for the agents, with which they can interact in effect. This notion comes of course very close to Wagner's ideas on the social constitution of "objects". We would like to add that *any* form of second or higher order coordination could constitute objects; the latter need not be made explicit in language. Non-linguistic rituals, dances or melodies too can communicate "this means", "this is play", "this is as if", and so forth without linguistically representing such a message.

Consequently, when the coordinating behavior of two or more experiencing agents obtains a recursive character, *an observer* may come to the conclusion that they have a "shared" reality. Maturana and Varela call such a seemingly shared reality a "consensual domain" (Maturana & Varela, 1980; Varela, 1979). The word "shared" is misleading however, as we stated above, because what seems to be shared actually belongs to the descriptive domain of an observer – notice that the observer and the actor/agent may be one and the same organism. A consensual domain is in fact a "co-operative domain of interactions" (Whitaker, 1997). Therefore, when we speak about culture as a socially shared reality, we implicitly or explicitly refer to the consensual coordination of individual actions that constitutes this "shared" reality.

Experiential closure implies the impossibility of shared experience. Moreover, it implies that the experiences of agents differs by definition. Consensual coordination of actions is therefore a much more accurate description of the process underlying meaningful world construction (as is Wagner's calibration or orchestration). And that world is inherently an enacted one. "Coordinating", here, is about arranging differences. It should be the object of analysis to understand how this consensual coordination takes place in real life interactions.

Only in the case of such consensually coordinated patterns of behavior, can we justly speak of intrinsically social interactions. In these interactions, the identity – as experientially closed systems – of all the agents that are parties to the interaction must be constitutive for that interaction. Consider the following example: while driving your car you hit a biker; by accident and only mildly; fortunately nobody gets injured, but still, you hit him. In our view, that interaction cannot be labeled intrinsically social. The experiential autonomy of the cyclist is *not* constitutive for the interaction pattern. To be sure, cycling, driving a car, even hitting a biker are social *actions* since these activities are charged with cultural artifacts, prescriptions, meanings and so on. Nevertheless, intrinsically social the interaction is not. Now consider the situation in which the cyclist just scared you by popping up out of the blue in front of your bumper, swearing and ridiculing your driving style. You get a little frustrated and almost by accident you hit the cyclist, only mildly, fortunately nobody gets injured, but still... In this case, the other party is constitutive for the social interaction since he does contribute to the interaction as experiencer; his identity or autonomy is at stake in the course of the event. This, we contend, *is* an example of an intrinsically social interaction.

Final Remarks

Rather than asking for the ontological status of social or, for that manner, collective representations (Farr, 1998), we argued that social psychologists should try to understand the epistemological nature of these and other purportedly social phenomena (such as scripts, models, scenarios and so forth) in the first place. We must understand how description, action, observation, and cognition are inherently social from the outset. Enactivism can avoid the epistemological and conceptual pitfalls of (shared) social re-presentationalism. It identifies the observer-dependent nature of alleged shared social processes and phenomena. As such, sharedness has an epistemological rather than an ontological status.

Similarly, Wagner's SRT enactivism focuses on concerted or consensually coordinated interactions of experiencing agents. Since we principally have no access to the experiences of others, we cannot share similar – let alone the same – experiences, representations, scripts, models, and the like. What people "have in common" is not a set of ready made ideas but a history of interlocked conduct; the experiencing agents are parties to consensual domains. That should be the unit of investigation when designing a psychological study of culture, or for that matter, a psychology of intrinsically social processes.

Notes

1. Some authors conceive of the social psychological phenomena with reference to situational factors or the social context (see Cole, 1996; see also Greenwood, 1994, p. 99). In our opinion, as far as these theories acknowledge an agent, it brings us again back to the conceptions of the social as discussed in this text. We therefore do not discriminate a third orientation, here, in which `the social' is understood as social context or the like.

2. As opposed to sociological social psychology, the discipline that is concentrated on the social structures individuals embody (Graumann, 1986, p. 98).

3. Elsewhere (Baerveldt & Verheggen, 1999a, b) we deal in detail with the formal arguments underlying the notion of experiential closure.

REFERENCES

Allport, F.H. (1924). *Social psychology*. Boston: Houghton Mifflin.

Baerveldt, C. & Verheggen, T. (1999a). Enactivism and the experiential reality of culture: Rethinking the epistemological basis of cultural psychology. *Culture & Psychology*, 5 (2), 183-206.

Baerveldt, C. & Verheggen, T. (1999b). Towards a psychological study of culture. Epistemological considerations. In W. Maiers, B. Bayer, B. Duarte Esgalhado, R. Jorna, & E. Schraube (Eds). *Challenges to theoretical psychology*. North York, Canada: Captus, 296-303.

Cole, M. (1996). *Cultural psychology: A once and future discipline*. Cambridge: The Belknap Press of Harvard University Press.

D'Andrade, R.G. (1995) *The development of cognitive anthropology*. Cambridge: Cambridge University Press.

Farr, R.M. (1998). From collective to social representations: Aller et retour. *Culture & Psychology*, 4(3), 275-296.

Fischer, A. (1991). *Emotion scripts: A study of the social and cognitive facets of emotions*. Leiden: DSWO Press.

Graumann, C.F. (1986). The individualization of the social and the desocialization of the individual: Floyd H. Allport's contribution to social psychology. In C.F. Graumann and S. Moscovici (Eds), *Changing conceptions of crowd, mind and behavior* (pp. 97–116). New York: Springer.

Greenwood, J.D. (1994*). Realism, identity and emotion: Reclaiming social psychology*. London: Sage.

Maturana, H. & Varela, F.J. (1980). *Autopoiesis and cognition: The realization of the living*. Dordrecht: Reidel.

Searle, J.R. (1995). *The construction of social reality*. New York: The Free Press.

Smith, R. (1997). *The Fontana history of the human sciences*. London: Fontana Press.

Strauss, C. & Quinn, N. (1998). *A cognitive theory of cultural meaning*. Cambridge: Cambridge University Press.

Varela, F.J. (1979). *Principles of biological autonomy*. New York: Elsevier North Holland.

Varela, F.J., Thompson, F., & Rosch, E. (1991*). The embodied mind: Cognitive science and human experience*. Cambridge: MIT Press.

Wagner, W. (1996). Queries about social representation and construction. *Journal for the Theory of Social Behavior*, 26 (2), 95-120.

Wagner, W. (1998). Social representations and beyond: Brute facts, symbolic coping and domesticated worlds. *Culture & Psychology*, 4 (3), 297-329.

Whitaker, R. (1997). Self-organization, autopoiesis, and enterprises. Retrieved June 12, 1997 from the World Wide Web: http://www.acm.org/sigois/auto/main.html

CULTURAL PSYCHOLOGY MEETS EVOLUTIONARY PSYCHOLOGY:
Toward a New Role for Biology in the Study of Culture and Experience

Paul Voestermans and Cor Baerveldt
University of Nijmegen

SUMMARY

In this article we argue that evolutionary psychology's study of culture in the framework of memetics and in terms of modules in the brain, supposedly designed in response to adaptive problems in the stone age, suffers from a few shortcomings. Therefore, the central issue of cultural psychology, that is understanding in psychological terms the patterning of behavior, remains untouched. First, the notion of causality, which is central to the Integrated Causal Model approach as an alternative to the Standard Social Science Model, is too narrowly defined. Second, the animal nature of the human species is presented in insufficient detail. The brain is cut loose from its embodied existence and treated as an isolated entity. Brains exist in the plural and develop in the intrinsically social group, as we argue. A more viable brain-approach to culture is called for. Enactivism, as the central tenet of this new approach, emphasizes the brain as an embodied control structure which operates in a community of experiencers.

INTRODUCTION

It is quite surprising how quickly cognitive scientists who – in the spirit of Ulric Neisser's 1976 book *Cognition and Reality* – reclaimed the study of consciousness as the proper subject for psychology, adopted the evolutionary psychology framework. Evolutionary psychologists are organized in various programs to study, among other things, social psychological issues, issues of mating, sex and gender, and culture. They claim to have something important to say about how the mind works. Natural selection and adaptation are chosen as the hallmarks of a new science of the mind. A rather polemical stance is taken in stressing the importance of a causal model for a proper study of the mind. Psychologists should it is said line up with biologists and together with them construct a real science.

In this article we will deal especially with psychologists, who in close cooperation with evolutionary biologists, human ethologists, cognitivists and neuroscientists, propose a new science of the mind and a new approach to culture. We call them evolutionary psychologists. We are well aware of the fact that there exists a wide variety, but only a few of them deal explicitly with culture (e.g. Barkow, Cosmides & Tooby, 1992; Tooby & Cosmides, 1992). To them we address ourselves. We will first give an account of the basic orientation and assumptions by describing what evolutionary psychology is about. Then we will try to assess its importance for psychology and for a psychology of culture in particular. Our central question will be whether evolutionary psychology's basic orientation and principles are useful for an understanding of culture. What we have to say hopefully leads to a better integration of evolutionary biology's insight into cultural psychology than is the case now.

THE BASICS OF EVOLUTIONARY PSYCHOLOGY

Evolutionary psychologists are much concerned with the behavior-generating principles in the brain, which came into existence under the pressure of adaptive problems in the environment. They want to get rid of the *Standard Social Science Model* (SSSM) of the social and behavioral sciences. In their view this model is defined and defended by, for example, Geertz (1973) and Montagu (1964) and it holds that culture is some sort of superstructure, built upon the natural basis that evolution has provided. It also holds that culture is a symbolic system, which brings all kinds of behavioral structures from the outside inside the human being. The SSSM is a relic from thoughts entertained already long before Darwin. At that time the human mind was not considered to be part of nature. It was a pre-given device (from divine origin) which stood open to the outside world and took its content from the social world. The evolutionary psychologists are convinced that this assumption is still a vital part of the SSSM. Central to this model is the idea that the mind operates on the basis of the free social construction of its content. This idea lies also at the basis of a few incorrect presuppositions with respect to culture, so the evolutionary psychologists argue. The most important one is that culture is somehow transmitted to a brain that functions as a "general purpose machine". To this machine belong the abilities to learn and to imitate others. General intelligence and rationality belong to it as well. The idea is that these functions are all free of content. Let us quote what the evolutionary psychologist have to say on this score: "all of the specific content of the human mind originally derives from the outside – from the environment and the social world – and the evolved architecture of the mind consists solely or predominantly of a small number of general purpose mechanisms that are content-independent, and which sail under names such as "learning", "induction", "intelligence", "imitation", "rationality", "the capacity of culture" or simply "culture" (Cosmides & Tooby, Internet Primer, 1997, p. 3).

What is the alternative proposed by the evolutionary psychologists? In the course of evolution a few regulative, functionally specialized circuits in the brain have been devised. They are designed for the execution of behaviors which are functionally organized around adaptive problems our stone age forebears encountered. There is some convergence on the part of neuroscientists, evolutionary biologists, and cognitive psychologists on the issue of how the brain as a physical system processes information in order to generate certain behaviors. This convergence aims at the understanding in terms of "computations" and "information processing" of a variety of behaviors, ranging from perception and cognitive functioning (Cosmides & Tooby, 1994) to sex and mating behavior (Symons, 1979) and several social psychological phenomena (Simpson & Kenrick, 1997). Those who adopt the SSSM have (it is said) assumed too readily that "all significant aspects of adult mental organization are supplied culturally". Linking the production of culture solely to "general purpose learning mechanisms or content- independent cognitive processes" denies the relationship between biology and psychology and suggests too strongly that human being are instinctually "underprepared". Learning becomes too much of a "window through which the culturally manufactured pre-existing complex organization outside of the individual manages to climb inside the individual" (Tooby & Cosmides,1992, p. 30). Content-specific brain mechanisms are neglected.

EVOLUTIONARY PSYCHOLOGY'S EXPLANATION OF CULTURE

If evolutionary psychologists depart from the assumption that human beings have a brain which consists of specialized modules from which the content of their behavior derives, how then do the evolutionary psychologists look at culture? They claim that they can explain culture.

Culture is quite important in the eyes of evolutionary psychologists. Humans are the only species "that has an extra medium of design preservation and design communication" (Dennett, 1991, p. 338). Culture "can swamp many – but not all – of the earlier genetic pressures and processes that created it and still coexist with it"(ibid.). The way evolutionary psychologist try to deal with culture has two aspects. One follows directly from the line of argument that starts with a critique of the general purpose machine, the other is developed as an analogue to genes. In the latter case, culture traits are turned into "memes" to which the concepts "variation", "replication" and "fitness" apply equally well as in genetic theory. People's ideas tend to survive by using the individual as a reproductive device; a replica is made, sometimes with some variation, and once the whole thing fits into a certain environment, the idea carries on (Blackmore, 1999). This is supposedly true for crucial inventions, a piece of music, a moral imperative, playing chess, and for material things we can no longer do without (Dawkins, 1989). Memetics, as the science of memes is called, tries to explain cultural patterns this way, and tries to come to grips with persistent behaviors and ideologies. Dennett (1991, p. 353 ff.) in his enthusiasm for memetics, has pointed out that memes are conceptually useful and interesting, because of the analogy with genes. "Gene" as a concept for information, does its work irrespective of how it is materialized. What is important is its syntax-like structure which can be read off in order to create functional organs. The same holds for memes. They carry information irrespective of how they are materialized. The individual is merely the vehicle by means of which memes replicate themselves. In memetics one wants to get rid of the acting person in the same way as in evolutionary psychology in general, where algorithms and macros take over the role of a conscious agent in order to do away with metaphysical categories like "mind" and "God". Memes as cultural traits are self-preserving, using the individual mind as bearer of the traits. Memes are responsible for the persistence of certain traits, even those that do not directly favor the group in which those traits spread themselves around.

What lies at the basis of this Darwinian view of culture? In applying evolutionary psychological principles to culture, a distinction is made in cultural phenomena. The primary set contains representations or features which exist in a single brain. Next you have the set of phenomena that come into being in other brains. These stem from the interaction between features of the source and of the receiver. What is brought about are "inferential mechanisms in the observer to recreate the representations and elements in his or her own psychological architecture" (Tooby & Cosmides, 1992, p. 118). This secondary class is termed "reconstructed culture", "adopted culture" or "epidemiological culture". Unlike the standard social science view, this emphasis on inference implies that much learning is *not* the basis of transmission. The central idea of evolutionary psychologists of culture is that in this inferential process it is content-specific and evolutionarily-produced psychological mechanisms in the brain that do all the work and play a crucial role. Memes are part of that. Culture thus is something brought about in and by separate brains. On the one hand one has the brain as the survival apparatus of memetic cultural traits, on the other hand one has the brain as a set of specific modules which determine the content of various cultural behavioral patterns.

THE CENTRAL ISSUE OF CULTURAL PSYCHOLOGY

In an attempt to convince us of an aimless, mindless, and purposeless cosmos full of macros and algorithms, memes and modules, evolutionary psychologists tend to forget that the brain is not a mere controlling system, but exists in an embodied form – and moreover is not singular, but plural. For an adequate understanding of culture, single brains are insufficient; what is crucial is an awareness of the mutually attuned and coordinated bodies of which the brain is a part. Once it becomes clear in these days of raging wars between cultural groups in Europe, Africa and Asia, that the civilizing offensive of the west runs counter to rather immutable cultural forms of behaving and is, as an enterprise of modern nations, itself a source of strain, it is rather strange to reduce culture to modules and memes of all sorts. Of course, the received definition of culture as the system of meaning and the sum-total of humankind's higher achievements, leads to the view that culture is a set of traits or elements. Yet, culture is more than that. As a concept, coined in the nineteenth century to delineate peoples' way of life, it is used to pinpoint the forms of behavior that have certain characteristics, which typify the individuals of a cultural group. Culture is not just Beethoven and chess, the combustion engine or the airplane. Culture is also the personal, individual behavior which is characterized by an almost automatically produced pattern. How cultural forms or patterns *become desire and start to motivate people*, that is to say, how cultural patterns of behavior cease to be mere empty form and empty conventions and become a demonstration that something really is at stake, is the central issue for a cultural psychology. It cannot be researched on the basis of the rather one-sided metaphors of computations, modules and memes. Understanding how individual brains and bodies coordinate their behavior with respect to one another and with respect to the environment, requires a conceptual apparatus to be designed for that purpose in order to guide our empirical research. A few bits and pieces of our biological heritage and animal nature are not enough. We hope to show that brain in the singular, hardly with a real body – *and solely in that form to be considered of evolutionary importance* - is one of the great misconceptions of our time. This preconceived idea puts biology out of play in the attempt to understand human motivation and ideation. What we need to understand is foremost how people produce – among themselves, in mutual relations – ideas and strivings, in which they firmly believe and which motivate them with almost the power of a physical process.

The conception of culture of the evolutionary psychologists bears the traces of this wrong emphasis on the isolated brain. The problem of culture to which we so badly need to address ourselves, is to understand how the bodily conditioned exchange with the environment and other people is psychologically involved in the production of culture. That problem is hardly dealt with in the proposed psychological alternative to the SSSM, the so called Integrated Causal Model (see Cosmides & Tooby, 1997), for two reasons, which we will elaborate subsequently:

First, the defence of the *Integrated Causal Model* (ICM) against the SSSM blocks the study of the causes of behavior by limiting causality to a rather narrow version of it; and second, in an attempt to put human beings on a par with the higher primates, it is not made sufficiently clear what is specific about the animal side of the human species. In a final section we hope to show that postulating humans' possession of a rather specialized brain, which is designed for the solution of adaptive problems from a remote past and which consists of autonomously operating built-in circuits or modules, does not help our understanding of culturally informed behavior – especially not if the emphasis is on an isolated brain only. We are in need of a more cooperative stance on these matters from biologists and psychologists together.

THE NARROW VIEW OF CAUSALITY

Let us now try to answer the question, why causal relationships and causal mechanisms are emphasized so much in the writings of evolutionary psychologists (see, for instance, the "Primer" on evolutionary psychology by Cosmides & Tooby). It is quite understandable that causal-analytical procedures, which had been so successful in advancing secularized solutions to problems of food, shelter and health, were seen as potentially equally useful for the advancement of rational solutions to problems associated with politics and policy.

Yet the evolutionary psychologists oppose those social scientists who refuse to apply the laws of biology. What rankles the evolutionary psychologists in particular is the claim of social scientists that "environmentalism" and being "biophobe" – that is, considering biological explanations as something fearful to the extent that such explanations need to be avoided at all costs – have moral appeal, in that it is easier to fight against sexism and racism from an environmentalist's perspective. Therefore, biological determinism is declared wrong at the outset. The evolutionary psychologists believe that the nasty things that set one cultural group against another do not come from human nature. On the contrary, we are invited to replace the plasticity of human nature with a universally shared species-typical and species-specific architecture in which a variety of causal mechanisms do the work. This universal architecture harbors all kinds of nice devices, one for language, one for mating, one that triggers a jealous reaction, one for the detection of cheating, one for violence directed at out-groups and so on and so forth. All kinds of species-specific configurations are involved in the patterning of social behaviors, and evolutionary stable strategies (ESS) have done the filtering work by causing viable strategies to be preserved and non-viable ones to become extinct. Such processes take care of the transmission of certain genetic features. There simply is one class of causes that is preferred by evolutionary psychologists. These causes are represented by a rather odd metaphor: "the selfish gene". Genes take care of everything. Yet, it is quite astonishing how little is said, for example, about the entire *process* that supposedly makes foster fathers more aggressive towards children, compared to the biological fathers. We have to admit that the writing about this type of aggression in the opposite camp of the SSSM is quite disappointing as well. There is little concern with sub-personal processes and if such processes are considered at all, they are rarely analyzed in a plausible or viable way. By sub-personal or sub-symbolic processes we mean those behavior-generating mechanisms that take care of automatically produced behavioral forms. In the SSSM explicit verbal accounts are often preferred, which makes the type of explanations in which no causes but "reasons" or "goals" are involved, look rather silly. Such a state of affairs adds to a strong emphasis on causes by evolutionary psychologists. Yet solid biological determinism requires some idea about the nature of the process behind sub-personal or sub-symbolic factors.

What is most discomfiting about the ICM, is that it truly misdirects research into the *ideational* basis of the production and styling of behavior. In the ICM approach there is no room for notions like motive, means, ends, reasons, affective structuring, desire, personal style etc. Instead, one encounters a wide-ranging fear that together with a concern for these matters, first "mind" and maybe even God creep in again. Moreover, as Kitcher (1985) has pointed out, evidence is almost non-existent to support the proposal that the narrowing down of causes to a few hard-nosed concepts is fruitful.

One of the things that needs a much more refined approach is the nature-side or animal side of the *animal rationale*, the human species. That is our second point. The "adaptation-causalism" of the evolutionary psychologists needs refinement by showing what is specific for the human species as a natural kind.

THE HUMAN SPECIES

Humans somehow unite within themselves the animal and reason. One would expect that evolutionary psychologists would give a clear exposé about what type of animal is involved and how reason comes about. In order to turn psychology into a branch of biology, one would expect fairly exact information on the way our animal inheritance contributed to the "design" of specialized circuits in the brain. Evolutionary psychology offers at the same time too little and too much. It offers too much because of the things that are, in a broad gesture, linked up with locating the human mind in the stone age. We all still possess a stone-age mind, a brain that took shape in an environment full of adaptive problems, whose influences have no bearing any more on the modern requirements for a well-functioning brain. And it offers too little, since it is quite astonishing how much evidence with regard to biological contributions to the symbolic evolution of the human species is left unused by the evolutionary psychologists. No details are given about the habitat in which "the brain" developed. It is not that evolutionary psychologists just forget about the details, they pass over vital species-specific features of the human species as animal. Here we list a few of these.

One brain is no brain. Fossil remains found near Laetoli in Tanzania testify to the fact that the hominid life form dates back about 4 million years. The first as *homo* classified fossil dates back 2 million years. The *homo sapiens-sapiens* lived 200,000 years ago in Africa. Form and size of the skull and DNA point toward a very specific type of animal. In a period of about 3 to 4 million years the size of the brain increased from 400 ml to 1400-1500 ml, while the body size did not change much (Holloway, 1996). There are quite a few indications that manipulative skills, acted out in concert with other members of the species who carried out comparable movements, contribute to the specification of neural structures, not only ontogentically, but phylogenetically as well (Lock & Peters, 1996). We are not suggesting that psychologists should become paleontologists, but these indications contradict the evolutionary psychologists' focus on quantitative increases in the size of isolated brains in order to explain cognitive skills. They rather point to the fact that the operations and the evolution of a distinctly human brain are probably best understood in terms of a mutual coordination *between* brains (Singer, 1997, 1999). There are some indications that the manipulative skills of the species *Homo* have played an important part in the specification of the neural circuitry. These skills were laid down in the brain structures as a consequence of their development in the human group. The production of functional and skillful movements involves not just eye-hand coordination, but also the mutual coordination of actions in the human group. Let us call these coordinations that are bound to the community "first order consensual coordinations" (the eye-hand movement being merely a coordination). Such first order consensual coordinations of action can be found among all kinds of social animals. A very particular, and much more complex situation arises, however, when those consensual coordinations of action become themselves consensually coordinated. Elsewhere in this volume we argue that second order consensual coordinations of action can be found in "as-if" behavior, like play, or threat, or deceit, and also in symbolic behavior. These second order consensual coordinations one finds among animals as well. They characterize fights for dominance among animals, for example. But they clearly evolved to a very sophisticated extent in the human group. They often have a ritual, rather than a linguistic or symbolic form. Rituals are sub-symbolic processes which create order without the use of any symbolic or propositional system. Rituals can be fully automatic Voestermans, 1999). Their impact on cognition and the evolution of brain structures is something to be studied in its own right, on a par with perception and the motor actions. That should be done in relation to the attempt to delineate its impact on the ideational processes that create motives of all sorts. Maybe language has its origin in the way that those second, and higher order consensual coordinations of action is achieved (Baerveldt, 1998; Baerveldt, Voestermans & Verheggen, this volume). We will return to that.

Psychologists have a clear role here in elucidating paleontological findings. How crucial was the fact that the production of cultural artifacts was a group process? By stressing merely the adaptive problems that created the stone age mind, evolutionary psychologists miss the point.

Our primate past. Human chromosomes resemble those of the higher primates, particularly, the bonobo's, the chimpanzee's, and the gorilla's. It is tempting to conclude that the human animal is the "third chimpanzee"(Diamond, 1992). In making such comparisons, one often hastens to add that this "third chimp" has a much more elaborate culture. Yet, to turn culture into something all the chimps, including the "third" one, have in common, should be done cautiously and in a conceptually and empirically adequate way. One of the things evolutionary psychologist hardly do, however, is to demonstrate the role of sub-symbolic processes in so called culturally informed behaviors, that is to say, in behaviors of a distinct pattern in which certain objects (tools) or means (signs etc.) are used in characteristic ways. The genesis of life forms in general throughout the animal kingdom of primates, including the human animal, is something to be quite precise about. The shadow of culture in the animal world (Bonner, 1980) is nothing compared to what humans derive from their culture. But one cannot make culture into something humans and animals simply share. Bonobos are certainly worth comparing with humans. One can demonstrate, for example, that behavioral change does not require explicit instruction, whereas there does not exist a strict genotypical determinism either. Maybe this is the same among humans. But one can hardly object to a bit more attention being given to the variety and distinctiveness of sub-symbolic processes among animals and humans as well. That should be done in a rather precise way.

Skill and language. The human hand has the special feature of being able to place the thumb opposite every other finger. Humans walk upright and have white finger nails... One can go on like that. To prevent getting lost in a sea of differences, some should be marked. The manual skill and upright position are important for the development of a skillful manipulation of weaponry, but also of other kinds of manipaulation. One would like to know what the implications are of these skills for the development of symbolic forms of behavior among humans and animals. There are some indications that the human brain evolved in connection with the bringing to perfection of two things: the extremely complicated coordination of the eye and the hand, which is necessary for throwing and slinging (eg Calvin, 1986), and the development of second-order coordinations in the band of animals which fostered the emergence of communicative skills (eg Deacon, 1997). The influence of these coordinations on the construction of artifacts and particularly on communication is an issue in its own right, to be dealt with carefully. Here one-sided evolutionism and biological reductionism are of no help. On the contrary, "biologizing" psychology leads to evading the issue: how the hardware is involved not so much in determining behavior, but in providing bodily structures that can become part of the software so to speak. Here language enters in a rather special way.

Language is much older and more widespread than initially believed; it was already present in human groups who did not evolve further, as fossils of the place of tongue-bone in the Neanderthals suggest. However, the physical aspects of language production are not the most important, since the deployment of language is fully present in the use of manual signs, for example (Place, 2000). This implies that language needs to be viewed in the same respect as other consensual coordinations of action, that is, in its important role in the human group. Language is a form of second-order consensual coordination, a coordination of coordinations. As such it is not a matter of an isolated brain, any more than the first-order consensual coordinations are. It is quite probable that language originated in connection with the skills we talked about earlier. Maybe it is more important to look for these features than to emphasize the basis of language in brain structures of some sort. These structures can be the consequence of the way language has been developed from coordinative skills. That is the reverse of Pinker's claim that these structures serve as a point of departure in analyzing language as a tool (Pinker, 1994). Of course, without a brain there is no language, that is for sure, but that is not the point. Language is a human tool for getting attuned to one another, and for the mutual coordination of actions (Baerveldt, 1998; Baerveldt, Voestermans & Verheggen, this volume). Such a tool needs to be studied in an evolutionary psychological frame, starting from the assumption that humans have in common with the animals certain sub-symbolic processes. In the human species the development went much further, in the direction of symbolic meaning (Lakoff & Johnson, 1999). Culture should not be equated with higher mental functioning, or with this symbolic superstructure alone, but foremost with the experiential coordination of actions through which certain skills are produced.

Sub-symbolic processes in skill acquisition, involving everyday automaticity and embodied affective structures, are important for the way culture "ticks" (Voestermans, 1999). The processes involved in these skills need specification in such a way that humans indeed become what they are: evolved products of the way certain life forms already developed in animals.

A VIABLE BRAIN-APPROACH TO CULTURE

Evolutionary psychology is to be commended for trying to put culture on the psychological agenda. Culture has been rather exclusively the research domain of sociologists and anthropologists. There is nothing wrong with that, except for a certain one-sidedness. Culture has been primarily seen as context, as part of the environment in which behavior takes place. From an enactive perspective (Baerveldt, 1998; Baerveldt & Verheggen, 1999; Baerveldt, Voestermans & Verheggen, this volume) such a view of culture runs the risk of evading the issue. Emphasizing context leads to a preoccupation with cultural differences, using research tools to assess the effects of culture on the individual or on the behavior of members of a cultural group. Culture as a prefixed "out-there" reality, as an already given social world, wrongly becomes the source of the content of the specific human mind. Meanings, in other words, are injected into individual minds. Evolutionary psychologists rightly focus on culture as something the mind produces. What, then, is a viable brain approach to culture?

First, it is important to allow for a central role for biology in constructing meaning. It should be acknowledged that despite all the criticism, evolutionary psychology is on the right track in emphasizing knowledge of brain structures as vital to a proper understanding of culture. Culture should not be put in opposition to biology. It is more fruitful to devise a biologically informed theory of meaning. In that regard, it is quite right to emphasize the so called cognitive unconscious. Sub-symbolic processes are of prime importance in researching culture. However, what the study of the cognitive unconscious reveals, is quite a different view of biology's part in the constitution of meaning than evolutionary psychologist would have us believe. Evolutionary psychologists are often satisfied once they have pointed to the ingenious specialized circuitry of the brain. One circuit for the detection of shape, one for motion, one for direction, one for judging distance, one for color, facial recognition and so on. It is easy to list them, it is easy to postulate that they are organized in higher level circuits, but it is not easy to explain how minds get attuned to other minds, and what the impact of such coordination has actually been, and still is, on cognitive functioning up to the level of conscious awareness.

What needs further elucidation is how experience, locked away, so to speak, in the cognitive unconscious, is involved in the creation of domains of understanding and practice, the so called "consensual domains" (Baerveldt & Verheggen, 1999). A viable brain-approach to culture necessitates the exchanging of an all too formal approach to brain processes, including language, with an approach in which one is concerned with the embodiment of a control structure – the brain – in a "community of experiencers", equipped with similar brains and similar bodies. Cognition needs to be placed into the body *and* the brain in such a way that beliefs and desires, needs and wants are not merely seen as resulting from propositionally organized thought in the isolated head, but from consensually coordinated action.

No actor – be it the human one or the animal one, although in this latter case the matter is obvious -- can have access to his, her or its own experience apart from the way in which this experience is recurrently brought to the attention of others by the way meaning is co-constructed. These so called "lived" meanings entail an area of interlocked conduct of which the environment is part as the triggering instance. Evolutionary psychologists have refrained from observing and conceptualizing body and brain in concert. They took recourse to an abstract machinery of selective pressures and adaptive problems. They did not reckon with the fact that socially coordinated actions in a group of like brains and bodies can provide a starting point for a viable reconstruction of how meanings get produced.

REFERENCES

Baerveldt, C. (1998) *Culture and the consensual coordination of actions*. Ph.D. thesis. Nijmegen Cultural Psychology Group.

Baerveldt. C. & Verheggen, T. (1999). Enactivism and the experiential reality of culture: Rethinking the epistemological basis of cultural psychology. *Culture & Psychology, 5* (2), 183-206.

Barkow, J.H., Cosmides, L., & Tooby, J. (1992). *The adapted mind. Evolutionary psychology and the generation of culture. New York: Oxford.*

Blackmore, S. (1999). *The meme machine*. Oxford University Press.

Bonner, J. (1980). *The evolution of culture in animals*, Princeton, NJ: Princeton University Press.

Calvin, W. (1986). *The river that flows uphill: A journey from the Big Bang to the Big Brain.* New York: Macmillan.

Cosmides, L. & Tooby, J. (1994) Beyond intuition and instinct blindness: Toward an evolutionary rigorous cognitive science. *Cognition, 50*, 41-77.

Cosmides, L. & Tooby, J. (1997). Evolutionary psychology: A primer. Internet <http://www.psych.ucsb.edu/research/cep/primer.html>.

Dawkins, R. (1989). *The selfish gene*. Oxford: OUP. .

Deacon, T.W. (1997). *The symbolic species: The co-evolution of language and the brain.* New York: Norton.

Dennett, D. C. (1991). *Darwin's dangerous idea. Evolution and the meanings of life.* New York: Simon & Schuster.

Diamond J (1992) *The rise and fall of the third chimpanzee*. New York: Harper Collins.

Geertz, C. (1973). *The interpretation of cultures*. New York: Basic Books.

Holloway, R. (1996). Evolution of the human brain. In A. Lock & C. Peters (Eds) *Handbook of human symbolic evolution*. Oxford: Clarendon Press

Kitcher, P. (1985) *Vaulting ambition. Sociobiology and the quest of human nature*. Cambridge, MA: MIT Press.

Lakoff, G. & Johnson , M. (1999) *Philosophy in the flesh. The embodied mind and its challenge to western thought*. New York: Basic Books.

Lock, A. & Peters, C. (Eds) (1996). *Handbook of human symbolic evolution*. Oxford: Clarendon Press.

Montagu, M. (1964). *Culture: Man's adaptative dimension*. Chicago: University of Chicago Press.

Neisser, U. (1976). *Cognition and reality*. New York: Freeman.

Pinker, S. (1994). *The language instinct*. New York: Morrow

Place, U.T. (2000) The role of the hand in the evolution of language. Psycoloquy, 11. Internet: ftp://ftp.princeton.edu/pub/harnad/Psycoloquy/2000.volume.11

Simpson, J.A. & Kenrick, D.T. (1997). *Evolutionary social psychology*. Mahwah NJ: Erlbaum.

Singer, W. (1997). The observer in the brain. Invited address at the New Trends in Cognitive Science Conference, Vienna.

Singer, W. (1999) Neurobiology. Striving for coherence. *Nature*, *397* (6718), 391-393.

Symons, D. (1979). *The evolution of human sexuality*. New York: Oxford.

Tooby, J. & Cosmides, L. (1992). The psychological foundations of culture. In J.H. Barkow, L. Cosmides & J. Tooby (1992) *The adapted mind. Evolutionary psychology and the generation of culture*. New York: Oxford, p. 19-136.

Voestermans, P. (1999). Cultural psychology looks at culture. In W. Maiers, B Bayer, B. Duarte Esgalhado, R. Jorna & E Schraube (Eds.) *Challenges to theoretical psychology* (pp. 304-312) North Ontario: Captus.

THE TAJFEL EFFECT

Steven D. Brown and Peter Lunt
Loughborough University; and University College, London

SUMMARY

This paper explores the relationship between social psychology and social theory by following the development of Social Identity Theory (*SIT*). It is argued that the current state of *SIT* is profoundly shaped by a range of intellectual and moral strategies adopted by Henri Tajfel. This "Tajfel effect" manifests itself as a particular form of individualist analysis developed within *SIT*, coupled with a wholesale exclusion of social structure. Combined together, these tendencies undermine *SIT*'s ability to describe how both categorisation and social change arise within a shifting and complex modern social landscape.

INTRODUCTION: TAJFEL'S LEGACY

In his introduction to *Human Groups and Social Categories*, a collection of published work spanning thirty years, Henri Tajfel adopts a confessional voice. There is a progression, he claims, between his initial explorations in "New Look" psychology, the subsequent pan-European studies of ethnocentrism and later work on inter-group relations. This progression is described in terms that are counter-intuitive to a scientific sensibility. It consists of a journey which attempts to retrace its path, a passage away from current achievements and back towards the starting point, prior to the author's entry to the academy. "[W]hen I look back today at the variety of things I have done between 1945 and 1980", Tajfel writes, "it often appears to me that I have never been so useful again as I was in the few short years immediately after the war, when I had an opportunity of helping to bring back to the surface a few dozen people, hardly younger than I was myself at the time" (1981, p. 10).

The mode these words are written in is the autobiographical. Here the search for origins, the setting forth to capture "lost time", is expected. To this it must be added that Tajfel belonged to that generation of academics, European refugees and survivors of the Shoa, for whom the search for meaning in the overwhelming sense of loss is unbearably poignant. It commands our belief that the academic careers of this generation were directed by the horrors they witnessed. But unlike some contemporaries – say, Bruno Bettelheim or Zygmunt Bauman – who chose to discuss the carnage of wartime Europe directly, Tajfel's legacy to us is a work of *theory* and in his retrospective account this legacy is presented as a personal struggle through different types of psychological theorising. Social identity theory simultaneously completes Tajfel's personal journey and the maturation of social psychology as a distinct discipline.

How are we to respond to this way of characterising one of the most important theories of contemporary social psychology dealing with prejudice, one of the central questions of the field? Tajfel puts his reader in a difficult position. One may dispute a work of commentary through claiming that its interpretation of events or of a text is flawed or in some way unwarranted. But one cannot do this with a theory. The fate of theory is instead tied to its conceptual coherence or logic and its application, in the experiments in which its terms are operationalised, or the empirical findings which the theory organises. Theory is meant to be distinct from its origins in a way that commentary, which depends so intimately on the viewpoint and social standing of the commentator, does not. Tajfel's legacy – social identity theory – ought then to be evaluated as entirely distinct from Tafjel himself. It should be possible to completely erase the autobiographical from the theoretical. Yet this is clearly not how the social identity tradition has developed. Tajfel's presence is still acutely felt within the tradition, as born out by a recent festschrift (Robinson, 1996). And this continued reference to Tajfel is not limited to retrospective collections but is a central feature of most writing in the *SIT* tradition. It is standard for originating or founding figures to be extensively cited (another example from social psychology would be the many references to Fritz Heider in Attribution Theory). However, it is our contention that, in the case of Tajfel, this referencing is something beyond the deference due to the leader of the field. Indeed the manner in which Tajfel is invoked by researchers in the social-identity tradition is entirely different from the way one would usually expect a figurehead to be recalled. Take the following instance, where Amélie Mummendey recalls:

> ... a trip from Düsseldorf Airport to Münster [during which] Tajfel
> narrated me the following episode. At a gas station somewhere in England
> where he had stopped to take gas, he noticed that the employee, a young
> man of 16 to 17 years, wore a necklace with a golden swastika. Henri got
> out of the car, addressed the young man, asked him whether he really knew

the meaning of this symbol and then pulled a substantial British pound note out of his wallet. While presenting this bank note he taught the boy a lesson about Nazi-crimes, discrimination, hostility, torture, murder and even genocide. As a result of this lesson his pupil promised to throw the necklace away and never wear swastikas or symbols of this kind ever again (Mummendey, 1995, p. 657).

This is a fascinating extract. It contains an unusual amount of detail, a technique which discursive psychologists have identified as an attempt to place the reader directly within the episode recounted, encouraging them to see through the eyes of the narrator (Potter, 1996; Woofitt, 1992). Mummendey tries here to bring the audience directly into Tajfel's presence. What is it that she wants us to see? Her purpose becomes clearer as the article progresses. Social discrimination, the ostensible topic of the article, is framed by citing Tajfel and Turner's technical description of the results of the minimal group studies:

> [T]he mere perception of belonging to two distinct groups – that is social categorization per se – is sufficient to trigger intergroup discrimination favouring the ingroup. In other words, the mere awareness of the presence of an outgroup is sufficient to provoke intergroup competitive or discriminatory responses on the part of the ingroup (Tajfel & Turner, cited in Mummendey, 1995, p. 659)

The difference between the two extracts could not be more apparent. In the latter, social discrimination is present only by analogy with the actual "discriminatory responses" made by participants in minimal group experiments. It is one story that can be told about what happens when people are invited into laboratories and asked do some unusual things (like view slides of paintings and fill out peculiar looking forms). If that story seems plausible to a contemporary audience, it is because it is now underwritten by the theoretical edifice which was subsequently erected upon the studies. But in the first extract, what is presented is a very different kind of story about social discrimination, recounted by an individual who is both a Jewish émigré and the author of a theory which has been used to account for prejudice. In this story, prejudice appears symbolically in the form of the swastika worn as jewellery. Significantly, Tajfel chooses to confront its wearer not by explaining the mechanics of social categorisation and intergroup differentiation but instead by recounting the life of the symbol and events with which it was associated. History is asserted over theoretical generalities.

So perhaps what Mummendey wants us to see is the ironic distance which existed between Tajfel the émigré and Tajfel the academic, a gap which Tajfel himself made salient by choosing to repeat the story to a German social identity-theorist during a trip to Münster. What the story also does though is to remind us of the complex relationship between what Billig (1996) terms the "particular background" of Tajfel's work and the subsequent tendency to "universalise" the resulting theory of intergroup discrimination. As the social identity tradition has developed, it has become more markedly experimental, and so less likely to deal directly with actual instances of the phenomenon which lay at the heart of Tajfel's original concerns with fascism. But this move is problematic for a tradition which relies so heavily upon an original analogy between a particular kind of experiment and specific sets of social acts. The danger is that the more experiments we consume, the more difficult it becomes to comment directly on fascism. Hence there is a need to continually reinvigorate the analogy by bringing the actual phenomenon back in. And this is what invoking Tajfel and his biography serves to do. What Mummendey wants us to see is the continued strength of the analogy as embodied by Tajfel himself.

Drawing on Deleuze and Guattari, we propose to call this invocation the "Tajfel effect". Deleuze and Guattari emphasise that the reiteration of a proper name – such as "Tajfel" – does more than simply acknowledge a founding figure. Invoking a name is a social act which generates effects in the immediate context where it is written or spoken. Deleuze & Guattari claim that it is possible to classify such effects:

> The theory of proper names should not be conceived of in terms of representation; it refers instead to the class of "effects": effects that are not a mere dependence on causes, but the occupation of a domain, and the operation of a system of signs. This can be clearly seen in physics, where proper names designate such effects within fields of potentials: the Joule effect, the Seebeck effect, the Kelvin effect. History is like physics: a Joan of Arc effect, a Heliogabalus effect – all the names of history and not the name of the father (Deleuze & Guattari, 1983, p. 86).

Thus just as physicists use proper names to designate particular kind of natural effects, so historians might similarly assign the proper names of historical figures to designate certain kinds of social effects. As psychologists we do something similar when we speak of circumstances where the relationship of experimenter to participant typically gives rise to a predictable social phenomenon as a "Hawthorne effect". In this sense the "Tajfel effect" can serve to designate a particular kind of interaction between the theoretical, experimental and biographical elements of a tradition of research which operates to prevent the tradition becoming disconnected from the phenomenon which it purports to explain. We will now explore this effect as it operates on both the individual and the social dimension of *SIT*.

SIT AND THE INDIVIDUAL

The social identity tradition finds its core statement in Tajfel's (1981) promotion of a "mid-range" solution to the problem of integrating individual psychology with social theory. Tajfel framed this move through a rejection of competing "psychological individualist" approaches to explaining large scale conflict. His ire was centred upon the banality of an apparent logic where mass action is seen as the cumulative effect of individual behaviour. Such an account crucially assumes that there is a uniformity in the individual responses made to particular environmental cues (e.g. aggression in response to frustrating stimuli). From which it follows that everything is to be explained by looking to the prevalence of certain individual characteristics, such as "authoritarian personalities". Tajfel points to the relative poverty of this approach when it comes to matter of historical specificity:

> The selection for the gas ovens in the concentration camps of World War II was undoubtedly, to some small extent, affected by the individual characteristics of those who were so selected, by the individual whims or "personalities" of the selectors or by some personal relationships which may have developed here and there. All this hardly amounts to more than a wrinkle if it is our aim to understand the most significant general aspects of what has happened (Tajfel, 1978, p. 42).

The "significant general aspects" of "what has happened" are only poorly grasped by referring to the motivations or personal character of given individuals. The intended target of Tajfel's critique is the work of Berkowitz (1962) and of Adorno and colleagues (1950). But it is also apparent from his choice of example that the critique of individualism made here is not to be understood purely in terms of its analytic or explanatory shortcomings. Note that Tajfel talks of "understanding" rather than "explaining" the Shoa (see Billig, 1996). This makes his charges against Berkowitz and Adorno, both Jewish academics involved in producing work on conflict and prejudice, appear more highly charged. Their failing is to have produced work which potentially allows the academic community to imagine it has fully accounted for genocide. As Billig makes plain, complete accounts of the Shoa act as precursors for the disposal of its historical specificity. They are attempts to "put an end to the matter". So although in many ways Tajfel's work broadly resembles the experimental and quantitative approach adopted by Berkowitz and Adorno, his subtle stress on using the resultant data to further understanding over explanation enables him to strike a balance between the intellectual obligations of being a Jewish émigré academic and the "non-negotiable theoretical principles of the day" (Wetherell, 1996, p. 277).

In this sense, Tajfel's critique of psychological individualism can be seen as an intellectual strategy rather than a narrowly epistemological move. And what then becomes evident is that the strategy Tajfel pursued involved its own risks. For example, the theory which emerged from his opposition to Berkowitz and Adorno had to carry the burden of the obligations which he considered to have been so easily discarded by psychological individualism. This means that part of Tajfel's legacy is the necessity of displaying the *moral* superiority of social identity accounts of prejudice and conflict from competing individualist accounts through an engagement with "real life" issues. Yet, because experimentation and the commitment to a mid range theory were also part of Tajfel's strategy, this engagement is necessarily strained by a push toward theoretical elaboration. The analytic then comes to dominate the moral. Which in turn creates a situation where moral obligations can only be met by repeating the failings and potential dangers presented by rival accounts (see Turner, 1999; Turner & Oakes, 1997).

The precariousness of Tajfel's intellectual strategy is also apparent in the centrality of the minimal group paradigm to social identity work and the resulting conception of the relationship between society and individual in terms of a continuum of behaviour ranging from the purely interpersonal to the purely intergroup. The analytic and experimental focus on behaviour oriented his work to what was overt and visible in the phenomenon in question. Nebulous entities such as "social forces", the stock in trade of the critical sociologist, or "unconscious drives", the bedrock of psychoanalysis, are deliberately disqualified. It is worth recalling that these two forms of thought which Tajfel sought to expel from nascent social identity theory – psychoanalysis and neo-Marxist social theory – were precisely those which the critical theorists of the Frankfurt School, of whom Adorno was the best known, had used to develop their critiques of the conflicts inherent to modernity (see Adorno, 1973; Marcuse, 1968). But if Tajfel's aim here was to reduce abstraction, the result was to create an analysis of social groups seemingly disconnected from individual desires or broader socio-historical movements. We are left with the puzzling spectacle of the seemingly counter-intuitive behaviour of experimental subjects. As has often been noted (Billig, 1985; Michael, 1990; Wetherell & Potter, 1992) experiment and theory together then constitute an abstract account of an idealised group.

But such critiques of the universalising tendency in social identity analysis miss a further subtle aspect of Tajfel's strategy. The question to which Tajfel returns constantly in *Human Groups and Social Categories* is how it is that group members enact categorisation in their behaviour in such a way that they foreclose upon moral choice. How, in other words, do people not feel the full moral burden of their decision to "create concentration camps, to drop the first A-bomb, to burn Dresden or the ghetto of Warsaw, or to kill "suspect" women and children in Vietnamese villages" (Tajfel, 1981, p. 38). Tajfel's answer is that a prior act of judging using "clearly defined categories of social situations" (p. 39) makes this possible. One adjudges the out-grouped other to be unworthy of serious moral concern. Now what the minimal group paradigm does is to make concrete the scene of this prior judgement. It is not allowed to slip entirely under the cover of a blanket explanation. Tajfel wants to isolate the initial scene of judgement, make it stand full square at the heart of prejudice and to restore to it the full and proper range of cognitive, emotional and moral weight. But when subsequent social identity work grasps the scene of judgement as a purely perceptual matter, a question of how the individual perceiver discriminates and apportions the stimuli they encounter, then this aspect of Tajfel's strategy falls away entirely. Judgement is reduced to perceptual event, what Wetherell and Potter (1992) describe as a "social spectacle" laid out before the attentive gaze of a "solitary observer", apparently disconnected from history or society.

What we have been calling the "Tajfel effect" then manifests itself in response to the tensions which have emerged as the social identity tradition tries to balance out the various moral obligations and intellectual strategies initiated by Tajfel. One unwitting consequence of this delicate balancing act has been the production of a form of individualist analysis - the perceptualist strand - that not only lacks much of the sophistication of rival approaches, but also fails to carry forward Tajfel's own moral concerns. As we will now go on to describe, similar problems exist around the conception of social structure in social identity work.

SIT AND SOCIETY

In social identity work, everyday cognition is viewed as a ongoing process of categorical activity. Stimuli relating to both self and environment are sorted into mental categories following the act of perception. Self-categorisation theory adds to this that these mental categories are arranged in a logical hierarchy, such that the relationship between any given pair of categories can only be fully appreciated by invoking their structural relationship to a higher level or superordinate category (cf. Rosch, 1978). Now the obvious problem encountered by this position is that of relating mental category to world – how can we be sure that the structure of mental categories, let alone their content, is an adequate representation of the world as it is encountered by the individual? A failure to supply such a guarantee threatens to let loose the spectre of rampant subjectivism, where there are as many variants on the structure as there are individual perceivers.

The solution most usually adopted is, following Tajfel, to claim that mental categories are in essence transformations of pre-existing social categories, which in turn reflect the givens of social structure. These include "power, status, prestige and social group differentials" (1981, p. 14) underpinned by wider socio-economic determinants and constraints. To be a member of any society is to experience oneself as positioned in the social categories which necessarily emerge from its structural-functional organisation. Turner and colleagues (1994) use this insight to advance the idea that both the structure of psychological process and the contents which they organise are shaped by the interaction of the individual with their particular social environment. Individuals "internalise" social structure in the form of social categories, which then act as a template for the emergence of individual cognitive categories. Hence the representational chasm which exists between mental category and world is bridged by an interactionist account of how psychological processes emerge.

Interactionism of this kind does not, however, put an end to the problem. As Abrams (1999) shows, the relationship between a given category and the attributes which make up its presumed contents can be highly mutable depending upon the context in which the category gains salience. The self-category "parent" may, Abrams notes, be defined in entirely different ways when it appears in the course of a course of school meeting (e.g. concerned, involved, intellectual) from the use an adult may make of it at home (e.g. loving, fun, responsible). If categories are mutable in the way Abrams suggests, then this tends to undermine the idea that categories have a clear, logical structure. Indeed this point has been exploited by discursive critiques of self-categorisation theory which have accused Turner et al of failing to distinguish between the logical conception of hierarchical semantic structure and the actual practice of creatively mobilising categories-in-use during talk (Billig, 1997; Edwards, 1997; Wetherell & Potter, 1992).

Yet limits can be placed upon the mutability of categories by pointing to the determining power of social contexts to establish an authoritative definition of who or what is to count as an proper instance of a particular category. This position is implicit in Abrams (1999) examples of universities, schools and hospitals as settings where the evaluative dimensions of social categories like "doctor" or "parent" are relatively fixed. It then becomes reasonably clear who can be properly called a doctor or parent, the range of attributes to be held relevant and the nature of their obligations to others. Turner and Oakes (1997) claim that social groups themselves act as limit contexts because they subject varying interpretations of categories to "processes of discussion, argument and collective testing" (p. 369). In this way, social structure is conceived by social identity work as both the origin and final limit to processes of categorisation.

But since social identity theory is premised upon the exclusion of social theory, it lacks a vocabulary or indeed any analytic grasp of the very notion of social order. Because it cannot speak in any meaningful way about social stratification, social identity work can only assume that a single social order exists in the hierarchical form posited by the interactionist account of the relationship between world and mental categories. Without a discrete hierarchies "out there" in the world, the model of hierarchies "in there" as internalised social categories becomes unstable.

Once again, on the question of social order Tafel's work is more subtle than it might first appear. In his later work Tajfel (1984), whilst not conceding to engage with social theory directly, promoted the idea of "social myth" as a mediating concept between social structure and psychological processes. Social myths – derived from the work of Moscovici and of Bourdieu – are shared symbolic representations of social order and the broader environment. They serve as the background against which individual thinking can gain some purchase on the world. The insertion of social myth into social identity theory means that persons never encounter the world directly, but can only do so by way of a symbolic order which has enveloped and shrouded "real" social structure. Now what this means is that the context in which categorisation occurs is itself symbolic – therefore mutable – and so cannot serve as a pure limit on the definition of categories. Parents and doctors experience schools and hospitals as symbolically charged environments rather than as clear and distinct contexts where the social order makes categories self-evident.

Tajfel's turn toward myth provides for a "cut down" version of society, one where it is possible to talk of social order as it appears in social myth without having to engage with the brute realities of history, economics or political ecology (subjects, Tajfel suggests, best left to other social sciences). But this move makes it impossible to distinguish what is ground from what is grounded, that is, category from context. Tajfel holds to the idea that there is a single social order to all this somewhere, but does not allow that order to enter into the analysis directly. It is as though there were a single structure that organised both cognitive processes and the organisation of everyday life, but this "real" structure could not in itself be analysed, existing somewhere off in the background, perpetually just out of reach. Hence social identity theory is set off as an approach which studies processes at level of the individual, but cannot conceive of any such processes occurring at the level of the social.

REFERENCES

Abrams, D. (1999). Social identity, social cognition and the self: The flexibility and stability of self-categorization. In D. Abrams & M. Hogg (Eds), *Social identity and social cognition* (pp. 197-229). Oxford: Blackwell.

Adorno, T.W. (1973). *Negative dialectics*. London: Routledge & Kegan Paul.

Adorno, T.W., Frenkel-Brunswik, E., Levinson, D.J., & Sanford, R.N. (1950). *The authoritarian personality*. New York: Harper and Row.

Bauman, Z. (1989). *Modernity and the holocaust*. Cambridge: Polity.

Berkowitz, L. (1962). *Aggression: Its causes, consequences and control*. New York: McGraw Hill.

Billig, M. (1985). Prejudice, categorization and particularization: From a perceptual to a rhetorical approach. *European Journal of Social Psychology, 15*, 79-103.

Billig, M. (1996). Remembering the particular background of social identity theory. In W.P. Robinson (Ed.), *Social groups and identities: Developing the legacy of Henri Tajfel* (pp. 337-357). Oxford: Butterworth-Heinemann.

Billig, M. (1997). Discursive, rhetorical and ideological messages. In C. McGarty & S.A. Haslam (Eds.), *The message of social psychology* (pp. 355-373). Oxford: Blackwell.

Deleuze, G. & Guattari, F. (1983). *Anti-Oedipus: Capitalism and schizophrenia*. Minneapolis: University of Minnesota Press.

Edwards, D. (1997). *Discourse and cognition*. London: Sage.

Marcuse, H. (1968). *Negations*. Boston: Beacon Press.

Michael, M. (1990). Intergroup theory and deconstruction. In I. Parker & J. Shotter (Eds), *Deconstructing social psychology*. London: Routledge.

Mummendey, A. (1995). Positive distinctiveness and social discrimination: An old couple living in divorce. *European Journal of Social Psychology, 25*, 657-670.

Potter, J. (1996). *Representing reality: Discourse, rhetoric and social construction*. London: Sage.

Robinson, W.P. (Ed.) (1996) *Social groups and identities: Developing the legacy of Henri Tajfel*. Oxford: Butterworth-Heinemann.

Rosch, E. (1978). Principles of categorization. In E. Rosch & B.B. Lloyd (Eds), *Cognition and categorization* (pp. 24-48). Hillsdale, NJ: Erlbaum.

Tajfel, H. (1978). Interindividual and intergroup behaviour. In H. Tajfel (Ed.), *Differentiation between social groups: Studies in the social psychology of intergroup relations*. London: Academic Press.

Tajfel, H. (1981). *Human groups and social categories: Studies in social psychology*. Cambridge: Cambridge University Press.

Tajfel, H. (1984). Intergroup relations, social myths and social justice in social psychology. In H. Tajfel (Ed.), *The social dimension: European developments in social psychology, vol 2* (pp. 695-715). Cambridge: Cambridge University Press.

Turner, J.C. (1999, July). The prejudiced personality and social change: A self-categorisation perspective. Keynote address to XIIth General Meeting, European Association of Experimental Social Psychology, Oxford.

Turner, J.C. & Oakes, P.J. (1997). The socially structured mind. In C. McGarty & S.A. Haslam (Eds), *The message of social psychology* (pp. 355-373). Oxford: Blackwell.

Turner, J.C., Oakes, P.J., Haslam, S.A., & McGarty, C.A. (1994). Self and collective: Cognition and social context. *Personality and Social Psychology Bulletin, 20*, 454-463.

Wetherell, M. (1996). Constructing social identities: The individual/social binary in Henri Tajfel's social psychology. In W.P. Robinson (Ed.), *Social groups and identities: Developing the legacy of Henri Tajfel* (pp. 269-284). Oxford: Butterworth-Heinemann.

Wetherell, M. & Potter, J. (1992). *Mapping the language of racism: Discourse and the legitimation of exploitation.* Hemel Hempstead: Harvester Wheatsheaf.

Wooffitt, R. (1992). *Telling tales of the unexpected: The organisation of factual discourse.* Hemel Hempstead: Harvester Wheatsheaf.

DISCOURSE ANALYSIS AND STRUCTURAL SUPERVISION

Arnd Hofmeister
University of Western Sydney, Nepean

SUMMARY

Structural Supervision is a conceptual framework, which allows us to analyze problems in the working environment without personalizing them by the use of discourse-analytical and subject-scientific instruments. It is an attempt to combine supervision with an emancipatory impulse. In this paper I sketch the basic assumptions and the analytical framework with its theoretical implications. Following from there I describe the different steps of a supervision process. Finally I give an example of a supervision process in order to illustrate the advantages and problems of this approach. The example is taken from work with the Sanctuary Movement in Germany.

INTRODUCTION

"Structural supervision" is a conceptual framework which has been developed to overcome the limitations of traditional theories of supervision within the context of the workplace. Approaches derived from systems theory, which concentrate in their analysis on system relations, tend to conceptualize systems as more or less closed. Therefore, they cannot transgress the status quo and instead the problems that arise within the given conditions are merely displaced. Psychoanalytic and humanist theories of supervision focus in their analysis of problems predominantly on interpersonal relations within the work context. Consequently these approaches individualize and personalize problems.

The structural supervision approach tries to avoid these dangers by using discourse-analytical instruments for analyzing problems in their structural relations and in their concrete articulations. In doing so this approach overcomes the dilemma of the dichotomous formation of the individual-society opposition. It allows the clients to comprehend the way they are articulated within different conflicting discursive and non-discursive structures without reducing them to mere functions of the system, because it tries to reconstruct the specific problem-articulation from the clients' standpoint. Finally structural supervision tries to empower the clients not merely to manage their problems in the restrictive framework of the given conditions but to develop possibilities for action which transcend those frameworks within an emancipatory perspective. To illustrate these abstract issues, and to demonstrate their practical significance, I conclude with an example of the supervision of a group who work in the sanctuary movement (a movement which takes care of refugees threatened with expulsion from Germany).

THE BASIC CONCEPT OF STRUCTURAL SUPERVISION

Structural supervision is based on the assumption that dynamics and conflicts within work processes emerge at specific places, which are characterized by discursive and non-discursive structures and practices. These overlap, become knotted and form a web, in which people act, spin a web around and in which they are caught. The aim is to make these different discursive practices and structures visible, in order to enable clients to become "action-potent" within these webs.

As an analytical framework structural supervision distinguishes between discursive and non-discursive structures and practices of both an inner and an external web. The distinction between discursive and non-discursive structures and practices in supervision is necessary and difficult at the same time, because non-discursive structures organize the field of the visible while supervision as a discursive practice organizes the field of the sayable (Deleuze, 1986). Looking for non-discursive structures allows us to take a critical look at taken-for-granted conditions and relationships within the working environment, which might be important for understanding the problem (Hofmeister, 1998). Non-discursive structures and practices, such as institutions and economical conditions, are very stable. They regulate working processes without even being recognized. Furthermore they cannot be changed easily. In consequence their significance for problems arising within working conditions is often dethematized. Discursive structures and practices on the contrary are flexible, they inhabit different non-discursive structures, build links between them and provide modes of articulation within these non-discursive structures. Altogether discursive and non-discursive structures and practices have to be understood as an apparatus of knowledge and power, which regulates the working process within societal conditions.

The focus for analyzing the inner web of a working place is on the microeconomics of the employee-employer relationship, the financial and personal management, work-concepts, power-relations and hierarchies as well as personal relations from a class and gender-analytic perspective. The structures and practices of the external web include the macroeconomics of the work relations, and the official tasks and functions in terms of the wider institutional net (cf. Holzkamp and Markard, 1989).

Discourse analysis serves to analyze the internal and external web as well as the subject's articulations within these webs during supervision. According to Foucault (1969) discursive practices are not to be understood as the activity of one or several subjects. They are to be understood as an ensemble of rules determining the formation of the subject-matters which can be brought up, the subject positions, which can be taken up, the concepts which can be used and the theories which characterize this practice. In each work-relation there are various discourses crossing in this specific place. These discourses differ from each other in definiteness and stability, e.g. judicial discourses are more definite than conceptual ones. The articulations of the subjects take place within this discursive web. These articulations, especially if they describe a problem, are predominantly *narrated*. The specific quality of narrations is their ability to connect various discourses in one articulation while at the same time ignoring the contradictions and conflicts (differends) between these discourses. A narration describing and explaining a problem, is in effect a kind of "grand narrative", because the narrator tries to present, in a plausible way, why he or she is changing from one discourse to another. In many cases the actual problem is the result of suppressed conflicts between different discourses. I am using the term conflict (*differend*) here in the Lyotardian sense (Lyotard, 1983). According to Lyotard a conflict (*differend*) emerges where two sentences belonging to two different discourses are connected without any consensual rule for connecting them. While connecting, the conflict is transformed into a "law-suit", in which the rules of at least one discourse are suppressed and the claims of value are condemned to silence.

The supervisor's task is not to put these different discourses into an order, but to recognize these conflicts, finding transitions between them. The request for clarity results from scientific discourse. However, clarity is not a condition sine qua non for being capable of acting, because this ignores the fuzzy-logic of practice, which is ambiguous (Bourdieu 1980; Bourdieu & Wacquant 1992). A different supervision concept may help the supervised persons in the long run in solving problems by themselves, by understanding the specific logic of their practice. Furthermore, to imagine absolute clarity or enlightenment may function terroristically since differences, ambiguities and contradictions may be ignored, leading to boring lectures or ideological productions by the supervisor (see Horkheimer and Adorno, 1969). This in turn might evoke resistance from the supervised persons, destroying any possibility for constructive work.

THE PROCESS OF STRUCTURAL SUPERVISION

In what follows I want to describe the different steps of a supervision process: more precisely the first contact, the first session, and the structure of following sessions. During the first contact the focus of the evaluation is as extensively as possible on the discursive and non-discursive structures of the internal and external web. This includes the institutional background, the working conditions and the reason for the request for supervision (who is asking for supervision for whom and why). The institutional background means the institutional framework, its development and change, its internal structure, its referring groups, its environmental setting and tasks. Working conditions include basic theoretical concepts and assumptions, methods, and how the institution is financially equipped.

The actual problem needs to be posed in exact terms, specifying its appearance and typical form. Preparing the first session means to develop a structural framework, within which a location of the problem and a discussion of its articulation are possible, in order to find other ways for articulating it. Reflecting the problem and its context before the first supervision session serves to hold the societal dimensions of problems and conflicts in mind, avoiding the danger of merely following the perspectives suggested by the clients and to get stuck in the immediacy of the problem. On the other hand the supervisors need to be careful not to mix up the first structural analyses with the processual work of concrete problem-analysis, thereby thinking that they have understood the "real problem".

The first session is very important. A first relationship between the supervisor and the clients is established; then the supervisor attempts to learn more about the institutional reality. At the same time the supervisor is also forming an idea of how the clients make sense of themselves within these structures, and in terms of what discourses they articulate their problems. Therefore, the supervisor asks only information-seeking questions to fill in the gaps of what remains unclear and what was left out according to the first structural analyses. He or she asks each participant for the reasons for supervision and for a definition and description of the presenting problem. The reasons given for supervision are important for getting an idea about the motivation for supervision, whether it is seen as a voluntarily desired reflection of one's own working practice or as a necessary duty. The actual problem's description and definition is the initial point for the further supervision process. The client's articulation is mostly held in the form of a narration, which brings together different discourses structuring his/her work without making the conflicts and contradictions between these discourses obvious. Furthermore it shows which discursive and non-discursive structures and practices are not considered relevant for this problem. During that phase each comment and discussion should be stopped. Only then does the supervisor put his or her first structural analyses in exact terms. He or she tries to distinguish the discourses in which the clients articulate their point of view and tries to find out where within these articulations are contradictions, conflicts and ambiguities in order to differentiate the analysis of the problem.

Though avoiding discussion within the group of clients, this session now allows the first evaluation of group or team constellations and dynamics. Their different narrations are no first, "lonely" or "authentic" ones but rather the temporal result of the conflict's history. They can also be read as a situational response to the assumed position and role of the supervisor as well as to the other statements. With the assumption of the dialogical structure of narrations each statement is not only an element of a discourse, but also a response to other statements within the team, group and institution and is therefore relevant for understanding the group dynamics. After reflecting on these levels of conflict the supervisor has – according to present experiences – a viable concept for understanding the problems. How to continue, however, depends on the contractual agreements.

In short term supervisions (in other words, in organizational counseling), interventions are geared to the analyses. Often this is very confronting and only effective if the actual structure of the group, team or institution is in a process of change. In what follows the focus is on continuous supervision processes. The structure of the second and following sessions is then characterized by a "normal form" expectation (Giesecke and Rappe, 1982), which is the result of discursive structures within supervision processes. These are reproduced by complex, intersubjective patterns of expectation. Such "normal forms" are structured in five phases, which are connected by four coordinating points regulating the supervision process. They start with a pre-phase in which the conditions for a supervision are founded. At the following coordination point the supervisor has to draw a link to the negotiation phase, where each client sketches his or her problem. After a brief period of negotiating the supervisor needs to decide whether there is enough ground for working on one problematic case or situation or rather for working on thematic questions, including moments of group-dynamics. In the third phase the narration of the problem follows, which is regulated by the "narration-forces". Each narration has to follow three different forces (Schütze 1976): the force to condense, i.e. to select the important information due to the limited time of each narration; the force to specify, i.e. to give details for being comprehensible; and the force to close the *Gestalt* of the narration, i.e. to bring it to an end. Therefore it finds a "natural" end.

After some inquiries the supervisor commences the "dealing" phase, which is characterized by further questions, demands, and descriptions, by first conclusions and some reconstructions of the problem. At the coordination point to the final phase the supervisor summarizes the problem and the results of the dealing phase, and might comment on the development of the discussion and on the group processes.

THE STRUCTURE OF PROBLEM-ANALYSES

Having outlined the structure of a supervision session I want to describe how structural supervision handles a problem: first by using an abstract model and second, by giving an example. After the problem narration the dealing phase starts with further questions, which serve to make the contradictions and conflicts apparent. First it is useful to avoid focusing on one discourse, because questions directed at one concrete discourse interpellate subjects as the subjects of statement of this discourse – potentially, just reconstructing the whole problem in terms of this very same discourse. Consequently all conflicts and ambiguities of the problem are artificially "straightened out". Questions during the dealing phase should rather keep the problem-narration in all its statements present.

When the description of the problem is rich enough and conflicts and contradictions have become more evident there are different forms of clarifying interventions. If there seems to be an adequate discourse or idiom to rephrase the conflict (e.g. the conceptual foundations of this team or institution, or judicial discourses), the supervisor now starts to interpellate the subjects as subjects of statements of this conceptual or judicial discourse. The problem's description is usually overdetermined, but to become action-potent there has to be a reduction of complexity for developing strategies to deal with the problem. Interpellating the clients as the subjects of judicial or the conceptual discourse means that they rearticulate the problem in one of these discourses, hoping that this discourse allows to grasp the central dimensions of this problem. If the subjects are rearticulating the problem in these terms, then they have recognized some of the structures in which they were caught. However, if the clients are merely starting to describe and discuss the former problem again then the intervention has failed. Reasons may be found in a false analysis of the problem, or in deeper constellations of conflict. One possibility that now emerges is to interpret the group-reaction, thus transforming the conflict into a group conflict, in order to find the reasons why the group evades this issue. If the articulations are contradictory because of the work relations and opposing interests our aim is to keep these contradictions open, since every attempt to solve them leads consequently to a hidden return of the problem.

A very important component of the supervision process and in many ways the most complicated one, concerns the role and function of emotions and personal relations within this process. Conflict-narrations and discussions are always accompanied by emotional valuations. On the one hand these valuations are linked to the concrete situation, indicating what possibilities to solve this problem are expected (Holzkamp-Osterkamp, 1991). On the other hand emotions are easy to displace and may be regarded as a relative autonomous sphere. (The psychoanalytic thesis of the ambivalence of emotions supports this second conceptualization. This ambivalence between anxiety, as a defensive motive, and wish, as an extended motive, runs parallel as an analytical dimension to the thematic work). Group dynamics and conflicts are often the result of processes in which ambivalences are dissolved. Each pole, as a consequence, is personalized with one group or team-member fighting against his own ambivalences in his or her opponent. Therefore emotions within supervision processes are to be conceptualized as a discourse, in which they are structured and which supply different possibilities for their articulation.

AN EXAMPLE: THE SUPERVISION PROCESS OF A SANCTUARY MOVEMENT GROUP

To illustrate these very abstract reflections I wish to give an example. This example is the description and analysis of a supervision team-workshop of a group who work in the German sanctuary movement. This movement takes care of refugees who are threatened with expulsion by the German authorities, and gives them a refuge in church premises while trying to change the authorities' decision. Some background information concerning the situation of refugees in Germany will help to clarify this situation. People who have found refuge within the church are relatively safe in regard to deportation to their home countries compared to the situation of other refugees. Within the church the police are generally not allowed to persecute people. Consequently, in order to remain safe, these refugees have to live in the churches, where members of the above-mentioned group are taking care of them. Though these people - the church members - are all convinced of the worth of their work, and although they are symbolically and materially supported by their parish, their cooperative work is not unproblematic; they are dealing with many problems among themselves.

After the sanctuary movement had established the first contact with us (the supervision-group), they sent material to us through which they wanted to explain the reasons for working on such a project. We tried to get an idea of the different structures of the external and internal web. Reading through the given literature we discovered many contradictory structures and ambivalent discourses arguably

102

predestined to produce problems. The external conditions force those people to cooperate with state structures to obtain a right of residence for the refugees. At the same time they have to fight against these state structures. Furthermore there is the internal ambivalence for these "respectable and God-fearing people" who revolt in only this way against state structures, whilst at the same time considering themselves as good citizens. It is often difficult for them to understand,why a "democratic state" expels refugees and how this aspect of politics is linked to other dimensions of politics.

The state's official position acts strategically: the government wants to get rid of refugees, but it does not want to have too much negative publicity. The institutional church structure causes difficulties as well. Most people who work in this group do not hold any official position in this institution. They work as volunteers. Their private lives, their engagement in this work and their social contacts are mixed together, the borders between work and leisure time become unclear. Finally, the whole work is overdetermined by a moral discourse. In their own information booklet they write that for them neither guilt, nor nation nor other facts are reason enough to deport people, to torture them or send them to their death. This absolute moral standpoint does not recognise any ambivalence; in this view the refugees are pure victims and Christian duty demands that they be helped. Any ambivalent feeling about the refugees seems to endanger their whole work. From our own experiences with refugees we knew that they themselves are much more contradictory than we may want to admit. On the one hand those who manage to come to Germany are not necessarily the poorest ones. They have their own histories and sometimes a criminal background in Germany; on the other hand they are persecuted and while having to return to their country they are threatened by poverty and persecution or by torture and death. But because they are first of all victims one must not talk about one's own doubts.

For all these reasons we decided that it might be important to focus on the moral discourse in the supervision process. In the first phase of this workshop everybody told his or her view on their work and their problems. Later they started arguing about the possibilities and limits of their work. The conflicts were all articulated by personalizing the issues. Some interpreted the whole problem of their work as a political one with the consequence of fighting for political solutions, while others focused on the individual distress which they wanted to avert. Some asked for more regulating structures and professionalization to get distance from all the problems to avoid a burn-out of the collaborators. Others were scared of neglecting the direct contact with the refugees, who needed personal support.

Against the background of our first structural analysis we saw that the ambivalences of these different discourses were separated into two positions, fighting each other. In our first intervention we tried to work out the difficult situation of such work. But the effect was against our intention, in the way that the group constructed a group-identity in contrast to the state-structures. We started once again focusing on the different positions and trying to reinstall the first argument. We now tried to "irritate" each position by asking questions analyzing their problems. As a result they turned aggressive, because everybody knew about his or her own doubts and understood very well the other position. In the moment when they started to discuss their positions again we interpreted the situation as a result of the ambivalences and contradictions of these structures and emphasized that the personal conflicts are the attempt to solve these structural contradictions within the group – which is impossible. Then we tried to reinterpret these conflicts as necessary and productive for a group working in such a conflict-laden field, as long as they do not start to personalize these conflicts.

In the next phases we tried to work on different conflicts so that the participants understood their own ambivalence. We discussed the problems of drugs, sexuality and violence in their work with refugees. We touched on a lot of topics which are difficult to discuss because they form part of the conservative cliches and propaganda about refugees as criminals and so on. The basic moral position of this group became more differentiated. Refugees were not only seen as victims but also as perpetrators, but without condemning them. Personal decisions e.g. for not supporting a violent man also became acceptable, so as to work with them without personalizing (in this case gendering) this issue. In the end the workshop created the idea of a *cooperation in critical solidarity*, while knowing that the societal conditions and the politics are working against an improvement of the refugee's situation and that this "harmony" remains only a "fleeting" experience.

This is only an outline of a process of structural supervision. The concrete practice is much more conflict-laden, but I hope that I have shown how productive discourse-analytical instruments can be for analyzing problems in working relations and group conflicts. We know that most conflicts cannot be solved, but we can at least try to ensure that we are all governed a little less.

REFERENCES

Bourdieu, P. (1980): *Le sens pratique*. Paris: Les Editions de Minuit.
Bourdieu, P. & Wacquant, L.J.D. (1992): *An introduction to reflexive sociology*. Chicago, IL: University of Chicago Press.
Deleuze, G. (1986). *Foucault*. Paris: Éditions de Minuit.
Foucault, M. (1969). *L'archéologie du savoir*. Paris: Éditions Gallimard.

Giesecke, M. & Rappe, C. (1982). Setting und Ablaufstruktuiren in Supervisions- und Balintgruppen. Ergebnisse einer kommunikationswissenschaftlichen Untersuchung. In D. Flader et.al. (Eds) *Psychoanalyse als Gesräch, Interaktionsanalytische Untersuchungen über Therapie und Supervision* (pp 208-299). Frankfurt/Main: Suhrkamp.

Hofmeister, A, (1998). *Zur Kritik des Bildungsbegriffs aus subjektwissenschaftlicher Perspektive, Diskursanalytische Untersuchungen.* Hamburg: Argument-Verlag.

Holzkamp, K. & Markard, M. (1989) Praxis-Portrait. Ein Leitfaden zur Analyse psychologischer Berufstätigkeit. *Forum Kritische Psychologie, 23,* (5-49).

Holzkamp-Osterkamp, U. (1991). Emotion, cognition and action-potence. In C. Tolman & W. Maiers (Eds) *Critical psychology: Contributions to an historical science of the subject* (pp. 102-133). New York: Cambridge University Press.

Horkheimer, M. & Adorno, T.W. (1969). *Dialektik der Aufklärung, Philosophische Fragmente.* Frankfurt/Main: Fischer.

Lyotard, J.F. (1983). *Le Différend.* Paris: Les Édition de Minuit.

Schütz, F. (1976): Zur Hervorlockung und Analyse thematisch relevanter Geschichten im Rahmen soziologischer Feldforschung. In: Arbeitsgruppe Bielefelder Soziologen (Eds) *Kommunikative Sozialforschung* (pp 159-220). München.

FORMING CULTURES THROUGH VIRTUAL SOCIAL COMMUNITIES

Claudia Orthmann and Lars Näcke
Free University of Berlin

SUMMARY

This contribution deals with the specific topic of virtual social communities which are gaining more and more importance in our world. However, it does not proceed on the assumption of existing "real" social networks/relations being substituted by virtual ones. Rather, it is the possibilities and limits for virtual communities complementing the former kind that are to be discussed. By means of existing, constantly further developing communities the role of virtual communication for a discourse in the sense of "doing culture" is examined as an example. Virtual social communities offer to science forms and perspectives yet to be manifested: spaces for intercultural as well as less hierarchically structured discourses. In conclusion, a concrete model for the realization of this claim will be presented.

INTRODUCTION

As an introduction to the specific topic of virtual social communities we are first going to explain theoretically the term "social community" and link it to the Internet. The possibilities and limits of extended ranges of action will be dealt with particularly in regard to the "scientific community", and - proceeding from existing opportunities offered by the Internet for virtual communities – we shall discuss in detail the most promising opportunities, from our point of view, for the social sciences. In our opinion, virtual communities offer a good starting point for intercultural scientific discourses in which all participants have equal opportunities and voices. The structures of the Internet make the balanced negotiation and construction of science possible, if the chances are used. However, more than good will is required to reach this goal. Apart from global problems on economic grounds, there are many obstacles to be surmounted on a local level. Due to these local difficulties we cannot yet present a completed model for the realization of a worldwide, balanced intercultural discourse but can only try to create first bases and a theoretical intellectual impetus for surmounting the local problems.

SOCIAL NETWORKS AND COMMUNITIES

In the psychological context the social network is mostly characterized by the emphasis of supporting elements. Social networks are understood as "a range of interpersonal exchanges that provide an individual with information, emotional reassurance, physical or material assistance, and a sense of the self as an object of concern" (Pilisuk & Parks, 1980, cited in Krebs, 1998, p. 2). In connection with the scientific discourse it is not the *total* network of a person, which comprises all conceivable relationships of this person, but the *partial* network that plays a role (Pfingstmann and Baumann, 1987). The partial network means only a section of the total network, making reference to specific kinds of social relations, as for example scientific ones. The characterizations of networks are closely connected with the concepts for social support (Krebs, 1998). Whether one deals with the interaction and communication within the constructions of "network", "group" or "community", all three forms also appear as social structures in the Internet. Döring (1998) distinguishes three types of groups in the Internet: virtual small groups (with only three to five persons), virtual social networks and virtual communities. The small groups form themselves due to formal reasons (mostly in the fields of work and education), whereas the interaction in virtual social networks is based on a common subject and is therefore more an organic social form. The networks differ from social communities in that their members do not feel themselves as being an entirety and do not develop a feeling of solidarity worth mentioning. As with Hahn & Batinic (1998), the emphasis of networks lies on making available social capital which can be used for the seeking of information and advice. Rheingold's often cited, socio-psychologically oriented definition is to be used as a definition of social communities within the scope of this contribution: "Virtual communities are social unions which arise in the net when enough people have these public discussions long enough and invest their feelings so that a mesh of personal relationships is created in the Cyberspace" (Rheingold, 1994, p. 16). With the vision of a worldwide scientific discourse we are thus moving between networks and communities, as on the one hand the scientific discourse is a subject relatively clearly distinguishable from, for example, "MUD" (Multi User Domain) players or fans of Cybersex and changes organically, thus moving close to networks; and on the other hand a feeling of solidarity is an important part of the scientific *community*. The use of Rheingold's definition of virtual communities is not to give the impression that we aim at a romantic, empathic discourse. No, even if personal aspects are part of every communication, it is to be understood in an abstract sense regarding the virtual scientific community. Indispensable also for the scientific discourse in the Internet is the awareness of a community, an awareness which, even if not always understood positively, has always existed in science. This feeling of solidarity which has constituted itself so far by means of the membership of a discipline, a school, by a special comprehension of methods etc., gains new dimensions in the Internet.

In the framework of this paper we want to discuss the possibilities and limits of additional virtual communities. It is not a question of substituting the existing "real" contacts in science by purely virtual ones, but that the local discourse is to be extended. The beginnings existing at present in the Internet have to be developed, since in the computer-mediated discussion in the field of science the existing ways of communication and styles have so far only become faster and shorter – a conceptual change has not come about. By means of three concrete examples the present state of the use of computer-mediated communication in science is sketched from our point of view:

1. The advantages of computer-mediated communication, such as independence from place and time, have been recognized but have been realized above all by replacing formal letters by emails – which often are not less formal.

2. Cooperation via the Internet as it is propagated by industrial and organizational psychology mostly succeeds only on the level of small groups and therefore offers no model for the discourse in science in general.

3. Discussions with regard to scientific contents continue to be led mostly on a local basis. Only in single cases - and then mostly in mailing lists – is there an interdisciplinary and intercultural exchange.

With email and mailing lists two opportunities of Internet usage have been mentioned above which form the bases of communication of the virtual networks and communities. These forms and others are now going to be described in detail and located with respect to existing virtual discourses.

POSSIBILITIES FOR THE USE OF INTERNET STRUCTURES

A prerequisite for the extension of the contacts is *online presence*. In most of the institutions of the western industrial nations online presence is already a matter of course. Other nations have hardly arrived in the computer age regarding their technical equipment so that Internet access is an almost impossible enterprise due to the technical conditions (telephone connection, electricity, etc.). Those who have no problem with their access even to the World Wide Web present themselves mostly with their own homepages as individuals, institutes, research groups, etc.

Global exchange does not have to take place immediately on a high-tech level, as for example by means of online conferences, but it can begin in a quite unspectacular way with common *text work* in the sense of a text workshop. The more up-to-date word processing programmes additionally support these interactive ways of working by respective functions. Even though we were not separated by many kilometres, the present paper was written in this way for reasons of working economically. Furthermore, by means of so-called "Applets" and "Scripts", the Internet structures make the addition of new contributions to existing texts possible. These *"online stories"* which are being tested by us in seminars with students at the Free University of Berlin include in most cases very creative ideas and encourage cooperative working.

Online publications also have to be seen in this context. These involve the reader more than print media do, as the authors can be reached directly and easily via email. Some authors explicitly invite remarks and criticism, enable the reader to add links or comments or offer a guest book. This way, the idea of peer-review achieves a totally new dimension. Not merely a pre-defined, selected partial scientific community but an unrestricted circle of readers has the possibility to evaluate other people's work. Apart from the interactive modification of the publications there is also the opportunity of presenting state-of-the-art science. Out-of-date assumptions can be quickly revised in the Internet. However, such an understanding of a worldwide scientific discourse also poses problems. Copyrights have to be redefined and even linguistic aspects have to be considered. English is the acknowledged international language of science and of the Internet; however, a certain willingness is necessary to leave certain words in the original in order to prevent a "colonization of the language" and ensure the respective cultural specificities, as the translation of a concept or a term does not always allow the transformation of the cultural meaning too.

One possibility of the exchange via the Internet, however a technically very expensive one, is offered by the above-mentioned online conferences where sound and picture are sent via the Internet by means of corresponding interfaces (microphone, video camera etc). However, the advantages of this kind of synchronous communication have so far been brought to nothing because of the insufficient speed of data transmission. Therefore many conference attempts fail after frustrating, fruitless questions like "Hello, can you hear me? I can see you but I get no sound! Hello?" For these reasons online conferences have so far played a minor role and will only be relevant and important for the scientific discourse in the future in the wake of the continuing development of the Internet.

On a chat channel (IRC or lately also web based channels) several persons can communicate with each other simultaneously (mostly text based, but more and more also graphically supported). Whereas informal chat channels with a general, social reference are very common, chat channels devoted to scientific subjects have been infrequent so far (Döring, 1998). However, this form of communication offers an immense potential for science and will be dealt with later in detail.

Of increasing importance in teaching (but also in research) are Web-boards, also called discussion forums, where news can be "pinned" to a site just like to a notice-board. All of the Internet users can potentially participate in the asynchronous discussion. College freshmen as well as experts may benefit from the contributions. Apart from the notorious "FAQ's" (Frequently Asked Questions) even beginners can introduce new views and discover fundamental errors by asking questions. In seminars with students of educational science and psychology at the Free University of Berlin it turned out that the discussion forum installed as a supplementation of the discussion regarding the contents, was being transformed very quickly by the students to serve their own purposes. Despite the participation of external interested persons and experts, the forum was additionally used for organizing papers, structuring theses and criticising the teaching assistant. This shows that forecasts on the future usage of the Internet in science can only be made regarding tendencies: the net develops in accordance with its users.

In the virtual scientific discourse it is the mailing lists which have asserted themselves. Mailing lists are understood as a forum for writing regarding a defined topic. Contributions, so-called "postings", are sent to the list by one participant and thus, according to the principle of mail distribution, to all subscribers to the list. Advantages (such as independence from place and time, the possibility of keeping archives) and disadvantages (such as the discontinuous course of discussion, digression from the topic, and considerable fluctuation of the participants) of this kind of communication cannot be set off against each other in general but have to be evaluated for each list separately. In our opinion, open mailing lists offer a good basis for intra- and interdisciplinary communication between scientists of any discipline. By the term "basis" it is being suggested that the implementation of this communication and of the aspired-for common construction of science has yet to be attained, for there are still many examples of cultural and social role attributions being employed even in such lists in order to realize prejudices or exclusions. One example is the list Transcultural

Psychology*[1]. The following sentence can be found in the self-description of the list: "Please don't be shy about posting questions or issues you want to discuss with the list members. There is a wealth of experience on this list and I hope that we all can learn from each other." This sentence reads well and invites people to bring in topically relevant aspects of any kind. Unfortunately, the authors discovered that the list could not live up to its expectations, for when a list member brought up the subject of ethnic discrimination and marginalization in science and everyday life due to colour of skin or social status, it was suggested to this person, and to other list members who supported the discussion and tried to continue it, that they should leave the list or discontinue this kind of discussion. It is remarkable that the supporters of the exclusion were just those scientists who held the socially highest positions, namely doctors and professors. In the end, the conflict culminated in a division of the list.

The last and most far-reaching possibility of how to use the Internet in developing a global scientific discourse lies with online institutes. These institutes comprise individual persons who work in very different institutions in "real life" and have united in the Internet because of similar interests and focuses. Good examples are the Virtual Faculty* and soon also the homepage* of the research group Culture, Development and Psychology, at the Developmental Psychology Unit at the Free University of Berlin. In common online projects, mailing lists, discussion forums, publications, E-Zines (electronic magazines or online newspapers which exist only in the Internet), courses, and so on, the members of the online institutes present themselves as a virtual community. Online institutes have so far come closest to our concept of a virtual scientific community. They can act in a balanced, interdisciplinary and intercultural way. Of course, like in the case of all communication possibilities presented, the Internet per se is no guarantee for this form of discourse. However, with the corresponding attitude of the individual the Internet can encourage it tremendously.

FORMING CULTURES WHILE USING THE COMMUNICATION POSSIBILITIES OF THE INTERNET

How can the above-mentioned possibilities of communication via the Internet be used in order to achieve what we have announced as "forming cultures" in the title of this paper?

As we have just pointed out, we prefer the form of online institutes as forms of representation, communication and work besides the real face-to-face interaction. Net communication via online institutes serves above all the forming of a necessary self-appreciation of scientific groups and communities. The advantage of communication via the Internet is its relative independence compared with "common" forms of (scientific) communication which are always linked to power structures and social and cultural prejudices and forms of interaction. Online institutes represent a kind of meta-structure, similar to a university, under the auspices of which all forms of scientific interaction possible can be united. It is, for example, conceivable to offer open mailing lists which could come close to their demand for a balanced discourse in that the team of moderators of such a list is composed of persons with a great variety of cultural backgrounds and social positions. However, it is particularly important not to repeat seemingly "normal" representations of social reality without reflection. The status of female scientists may serve as an example. Despite their increasing presence in the scientific landscape they do not experience a true equality of rights. If, for example, one looks at the percentage of women in the highest positions of scientific institutions in Germany, they represent only a very small part, whereas their number in lower and subordinate positions in social sciences and the humanities have by now exceeded fifty percent. However, implicit exclusion also has to be reflected and implemented accordingly. In western society women still represent the "marked gender" whereas the male gender has established itself as the "unmarked", universal one and therefore is not or cannot be made a topic (see for example the writings of Donna Haraway, Luce Irigaray, Judith Butler).

Another challenge is represented by the "chats", a form of communication which have hardly played a role in scientific contexts so far. Chats are particularly suited for less hierarchically structured and more equal communications since there potentially everyone has the possibility to create him- or herself as a person and to act seemingly independently from their real social and cultural background. We are the way we are creating ourselves. Thus it gets difficult to apply certain prejudices to persons and to update them in the form of actions, for example an exclusion. Potentially everyone can represent, externally, a neuter which in the course of the communication can be filled with the respective personal experience and knowledge. In such communications cultural origin, colour of skin etc. cannot take such dominant roles as in face-to-face interactions since perception and therefore traditional ways of thinking are available in a limited form. Another possibility is the presentation of oneself as a member of the opposite sex, so to speak as an opportunity to experience the "other being" with its respective advantages and disadvantages. However, this is not supposed to mean that in doing so these problems are to be abstracted, possibly even negated. On the contrary, they should always be genuine elements of all scientific communications in order to make a topic of, disclose, and question the still dominating arrogance of the western scientific landscape, as it has spread over the whole world, thus making possible, at best, new ways of thinking and of interaction.

Online institutes potentially enable all net users to participate for they have free access via the net. Everyone, scientist or "layman", can be part of such a community. The explicit inclusion of the "layman" which is demanded here aims in two ways at a different way of dealing with forms of cognition and the resulting forms of knowledge. On the one hand, the term "layman" comprises the non-scientist. With this meaning, a form of knowledge is being referred to which so far has not yet been included as a recognized form in the generation of knowledge. On the other hand, the term aims at the inclusion and the equal treatment of so-called "indigenous theories" as they have been and are being formulated by scientists who refer to just such a "non-scientific knowledge" of their respective cultures (Kim, 1997).

The ideas and visions presented by us here concerning the usage of existing forms of communication and presentation of the Internet are only conceivable, however, if they do not remain theoretical concepts but are implemented. Of course, this is not realized just by an implementation of the possible formal structures (the homepage etc.) on a technical level but by a simultaneous change in the "real forms of thinking and acting".

WHY *SOCIAL* VIRTUAL CULTURE? The Development of Ethics of Interaction in the Internet

From this point of view it becomes clear why we have spoken in the title explicitly of "social" virtual cultures. So far the "potential of net communication is being considered too much in a one-dimensional way, social factors are not enough taken into consideration" (Jarren, 1998, p. 14). All of the possibilities of the Internet use demanded above for achieving a less hierarchically structured communication are political elements of human life. Due to its potential accessibility alone, the Internet is suited for the implementation of different political action, for the "political order becomes visible through public action and thus experiences ... its legitimation" (Jarren, 1998, p. 15). However, political action cannot remain limited to virtual realities, for politics means acting in real places and is bound to certain social rules. Thus the term "social", apart from the aspect of feeling as is discussed below, refers to rules which explicitly determine the forms of interaction. "Culture", on the other hand, is to refer, among other things, to all those implicit rules which reconstitute themselves in interactions (see especially Capurro, 1998).

Therefore the authors think it necessary to make explicit rules which are constantly moving -- meaning that they can be questioned and changed at any time. Examples are the "netiquette" or the rules behind the sign of the "blue ribbon" in the Internet as well as the information ethics* which were formulated in cooperation with UNESCO. However, such rules have to be supervised and guaranteed by institutions. The authors are aware of the difficulty of not falling back into the old structures and ways of interaction, but it is in such communities like the online institutes, which are small compared with the Internet, that we see possibilities to prevent this – because the online institutes are to be understood as supra-regional and intercultural forms of scientific interaction. In the opinion of the authors, however, this is not sufficient. Besides these explicit rules which can be formulated and written down, it will be necessary to create a certain ethical attitude among the participants and the visitors of the online institute. This cannot be done by way of formal guidance and regulation. The forming of an ethical attitude is both precondition and result of interaction and conscious action, for example by questioning recognized knowledge due to a certain attitude. In the "real" scientific context such ethics are just in the course of being formed by the movement of "Cultural Psychology" where the attempt is made to oppose all those mechanisms which lead to the exclusion of persons and thus of knowledge and possibilities of knowing in scientific interactions or work forms. Behind this movement there is an ethical attitude which aims at the acceptance of difference concerning cultural and social backgrounds. Such an attitude has to be taken up and transported by online institutes, too. Therefore it is not surprising that the two examples mentioned above also come from Cultural Psychology.

It now remains to be clarified how such an attitude can be formed or imparted. For this purpose the concept of "Doing Culture" is to serve us, a concept formulated by Chung-Woon Kim (1997) and the implementation of which is tried by the research group "Culture, Development and Psychology". Kim proceeds on the assumption that the deconstruction of western models of thinking and theories is a starting point of such an ethical attitude. However, this deconstruction must not only be understood as a cognitive reflection. "On the contrary, it is a real social process of action" (Kim, 1997, p. 316). Since we understand "virtual reality", as mentioned in the beginning, to be an extension of our human forms of interaction, this sentence is relevant here, too. According to Kim, feeling is the key to reflection. "Reflection is not possible until the social and cultural position of the other person can be comprehended ... only then can one's own position be reflected. Through the inclusion of the dimension of feeling the ability to comprehend totally differs from understanding. Reflection is no property of the logical philosopher or the speculative rhetorical speaker. A reflecting person is a feeling thinker or a thinking feeling person" (Kim, 1997). The dimension of feeling is still not understood as a real moment of social virtual communities. Whoever has gone into "virtuality" once in order to make social contacts will soon find out that feelings are constant companions of online communications. There are explicit forms to express one's feelings, like the emoticons, but the language itself seems to include a dimension which knows how to compensate certain reductions of our perception. Electronic language in connection with one's own respective interpretation becomes a sensually perceptible entirety which transports not only information, as it is mostly assumed, but also meanings and moments which can be felt. For example, one is shocked by the death of an intensive communication partner (see Argyle, 1996) or likewise, if not more, hurt by an attack on one's own person.

Accordingly, reflection is understood here as an interactive communication process or as the result of the same and is possible only "if the communication partners can make clear to each other the difference of their perspectives. They are interacting for just this purpose" (Jarren, 1998, p. 18). A "feeling thinker" is therefore a person, a male or female scientist, who is able not only to see the limits of his/her own possibilities of knowing due to the "social" confrontation with people who think differently, but also to go deeply into the knowledge system of the other person, e.g. an indigenous theory, and to perceive it as a real option. This is certainly no new position, however it is still waiting to be implemented. To us it is a matter of course that under the circumstances given such a use of the Internet is still limited to certain, mostly western contexts and cannot be realized until the global economic inequalities concerning the participation in tele-presence can be abolished. In order to surmount them, everyone of us is invited to participate in opposing this kind of exclusion, either by means of support in the form of financial means or by making available their experience in dealing with technology and software. It would be conceivable, for example, to arrange for mentorships among scientists, research groups and universities via the online institutes.

FINAL REMARKS

What matters to us in our contribution is to show clearly the possibilities and limits of what the Internet has to offer in order to reach another form of scientific communication. At the same time it is important to point out how much the Internet is linked to really existing structures of action and thought and that a vision of a different interaction cannot be limited to the Internet but has to have effects on "real" interaction. To what extent the ideas and suggestions presented here can be realized remains on the one hand to be seen and yet at the same time in the hands of all of us -- for example by "forming virtual social cultures"...

Note

1.   *URLs etc cited:
       transcultural-psychology@listserv.nodak.edu
       http://www.massey.ac.nz/~ALock/virtual/welcome.htm
       http://www.cultural-psychology.de
       http://www.de3.emb.net/infoethics

REFERENCES

Argyle, K. (1996). Life after death. In Shields, R. (Ed.), *Cultures of Internet. Virtual spaces, real histories, living bodies.* London: Sage Publications, Chapter 8.

Capurro, R. (1998). Informationsgerechtigkeit. Zwischen Selbstkontrolle und Weltinformationsordnung. *Medien Praktisch, 4/98*, 42-44.

Döring, N. (1998). *Sozialpsychologie des Internet- Die Bedeutung des Internet für Kommunikationsprozesse. Identitäten, soziale Beziehungen und Gruppen.* Unpublished dissertation, Free University of Berlin:.

Hahn, A. & Batinic, B. (1998). *Zukunftsperspektiven: Psychologie und Internet am Beispiel ausgewählter Online-Projekte.* Vortrag gehalten im Rahmen der 40. Tagung experimentell arbeitender Psychologen (TeaP) in Marburg 6.-9.4.98. URL: http://www.psychologie.de (22.1.99).

Jarren, O. (1998). Internet - neue Chancen für die politische Kommunikation? In: *Aus Politik und Zeitgeschichte*, Band 40/98, 13-21.

Kim, Chung-Woon (1997). *Baustein für einen kulturpsychologischen Diskurs: Dekonstruktion des unilinearen Entwicklungsgedankens.* Unpublished dissertation, Free University of Berlin.

Krebs, N. (1998). *Soziale Unterstützung und Gruppenidentität in Mailinglisten.* Unpublished thesis Free University of Berlin:.

Pfingstmann, G. & Baumann, U. (1987). Untersuchungsverfahren zum sozialen Netzwerk und zur sozialen Unterstützung. Ein Überblick. *Zeitschrift für Differentielle und Diagnostische Psychologie*, 8 (2), 75-98.

Rheingold, H. (1994). *Virtuelle Gemeinschaft. Soziale Beziehungen im Zeitalter des Computers.* Bonn/Paris: Addison Wesley.

III PERCEPTION, COGNITION AND REASONING

POINTS OF VIEW AND THE VISUAL ARTS:

James Turrell, Antonio Damasio and The "No Point of View"
Phenomenon

Ciarán Benson
University College Dublin

SUMMARY

This paper distinguishes types of point of view and their relationships to phases in the history of Western visual art.[1] This supplies a context for considering the phenomenon which is the focus of the analysis, the experience of "no point of view". The Ganzfeld Sphere created by the American artist James Turrell comes closest to enabling the perceptual experience of no-point-of-view with its dissolution of the phenomenological categories of inside-outside and here-there. In particular it seems to enable viewers to *see their seeing*. Using the work of the neurologist Antonio Damasio, the paper concludes with the speculation that Turrell has created the conditions which isolate for attention a particular neural representation of the body being changed by an object which Damasio proposes as central to subjectivity.

INTRODUCTION: THE LANGUAGE OF LOCATION

There are many words for "location" and "being located" in English. They include up/down, front/back, above/below, inside/outside, on/off, here/there, towards/away and now/then. Between them, these constructs form one set of coordinates for psychological location, the perceptual-motor field, which includes our sense of being spatially and temporally located (Paillard, 1991). A second set of coordinates, essential to being a self and a person, locates a self in relation to other selves both socially and morally. Here the key constructs are I/you, us/them, is/is not, have/not have, yours/mine, and for/against.

It is hard to think of any more important pairs to add to this list, which is to say new constructs which could not be generated from these primary ones. This is a working list to which we can address a number of questions. For example, in terms of psychological development is one of them a primary one from which the others are subsequently derived? Does the "sense of here/there", for instance, developmentally precede the "sense of I"? Do newborn babies function exclusively at a perceptual-motor level such that senses of here/there, up/down, towards/away, develop before and ground the senses of me/you, yours/mine, us/them, for/against? Is the linguistic structure of our psychological lives modelled in some way on the structures of our physical location? (Bloom *et al.*, 1996).

Central to both sets of constructs is the further idea of a "boundary" as somewhere or something at which one pole of the construct ends and another begins, where for example our "inside" ends and the "outside" begins. With here/there or up/down there is the idea that the boundary is spatial. But at what point does "there" experientially become "here"? And what is the nature of the boundary between "you" and "me", or "me as I now am" and "me as I then was", say ten years ago?

The ways in which we think and speak of ourselves and of our positions in the various aspects of the world are permeated by our use of metaphors based on our language for physical location. Amongst many other classes of metaphor, George Lakoff and Mark Johnson highlight the role of what they call "orientational metaphors" in shaping "part" of such experiences, or enrolled as co-constructors of them how we think of things (Lakoff & Johnson, 1980; Lakoff & Johnson, 1999). They show how all of these metaphors, and many others, are coherently grounded in experiences that are physical, social or cultural.

The arts are the most accomplished metaphorical realm created by human beings. Becoming more than oneself depends in part on the inventiveness of artists and of their traditions (Benson, 1993). Within the visual arts, entry to the work that art does has relied on ideas and practices of perspective and perspective-creation. In this paper I want to distinguish four kinds of case: any point of view, a defined point of view, one's own point of view, and no point of view. These I take to be, very roughly, successive emphases in the history of Western art, partly dependent for their emergence on technological developments. My particular interest is in a contemporary "no point of view" experience and its implications. My extremely brief treatment of the first three cases should therefore be read as background and context for this fourth case.

Medieval artworks create a pictorial space that is "flat", without engaging "depth". Medieval cosmology and medieval art were intimately linked, as Margaret Wertheim argues (Wertheim, 1999). Space and time were understood as being heterogeneous and discontinuous. Below, here on earth and above the stars matched regions of Hell, human life, and Heaven respectively, as Dante mapped them. Pre-linear perspectival pictures make no demands on spectators' viewing positions other than that the picture should be visibly in front of them. Within limits of visibility, any point of view will do since the structure of the picture does not anticipate and require a particular perspective. The psychological engagement of the spectator, however intense it may be in other respects, does not privilege where the spectator is. The picture does not have the sort of "depth" which requires a "point of entry". The correlative experience, at least as we view it today, can be characterised by a quality of "distance" and "otherness" compared with what followed upon the development of linear perspective. Prior to linear perspective the construction of pictorial space depended on cues such as interposing one figure before another, relative size, and so on. We can only guess at the detailed psychology of "how they felt to be seen" at that time (Damasio, 1999).

The development of linear perspective is not unrelated to emerging ideas of space as unified and continuous. The technology of linear perspective enabled the making of perceptually compelling virtual spaces into which spectators could be temporarily relocated. It is a technology that requires a defined point of view for optimal experience, one that defines in advance where the viewer should be. It created that pictorial "doubleness" which formed the antithesis for so much art in the twentieth century, what Richard Wollheim has called the "twofoldness" of pictures (Wollheim, 1987; Rock, 1995). We can look "into" pictures to see what they are "about", but we can also withdraw that attention and re-focus on qualities of the pictorial surface. From the Renaissance to the twentieth century, "looking-in" was the dominant mode of psychological participation in pictorial art. There was an optimum point of entry for this "looking in," one which was pre-determined by the pictorial composition itself. That was the picture's point of view.

We have literal, perceptual points of view which have to do with our positions in space. We metaphorically extend the phrase to cover our positioning on issues of understanding, morality and social standing. In the always changing flow of consciousness it is useful to think of "my point of view" generically, as meaning something like the coherent succession of types of point of view which characterise a particular phase of that stream of consciousness which I feel to be my own. In experiences of art, a visual point of view can be recruited to serve other points of view such as favoured forms of feeling, or orientations of a church or political movement, for example. The geometry of linear perspective enables the artist, in addition to creating a powerful illusion of depth, to feed this into the narrative of the painting so that the spectator's eye may be drawn to some central character or action, or even for concealing allusion in the work (Kubovy, 1986).

The power of the technique is greater than this since the compelling visual appearance of this new pictorial space changes its relationship with the actual space in which the spectator begins looking at the picture. Artists like Andrea Mantegna recognised this in works like *Saint James Led to Execution* (1454-57) and began to explore ways of, as it were, deliberately linking virtual and actual space so as to create new psychological experiences.

Viewers of this Mantegna feel themselves to be located at a point on the bottom of the picture plane where the shield of the man standing to the right of the arch touches the ground. Yet their line of sight must be tilted upwards, so powerful is their feeling of being placed at its centre of projection. Kubovy has analysed how Mantegna used his understanding of perspective to create a discrepancy between the direction of the spectator's gaze (upwards) and the direction implicit in the orientation of the picture plane (horizontal). The psychological result is "a vibrantly tense work full of foreboding" (Kubovy, 1985, p. 148).

Modernist artists fully understood the technology of linear perspective, its achievements and its expressive exhaustion. This understanding is the basis for my distinction between the "any point of view" of pre-linear perspective images and the "own point of view" of twentieth century modernism. In Modernist work, it is the "looking at" facet of the twofoldness of pictures that is required of the spectator rather than "looking in". But that "looking at" requires a subject with a degree of choice about looking and interpreting which is radically different to that of a medieval worshipper before an icon. Modernist work requires autonomous spectators in self-conscious possession of their own points of view. That is the crucial difference in the psychology recruited by medieval pictorial flatness and modernist two-dimensionality. One might rather grandly suggest that refusal of depth and redundancy of point of view go together in an epoch of unified space-time.

This cursory review of how Western art has deployed understanding of viewpoints – "any", "defined", "own" – allows me introduce a deployment that seems to me to be particularly interesting, but for which I would resist the description postmodern. This is the idea and experience of "no point of view" and its experiential uses. Part of its interest has to do with the quintessentially modern preoccupation with "interior space" and the "interior depths" of self, as well as with questions of "personal boundaries," of where "you" end and something else begins (Taylor, 1989: Benson, 2001).

GANZFELDS, THE "NO POINT OF VIEW" PHENOMENON, AND SEEING ONESELF SEE IN THE ART OF JAMES TURRELL

In each of my three previous cases the art with which self engages is object-based, imagistic or thematising of surface qualities, and it invites the deployment of a focused attention and a point of view of some form or other. What, though, is the quality of subjectivity when there is no object, no imagery, and no point of view? The strikingly innovative work of the American artist James Turrell allows us to address this question. Turrell's sophisticated work with light itself creates highly distinctive experiences which utilise the twofoldness of *perception* in contrast to the twofoldness of the *pictorial*.

For over sixty years psychologists have been interested in what are called *Ganzfelds* . These are total visual fields of uniform light but with no visible image or object. In the ordinary world, experiences of anything like a total visual field of uniform light are extremely rare. Real world examples of something like a *Ganzfeld* would be what explorers call Arctic "white-outs" or what pilots rarely experience in a total envelope of fog.

From the 1930s onwards, Gestalt psychologists like Wolfgang Metzger and Kurt Koffka experimented with *Ganzfelds* (Metzger, 1930; Koffka, 1935; Avant, 1965; Adcock, 1990). In the 1950s and 1960's the American psychologist J.J. Gibson and his co-workers further explored the psychology of total visual fields and came to the conclusion that what was to be seen was *nothing* in the sense of no-thing (Gibson 1979). It was rather like looking at a sky in which there is no object and no distance. This "empty medium" reduced perception to very basic levels. Locating ourselves in space, it should be remembered, is achieved by relating ourselves to other objects in terms of relative distance. Parallel to this research were inquiries into sensory deprivation and the experiences of disorientation and dislocation which result from being deprived of such stimulation (Vernon, 1966). These types of experience intrigued Turrell. Born in Los Angeles in 1943, he trained as a psychologist before becoming an artist. His utilisation of his observations on seeing are amongst the most astute available.

With some exceptions such as art which depends wholly on touch, the visual arts self-evidently depend on sight and light. Most often this light is reflected light: reflected from pictures, sculptures, buildings. It may also be translucent, as with stained glass. Light is central to the evolution of life. The brain itself, it is speculated, originated in light sensitive organs. At every level of human life, even for those born blind, light is centrally important since even the congenitally blind can in their own way visualize. Their brains are the outcomes of an evolution of seeing even if they cannot see. Susanna Millar, in her book on understanding and representing space in blind and sighted children, tells of a young and ardent soccer fan of her acquaintance who is blind and who had regularly listened to commentaries on football matches but who visualized the pitch as having one goalpost in the middle into which both sides kicked the ball (Millar, 1994, p. 177).

There is no tangible barrier blocking an actor on a stage from seeing the audience: stage light is the barrier. There is no physical barrier blocking our seeing the stars during daytime: sun lighting the atmosphere is the barrier. Diminish the light and the audience and stars become visible. These examples introduce the ideas underpinning Turrell's work. Light is his medium, and making available for attention the *act of seeing* is his aim. There is no object in his work, in the sense of something solid, other than the constructions which frame the experiences of the viewers. There is no image because Turrell deliberately wants to avoid associative, symbolic thought. There is no focus or particular place to look. As he says himself, in his works "You are looking at you looking" (Adcock, 1990, p. 26).

TURRELL'S GANZFELD SPHERE AND ACCOUNTS OF PARTICIPANTS' EXPERIENCES

In 1996 Turrell constructed his *Ganzfeld Sphere* in the National Sculpture Factory in Cork, Ireland. The *Ganzfeld Sphere* is a real sphere into which the viewer is inserted lying on a tray in a procedure that is similar to having a body-scan. Once the spectator is inside the sphere, lying flat and looking upwards, a technician manipulates the internal lighting of the sphere. As far as is possible there are no visible reference points nor features upon which to focus. The spectator has the experience of being surrounded by light of different hues which change at different tempos. The subjective result is remarkable.

By removing all possible reference points, bar one's own nose which is a prominent but normally unnoticed protuberance in our field of vision and such feelings as come from the body lying on a hard surface and some ambient sound, Turrell creates a unique type of experience which challenges our sense of being located. He enlists a series of psychological phenomena using light of different hues and rhythms which are otherwise difficult to observe or feel in the complex flux of ordinary experience.

A sample of reflections from spectators on their own experiences illustrates what is involved. I selected these from over 400 in the Visitors Book in order to suggest the effects on the phenomenology of "inside-outside" and the orientational language which people use to describe these experiences.

First let me take the issue of body boundaries, our sense of where we end and the rest of the world begins. Turrell's *Ganzfeld Sphere* makes uncertain our senses of here and there, of inside and outside, of this and that. He does this, as I have said, with no imagery or symbols upon which to focus or take our bearings. He induces the experiences with fields of light alone, partly by what is there and partly by excluding what is normally there. Typical comments left by individual participants illustrate the experiential correlates of the "no point of view" phenomenon:

"Sometimes I didn't know whether my eyes were closed or open"
" I really felt as if the roof of the dome was the outer membrane of my eyes"
" I felt the colours inside my head, rather than around me"
" What I thought most interesting was the sensation that I had closed my eyes when I had not, my eyes at times felt paralysed, great after images like seeing into your own retina, from the inside"
" ...sense of time vanishes as well as immediate sense of location"

Whereas the focus of traditional pictorial art is on *what* is seen, Turrell's express intention and achievement is to enable the *act of seeing* itself to be foregrounded.   The import of this is a challenge to our common-sense notions of location, boundary and point of view at a very basic level.

Furthermore, visual perception includes *a feeling of the body as we see* and that bodily feeling is larger than seeing alone. Synaesthesia, which has to do with the interrelations of the senses, is one aspect of this. In the case of the *Ganzfeld Sphere*, we have repeated reports of the tangibility and touchability of the light as though the senses of the skin were recruited as part of the act of seeing:

" You forget time and space in the sphere. I feel the cold of the blue and the heat of the red."
" Dreaming with open eyes. Feelings of cold and deep blue sea."
" The first time I have ever truly experienced the weight of colour, without any other reference to shape, form, etc.."

The effects of all this were frequently described as calming, relaxing, womb-like, uplifting, meditative and so on.

THE "NO POINT OF VIEW" PHENOMENON IN THE LIGHT OF DAMASIO'S THEORY OF CONSCIOUSNESS

Art vigorously engages and shapes human psychology. How might contemporary psychology begin to explain some of the phenomena of location, point of view and object exemplified above? I want to offer some speculations which use aspects of Antonio Damasio's theory of neural representation as a possible basis for the phenomena which James Turrell has made so impressively his own.

A feature of normal lives is their stability. People are generally quite confident that they know who they are and where they are. Apart from the dislocation caused by bereavement or moving to a new country, for example, our ability to confidently take our bearings and know where we are physically and socially is not often called into question (Benson, 2001). Our obvious competence belies how such an astonishingly complex feat can be achieved with such relative ease. Merleau-Ponty wrote that "My body is the fabric into which all objects are interwoven" (Merleau-Ponty, 1981, p. 235). This is the same basic idea which the neurologist Antonio Damasio develops (Damasio, 1995 and 1999).

Neurologists and neuropsychologists have theorised for some time that there are neural networks underpinning a foundational body-self, or neuromatrix or neural self (Melzack, 1989). Damasio elaborates the notion of a "neural self"(Damasio, 1995) or "proto-self" (Damasio, 1999) and outlines its significance for locating what happens to us, whether within the boundaries of our bodies or outside them. He suggests that the brain evolved in the first instance, as a means of "Representing the outside world in terms of the modification it causes in the body proper, that is, representing the environment by modifying the primordial representations of the body proper whenever an interaction between organism and environment takes place" (Damasio, 1995, p. 230).

These representations are distributed over several regions of the brain and are coordinated by neuron connections, in which the musculoskeletal frame and skin play, in Damasio's view, an important role. This map of the body is dynamic and constantly renewed. If this is valid, it would mean that we should think of most physical interactions with the environment as happening *at a place within the body boundary* since sense organs exist at a location within the body boundary, such as seeing at the eyes.

Signals from the "outside" in this physical sense are always *double*. There is the seeing of something as a *non-body signal*, but there is also a *body signal* which comes from a place in the skin where the special signal entered, such as the eyes in the head. Therefore in addition to seeing what you see, you *feel-yourself-seeing* with your eyes. Visual perception is "a feeling of the body as we see" (Damasio, 1995, p. 232). However, unless things go wrong and demand attention, as for example when we feel pain, perception of the body generally remains in the background.

Turrell's work with experiences of light itself is playing with just that doubleness of perception which is the focus of Damasio's ideas on body-representations in the brain. For Turrell, as we saw, it is *the feeling of seeing itself* which is the focus of his work. On the other hand, the psychology of Renaissance perspective was very much about the other aspect of doubleness, situating the spectator the better to see what was there to be seen. In much modernist painting the particular doubleness in play was not that "seeing itself" as against "that seen," but rather "looking at" rather than "looking into." This was a play with surface qualities while eschewing the qualities of virtual depth. Where spectators feel themselves to be is very different in each type of art.

As the body is represented in the structure of the brain, "symbols" of the body may be used "as if" they were current body signals. The pain of phantom limbs after amputation is a case in point. What are called "as-if loops" in the brain have great significance for our understanding of how we locate ourselves and our feelings. This is again relevant for any consideration of the emotional dimensions of experiences of art. But the general point is that these representations of our body are vital to our sense of how and where we are. Furthermore, they change, review and renew from moment to moment (Damasio, 1995, p. 235). This idea of the neural or proto-self incessantly renewing itself is in keeping with the more complete idea of self, especially as developed by William James, as a process always flowing and moving on as part of the present thoughts which compose the stream of consciousness (James, 1950). Is there any neurological evidence for this?

ANOSOGNOSIA AND THE INCESSANT RENEWAL OF BODY-MAPS

Damasio observes that when a patient suffers neurological loss their descriptions of what has happened to them suggests that they "locate" the problem to a part of their persons which they are surveying from the vantage point of their selfhood. "My God," a patient might say, "what is happening to *Me* ? I cannot move my arm." But there is a curious form of brain damage where this does not occur. This is the condition of *anosognosia* where the person may, for example, be totally paralysed down the left half of the body but be completely oblivious of the problem. For them, nothing is wrong and things are fine, even though they cannot feel the left half of their body, or move their left arm or walk. Their form of brain damage yields no internal information which would automatically tell them that they are catastrophically damaged. Even when confronted with the fact of the damage by others they seem relatively unconcerned. This has a particular theoretical significance for the idea of a "neural self" and for some general idea of how the world, including ourselves as part of it, remain stable while at the same time being unceasingly updated.

In cases of complete anosognosia sufferers never refer the trouble to themselves nor can they say when it started. To do so would involve referring to themselves in terms of a time before damage which they could contrast with the time after damage. Damasio interprets the condition of complete anosognosics as a partial demolition of the substrate of the neural or proto-self such that current body states cannot be processed. For these unfortunately unperturbed people the incessant renewal by the brain of the representation of their bodies has ceased, and they are left with an old representation of a healthy body and the new but ignored fact of a damaged one. The updating of the brain's body-representation and/or its availability to consciousness has ceased. Their dilemma provides evidence for the view that the neural foundations of the body are all the time being remade outside the awareness of the person. Of course, to speak of a neural self is not to argue for a "single central knower" nor is it to suggest that such an entity would reside in a single brain place.

From a neuropsychological perspective the constancy of our point of view must be rooted in an endlessly renewed but relatively stable series of biological states and this must lie at the heart of our ability to orient and locate ourselves in the world. Speaking of the neural foundations of self, Damasio says that "At each moment the state of self is constructed, from the ground up. It is an evanescent *reference state* [emphasis added], so continuously and consistently *re*constructed that the owner never knows it is being *re*made unless something goes wrong with remaking" (Damasio, 1995, p. 240). We still have little idea about how our distinctively human subjectivity and consciousness emerges but Damasio's suggestion is

> that subjectivity emerges ... when the brain is producing not just images of an object, not just images of organism responses to the object, but a third kind of image, *that of an organism in the act of perceiving and responding to an object* [emphasis added]. I believe the subjective perspective arises out of the content of the third kind of image (Damasio, 1995, p. 243).

He goes on to argue that subjectivity is produced by "successive organism states, each neurally represented anew, in multiple concerted maps, moment by moment, and each anchoring the self that exists at any one moment" (Damasio, 1995, p. 235).

AN INTRIGUING QUESTION

Could it be that Turrell has isolated phenomenologically, and exploited aesthetically, representations of this third kind, "images of the organism in the act of perceiving" precisely by his elimination of the object? If he has, then could his phenomenological dissolution of the operative boundaries of routine categories like "inside-outside" and "here-there" result from creating conditions (no object, no point of view) in which this representation of the act of seeing is quarantined from the other putative types of representation comprising our sense-of-self-in-the-world, namely "representations of the object of perception" and "representations of organismic responses to an object"? It is an intriguing possibility.

Note

1.   This paper is part of a wider project: see Benson (2001).

REFERENCES

Adcock, C. (1990). *James Turrell: The art of light and space.* Berkeley CA: University of California Press.

Avant, L.L. (1965). Vision in the Ganzfeld. *Psychological Bulletin,* 64, 246-258.

Benson, C. (1993). *The absorbed self: Pragmatism, psychology and aesthetic experience.* London: Harvester Wheatsheaf.

Benson, C. (in press for 2001). *The cultural psychology of self: Place, art and morality in human worlds.* London: Routledge.

Bloom, P., Peterson, M., Nadel, L., & Garrett, M.F. (Eds) (1996). *Language and space.* Cambridge, MA.: MIT Press.

Damasio, A. (1995). *Descartes' error: Emotion, reasoning and the human brain.* London: Picador.

Damasio, A. (1999). *The feeling of what happens: Body and emotion in the making of concsiousness.* New York: Harcourt Brace & Company.

Gibson, J. J. (1979). *The ecological approach to visual perception.* Boston: Houghton Mifflin.

James, W. (1950). *The principles of psychology.* 2 Vols., New York: Dover Publications.

Koffka, K. (1935). *Principles of gestalt psychology.* New York: Harcourt, Brace and Company.

Kubovy, M. (1986). *The psychology of perspective and renaissance art .* Cambridge: Cambridge University Press.

Lakoff, G. & Johnson, M. (1980). *Metaphors we live by.* Chicago: University of Chicago Press.

Lakoff, G. & Johnson, M. (1999). *Philosophy in the flesh: The embodied mind and its challenge to western thought..* New York: Basic Books.

Melzack, R. (1989). Phantom limbs, the self and the brain: The D.O. Hebb Memorial Lecture, *Canadian Psychology,* 30, 1, 1-16.

Merleau-Ponty, M. (1981). *The phenomenology of perception.* London: Routledge & Kegan Paul.

Metger, W. (1930). Optische untersuchungen am Ganzfeld, 11. Zur phänomenologie des homogenen Ganzfelds. *Psychologische Forschung,* 13, 6-29.

Millar, S. (1994). *Understanding and representing space: Theory and evidence from studies with blind and sighted children.* Oxford: Clarendon Press.

Paillard, J. (Ed.) (1991). *Brain and space.* Oxford: Oxford University Press.

Rock, I. (1995). *Perception .* New York: Scientific American Library.

Taylor, C. (1989). *Sources of the self: The making of the modern identity.* Cambridge MA.: Harvard University Press.

Vernon, J. (1966). *Inside the black room: Studies of sensory deprivation..* Harmondsworth: Penguin.

Wertheim, M. (1999). *The pearly gates of cyberspace: A history of space from Dante to the internet.* London: Virago Press.

Wollheim, R. (1987). *Painting as an art.* London: Thames & Hudson.

BEYOND REPRESENTATIONALISM:
A Dynamical Approach Transcending Symbolism in Cognitive Psychology

Donald L. Rowe
University of Wollongong

SUMMARY

Representationalism has defined the premise that cognition must involve a capacity to manipulate symbolic information. Although this approach has provided a good metaphoric and descriptive view of cognition, it ignores the distinct neural properties of the brain. This chapter has explored this problem by providing a more neurologically plausible account through the use of dynamical and chaotic systems theory. Symbols or representations were suggested to be epiphenomenonal to actual neural function and were considered as descriptions of behavior rather than cognition. Instead such entities were presumed to be embedded and decomposed in low level chaotic activity of the brain in such a manner that their localisation to specific neural entities was not a critical factor. The formation of knowledge, memories, or action was considered as an emergent property of distinct neural patterns of activity that result from the interaction of various neural groups.

INTRODUCTION

A capacity to manipulate symbolic information to form complex relations has been recognised as an essential component of higher cognition (Fodor & Pylyshyn, 1988). This has motivated researchers to develop computational systems utilising multi-dimensional symbolic storage systems (Halford, Wilson & Phillips, 1998). However they have failed to question the validity of the motivating premise and in doing so have ignored the distinct and dynamic neural properties of the brain. In reality the brain does not manipulate symbolic information nor does it form complex interrelations, such apparent activity is epiphenomenal to the actual neural function. Instead the brain operates as a dynamical system travelling through a kaleidoscope of uniquely generated patterns of neural activity. This paper addresses this issue by examining a number of neural network architectures to provide a more complete theoretical framework for the generation of a knowledge entity.

It is necessary to qualify the level of description provided by this paper. A reductionist approach examines the brain on a neurophysiological level such as looking at the dynamic functions of cellular membranes and ion channels in neurons. However, complex, self-organising systems tend to be unpredictable at this level of detail. Therefore, this paper focuses on a "level of structure" that is roughly predictable (Goertzel, 1996, p. 135) where the smallest relevant psychological entity is not the individual neuron, but the interconnection and interaction of neural groups (Edelman, 1987). This involves the use of dynamical systems analysis that models the formation of various attractor states which represent components and transitions in cognitive function.

While the dynamical systems analysis is a valid portrayal of the activity within neural networks it is not particularly clear about the specific neural architecture of the system, apart from it being nonlinear. Here, it is assumed that the mind's activity is an *emergent property* generated by a distribution of synaptic weights and patterns that are generated between interconnected units or neurons. The transitions that occur within these synaptic weights can be represented as a flow of energy cycling between points of stability and instability. In this paper I will only briefly touch on the possible architectural requirements needed to produce such systems and it is well realised that the formulations are only preliminary.

DYNAMICAL SYSTEMS THEORY

A key feature of a dynamical system is nonlinearity. In linear systems or single layer neural networks, output values are governed by simple linear relationships that transform the input signal to the output signal. In multi-layered neural networks, output values are representative of not only changes in the input layer but changes in the "hidden" or "middle" layers, resulting in system nonlinearity. A further important distinction is that nonlinear systems have emergent properties whereas linear systems do not. In the nonlinear system input entities may be transformed to produce a new set of entities. In the linear system the input entities alter in magnitude but maintain their distinct identity.

These emergent properties can be modelled by considering the path of a number of *trajectories* through state space. This is a graphical representation of all the possible states that two variables may take on. The collection of all the possible trajectories generated for different initial conditions forms what is called a phase portrait, which can be used to represent various types of attractor states. The type of system attractors governs the behavior of these trajectories such that they may follow point, cyclic or chaotic patterns. Of particular interest are *chaotic* or *strange* attractors as these display a very high sensitivity to initial conditions and have fractal nature characterised by boundaries of infinite complexity and variability (see Barton, 1994, for further descriptions).

The phase portrait resembles a pattern of basins or points of local minima. These basins are points where the system potential energy is at a local minimum. Trajectories tend to converge towards these basins in an attempt to reduce the potential energy and instability of the system. The pattern of the phase portrait is dependent upon a number of parameters such as the system dynamics, initial starting conditions, and the interaction of the various entities or agents. The phase portrait may fluctuate erratically until a suitable pattern of stability has developed to reduce the system energy to an overall minimum. These transitory conditions are known as *bifurcations*. Complex dynamical systems in the brain contain a number of interacting dynamical subsystems undergoing continuous bifurcation and the formation of complex attractor states.

Elman's Natural Language Model

The first model examined is Elman's (1995) connectionist language model based on *a simple recurrent network* architecture. Of particular interest is Elman's dynamical analysis of the network properties and its ability to model natural language processing. The model consists of three fully interconnected layers of units. A hidden layer is also connected to a layer of *context* units via one-to-one connections. This forms a feedback loop enabling the network to save activation patterns at any one step in time. This provides the network with an ability to store a number of grammatical rules.

The network was trained on a set of 10,000 sentences using a small lexicon of 29 nouns and verbs. Each word was assigned a localist vector, identifiable by a single randomly assigned bit, hence there was no correlation between the input representation and the properties of the word. Learning was facilitated through an error correction algorithm called back-propagation and the task of the network was to predict successive words. At the conclusion of training, a comparison of the network's predictions with the cohort revealed a high degree of success (0.852; a perfect performance would have been 1.0).

The pattern of activation weights formed with each successive prediction by the network was analysed and the results plotted on state space diagrams

(Elman, 1995). Observations revealed that the network had discovered several major categories of words as indicated by the clustering of similar words or point attractors in specific regions of state space. The syntactic rules binding specific localised points or words could be observed as trajectories through state space converging towards attractor points representing each successive word in a sentence. The emergent properties displayed by dynamical systems also meant that the network was able to respond sensibly to novel inputs presented in a familiar context.

Even though the network is able to sequence words appropriately and infer a valid categorical structure within the lexicon it knows nothing about semantic content of the words, and it is limited to the formation of only simple point attractors rather than more complex phase portraits produced by periodic and strange attractors. Although Elman did not consider his network to be the complete picture, it did require a more complex semantic structure mapped onto each of the attractor points. This motivated the proposal for a hybrid architecture combining Elman's "syntactic" network with another neural system capable of representing hierarchical knowledge structures.

Hybrid and Dual Network Models

There is considerable support for hybrid architectures considering the number of neural tracts throughout the brain specialised for associative functions and connectivity between brain regions (see Shepherd, 1998, for details). Many authors have considered mapping lower order cognitive *discriminative* functions onto higher-order cognitive representations (e.g., Gobet, 1998). Goertzel (1996) referred to this as a *dual network* structure suggesting that within the basic six layers of the brain, the pyramidal cells with their columnar structure may act as a "skeleton" of cortical organisation. These specialised neural groups in the brain may form a system of attractors that function as a two-dimensional associative memory such that items related to each other are stored near each other (Goertzel, 1995). These attractors may act to funnel neural flow or trajectories into strange attractors capable of forming multidimensional representations. Thus, the next step was to look at the neural and computational feasibility of symbolic or multidimensional knowledge structures in neural network models.

Relational Knowledge Theory

The connectionist approach to symbolic representation requires mechanisms that provide bindings of properties and relations to sets of individual concepts or objects. The most suitable model appeared to be a connectionist network capable of representing higher-order relational structures (Halford et al., 1998). The model had distinct advantages over traditional connectionist networks in that the associative links between vector representations were not limited to meaningless associations but could now form meaningful relations and hierarchical knowledge structures. Halford and his colleges had also accumulated a growing body of empirical evidence to support a theory of relational knowledge (e.g., Halford, 1996).

The model utilises a system of tensor product bindings. This reproduces a related vector through a system of matrix equations involving a tensor product multiplication of the available vectors. Each vector maintains its own localist identity and the required activations for a particular structure are superimposed on top of each other in a single set of binding units. This is different to the usual multi-layered networks where dimensions are distributed from the input to the output units resulting in a loss of individual identities (Halford, 1996).

The network by nature is nonlinear but each relational or tensor node is somewhat fixed in its representational power, although this is an inherent component of the theory and is referred to as *relational complexity*. With increases in the dimensionality of a given node the system requires a monotonical increase in the number of binding units with an associated increase in computational expense. This places constraints on the system at Rank 5 tensor and above, though this does coincide with the limits of human analogical transfer ability and relational representation (Halford et al., 1998). A simple way of conceptualising this ceiling on relational complexity is by considering the difficulty individuals have conceptualising a 4-way ANOVA, which is a rank 5 tensor. While this is a satisfactory prediction for purposes of analogical reasoning and transfer it does not resolve more complex cognitive processes involving the linking together of a number of relational structures in a complex sequence of operations.

A partial solution is that complex relations greater than Rank 5 undergo a *segmentation* and *chunking* process (Halford et al., 1998). Segmentation involves the decomposition of complex tasks into smaller segments or chunks that can be processed serially without exceeding limits of parallel processing. Chunking involves recoding complex relations into simpler relational structures of a lower rank or dimension (Halford, 1996). While there is substantial evidence supporting the chunking or decomposition of representational items (Gobet, 1998), the use of the terminology does little to say how the process occurs and is somewhat misleading in its presumptions.

LIMITATIONS OF THE MODEL AND NEW FORMULATIONS

It is unlikely that the brain computes tensor products and this type of computational system is inherently non-emergent. The tensor product system and the chunking of information also implies a localist representation essential for maintaining the unique identities for each vector representation. This in particular implies a rigidity in brain structure and a dedication of processing units to specific vector representations leading to an inefficiency and an inflexibility in the computational power of the system. While not denying that some level of localised neural specialisation does exist within the brain, the localist approach steers away from the brain's distributed organisation and the emergent properties that are involved in memory and knowledge reconstruction. In this sense, multidimensional or hierarchical structures are not stored or localised in the brain. They are emergent and arise from patterns of activity within and across neural groups, such that relatively simple computational algorithms and structure can result in representations that display a potentially infinite variability and complexity. Once the representation has dispersed as a result of a transition in attractor states the *representation is not necessarily bound to the particular neural units* that formed the initial representation, nor is it identifiable within those units.

Dynamical Systems and Emergent Behavior

Dynamical systems theory would predict that information is decomposed into simple components, in such a manner that we are able to derive complex memories out of much simpler units. This emergent property is extremely important in human memory, particularly since the brain has a finite capacity. For example, Goertzel (1995) estimates that the brain is exposed to 100 billion billion bits of information during an average lifetime, but it can store only 100 thousand billion bits. This means only one out of every million pieces of information can be "permanently" retained. This has raised a related question; if the brain does have a finite capacity, where does this additional information go, and is it really lost? Experiments such as cued recall would suggest that the information is not lost, but is reproducible depending on stimulus cues (e.g., Kolers, 1976). Therefore, if information is not lost and the brain does have a finite capacity, it would seem uneconomical to store every piece of information as explicit exemplars, as in the Tensor Product model. Clearly people don't remember everything that they have been exposed to but much of what they do encounter is reproducible due to environmental cues and the emergent properties of the neural system.

Mandelbrot and Julia Sets as Catalogues of Emergent Behavior

The emergent and dynamic property of the brain's neural activity can be further explained by considering examples of some other dynamical systems that produce formations known as Julia sets or Mandelbrot sets. To derive the images of these sets, one takes all initial starting conditions and enters them into a given mathematical system or quadratic function. Those that do not zoom out to infinity form a Julia set and are plotted as a graphical representation. Julia sets are "self-similar", in that their fractal structure reveals repetitions of patterns that display symmetry between levels of magnification, but on the observable level only smaller. Mandelbrot sets are not self-similar and display a fractal structure of increasing variability and complexity, but still self-organised. Mandelbrot type sets can be considered as a catalogue of different Julia sets and are more similar to natural examples due to their asymmetrical structure.

Recall earlier that a dynamical system acts to reduce the potential energy of the system by converging on the most stable attractor states or the pattern of basins that result in points of local minima. However, changes in system constraints produce instability within the system that increases potential energy. To reduce energy levels the attractor states within the system must bifurcate to alternate forms, thereby lowering the system energy.

The Julia sets can be considered as a catalogue of the transitions that occur in complex system behavior as a result of changing parameter values, dynamic interactions and bifurcations to new attractor states. The Julia set represents the boundary between a group of trajectories that are potentially useful (finite trajectories), and a group that are not, those trajectories which tend to infinity. If we draw an analogy to the mind, there is obviously no value in the mind searching for trajectory paths that diverge towards infinity, and such divergent states would be a waste of time and energy. Therefore, the mind has a preference for converging towards stable states, hence as the mind functions it must keep its parameters within the appropriate Julia sets or bounded trajectories, to maintain minimal levels of system energy. Movements within the fractal boundaries of these sets represent transitions of mental processes, and as the system changes and grows, these fractal boundaries permit an enormous level of evolution and variability (Goertzel, 1995).

Fractal Structures in the Mind

Now how does this relate to Halford's work on relational knowledge representations? In reality there are now no distinct relational structures but transitions in neural activity and formations that have multi- or fractional dimensionality. There is still a limit on relational complexity, but this is dependent on the type of neural groups dedicated to this task that display a property of instability and transient "short term" states, only capable of maintaining stable formations for a short period of time. The complexity of the attractor formations is affected by the plasticity of neural groups and is a property of the mind's ability to explore attractor states and bifurcate to more complex states of activity. It requires energy and the synchronisation of the appropriate neural groups, and is dependent upon the structural history of the neural groups.

Technically, in the dynamical systems model, relations are no longer limited to rank 5 tensors and theoretically each relation can have an infinite number of other relations due to their fractal properties. This is what the concept of chunking appears to be referring to in terms of moving through different levels of relational structure, such that exploring fractal boundaries leads to more complex relations, whereas moving away from fractal boundaries reveals a simpler (or "chunked") relational structure. Therefore in Halford's network each relational node is now envisaged as an attractor point capable of bifurcating to form periodic and strange attractors, thus adding dimensionality through a complex pattern of neural activity.

Applications in Psychophysiology and Abstract Thought

The application of dynamical systems in psychology is not novel (see Abraham, 1996; Alexander & Globus, 1996, for similar proposals), although generally no one has actually proposed how a dynamical systems model of brain function may be implemented on a computational and theoretical level. Exceptions include Robert Gregson who has developed a system of nonlinear equations known as "Gamma recursions", a special cubic equation that generates Julia-like sets and has been successfully used to model a number of nonlinear patterns occurring in psychophysics (e.g., Gregson, 1996). The nonlinear analysis of EEG data has also shown that complex problem solving exercises result in an increase in patterns of chaotic behavior (A. M. Gregson, Campbell, & Gates, 1992). Another good exception is Walter Freeman and his colleagues who have been successful in modelling dynamical properties of the olfactory system (e.g., Freeman, 1991). A more recent development has been a computational system of cortical electrical activity that models human EEG data (Rennie, Robinson, & Wright, 1999; Robinson, Rennie, Wright, Gordon, & Bahramali, 2000).

In Freeman's model the olfactory system is considered to be a structured strange attractor displaying low level chaotic activity. The olfactory attractor network is highly sensitive to small changes in olfactory input, as characteristic of chaotic systems. This leads to highly divergent trajectories that search for more stable states to compensate for the instability created by the input. The structure of the strange attractor contains different regions that correspond to different smells. Exposure to an odour increases the chaotic activity until it settles into a specific region of the attractor leading to discrimination of the smell. Alternatively the system explores the fractal boundaries of the attractor, thereby generating new attractor states for novel odours. Transitions bring stability to the system, and lower points of potential energy, through bifurcations to more stable periodic, limit cycle attractors that are confined to small regions of the attractor.

Freeman's work provides a particularly important step if we consider the evolutionary history of the frontal lobes and the olfactory system (see Johnson, 1991). While the olfactory system was extremely important for our human reptilian ancestry it is of less importance to us today, but through specialisation it has led to the development of the frontal lobes or the neocortex. It is likely that the neural requirements for olfaction are similar to the neural requirements for abstract thought. The type of neural network necessary to produce such systems requires a large number of sprawling and combinatory connections (Goertzel, 1995). It turns out that the neural structure of the olfactory bulb does appear to permit considerable combinatorial complexity (Shepherd, 1990), and the synaptic organisation in the olfactory system closely resembles the basic circuits in the hippocampus and the neocortex (Haberly, 1990).

We have seen that the dynamic activity of a localised set of neurons has the capacity to form various attractor states through bifurcations caused by changes in system parameter constraints and the associated instability. We also know that the brain consists of a large number of specialised brain nuclei or neural groups that form an interactive whole brain network. So the next question is, what is the effect of coupling neural groups and what are some of the dynamic mechanisms through which these groups interact?

Brain Connectivity Through Recursive Networks and Modularity

The human brain is estimated to contain between 10^{10} and 10^{11} neurons (Anderson, 1995). This presents a certain connectivity problem such that if all neurons were fully inter-connected the brain would have a circumference of 10km (Heemskerk & Murre, 1991). This problem is overcome by a distinct modular structure (Fodor & Pylyshyn, 1988), such that complexity exists on multiple levels between and within brain nuclei or modules (Alexander & Globus, 1996). What we find is that each neural group has a maximum level of connectivity that may be supported. Moving up from this to the subneural group we also find a maximum level of connectivity that may be supported between neural subgroups. This type of connectivity between ever increasing macro groups of neurons continues in a modular and recursive fashion creating neural networks within neural networks.

This leads to a vast level of neural connectivity and interaction within the brain, exactly what is needed for fractal and chaotic dynamics.

Communication and Connectivity through Synchronous Oscillations

The modular and recursive structure within the brain permits an enormous amount of communication. This has been examined in the form of synchronous oscillations (e.g. Gray & McCormick, 1996), and these mechanisms have been shown to be a fundamental component in the development and organisation of cortical circuitry (Sandyk, 1998; Wallenstein & Hasselmo, 1997). Analogies have been drawn to oscillatory neural networks that are represented by non-strange oscillating or periodic attractors that exist at the edge of chaotic activity (Alexander & Globus, 1996; Freeman, 1991). Others have considered this synchronous oscillatory activity to function as a system of phase-locked loops, critical in feedback activity from the cortex to the sensory areas (e.g., Damasio, 1989).

The dynamics of synchronous oscillations across neural groups makes intuitive sense. Mathews and Strogatz (1990) provide a detailed analysis of the interaction limit cycle oscillators that may well apply to the interaction of neural networks in the brain. Neural networks with synchronous patterns are going to have very similar trajectories or attractor states, resulting in temporal and spatial compatibility between the neural groups. We can conceptualise this in the form of a holographic image of the attractor states of one network overlaying the attractor states of another. Once synchronised or locked, the two networks will remain the same to maintain more stable states, in effect linking the two neural groups. Otherwise, a change in the dynamics of one network may cause each network to diverge on separate paths to new attractor states which may in turn synchronise or interact with other neural groups.

The coupling of neural groups through synchronous oscillations can lead to a fractional or higher dimensional state space and potentially more complexity and variability. Abraham (1996) talks about the coupling of discrete systems or agents creating instability or a new dynamic and the necessity for each system to change to a more stable system state. He uses an example of two individuals, although each agent may be substituted for components of an organisation or social structure, or in our case, neural components of the brain. Abraham refers to each agent as two-dimensional oscillators such that the two-dimensional phase space of each agent is combined to form a four-dimensional space.

The degree of "strangeness" between each system or agent will affect the extent to which the coupling of the system creates chaos and the need for bifurcations to alternate states. The regions of attractor states that each system settles down to will also depend upon the uncoupled tendencies of each system, as reflected by the structural stability of each system over time. These patterns of structural stability are a function of hard-wired genetic algorithms, leading to a variation in the plasticity of neural groups. A high level of plasticity will be apparent in those networks where there has been the formation of new connections, or in those neural groups that are specialised for transient states such as in short term memory functions. Other networks such as those serving long term dedicated functions such as metabolic activities are going to display less plasticity and much more rigid periodic attractor states.

CONCLUSIONS, AND LIMITATIONS OF THE APPROACH

The application of dynamical systems in psychology is not very well understood by the majority of psychologists (Barton, 1994) and major developments have only really occurred in the last 10 years. Admittedly, there are limitations (e.g., Ayers, 1997), and attractor networks capable of representing abstract thought and behavioral sequences have not been constructed. However, Freeman's research presents a good start with his network of the olfactory system, the dynamic patterns of which are expected to closely resemble templates of abstract thought. Furthermore, existing connectionist architectures are in essence dynamical systems, and all network architectures composed of more than one layer of units display non-linear patterns of behavior. In Elman's network a transparent analysis of the neural activity in a connectionist model has been provided by using a dynamical systems approach. In this model the mental lexicon is considered to comprise localised regions of attractor points in state space, and syntactic rules are trajectories which link these points together in a grammatical fashion. We can also extrapolate from Elman's network and consider each attractor point to have fractal boundaries that may permit complex semantic networks.

Most importantly, we see that symbolic items are not stored in the brain as localised vectors distributed across a number of specific neural components. Instead they are decomposed and embedded in low level chaotic activity. Due to the emergent and chaotic properties displayed in the system dynamics small changes within the system may result in the reconstruction of complex neural activity leading to the formation of memories, abstract thought, and action.

The modelling and testing of the brain as a nonlinear system that is inherently on the "edge of chaos" is a difficult task. The models in their obscurity may produce strange ("novel") results (albeit a criticism), but these patterns of behavior often turn out to be present in the natural world (see Lewandowsky, 1993, for examples). The numerical structure of the models permits testing and falsification of the model against various environmental constraints and initial starting conditions (Gregson, 1996; Rennie et al., 1999; Robinson et al., 2000). We don't necessarily know what is going to happen, but running the model through a number of iterations can allow us to find out. Goertzel (1996) has also emphasised that dynamical systems are not necessarily unpredictable due to the structural stability which they tend to display. If we look at the evolution of a system we do see predictability on the level of structure, we see general trends in the dynamics of the system, and periodic patterns of behavior that repeat themselves but which change form in subtle ways. We can use this information to extrapolate, and not necessarily compute the mathematical trajectories but as a result be able to conceptualise a system in a dynamical way to provide an in-depth level of understanding.

Note

1.   The author would like to thank his college Peter Leeson for his helpful comments and discussion while preparing this manuscript.

REFERENCES

Abraham, F.D. (1996). Dynamics, bifurcation, self-organisation, chaos, mind, conflict, insensitivity to initial conditions, time, unification, diversity, free will, and social responsibility. In R. Robertson & A. Combs (Eds) *Chaos theory in psychology and the life sciences* (pp. 155-173). Mahway, NJ: Lawrence Erlbaum.

Alexander, D.M., & Globus, G.G. (1996). Edge-of-chaos dynamics in recursively organized neural systems. In E. R. Mac-Cormac & M. I. Stamenov (Eds) *Fractals of brain, fractals of mind* (pp. 31-73). Philadelphia, PA: John Benjamins Publishing Company.

Anderson, J.A. (1995). *An Introduction to neural networks*. Cambridge MA: MIT Press.

Ayers, S. (1997). The application of chaos theory to psychology. *Theory and Psychology*, 7(3), 373-398.

Barton, S. (1994). Chaos, self-organisation, and psychology. *American Psychologist*, 49(1), 5-14.

Damasio, A.R. (1989). The brain binds entities and events by multiregional activation from convergence zones. *Neural Computation*, 1, 123-132.

Edelman, G.M. (1987). *Neural Darwinism: The theory of neural group selection*. New York, NY: Basic Books.

Elman, J.L. (1995). Language as a dynamical system. In R. F. Port & T. van-Gelder (Eds) *Mind as motion: Explorations in the dynamics of cognition.* (pp. 195-225). Cambridge MA: MIT Press.

Fodor, J.A., & Pylyshyn, Z.W. (1988). Connectionism and cognitive architecture: A critical analysis. *Cognition,* 28, 3-71.

Freeman, W. (1991). The philosophy of perception. *Scientific American*, February, 35-41.

Gobet, F. (1998). Expert memory: a comparison of four theories. *Cognition*, 66, 115-152.

Goertzel, B. (1995). *The miraculous mind attractor, chaos, complexity and the computational mind: A dynamical dialogue.* (unpublished MS)

Goertzel, B. (1996). A cognitive law of motion. In R. Robertson & A. Combs (Eds) *Chaos theory in psychology and the life sciences.* (pp. 135-153). Mahway NJ: Lawrence Erlbaum.

Gray, C.M., & McCormick, D.A. (1996). Chattering cells: superficial pyramidal neurons contributing to the generation of synchronous oscillations in the visual cortex . *Science*, 274(5284), 109-113.

Gregson, A.M., Campbell, E.A., & Gates, G.R. (1992). Cognitive load as a determinant of the dimensionality of the electroencephalogram. *Biological Psychology,* 35, 165-178.

Gregson, R.A. (1996). n-Dimensional nonlinear psychophysics: Intersensory interaction as a network at the edge of chaos. In E. R. Mac-Cormac & M. I. Stamenov (Eds) *Fractals of brain, fractals of mind* (pp. 155-178). Philadelphia PA: John Benjamins Publishing Company.

Haberly, L.B. (1990). Olfactory cortex. In G. M. Shepherd (Ed*.) The synaptic organisation of the brain* (pp. 317-345). New York NY: Oxford University Press.

Halford, G.S. (1996). Capacity limitations in processing relations: Implications and causes. Paper presented to ILAS 3rd Brain and Mind International Symposium on Concept Formation, Thinking and Their Development, IIAS, Kyoto, Japan, May 30-June 1.

Halford, G.S., Wilson, W.H., & Phillips, S. (1998). Processing capacity defined by relational complexity: Implications for comparative, developmental, and cognitive psychology. *Behavioral and Brain Sciences*, 21(6), 803-864.

Heemskerk, J.N.H., & Murre, J.M.J. (1991). Neurocomputers: Parallelle machines voor neurale netwerken. *Informatie*, 33, 365-464.

Johnson, G. (1991). *In the palaces of memory: How we build the worlds inside our heads.* Knopf.

Kolers, P.A. (1976). Reading a year later. *Journal of Experimental Psychology: Human Learning and Memory*, 2, 554-565.

Lewandowsky, S. (1993). The rewards and hazards of computer simulations. *Psychological Science*, 4(4), -236.

Mathews, P.C., & Strogatz, S.H. (1990). Phase diagram for the collective behavior of limit cycle oscillators. *Physics Review Letter*, 65, 1701-1704.

Rennie, C.J., Robinson, P.A., & Wright, J.J. (1999). Effects of local feedback on dispersion of electrical waves in the cerebral cortex. *Physical Review E*, 59(3), 3320-3330.

Robinson, P.A., Rennie, C.J., Wright, J.J., Gordon, E., & Bahramali, H. (2000). Direct prediction of EEG spectra from physiology. Submitted to *Physics Review*.

Sandyk, R. (1998). A neuromagnetic view of hippocampal memory functions. *International Journal of Neuroscience*, Vol 93 (3-4), 251-256.

Shepherd, G.M. (1990). Olfactory bulb. In G. M. Shepherd (Ed.) *The synaptic organisation of the brain* (pp. 133-169). NewYork, NY: Oxford University Press.

Shepherd, G.M. (1998). *The synaptic organisation of the brain* (4th ed.). New York, NY: Oxford University Press.

Wallenstein, G.V., & Hasselmo, M.E. (1997). Functional transitions between epileptiform-like activity and associative memory in hippocampal region CA3. *Brain Research Bulletin.*, 43(5), 485-493.

THE DIALECTIC OF CRITIQUE, THEORY AND METHOD IN DEVELOPING FEMINIST RESEARCH ON INFERENCE

Rachel Joffe Falmagne
Clark University

SUMMARY

Feminist critiques of rationalism as a masculinist cultural construction, and of logic as a component of this regime of truth, extend to the traditional psychological research on inference as well. This discussion explores issues entailed in reconfiguring the theoretical and empirical study of reasoning on new ground informed by critique, a task that I argue is necessary if feminist theories of logic are to avoid producing new canons through rationalist theorizing and if the study of reasoning is to be rescued from its domination by a rationalist tradition. An illustrative qualitative study of reasoning processes with a design and interpretive framework informed by the above critiques and by feminist perspective on epistemology, is used as a vehicle for exposing the meta-theoretical, theoretical and methodological tensions entailed by this transdisciplinary reconstructive project, the ramifications of critique for method and the theory-data problematic.

INTRODUCTION

This chapter[1] addresses the complex dialectic between critique, theory and method, the implications that these have for one another, and the problematic of developing a positive research program in the theoretical space opened by the critique. That problematic is discussed with reference to the process of developing a new feminist approach to the study of a particular kind of reasoning, but the scope of this discussion extends to other domains and to other critical approaches as well. The discussion is reflexive in that it focuses on process rather than product, and it exposes the various tensions involved. Those tensions, as dialectical tensions, are the main focus of this paper. The discussion also will have some autobiographical references because my own trajectory as a socially constructed agent of knowledge epitomizes the issues.

CRITICAL CONSIDERATIONS

The domain of study under consideration is *"deductive"* inference, that is, those processes through which people draw the entailments from prior information or select among contradictory accounts. *"Deductive"* is inflected because the term is understood broadly and, in effect, the aim of this research is to redefine the domain of study, as explained next. Research and theory on that domain so far have been configured by a rationalist philosophical tradition and by a cognitive research tradition originating in that philosophy. Logic (in particular modern symbolic logic) dominates the discourse of knowledge and the cultural fabric of Western cultures, through the status it has been accorded as a foundational system formalizing necessary inferences, linguistic meaning, and mathematical relations, and through its function as an epistemic and linguistic norm. Most cognitive theories, including some that I have proposed in the past, show their rationalist origin directly or indirectly, either through spelling out rationalist thought processes or through advancing alternatives motivated by the rejection of those assumptions. Although the study of reasoning has broadened since the original focus on logic as a presumed model of human thought processes and now often includes the pragmatics and the content of reasoning, logic remains the invisible backbone of the questions that are asked (Falmagne & Gonsalves, 1995, provide a review).

But in the last decade, several lines of feminist critique have called these assumptions into question and have problematized the status of logic. First, feminist theorists and *"postcolonial"* critics [2] have stressed that the so-called knowing subject is not generic, she/he is concrete, and has a particular, historically specific, social location. She/he views the world from a particular *standpoint* that derives from that structural location. In addition her/his self as knowing agent is constituted by the material conditions and the discourses that comprise that location. So, knowledge is situated both structurally and psychologically (e.g., Alcoff & Potter, 1993; Collins, 1990; Falmagne, 2000a; Harding, 1993; Hartsock, 1983; Mohanty, 1991). Most pertinent to logic, standards of justification are situated as well: there is no *"view from nowhere"*, no absolute standards for evaluating knowledge claims.

Second, critics have revealed that there are deep relations between rationality and masculinity. Importantly, these relations are at once historical, symbolic, social and psychological. Gender cannot be treated as an untheorized (empirical) individual variable: It is a multilevel social formation of which psychological processes are but one strand (Falmagne, 2000a). Analytically, it is crucial to distinguish symbolic gender from structural gender (i.e., the way in which gender structures the world socially) and from psychological gender. Lloyd (1993) discusses that reason, in the West, is part of the content of *symbolic* masculinity, and she rightly observes that this content can be appropriated by both real men and real women. Flax (1993), through close textual analysis, shows how Kant's formulation of the Enlightenment ideal of reason stemmed form his desire for the male child to separate from the private and the family and to outgrow his initial dependency on the mother. Hence, the very formulation of the (allegedly universal) norm of reason was grounded in a particular masculinist construction. Likewise, Bordo (1987) argues, based on a rich historical and psychological analysis, that Descartes formulated the ideal of objectivity as a "flight from the feminine", a way to "reimage knowledge as masculine" (p.5). So, Western discourses of rationality are a masculinist product. And of course masculinist norms have been hegemonic in Western cultures.

Finally, more recent critiques have focused on logic directly as a central component of the power/knowledge system (Foucault, 1980) of rationalism, and problematize the foundational status logic has been accorded. Nye (1990) provides a psycho-cultural critique of different moments in the history of Western logic and documents the motivations that drove the different men who developed these logics (all were men) and the functions of the logics in the social context of their time. And contributors to Hass and Falmagne (in press; see below) scrutinize either local aspects (e.g., specific logical constructs) or global aspects of logic (e.g., its very enterprise) and their links to systems of power.

RAMIFICATIONS OF THE CRITIQUE

These analyses profoundly destabilize current philosophical theories of logic and current cognitive theories of inference. The question prompting the present discussion is: What do we do next? Critique is crucial but is most useful when it is generative of a novel reconstruction of a domain. Rather than dismissing "deductive inference" as a domain of thought, my concern is to redefine that domain, reconfigure its methodological approach, and develop a new theoretical vocabulary for understanding inference. Here I concur with Wilson (1998; see also Falmagne, 2000b) on the critical potential of engaging with the scientific constructs that are the object of critique rather than dismissing the domain as irrelevant. Wilson writes: "Deconstruction has its effect by inhabiting the structures it contests .... A deconstructive reading of cognitive psychology places itself internally to that domain, and it is reliant on that domain for its coherence and efficacy" (1998, p.29). Going one step further, the remainder of this discussion explores issues entailed in the reconstructive project of developing substantive theory and research on feminist grounds informed by the above critiques. Such a reconstruction is, of course, provisional and itself subject to critical scrutiny, but I take it to be the necessary complement of critique.

Three complementary directions can be identified in that regard. First, philosophically, an area of current contention is whether (any) logic is antithetical to feminist theories of knowledge, as Nye argues, or whether alternatives can be developed on a feminist basis. For instance, Nelson (in press) sees logic as one element in an interdependent system of knowledge and therefore revisable based on feminist epistemology and methodology. In contrast, Olkowski (in press) draws from Deleuze's analysis to argue that logic inherently embodies systems of domination. Plumwood (1993/in press) insists that the oppressiveness of logic lies not in the abstraction of logical thought but in the specific constructs of the dominant logical theory, in which negation is based on hyper-separation, with the negated term a homogeneous universe unable to be identified independently, a feature consonant with the fundamental dualism of western thought. She explores notions of negation that avoid these metaphysical and discursive problems and therefore do not entail exclusionary modes of reasoning and oppressive practices. So in these (contrasting) works, the philosophical reconstructive project is to explore potential alternative logics guided by the feminist critiques.

A second, different strand of investigation is to expose the societal/political process through which regulatory norms are constructed and reproduced and those institutional processes that constrain or enable particular modes of thinking (e.g., Henriques, Hollway, Urwin, Venn, & Walkerdine, 1984), for instance the relations between (rationalist) pedagogical practices and linguistic and cognitive development (Walkerdine, 1988).

A third agenda is to develop the implications of feminist critiques for substantive research and theory on inference. Feminist critiques have opened a theoretical space for asking new questions about "deductive" inference, with new methods and within a new theoretical framework. As suggested earlier, the logicist worldview had exercised its hegemony on the study of reasoning not only substantively but also conceptually, in configuring the limits of alternative proposals. The task is to develop new constructs and new questions, liberated (to the extent possible) from this historical hegemony.

This process of "critical reconstruction" is complex and rife with meta-theoretical, theoretical and methodological tensions. In the following sections, the process of formulating a line of research informed by feminist theory and critique will serve as a medium (a concrete workshop of sorts) for exposing these issues. Of particular concern will be the dialectic between critique and method, and the epistemic ramifications of methodological choices for the knowledge produced.

The next section contains a brief vignette of the exploratory study in this line of research (Falmagne, 1997), as a concrete reference for the subsequent discussion. Clearly, this empirical research is but one ingredient of a broader transdisciplinary agenda, the explorations of alternative logical constructs by some feminist philosophers being another. If feminist theories of or about logic are to escape relying on abstract (rationalist) speculation, it is crucial to develop a transdisciplinary methodology that establishes an interplay between the thinking of concrete people and feminist theory (Falmagne, in press). The nature of that interplay is yet to be clarified, as discussed at the end of this paper, but the methodology must enable it to be formulated eventually.

THE "WORKSHOP" STUDY AND ITS THEORETICAL FRAMEWORK

Feminist analyses drawing from sociological, historical and political modes of inquiry describe in various ways the material and discursive gendering of the social order. Thinkers develop in their particular ethnic/racial, class, gendered societal locations and in the fold of gendered cultural discourses and social practices. Their modes of thinking are jointly configured by these processes of social constitution and by their agency in appropriating, resisting, rejecting or modulating cultural discourses and models and in transforming social practices (see Falmagne, 2000a for an elaboration of these ideas).

Three points are crucial in this view. First, gender is not an individual variable attached to individual persons. As a complex social formation, gender structures the world socially, symbolically, materially and institutionally. Second, gender is not a unitary category: it functions through its intersection with ethnic/racial, cultural and socioeconomic social formations in particular. Third is the dialectic between social constructive processes and agency.

The research examines the reasoning processes upon which different social agents draw in everyday "deductive" situations. The exploratory study in this program has been with young adult women, and I return to this point momentarily. The women were offered hypothetical problems and asked to think through contradictory accounts (e.g., two contradictory medical diagnoses; the arguments from the prosecution and the defense in a hypothetical trial, etc.). The hypothetical situations, however, were only suggestive models of the type of situation of interest: the women were urged to think of analogous situations in their life and to reason with these, and did.

The interview began with an exploration of each woman's societal location, cultural background and life history, so that she could be particularized and her reasoning interpreted in that context. The semi-structured interview then explored the woman's reasoning. The aim was to characterize "moments" of reasoning, not a woman's overall style as knower: One woman may reason differently at different moments or in different situations. Follow-up probes flexibly attempted to identify the modes of knowledge the woman deployed (for instance, social knowledge, concrete knowledge, personal knowledge, general deductive principles, intuition, other resources yet to be identified), the ways in which these were interwoven in her reasoning and the particular ways in which they were in tension. Of interest were the way in which this interplay is modulated by the specific situational context in which reasoning is deployed, and the constructive processes through which the woman appropriated the problem and constructed the functional context for her reasoning. One focus among others was on how thinkers negotiate rationalist discourses and other discourses within their specific cultural frameworks and (gendered) social locations, and how they appropriate, resist, transform or integrate these discourses. However, these theoretical questions were but loose heuristic guides to the interview process. Driven by the aim of developing a new theoretical vocabulary, the interview method could not be configured by pre-specified questions, as discussed in a later section.

Five key tensions emerge in this process: (1) the problematic of relying on women as the starting point of theory; (2) the tension between openness and focus in designing the interviews, and its repercussions on the knowledge produced; (3) issues involved in constructing the descriptive language; (4) the dialectic of the particular and the general in describing and narrating; (5) the implications of the data for feminist theories of logic.

Why Women as the Starting Point for Theory-Building?

A widely accepted feminist meta-theoretical principle posits that our thought must start from women's lives. This principle derives from the assumption that marginal locations are more likely to reveal the contradictions of the social order, and that hegemonic masculinist conceptions need to be subverted or enriched. First introduced by standpoint theorists (e.g., Hartsock, 1983; Smith, 1990) as a transposition of Marx's structural analysis of the standpoint of the proletariat to an analysis of a feminist standpoint, this notion has been further complexified by "postcolonial" critics (e.g., hooks, 1990; Collins, 1990) to capture the intersectional nature of standpoints. "Postcolonial" critics have further pointed out that a marginal group must function with both the dominant discourse and its own subjugated or resistant discourse, a situation conducive to recognizing social contradictions.

Thus, for reasons of theoretical strategy, the initial theoretical constructs must be grounded in the thinking of women. What is understood by this, however, is crucial. "Women" must be taken, not as a uniform empirical group indexable through a simple category, but as referring to concrete women occupying particular locations in ethnic/racial, socioeconomic, historical and cultural formations and discourses. As indicated above, gender, race and class are intersecting social formations co-constitutive of one another. Thus, both social locations and individuals must be conceptualized in that intersectional matrix.

A few tensions surround this strategy. At face value, the strategy may appear to carry implicit essentialist assumptions. However, in the theoretical context of this research, it does not. First, it is clear from this discussion that the aim is not to define "women's ways of knowing". The decision to start with women was strategic, not ontological. The strategy is to start to theorize "deductive reasoning" from non-hegemonic locations. Second, the participants are particularized within an intersectional matrix, both theoretically and data-analytically, not taken to be representatives of a simple category. Third, the association between rationality and masculinity is taken to hold as a *symbolic* association and involves gender as a social formation, not individual gender: reason and symbolic maleness can be appropriated by both concrete men and concrete women.

Yet, there is a complex dialectic between the symbolic order, social structure, social practices, and individual functioning. Symbols have repercussions for concrete human beings, who constitute themselves as knowing agents in the fold of symbolic representations, social practices, cultural discourses, and their structural positioning. For instance, the rationalist ideal of detachment and its relation to symbolic masculinity have been instrumental in constituting gendered aspects of the social order and the subjectivities of many western privileged white men. Thus, the fact that logic and rationalism, as cultural and institutional systems, share men's social location, at least in the west, is significant, as standpoint theorists and other critics have explained. In this effort to try to liberate theories of reasoning from their logicist history, the strategy of initiating the research by studying women is motivated by these considerations.

But a tension that complicates this strategy is the effect it may produce on the public consumption of the research. It is too often the case that complex questions of the kind examined in this research are reductively distorted into a "gender difference" interpretation. Thus it is crucial to develop narrative strategies and pragmatic devices to block this misinterpretation, or this misappropriation, at every moment of dissemination (Falmagne, 2000a): formal rationality as examined here is a cultural construction participating in a multilevel gendered social formation, not a property of individuals.

Interview Design: Tension between Openness and Focus

Complex issues attend the delineation of the reasoning domain (e.g., the problems presented to the woman) and the design of the interview. In a general sense, these issues face all qualitative research. However, their particular form is configured by the specific nature of the research. Here, they are linked specifically to this feminist reformulation of research on inference. Reconfiguring a domain entails, in part, transforming it while "inhabiting" it (to borrow Wilson's term). Thus, the issue is how to transform the domain without vacating it and thereby abandoning it to its traditional construction.

Open-ended interviews are the less constraining approach. However, the focus of the research is to capture the range of knowledges women brought into their reasoning as these were applied to "deductive" problems. Doing so involves removing the constraints of traditional methods and dislodging the narrow rationalist definition of what constitutes deduction, yet keeping the focus on a certain domain of reasoning even while reconfiguring it. This domain includes, roughly, contexts in which people assess the entailments of particular assertions, adjudicate contradictory accounts, or evaluate the soundness of arguments.

So, while the field of inquiry is broadened, the focus nevertheless remains on a "core" reasoning domain, loosely construed. In posing the hypothetical problems as loose models for the situations the women were encouraged to think about, a deliberate decision was to avoid posing moral dilemmas, which have been studied by others within a different framework and with a different genealogy; and to avoid decision-making situations strictly governed by cost-benefit considerations.

But drawing those distinctions presupposes a pre-theoretical demarcation between domains of reasoning, a demarcation that can be challenged. Yet, on the other hand, to leave the field wide open rather than attempting to focus on (a reformulated) "deduction" essentially entails abandoning the study of deduction to the rationalist tradition. Thus, there is a critical tension between openness and focus here. A broad, unconstrained net will preserve the natural intertwining of thought, but it dilutes the analytic focus. Reciprocally, delineating the domain of reasoning rests on pre-theoretical distinctions, which are then imported into the construction of findings and of theory.

This same tension is also inherent in the design of the interview. The interview was largely shaped by the woman, but also guided flexibly by concerns pertaining to the way in which she constructed the problem, the interplay of different resources at different moments, the contrasts between reasoning situations, or the way in which the woman's reasoning could be understood in the context of her societal location and formative discourses. These backstage questions generated probes in a flexible manner, adapted to each woman's language and to the preceding interview context. The inevitable fact that the questions that served as the guiding thread of the interview constrain the nature of the *"data"* takes on a particular force in this research, because of the conscious agenda, both in feminist theories and epistemologies and in the present research, to develop a theory of knowledge on new ground. For that reason, the way in which preconceptions and available discourses are inadvertently imported into the generation of *"findings"* is of focal concern. Yet, again, this observation does not entail shifting to an open-ended approach, for reasons just discussed.

These issues instantiate one aspect of the dialectic between critique, method and theory. The design of the interview is developed in a theoretical space opened up by feminist critique. At the same time the particular methodological choices that are made regarding the reasoning domain and the scope of the interview will configure the theories produced. Again, what is distinctive is that this issue, while integral to any research, is dramatized in this attempt to construct an approach to inference on new ground, because the demarcation of the reasoning domain is itself a theoretically meaningful and unstable problem.

Construction of the Descriptive Language

The aim is to develop a new descriptive and analytic language for reasoning, liberated to the extent possible from the logicist hegemony that has molded the history of logic and the research on reasoning (and my own thinking as a socially constructed agent). The epistemological issues involved in constructing this language are closely related, from the data-analytic angle, to the issues of interview design just discussed.

This descriptive language is guided by feminist theories, but guided in a dialectical way. New analytic categories are constructed by listening to the participants' language and mode of thinking with an open ear, although an ear tuned to feminist theory broadly conceived.[3] Thus the process involves being oriented inductively (and of course induction is not genuinely possible) but with the analytical guidance of feminist theories of knowledge. The dialectic between this *"inductive"* mode of processing and feminist constructs in the text analyst's mind is expected to produce descriptions that are both faithful to the *"data"* in a suitable sense, and relevant to feminist theorizing. At the same time, because the aim is precisely to develop a transdisciplinary methodology for studying inference, existing feminist discussions of logic or epistemology cannot dictate or restrict these descriptions. Metaphorically, they should suggest a register for listening but not particular notes.

One perplexing question is whether the problems of logic exposed by feminist critics are confined to its normative function or whether they contaminate the use of logical principles as part of the descriptive language. Addressing this question is beyond the scope of this paper. The arguable choice in this study was to identify abstract logical principles when they appeared to be utilized, and to examine how they were intertwined with other knowledges in the women's reasoning, with the understanding that doing so may be performing the rationalist mode in which we have been enculturated.

The (ubiquitous) theory-laden character of data is particularly complex in qualitative research, because qualitative methodology is interpretive. Therefore, the data-analytic tools are always inherently theoretical. As illustrated above, this becomes crucial when one aim is to dislodge the normative hegemony of logic, and the other is to inform the development of feminist theories of logic and reasoning through a cross-disciplinary methodology.

The Dialectic of the Particular and the General

There is an inherent tension between preserving the richness, concreteness and particularity of responses and participants, and capturing cross-sectional patterns. This tension has epistemic as well as narrative dimensions. Epistemically, for reasons discussed previously, it is important to understand each woman in her full particularity, grounded in the context of her life and her social location. At the same time, if the understanding gained from empirical research is to be somewhat cumulative, the outcome of the study cannot be a collection of individual contextual narratives. Thus, two needs follow. It is important to be attuned to convergences or contrasts that may emerge across particularized participants. And it is important to develop an analytic language for identifying "moments" of reasoning. For these reasons, the data analysis was two-pronged. It included narrative profiles aimed to particularize the woman in terms of her social location, her cultural and family history, and her pertinent life context, and to describe her modes of reasoning; as well as the descriptive categories cutting across participants discussed in the previous section.

A key feature of the methodology is that societal context is used interpretively, not causally and not in a generalizable sense. The aim is to particularize the woman in order to understand aspects of her reasoning more fully, not to make causal attributions regarding aspects of her context or yield generalized inferences about modes of thinking characterizing her (pre-defined) intersectional subgroup. Both these moves are misguided (Falmagne, 2000a). Although, of necessity, there are implicit generalities underlying any social interpretation, it is important to see that these are used *interpretively* to understand a *particular* reasoner.

Yet, along with the primacy of the particular, one wants to have gained from a participant an understanding that can enhance one's understanding of another as well, to some degree. If a broader understanding of reasoning in social agents is to be achieved, meaningful condensations are necessary, and there must be a degree of (selective) transferability to these interpretations. Hence the two principles are in tension. This problem, again, is both an epistemic issue as just discussed, and an issue of narration. Every moment of narrating, when patterns are discussed, necessitates deliberate rhetorical strategies to block mistaken causal readings and mistaken categorical generalization to the group or subgroup.

Status of the "Data" for Feminist Theories of Logic

As discussed earlier, this empirical work is one component of a transdisciplinary reconstructive project and it is crucial to develop an interplay between the thinking of concrete people and feminist theory. The relations between empirical research and theory construction (always complex) are particularly intricate in the case of feminist epistemology and feminist theories of logic, because these theories have quasi-normative as well as substantive aims, even in their feminist reformulations.

Those two enterprises, though interwoven, are distinct. Substantive theory construction (that is, developing a theory that represents, on some criterion of adequacy, the empirical data as they have been constructed and described), is the more straightforward enterprise, yet even so it involves the complex epistemic and narrative issues discussed previously.

With regard to quasi-normative theory construction of the kind explored by Plumwood, Nelson, and others, the relation between such theoretical reformulations and empirical results deserves central attention. Philosophical theory must be informed in *some way* by the actual thinking of concrete people occupying a particular location in ethnic/racial, socioeconomic, gendered and cultural formations, if it is to avoid the same rationalist mode of theorizing as that afflicting traditional theories of logic. As one instance, if logic is revisable as Nelson (1990; in press) has maintained, then, is it revisable based on the kind of data generated in this research, and what is the exact nature of the relation? One aim of the research is to motivate the exploration of these questions.

CONCLUSION

Three convictions inspire the work discussed in this paper. One is that critique is most fruitful when it yields a reconstructive project in the space it has opened. The second is that, in the case of logic and of "deduction", this feminist reconstruction must be transdisciplinary and that explorations of new feminist theories of logic and descriptions of the actual thinking of concrete people must inform one another dialectically. The third conviction is that, having exposed the hegemony of the rationalist tradition on the study of "deduction", it is of interest to reconfigure the domain rather than abandon it to that tradition. The research discussed, aimed at exploring the articulation between critique, theory and method in this feminist project of critical reconstruction, is a modest step in that direction. The discussion has focused on the dialectical tensions between openness and focus involved in the demarcation of the domain of study; the choice of interview design; the development of a new analytic language; and on the tensions attending other strategic choices, tensions that are inherent in any project of critical reconstruction, and are productive.

Notes

1.   The work discussed here was supported by a grant from The Spencer Foundation.

2.   The quotation marks are intended to reflect the misleading nature of the term "postcolonial": the postcolonial era has not arrived yet.

3.   The descriptive language involves categories, as languages do. However, importantly, these categories are not classification tools. The categories serve a heuristic function as "provisional pointers". They form a language enabling one to speak and to identify contrasts. These provisional categories are revised or enriched or transformed on an ongoing basis as concrete instances present themselves in the transcripts, especially if these instances are borderline or in tension.

REFERENCES

Alcoff, L., & Potter, E. (1993). *Feminist epistemologies.* New York: Routledge.
Bordo, S. (1987). *The flight to objectivity: Essays on Cartesianism and culture.* Albany NY: State University of New York Press.
Collins, P.H. (1990). *Black feminist thought: Knowledge, consciousness and the politics of empowerment.* New York: Routledge.

Falmagne, R. Joffe (2000b). Deconstructing cognitive psychology: A critical opening. Review of E. A. Wilson, *Neural geographies: Feminism and the microstructure of cognition. Theory and Psychology, 10*, 277-282.

Falmagne, R. Joffe (1997). *Toward a feminist theory of inference: Exploration of a cross-disciplinary methodology.* Paper presented at the enGendering Rationalities Conference, University of Oregon.

Falmagne, R. Joffe (2000a). Positionality and thought: On the gendered foundation of thought, culture and development. In P. H. Miller & E. K. Scholnick (Eds), *Toward a feminist developmental psychology* (pp. 191-213). New York: Routledge.

Falmagne, R. Joffe (in press). Toward a feminist theory of inference: The case for a transdisciplinary methodology. In M. Hass & R. Joffe Falmagne (Eds), *Feminist perspectives on logic.* Lanham, MD: Rowman and Littlefield.

Falmagne, R. Joffe, & Gonsalves, J. (1995). Deductive inference. *Annual Review of Psychology, 46*, 525-559.

Flax, J. (1993). *Disputed subjects: Essays on psychoanalysis, subjects, politics and philosophy.* New York: Routledge.

Foucault, M. (1980) *Power/knowledge.* New York: Pantheon.

Harding, S. (1993). Rethinking standpoint epistemology: "What is strong objectivity?" In L. Alcoff & E. Potter (Eds.), *Feminist epistemologies* (pp. 49-82). New York: Routledge.

Hartsock, N. (1983). The feminist standpoint: Developing the grounds for a specifically feminist historical materialism. In S. Harding & M. Hintikka (Eds), *Discovering reality: Feminist perspectives on epistemology, metaphysics methodology and philosophy of science* (pp. 283-310). Dordrecht: Reidel.

Hass, M., & Falmagne, R. Joffe (Eds) (in press). *Feminist perspectives on logic.* Lanham, MD: Rowman and Littlefield.

Henriques, J., Hollway, W., Urwin, C., Venn, C., & Walkerdine, V. (1984). *Changing the subject: Social regulation and subjectivity.* London: Methuen.

hooks, b. (1990). Choosing the margin as a space of radical openness. In b. hooks (Ed.), *Yearning: Race, gender, and cultural politics* (pp. 145-154). Boston: South End Press.

Lloyd, G. (1984). *The man of reason: "Male" and "female" in western philosophy.* London: Methuen.

Lloyd, G. (1993). Maleness, metaphor, and the "crisis" of reason. In L. M. Antony & C. Witt (Eds), *A mind of one's own: Feminist essays on reason and objectivity* (pp. 69-84). Boulder CO: Westview Press.

Mohanty, C. (1991). Introduction: Cartographies of struggle. In C. Mohanty, A. Russo, & L. Torres (Eds.) *Third world women and the politics of feminism* (pp. 1-50). Indiana University Press.

Nelson, L. H. (1990). *Who knows? From Quine to a feminist empiricism.* Temple University Press.

Nelson, L. H. (in press). Logic as an empirical enterprise. In M. Hass & R. Joffe Falmagne (Eds) *Feminist perspectives on logic.* Lanham, MD: Rowman and Littlefield.

Nye, A. (1990). *Words of power.* New York: Routledge.

Olkowski, D. (in press). Words of power and the logic of sense. In M. Hass & R. Joffe Falmagne (Eds) *Feminist perspectives on logic.* Lanham, MD: Rowman and Littlefield.

Plumwood, V. (1993/in press). The politics of reason: Towards a feminist logic. *Australasian Journal of Philosophy, 71*, 436-462. Reprinted in M. Hass & R. Joffe Falmagne (Eds) *Feminist perspectives on logic.* Lanham, MD: Rowman and Littlefield.

Smith, D. (1990). *Texts, facts and femininity.* London: Routledge.

Walkerdine, V. (1988). *The mastery of reason: Cognitive development and the production of rationality.* London: Routledge.

Wilson, E. (1998). *Neural geographies: Feminism and the microstructure of cognition.* London: Routledge.

GETTING RID OF THE HOMUNCULUS:
A Direct Realist Approach

Terence McMullen
University of Sydney

SUMMARY

One of the problems arising in the representationist approach to cognition is that of the homunculus. How can cognition occur unless there is an inner "little man" who knows both what the representations are and what they represent? Dennett's "intentional stance" account proposes a way out. By analogy with computer processes (e.g. we speak of "chess-playing" computers when, in fact, they know literally nothing about chess or anything else), it can be seen that human cognition can be analysed down to basic processing assemblies which are cognitively attenuated ("stupid", "pseudo-cognitive"). Accordingly there is no need for representations, and so there is no homunculus problem. Dennett's solution is unworkable: the notion of pseudo- or proto-cognition is unsustainable. Must the homunculus be reinstated? Not at all: the direct realist account of cognition as an irreducible *relation* provides a radical but coherent alternative.

INTRODUCTION: DANIEL DENNETT AND THE PROBLEM OF THE HOMUNCULUS

When Franz Brentano introduced, or rather, revived (as he saw it), the concept of *intentionality* in his psychology last century, he believed that the concept provided a criterion whereby the mental could be distinguished from the physical. The correctness of that controversial claim is not the subject of this paper. Insofar as Daniel Dennett's contemporary approach to psychology is based on an "objective, materialistic, third-person world of the physical sciences" (Dennett,

1987, p.5), he is no follower of Brentano, but he acknowledges a significant debt to him. Dennett has taken over the concept of intentionality, but has applied it in an instrumentalist or functionalist fashion. "Folk psychology", Dennett states, often has a pragmatic justification. A folk theory of human behaviour says that behaviour can be explained it terms of people's beliefs and wishes : "she went into the shoe-shop because she wanted a new pair of shoes and believed she could buy a good pair there". What folk psychology does, Dennett states, is to take an *intentional stance* to behaviour. "To a first approximation, the intentional strategy consists of treating the object whose behaviour you want to predict as a rational agent with beliefs and desires and other mental stages exhibiting what Brentano and others call *intentionality*" (Dennett, 1987, p.15). The strategy often pays off predictively, and can be used not only with humans, but with other animals, plants, and machines. For example, a vine grows up a pole because "it wants" to get to the sunlight; a chess-playing computer makes a particular move because it "is trying" to take its opponent's pawn. The essential feature of intentionality in Brentano's account is its "aboutness", i.e. all and only mental acts are directed upon an object, they hold onto a referent, and no complete description of a mental act can be given without noting its object. For example, one never just "hears" nor "sees", one "hears the bell" or "sees the picture"; one never just "doubts", one "doubts that the politician will keep his promises". The objects intended by mental acts exist in their own right, and thus the question can be raised of how it could be that an act is *about* something else. Of course, there are other questions raised about Brentano's theory, but they are not relevant here.

To Dennett, the physicalist, there is nothing special about human beings' psychological processes that mark them off in kind from computers. Both are information processing systems. They possess *syntax,* rules and procedures for dealing with incoming representations of the world, and those representations have *semantic* properties, i. e. they have meanings. A computer has no access to the semantics of its internal states; it does not know whether it is recording responses made in a Skinner box, is playing chess or is analysing Costa Rican public health data. Most human beings, however, think that they have access to the semantics of their internal representations, i.e., they know what they are thinking *about*; they have access to the intentional objects of their mental acts. Dennett has had much to say about human cognition and consciousness, but the focus of this paper is on one specific issue: Dennett's attempt to avoid the problem of the homunculus in his account of human cognition.

Representationist theories of knowledge claim that what is known are not the external objects of knowledge directly, but, rather, such objects are known indirectly or inferentially by means of encoded representations, symbols, of them. The internal representations were once called ideas, impressions, sensations and perceptions; some more recent names noted by Dennett are "hypotheses, maps, schemas, images, propositions, engrams, neural signals, even holograms" (Dennett, 1979, p.122). He is well aware of what would seem to be a fatal problem for representationism. It is this: representations, symbols, signs, call them as you will, do not carry any *intrinsic* properties which say what it is that they are representing , symbolising or signing. No symbol, whether a putative internal mental one or an external physical one, has any mark of what it is symbolising. The representationist in psychology, therefore, cannot give any account of the semantics of representations, without having to allow, somewhere along the line, the possibility of having independent direct knowledge of what is represented by a particular representation. It is often suggested at this point that an inner homunculus would have to be invoked, an homunculus who knows both what a given symbol is and what it symbolises. Once this step is taken a vicious regress results, because the homunculus can only know things through his representations of them, and a higher order homunculus will have to be invoked , and so on. Dennett notes in *Brainstorms* (1979) his dilemma: "psychology *without* homunculi is impossible. But psychology *with* homunculi is doomed to circularity or infinite regress, so psychology is impossible" (p.122). What is his solution? It is that internal representations can be replaced with "internal pseudo-representations" (p. 125) which will do just as well.

DENNETT'S SOLUTION

The problem of how internal representations can be meaningful when there is no scanner to read the meaning is described by Dennett as *Hume's Problem* (1978, p.122). Hume had no answer to it, but he had no computers and knew nothing of Artificial Intelligence (AI). Dennett's answer to the problem is through AI. Broadly, one can take an intentional stance to computers and regard them provisionally as housing a set of homunculi. Every homunculus can be seen as a set or collection of smaller homunculi whose "knowledge" is relatively circumscribed. Every smaller homunculus itself is nothing more than a set of even smaller ones, and so on, until a level is reached where the homunculi are so relatively ignorant that they are no longer homunculi in any serious sense, hence doing themselves out of a job. What seems to be a unit teeming with intelligence and intention is really nothing more than a cognitively blind system of machinery. Dennett writes :

> The AI programmer begins with an intentionally characterised problem, and thus frankly views the computer anthropomorphically: if he *solves* the problem he will say he has designed a computer that can understand questions in English. His first and highest level of design breaks the

computer down into subsystems, each of which is given intentionally characterised tasks; he composes a flow chart of evaluators, rememberers, discriminators, overseers and the like. These are *homunculi* with a vengeance; the highest level design breaks the computer down into a committee or army of intelligent homunculi with purposes, information and strategies. Each homunculus in turn is analysed into *smaller* homunculi, but, more important, into *less clever* homunculi. When the level is reached where the homunculi are no more than adders and subtractors, by the time they need only the intelligence to pick the larger of two numbers when directed to, they have been reduced to functionaries "who can be replaced by a machine". The aid to comprehension of anthropomorphizing the elements just about lapses at this point, and a mechanistic view of the proceedings becomes workable and comprehensible. (Dennett, 1978, pp. 80-81)

Again, dealing now with humans:

One starts, in AI, with a specification of a whole person or cognitive organism ... or some artificial segment of that person's abilities (e.g., chess-playing, answering questions about baseball) and then breaks that largest intentional system into an organization of subsystems, each of which itself could be viewed as an intentional system (with its own specialized beliefs and desires) and hence as formally a homunculus. In fact homunculus talk is ubiquitous in AI, and always illuminating. AI homunculi talk to each other, wrest control from each other, volunteer, sub-contract, supervise, and even kill. There seems no better way of describing what is going on. Homunculi are *bogeymen* only if they duplicate *entire* the talents they are rung in to explain. ... If one can get a team or committee of *relatively* ignorant, narrow-minded, blind homunculi to produce the intelligent behavior of the whole, this is progress. A flow chart is typically the organizational chart of a committee of homunculi (investigators, librarians, accountants, executives); each box specifies a homunculus by prescribing a function *without saying how it is to be accomplished* (one says, in effect: put a little man in there to do the job). If we then look closer at the individual boxes we see that the function of each is accomplished by subdividing it via another flow chart into smaller, more stupid homunculi. Eventually this nesting of boxes within boxes lands you with homunculi so stupid (all they have to do is remember to say yes or no when asked) that they can be, as one says, "replaced by a machine". One *discharges* fancy homunculi from one's scheme by organizing armies of such idiots to do the work. (op. cit. pp. 123-124)

Elsewhere (in Miller, 1983) Dennett compares a relatively "stupid" subsystem with a CIA field agent who is told nothing more than he needs to know, so that if he falls into enemy hands he cannot give the whole show away. In *Kinds of Minds* (1996) Dennett can find no qualitative difference between *sentience*, which allegedly conscious systems (humans) possess, and mere *sensitivity*, the capacity to respond to change, found in both the animate and inanimate world (e.g., litmus paper changing colour upon exposure to acid or alkali). The hypothetical CIA agent is now joined by a KGB one (p.58).

It can be seen that if Dennett's proposal, as outlined, works, then he has side-stepped the problem of the homunculus by showing that apparently cognitive events can be derived from non-cognitive ones: representations are really "pseudo-representations" and the metaphorical status of cognition is underscored.

DOES DENNETT'S PROPOSAL WORK?

There is a host of issues which could be taken up here, but this paper has only one thesis, viz., that the attempt to reduce apparently cognitive systems to non-cognitive ones must fail. The thesis is concerned with human cognition; whilst there is no denial of the possibility of cognition in brutes, that fact, if fact it be, is not of present relevance. It is granted that attributing cognition to computers is metaphorical - literally they know nothing. To take an intentional stance to computers, however, does not licence taking one to human beings. To be precise, the point to be made here is that one cannot derive cognitive activities from non-cognitive ones by breaking the former down to subsets of the latter, and this is because the concept of "completely stupid knowers" is self-contradictory.

Consider first Dennett's example of the CIA agent. Suppose that, say, President Castro is to visit Mexico again, and that the CIA hatches a grand plan to assassinate him in Mexico City. Only two or three people in Washington know of the grand plan, but to put it into operation many helpers are needed, who must be kept as ignorant as possible. One such helper, vital to the plan, is an ignorant, illiterate, somewhat intellectually retarded cleaner in Mexico City. He has never heard of Castro, let alone knowing anything of his imminent visit. All that he knows is that someone has paid him to leave a certain room in a public building where he works locked on a certain night. Relative to the grand plan he knows next to nothing. He is indeed grossly ignorant, but only *in relation to* the grand plan. But there are other relevant things that he knows, and he knows them perfectly well - for example, which room in the building is the one to be left locked, how to lock the room and which building he works in. He has to be able to remember which night is the chosen night .Furthermore, all of these items can be decomposed into relatively more basic cognitive items. For example "knowing how to lock a particular room" entails ability to recognise the right room, ability to recognise the right key, remembering all the while where it is kept, running-off the appropriate visual-motor cognisings relevant to turning a lock, and so on. At no point does one arrive at some absolutely "basic" level which entails, so to speak, content-less cognition. In other words his "stupidity" is not an absolute property of his cognitive capacity; relative to the grand plan he is constrained, stupid, blinkered, cognitively blind, but he engages in fully blown cognition, nonetheless.

It might be objected that this example fails to come to grips with the kind of job which Dennett sees as being done by the pseudo-cognisers at the bottom of the hierarchy, the ones which are so stupid that all they have to do is "remember whether to say yes or no". One might be tempted to say that the "scanning" at this level is nothing more than a mere mechanical gating device, where there is no question of cognition. A fisherman's net, for example, "distinguishes" big fish from little fish only in the sense that little fish can swim through the net and big fish cannot. The net itself knows nothing . Analogously, it could be said that the stupid homunculus's declarations of yes or no (however these may be made) correspond to the net's metaphorical "utterances" of big fish or little fish. This strategy, however, will not work. At this point the discussion must go a little beyond Dennett's scope, because he does not explore the conceptual assumptions entailed in the notion of "attenuated" cognition. The argument here is that such a notion must come down to the unsustainable claim that there can be knowledge of *propositionless terms* , i.e., knowledge of a discrete term independent of a context which would make it either a subject or predicate.

In the first place the homunculus, in having to *remember* when to say yes or no has to engage in a species of cognition, memory. In the second place a mere declaration of yes or no has no semantic value unless it occurs in a context, implicit or explicit. If someone comes into one's room and says "out of the blue" "yes" one would not know what was trying to be conveyed. One would ask "yes what"? Presumably then the visitor would go on to affirm some fact, some state of affairs. This is cognition. The utterance of a bald "yes" well might be fraught with great meaning -witness Molly Bloom's monologue in *Ulysses* - but that is only because it occurs in a context. All cognition involves direct apprehension, which is not necessarily conscious, of some independently existing state of affairs, some situation. All situations involve complexity in that a certain description (a predicate) does, or does not, apply to a certain location (a subject). Nothing can ever be stated as a single term; there can be nothing known or said which is not propositional, i.e., one thing , a predicate, is affirmed or denied of another thing, a subject. The declaration "yes" by itself may be meaningful of course, i.e. assert a proposition, but only if there is a context, as , for example, when "Do you want an apple"? brings the reply "yes". Here "yes" is a symbol of the state of affairs "I want an apple", just as the single symbol of a silhouetted cigarette crossed through intends the proposition "smoking is forbidden". The physical sign itself cognises nothing, nor does it intrinsically indicate what it is symbolising, but it is the means by which one cogniser, the signer, communicates an independent state of affairs ("smoking is forbidden") to another cogniser, the reader, who must already know the convention of the signing. For a detailed discussion of symbolism as a ternary relation see Petocz (1999).

Take the cognition "I perceive an apple". To follow Hume (1739/1888, p. 2) one might break it down into impressions of colour, taste and smell. The cogency of Hume's associated distinction between simple and complex perceptions, especially that of his atomism, will be ignored here. Suppose that there is a stupid taste homunculus in charge of impressions of sweetness. All he has to do is yell out "yes" when a sweet impression comes along in an act of tasting, and "no" when it does not. Can cognition be circumvented here? No. The taste demon must be able to discriminate between occasions of tasting or not tasting, otherwise he will be continuously calling out "no, no, no", with perhaps an occasional "yes", all day long. Let him therefore be made even more stupid. All he does is say "yes" when a sweet impression arrives. As has been stated, "yes" on its own means nothing unless it occurs in a context, and once that is the case then cognition is going on. Say, then that the demon declares "sweet" instead of "yes". This will not help at all. The single term "sweet" has no meaning on its own. When the demon calls "sweet" does he mean that "there is sweetness *here, now*"? If so, he is propositionalising, so to speak. Is he predicating sweetness of something else ("this taste is sweet")? Is he taking sweet as a subject, and predicating some other thing (term) of it ("the sweetness is cloying")? Is he affirming something ("this taste is sweet") or denying something ("this taste is not sweet")? His knowledge of the lusciousness of a good Rutherglen liqueur muscat will be minuscule compared to that of the drinker he works for, but at least he must always know something. Suppose that there could be a demon whose cognitive capacity is so attenuated that he can know only one subject," sweetness", and only one predicate, "present here, now". Of course the subject might be "angularity", "movement", or "linearity", to take examples from the perception literature. Suppose even further attenuation : he can cognise only when "sweetness is present here, now"; he can know literally only one thing. It is hard to conceive that there could be knowledge of only the positive copula, i.e., that if he can know that "sweetness is present here, now", he also could not know that "sweetness is not present here, now"; further, that there could be knowledge of a term only as a subject or only as a predicate, i.e. that one could know that "sweetness is present here, now", without being able to know the converse, viz., that "some things present here, now are sweet". Even so, as attenuated as that cognition is, it is a complete, fully blown piece of cognition, being *propositional* in form.

CONCLUSION

Cognition is an all-or-none affair . There can be no question of proto-cognition, "protominds" (Dennett, 1996, p. 162), pseudo-cognition, or attenuated cognition of any kind (e.g. knowledge of discrete terms). Of course there can be attenuated cognition in an everyday quantitative sense: "Without my glasses I can't see the lemon, only a yellow blob". There is no difference of "levels" of cognition here, the "yellow blob" is just as much a term as is the lemon. Certainly some knowers will be stupid in comparison with others, but the distinction is a relative one. If one begins with cognition it cannot be decomposed into non-cognitive elements. One can, of course, be interested in the neural conditions of cognition, a legitimate enquiry in its own right, but something which the psychologist takes as given.

Although Dennett's approach to cognition is reductionist or functionalist, he takes it seriously enough in humans to recognise that the issue of the homunculus is a genuine one for representationism. His solution of the semantics of cognition is unworkable. There is a way to be a cognitionalist and to avoid the necessity of the homunculus, and that is to give up the doctrine of representationism altogether. Direct realism, in arguing that what is cognised are situations existing independently of the cogniser, sees that the "semantics" of cognition is the question of identifying those independent situations in the world which are cognised. Cognition is a *sui generis* irreducible relation between the cogniser and the cognised, one which has no necessary connotation of consciousness (Anderson, 1927/1962). If there are no such things as internal representations of the objects of knowledge, then the question of how to read the "meaning" of such representations simply does not arise. To cognise is to directly apprehend situations existing independently of the cogniser. Formally, cognition can be described awkwardly, but accurately, as "propositionalising" i.e. as intending independent situations which are ontologically propositional in that every situation is a complex spatio-temporal unity of subject, copula and predicate. On this account, which derives from the most thoroughgoing philosophical realist of the twentieth century, John Anderson, just as ontologically there cannot be anything sub-propositional (e.g. ontological "atoms"), so epistemologically there cannot be anything known which is sub-propositional. Any supposed discrete item of knowledge can always be shown to be functionally the subject or predicate of an unstated, but implicit proposition. Anderson, a Scot, did most of his philosophical work in Australia, and is little known to psychologists, most of whom associate realism with J. J. Gibson, but it is Anderson to whom one should look for a rigorous, systematic exposition (see, e.g., Mackie 1985, Baker 1986).

Realism is not only free from the problem of the homunculus, it is free from other fatal problems facing representationism, such as that of solipsism, that of the dualism of supposedly "inner" and "outer" worlds and that of the status of representative mental entities as mere reifications. Dennett's functionalist rendition of cognition, which tries to be both representationist, but not "really" representationist, does not work: the choice has to be either the realist view of cognition as relational, or a radical behaviourism which denies cognition altogether. Of course, the radical behaviourist betrays an implicit acceptance of the fact of cognition in supposing that an opponent understands the meaning of the spoken or written claim "there is no such thing as cognition".

REFERENCES

Anderson, J. (1962). The knower and the known. In *Studies in empirical philosophy* (pp. 27-40). Sydney: Angus & Robertson. (Original work published 1927).
Baker, A. J. (1986). *Australian realism: The systematic philosophy of John Anderson.* Cambridge: Cambridge University Press.
Dennett, D. C.(1979). *Brainstorms: Philosophical essays on mind and psychology.* Hassocks. Sussex: Harvester Press.
Dennett, D. C. (1987). *The intentional stance.* Cambridge, MA : The MIT Press.
Dennett, D. C. (1996). *Kinds of minds: Towards an understanding of consciousness.* London: Weidenfeld & Nicolson.
Hume, D. (1888). *Treatise of human nature,* L.A. Selby-Bigge (Ed.). Oxford: Oxford University Press. (Original work published 1739).
Mackie, J. L. (1985). The philosophy of John Anderson. In *Logic and knowledge: Selected papers,* Vol. I, J. Mackie and P. Mackie (Eds) (pp. 1-21). Oxford: Clarendon Press.
Miller, J. (Ed.) (1983). *States of mind.* London: British Broadcasting Corporation.
Petocz, A. (1999). *Freud, psychoanalysis and symbolism.* Cambridge: Cambridge University Press.

IV SOCIAL CONSTRUCTIONISM AND METATHEORETICAL ISSUES

LOGICAL POSITIVISM AND GERGEN'S SOCIAL CONSTRUCTIONISM:

No Radical Disjunction in Twentieth Century Psychological Metatheory

Fiona J. Hibberd
University of Sydney

SUMMARY

K. J. Gergen's postmodernist metatheory of psychological science – a radical form of social constructionism – is judged by many to be antithetical to positivist philosophy. However, the radical aspects of logical positivism are masked by their expressed empiricist intentions and there are, in fact, significant similarities between this philosophy and Gergen's metatheory. Both subscribe to conventionalism and both (mis)appropriate Wittgenstein's meaning-as-use thesis. These semantic similarities have their roots in a shared anti-realist epistemology in that both retain a link to Kant – they support the idea that we cannot know things as they are in themselves because we cannot know them directly. In psychology, the tradition of anti-realist metatheory continues.

INTRODUCTION

Amongst those psychologists concerned with metatheoretical matters, there is general consensus that positivist philosophy of science has failed as a metatheory for psychology. Some have taken K. J. Gergen's postmodernism – a radical form of social constructionism – to be a coherent alternative to positivism, and the effects of this can now be seen in a number of psychology's current theories, e.g., theories of education and of psychotherapy. Others are more sceptical, arguing that Gergen's brand of social constructionism is ultimately self-defeating.

172

Notwithstanding these differences, most psychologists believe that Gergen's metatheory is the antithesis of positivism. In fact, this belief is not peculiar to psychology, but prevalent throughout the social sciences and certain areas of philosophy. My claim is that this "antithesis" view is false; there are significant similarities between Gergen's "post-modernist" social constructionism and "old fashioned" logical positivism. In this paper, I sketch some of the arguments which support this claim. A more detailed account is provided elsewhere (Hibberd, in press-a; in press-b).

GERGEN'S SOCIO-LINGUISTIC PARADIGM

Gergen has repeatedly pronounced on the status of psychology's theoretical and observational statements, and on the ontological status of psycho-social phenomena. His view is (i) that language generally and theoretical language in particular is not descriptive – it does not refer to any independent, objective truths, and (ii) that knowledge is mediated by socio-linguistic conventions; that we are bound up in a closed system of language (e.g., Gergen, 1994a, pp. 31-39).

The Received View of Logical Positivism and its Relationship to Social Constructionism[1]

The table opposite highlights some of the perceived differences between logical positivism and Gergen's metatheory. The folklore surrounding logical positivism is such that these differences appear clear and substantial. My claim is that they are not. The radical aspects of logical positivist philosophy have been camouflaged by their expressed realist, empiricist and foundationalist intentions. In reality, Gergen's metatheory and logical positivism are partially equivalent with respect to central tenets. These tenets are (i) conventionalism, (ii) Wittgenstein's meaning-as-use thesis, and (iii) the claim that reality cannot be known directly.

Conventionalism

Conventionalism is primarily a theory about meaning. Its central features can be stated as follows. First, the meaning of some or all linguistic terms (depending on how extreme a version of the thesis is being considered) is not given at all by the things in the world to which the terms purportedly correspond.

TABLE 1: Some Perceived Differences between Logical Positivism and Social Constructionism

LOGICAL POSITIVISM	SOCIAL CONSTRUCTIONISM
1. Claims that any theory consists of both analytic and synthetic statements.	1. Rejects the analytic-synthetic distinction.
2. Subscribes to empiricism and realism – driven by an objectivist ideology. Observation statements are derived solely from uncontaminated sense-data, and the factual content of a theory is given by an upward seepage of meaning from the soil of observational experience. Scientific knowledge is a reflection of the way the world is. There are independent facts about the world which may be described by theories.	3. Rejects empiricism, realism and the possibility of objective social science. The meanings of these so-called observation statements are not derived from experience. Meaning trickles down from a linguistic framework or forestructure which creates its own domain of facts. That which counts as scientific knowledge is, therefore, determined by these frameworks or forestructures, not by the way the world is.

Second: some terms, then, are non-empirical (conventional) and their meanings are given by non-empirical factors. Referential relations do contribute to terms meaning what they do, but reference is said to be to, or determined by, something other than the supposed referents. It is to other terms and to the precepts of the stipulator, or to certain norms or practices that terms refer, and this is said to make reference "internal" rather than "external" (this I refer to as "the condition of internal reference").

Third: when applied to theories, conventionalism holds that the meanings of some or all of the terms and relations within a theoretical framework (or system) are determined by other terms and relations in that framework and reflect or express certain norms, practices or precepts of the individual scientist or scientific community.

Fourth: for this reason, theoretical propositions which consist of these terms and relations are said to have a purely conventional status – to be non-empirical. They do not convey, or purport to convey, information about the world or, more specifically, about the subject of each proposition, i.e., the thing that each proposition is about. They cannot, then, be true (in any realist sense of the word). Nor, of course, are they amenable to confirmation or disconfirmation.

Fifth: the condition of "internal reference" makes the system of propositions implicitly analytic. A consequence of such analyticity is that any network of conventions (set of propositions) can be generated and then "applied" to any set of states of affairs.

A major, but not widely known, feature of logical positivism was its development of nineteenth century conventionalism (Coffa, 1991; Friedman, 1991; Uebel, 1996). Schlick, Reichenbach and Carnap, each in his own way, proposed that certain terms in a scientific theory are non-empirical because they "have no association or connection with reality at all" (Schlick, 1925/1974, p. 37). Meanings are given to these terms from within a non-empirical definitional system or framework, that is, reference is internal. Their meanings are, then, contextual, in the sense that they are relative to the system in which they are employed. Moreover, a system of conventions (framework) enables the "ordering" or conceptualisation of the object of knowledge (Carnap, 1928/1967; Reichenbach, 1920/1965).

In Gergen's conceptualisation of the status of theories in psychology, some important aspects of the logical positivists' conventionalism are (unwittingly) retained. For example, the condition of internal reference is invoked in Gergen's (1985) claim that mental predicates are defined in terms of other mental predicates. Furthermore, the positivist idea that a system of conventions enables the "ordering" of scientific knowledge is the very function Gergen has in mind when he suggests that:

... we gain substantially if we consider the world-structuring process as linguistic rather than cognitive. It is through an *a priori* commitment to particular forms of language (genres, conventions, speech codes, and so on) that we place boundaries around what we take to be "the real". (Gergen, 1994a, p. 37)

Moreover, this aspect of social constructionism perpetuates the logical positivist notion of *a priori*. Gergen (1994b) maintains that language conventions form *"linguistic frameworks"* or *"forestructures"* which (among other things) generate *"scientific facts"* (p. 415). In his metatheory, the ontological status of these *"frameworks"* is not simple. They consist of *a priori* elements, but they are said to be contingent upon the social conditions under which the terms (which comprise the frameworks) are employed. This medley, in which *a priori* elements coexist with the *a posteriori* social is also a feature of logical positivism. Both take *a priori* to mean not *"independent of experience"*, and not *"for all time"*, but *"before knowledge"* (see, for example, Reichenbach, 1920, p. 105).

In short, both social constructionism and logical positivism conceive of conventions and frameworks as linguistic in nature, and both claim that theoretical propositions are characterised by autonomy and analyticity. One difference between them is that of quantity. Gergen takes autonomy and analyticity to characterise *all* theoretical propositions, logical positivism only some.

Meaning as Use

The *a posteriori* aspect of conventionalism pertains to logical positivism's development of verificationism and Gergen's claim that language acquires meaning through its use in socio-linguistic practices. The feature which is shared by both in explicating these views is Wittgenstein's identification of the meaning of a word with its use.[2] This, together with Wittgenstein's broad conceptualisation of a grammatical rule and his belief that the identity of such a rule is revealed by the speaker's behaviour or practices, is evident in Schlick's post-1931 attempts to identify meaning with verifiability. Schlick, explicitly following Wittgenstein, broadens rules of grammar into rules of use. In Schlick's opinion, verification is logically impossible only when meaning hasn't been given to a sentence, and this is when the researcher hasn't stipulated what must be done (specified the methodological practices) for the sentence to be verified. The meaning of a sentence is given by such a stipulation. Moreover, in Schlick's (1936/1979) account, *"stipulation"* refers not only to *"what must be done"* but also to *"what is done"*. He suggests that "... we require the presence of certain complex situations, and the meaning of the words is defined by the way we use them in these different situations" (p. 458).

An important feature of Gergen's metatheory is that meaning is contextually dependent; the meaning of any term in a psychological theory is given by the context in which the term is used. Socio-linguistic practices are contextual and, by "context", Gergen means anything from the immediate environment in which terms, propositions, etc. are uttered, to a whole cultural tradition (Gergen, 1994a, p. 49, pp. 84-87). Gergen's justification for his notion of contextual dependency involves, in part, Wittgenstein's criterion of meaning-as-use. Words acquire their meaning through the ways they are used in social practices (Gergen, 1994b, p. 413), by their function within a set of circumscribed rules (Gergen, 1994a, p. 53). Like Schlick, Gergen also interprets the term "rules" liberally. "Rules" are the rules of the "language-games"; the context; the socio-linguistic conventions, and the patterns of social interchange. Meanings, he claims, cannot be fixed because contexts vary (e.g., Gergen, 1994a, p. 267).

Despite the modern flavour of Gergen's contextual dependency thesis, the resemblance between the two versions of Wittgenstein's account is noteworthy. Both Schlick and Gergen rely on the meaning-as-use criterion, both make use of the notion of "rules" as determining use (and, therefore, meaning), both interpret "rules" broadly, and both require a social context in which meaning is given. Although Schlick's and Gergen's views are not identical, it is through Wittgenstein's influence that Gergen has proposed ideas which were present in Schlick's later defence of the verifiability principle.

The received view of the relationship between Gergen's metatheory and operationism must also be questioned. Schlick's verificationism and Gergen's social constructionism are conceptually related to Bridgman's and S. S. Stevens' operationism (Hibberd, in press-b). Operationism, too, requires that attention be drawn to context of usage as a determinant of meaning. Of course, there are differences between Gergen's metatheory and operationism, but both maintain that it is not any hypothesised features of the phenomenon under investigation which contribute to a term's meaning, only the context of its use. In each case, (verificationism, operationism and social constructionism) meaning is identified with use – either with stipulation of the practices which put the term to use (Schlick), with the set of operations involved in the use of the term (Bridgman and Stevens), or with the context (the social practices) involved in the term's use (Gergen). Meaning is not associated with the objects, attributes, or situations that a term stands for.

Reality Cannot Be Known Directly

The semantic similarities between logical positivism and Gergen's social constructionism have their roots in a common anti-realist epistemology. Logical positivism claimed that empirical propositions reduce to a phenomenal language consisting of sense–datum statements (of the kind, "rectangular, white here now") because what we perceive directly are mind-dependent entities, namely, sense data. Whilst Schlick and Carnap recognised the difficulties in defending this phenomenalism (Schlick, 1925/1974, p. 28; Carnap, 1934, pp. 78-82), they did not question it. Their "solution" was to turn to conventionalism. A conventional system of propositions (which, they claimed, is not merely man-made but used only if scientists choose to use it) will provide a certain and intersubjective starting-point for scientific knowledge. The same cannot be said of sense data.

A major factor in their failure to question the proposition that what we perceive directly are mind-dependent entities, was that neither Schlick nor Carnap had completely detached himself from Kantian idealism. They claimed to reject the Kantian proposition that objects or things in themselves are unknown to us (see Schlick, 1925/1974, pp. 269-270). In Schlick's opinion, it is:

> [t]hrough the conceptual system of the sciences we actually know the *essence* of extramental reality. It is not *unknowable*, as phenomenalism has continued to maintain since the days of Kant; it is merely *inexperienceable*, not a possible object of acquaintance, and that is quite a different matter.
> (Schlick, 1917/1979, p. 285)

Here we have knowledge of the world, not through experience, but through the mediation of a conceptual system. In his claim that the inexperienceable is knowable, Schlick not only abandons empiricism but subscribes to the proposition that we cannot know things as they are in themselves, where "know" is taken to mean "direct knowledge of", a proposition which Kant would not have disputed.

This idea lies at the heart of Gergen's epistemology, although social constructionism is not phenomenalist and Gergen (1994a) rejects any connection with Kant. Gergen's well known repudiation of ontological issues (1994a, p. 72) is driven by the belief that such issues cannot, in principle, be attended to. His claim is that:

> ... because disquisitions on the nature of things are framed in language, there is no grounding of science or any other knowledge-generating enterprise in other than communities of interlocutors. There is no appeal to mind or matter – to reason or facts – that will lend transcendental validity to propositions. (Gergen, 1994a, p. ix)

Although Gergen's emphasis is on language and Kant's was on cognition, this difference should not obscure the main point. If we are bound up in a closed system of socio-linguistic conventions, we can never know reality as unmodified

178

because there is no direct access to a language-independent world. This is equivalent to Kant's "unknowability of things-in-themselves" and consistent with his interpretation of the noumenon as something that cannot be known, in the sense of knowing its characteristics.

Thus, the epistemological similarity between logical positivism and social constructionism is that both subscribe to the view that we can never know things as they are in themselves; that we can only know things as they appear after the "conceptual system of the sciences" (Schlick and Carnap) or the "linguistic forestructure" (Gergen) has stepped in between the scientists and the object of study, or been imposed on the object of study.

CONCLUSION

There can be no objection to Gergen retaining the ideas of his intellectual ascendants when those ideas are tenable. However, conventionalism, meaning-as-use and the thesis that reality cannot be known directly are not tenable (Hibberd, in press-a; in press-b). Conventionalism entails the fallacy of constitutive (internal) relations and rests upon a number of distinctions which cannot be upheld. The identification of meaning with use involves an incomplete characterisation of meaning and makes causation logically impossible. The assumption that reality cannot be known directly, that modification of some kind is necessarily involved in what is known, again involves the constitutive doctrine. This doctrine breaches the notion of independence which is the sine qua non of realism, yet presupposes it in the process.

Gergen's social constructionism is an extension of logical positivism's original identification of linguistic analysis with philosophy. Both replace a study of situations with a study of language and the circumstances of language-use. Both judge this stance as an essential corrective to the unwarranted metaphysical or ontological emphasis which the "naive" philosopher or psychologist is so reluctant to relinquish. Ironically, the very metatheory which some psychologists have adopted in order to escape the deficiencies of positivism, exhibits a number of similar deficiencies. Contrary to the received view, there is no radical disjunction in twentieth century psychological metatheory. The tradition of anti-realism continues.

Notes

1.   For brevity, I sometimes use the label "social constructionism" to mean "Gergen's social constructionism".

2.   Schlick and Gergen misappropriate aspects of Wittgenstein's thesis. Schlick (1936/1979) appears not to have considered Wittgenstein's judgement that verificationism does not apply to all kinds of sentences; that verificationism is a sub-class of all language-games. This may be due to the fact that whilst Schlick was writing his final papers on the verifiability principle, Wittgenstein's notion of language-games was not fully developed. In addition, Schlick (1936/1979) maintains "that the only explanation which can work without any previous knowledge is the ostensive definition" (p. 458). This, Wittgenstein rejects in his 1930-1932 Cambridge lectures (see Lee, 1980). One aspect of Gergen's misappropriation involves an interpretation of Wittgenstein's meaning-as-use thesis in the strict sense wherein the meaning of a word is its use and the use of a word is its meaning (see, for example, Gergen, 1986). Yet, in his *Last Writings*, Wittgenstein (1982) states that not every use is a meaning (p. 289).

REFERENCES

Carnap, R. (1928/1967). *The logical structure of the world: Pseudoproblems in philosophy*. London: Routledge & Kegan Paul.

Carnap, R. (1934/1937). *The logical syntax of language*. London: Kegan Paul, Trench, Trubner & Co.

Coffa, J. A. (1991). *The semantic tradition from Kant to Carnap: To the Vienna station*. Cambridge: Cambridge University Press.

Friedman, M. (1991). The re-evaluation of logical positivism. *The Journal of Philosophy, 88,* 505-519.

Gergen, K. J. (1985). Social pragmatics and the origins of psychological discourse. In K. J. Gergen & K. E. Davis (Eds), *The social construction of the person* (pp. 111-127). New York: Springer-Verlag.

Gergen, K. J. (1986). Correspondence versus autonomy in the language of understanding human action. In D. W. Fiske & R. A. Shweder (Eds), *Metatheory in social science* (pp. 136-162). Chicago: The University of Chicago Press.

Gergen, K. J. (1994a). *Realities and relationships: Soundings in social construction*. Cambridge: Harvard University Press.

Gergen, K. J. (1994b). Exploring the postmodern: Perils or potentials? *American Psychologist, 49,* 412-416.

Hibberd, F. J. (in press-a). Gergen's social constructionism, logical positivism and the continuity of error. Part I: Conventionalism. *Theory & Psychology*.

Hibberd, F. J. (in press-b). Gergen's social constructionism, logical positivism and the continuity of error. Part II: Meaning as use. *Theory & Psychology*.

Lee, D. (Ed.). (1980). *Wittgenstein's lectures, Cambridge 1930-1932,* from the notes of John King and Desmond Lee. Oxford: Basil Blackwell.

Reichenbach, H. (1920/1965). *The theory of relativity and a priori knowledge* (M. Reichenbach, Trans.). Berkeley: University of California Press.

Schlick, M. (1917/1979). Appearance and essence. In H. L. Mulder & B. F. B. van de Velde-Schlick (Eds) *Moritz Schlick: Philosophical papers* (Vol. I, pp. 270-287). Dordrecht: D. Reidel Publishing.

180

Schlick, M. (1925/1974). *General theory of knowledge*. (2nd ed.). Wien: Springer-Verlag.

Schlick, M. (1936/1979). Meaning and verification. In H. L. Mulder & B. F. B. van de Velde-Schlick (Eds), *Moritz Schlick: Philosophical papers* (Vol. II, pp. 456-481). Dordrecht: D. Reidel Publishing.

Uebel, T. E. (1996). Anti-foundationalism and the Vienna Circle's revolution in philosophy. *British Journal for the Philosophy of Science, 47,* 415-440.

Wittgenstein, L. (1982). *Last writings on the philosophy of psychology*. (Vol. I). Oxford: Basil Blackwell.

WITTGENSTEIN AND SOCIAL CONSTRUCTIONISM:

Methods of "Social Poetics" or "Knots in our Thinking"?

Gavin B. Sullivan
University of Western Sydney

SUMMARY

Given the increasing value placed on reflexive and discursive investigations in psychology by social constructionists, this paper examines the ongoing debate about the relevance of Wittgenstein's later philosophy to the practices of psychology. Shotter, for example, argues that Wittgenstein provides psychologists with "methods of social poetics". While the position adopted here is sympathetic to the view that a conceptual-discursive examination of the detail of our cultural and linguistic practices provides a valuable, shared and non-theoretical resource for potential multidisciplinary investigation, it is debatable whether Wittgenstein would countenance the "insertion" of his philosophical methods into the practices of psychology. Wittgenstein's aim was to disentangle psychologist's conceptual problems rather than present the discipline with radically new methods for the discipline which, as Shotter suggests, reject a central role for the "way of theory". Therefore, it is by engaging with Wittgenstein's philosophy to work through doubts about the conceptual adequacy of particular theories and the meaning of such phrases as "a Wittgensteinian practice in psychology" that we can begin to remove "knots in our thinking" about the enduring relevance of Wittgenstein's philosophical method to critical psychological investigations.

INTRODUCTION

In recent years a number of interpretations of Wittgenstein's (1953, 1967,

1974, 1976, 1979, 1980a, 1980b) later philosophy have emerged which can be contrasted with more traditional and limited examples of relevant philosophical exegesis.[1] This is not to deny that the philosophical work exemplified by authors such as Baker and Hacker (1985), Budd (1989) or Cioffi (1998) provides important detail about the strengths and weaknesses of Wittgenstein's particular remarks and arguments. However, one problem with strict philosophical interpretations of Wittgenstein's remarks about psychology and psychological phenomena is that they often fail to engage with the work of psychologists in clinical, research and pedagogical practice. While these divisions of intellectual labour have an obvious basis in the disciplines of philosophy and psychology, my main interest is the work of individuals within the human sciences who attempt to apply and extend Wittgenstein's philosophical remarks and methods.

Social constructionists, in particular, have taken on the difficult task of interpreting and applying Wittgenstein's philosophy by demonstrating the conceptual problems of social psychology and cognitive science. A further concern is to show that empirical and quantitative work often ignores discourse as the primary medium for creating and maintaining everyday reality (e.g., Harré, 1986; Harré & Gillett, 1994). The work of social constructionists therefore is more likely to address the relevance and limits of Wittgenstein's philosophy to theoretical and practical aspects of psychology. However, the focus of this paper is not to detail the connections between Wittgenstein's later philosophy and "new paradigm" studies in the human sciences which are based on or, at the very least, inspired by Wittgensteinian philosophical critiques of psychology[1]. Instead, I shall examine John Shotter's more specific (1992, 1996, 1999; see also Shotter & Katz (1996) and Katz & Shotter (1996a, 1996b)) "methods of social poetics" account of Wittgenstein's writings. And if the argument succeeds, it will demonstrate that the espousal of new Wittgensteinian "poetic" methods in psychology is itself an example of what Wittgenstein (1975) generally described as "knots in our thinking" (§2).

REFLEXIVE WORK WITHIN PSYCHOLOGY AND WITTGENSTEIN'S LATER PHILOSOPHY: Similarities and Differences

There are several reasons why theoretical and critical psychologists attempt to usurp aspects of Wittgenstein's philosophical work for their own non-philosophical ends. One central reason is that Wittgenstein adopts a critical stance towards everyday psychological activities and concepts by attempting to represent accurately our conversational and cultural practices. In many cases, Wittgenstein's work is the direct inspiration for the "turn to language" that is closely connected with an emphasis on reflexivity in psychology (Parker, 1998). So while Wittgenstein's (1953, 1979, 1980a) remarks in the *Philosophical Investigations, On Certainty,* and *Culture and Value,* for example, are often poetic, challenging and difficult to read, they nevertheless appear to have great potential for the human sciences. And the only limits on the potential to explore the rich connections between Wittgenstein's writings and psychology appear to be personal and practical since it is easily possible for individuals to use Wittgenstein's remarks to extend their own critical reflections on thought, the self and emotions from criticisms of particular theoretical and empirical work (e.g., Harré, 1986) through to the broadest debates about relativism and realism (e.g., Parker, 1998; Shotter, 1992).

Wittgenstein (1953) examines the details of "actual language" (§107) and adopts a descriptive approach to conceptual problems which leads him to avoids theoretical summaries of practices. Because of this descriptive approach his work acknowledges the "discovery" of discursive psychology: that it is often extremely difficult to represent clearly our conversational activities and related knowledge practices from within these activities and practices. Wittgenstein's (1953) alternative is to assemble "reminders" (§127) of our use of language especially where we are tempted to favour generalizations and "theories" over crucial discursive details. And Wittgenstein (1953) employs notions such as "form of life" and "language games" as philosophical tools to highlight and describe important differences within linguistic and cultural practices:

> Our clear and simple language-games are not preparatory studies for a future regularization of language—as it were first approximations, ignoring friction and air-resistance. The language-games are rather set up as *objects of comparison* which are meant to throw light on the fact of our language by way not only of similarities, but also of dissimilarities. (§130)

Because we always work within language, statements about getting outside of language to reality are revealed as nonsensical because such language-games, so to speak, do not provide a general theory of linguistic practices or describe a relation between language or thought and reality. For what useful purpose could be served by contradicting "grammatical propositions" such as "my images are private" (1953, §251), "every rod has a length" (1974, §83) or "theories are language games" other than to create examples of "idle", ungrammatical and nonsensical language (1953, §132)?

This is not to deny that there is an "outside" (cf. Wittgenstein, 1953, §103) to our practices in the more useful sense in which it is possible for us to offer mistaken accounts of cultural practices and linguistic communities other than our own: for example, to be wrong about an individual from another culture despite recognizing that commonalities of judgement and behavior in human "forms of life" provide the basis for our potential translation of their statements, expressions and actions. Rather, the main point in relation to psychology is to be clear about the limits of philosophy to represent more specialized discourses from the "outside" perspective of an individual who is not immersed in them. In this regard, Wittgenstein's dismissal of a pre-eminent role for philosophy because of its potential to produce only a "certain jargon" (1976, p. 293) makes it difficult to ignore the similarities between the reflexivity of Wittgenstein's "turn to language" and the increasing value placed on reflexive and discursive research within psychology.

However, the potential use of Wittgenstein's methods to advance the aims of psychology has largely been limited to those social constructionists who have not only engaged with Wittgenstein's remarks about "forms of life", "language games" and achieving an "übersicht" or "surview" of a domain of grammar (Baker & Hacker, 1985), but also have accepted Wittgenstein's (1953) criticism that the uneasy confluence of experimental methods and conceptual confusion in psychology continues to make "us think we have the means of solving the problems which trouble us; though problem and method pass one another by" (p. 232). The implications of the remarks that constitute Wittgenstein's comments on rule-following and the "private language argument" (Baker & Hacker, 1985) can also be found in discursive treatments of cognitive psychology (e.g., Harré & Gillett, 1994) and developmental psychology (Jost, 1995). Parker (1998) therefore argues that discursive work of this type:

> ... represents a critical reflexive movement away from mental paraphernalia in each individual's head towards a socially mediated and historically situated study of action and experience. (p. 1)

Thus it seems reasonable to claim that changes inspired by Wittgenstein's work (or similar philosophical perspectives) underpin the "increasing interest" in "approaches which locate the stuff of psychology in discourse in particular" and "social constructionist perspectives in psychology in general" (p. 1).

The effects of Wittgenstein's "vast influence in the field of social science" (Trigg, 1991, p. 209) can also be argued to have permeated to saturation point in some areas, with the result that it is now worthwhile to revisit Wittgenstein's work and to reevaluate uses of his philosophy by psychologists. The following questions are particularly germane because the answers provided by social constructionists may not be ones that Wittgenstein himself would accept. Does Wittgenstein really invite "us" to blur the boundaries between philosophy and particular human sciences when he suggests that "we" recognize the distance between conceptual problems and experimental methods (1953, p. 232)? Should we avoid the scientistic (and realistic) aim of trying to "penetrate phenomena" (1953, §90) because Wittgenstein says "nothing is hidden" (1953, §435)? Must we concede that "we may not advance any kind of theory" (1953, §109) and avoid all theories or explanations in psychology? Finally, should we realize that many of "our" considerations "could not be scientific ones" (1953, §109) if Wittgenstein is only attempting to make us acknowledge that philosophy "neither explains nor deduces anything" (1953, §126)?

Although it is tempting for psychologists to include ourselves within Wittgenstein's use of "us", Wittgenstein does not always talk of "our" problems in a way that is completely compatible with the aims and projects of social constructionists (see next section and also Rundle, 1995). For example, while the listed features of Wittgenstein's philosophy appeal to social constructionists, other Wittgensteinian remarks indicate that his philosophy should not be used to "reform" (1953, §132), "interfere with" (1953, §124) or provide foundations for existing language. Nevertheless, an "outside" philosophical perspective may still engage psychologists in the common task of removing conceptual problems that can be found in particular areas of theory and practice. As Wittgenstein notes:

> Philosophy unties the knots in our thinking which we have tangled up in an absurd way; but to do that it must make movements which are just as complicated as the knots. Although the result of philosophy is simple, its methods for arriving there cannot be so. (1975, §2)

On this view, it is plausible to suggest that a psychologist's concerns about mainstream accounts of the self or emotions, for example, might connect with Wittgenstein's remarks on privacy and his attack on the possibility of a private language. But Wittgenstein's remarks do not have the status of work within the discipline of psychology even though they have considerable potential to prevent inappropriate investigations, remove sources of confusion and help psychologists to achieve clarity. Wittgenstein's philosophical remarks and the work of social constructionists can therefore both be described as reflexive, as long as we remind ourselves of other crucial differences.

An example of such a difference is the need to be aware that an "outsider's" philosophical critique cannot result in a coerced or dictated transformation of psychology. For at a number of points, Wittgenstein makes it clear that he did not wish to impose his philosophical findings on the practices of others. In particular, Wittgenstein acknowledged the considerable potential for a descriptive philosopher to interfere in the practice of mathematics and in this respect, his remarks about the relations between philosophy and mathematics are "entirely analogous" (1953, p. 232) to an understanding of the relations between philosophy and psychology:

186

> The philosopher easily gets into the position of a ham-fisted director, who, instead of doing his own work and merely supervising his employees to see they do their work well, takes over their jobs until one day he finds himself overburdened with other people's work while his employees watch and criticize him. (Wittgenstein, 1974, p. 369)

Wittgenstein clearly felt that his role was to comment upon problems in psychology but not to take over the work of psychologists. By extension, psychology is obviously regarded by Wittgenstein as an autonomous discipline that is as free to entangle itself in conceptual confusion as it is to acknowledge the validity of philosophical criticisms. The richness of Wittgenstein's methods and remarks therefore present us with a dilemma in our activities as reflexive psychologists. Do we follow and expand upon what Wittgenstein has written in a largely accepting manner or do we instead engage with some of his remarks and thus accept that we will need to reacquaint ourselves constantly with the whole of his philosophy?

At the end of the *Philosophical Investigations*, Wittgenstein acknowledged a number of important similarities between his remarks on psychology and mathematics which can be used here to provide further clarification of the differences between the practices of philosophy and psychology. Wittgenstein noted, for instance, that:

> . . . what a mathematician is inclined to say about the objectivity and reality of mathematical facts, is not a philosophy of mathematics, but something for philosophical *treatment*. (1953, §254)

The main point for our discussion of psychology is that it is similarly not a philosophy of psychology to compare psychologists' talk about similar problems (although such statements do provide the basis for philosophical investigation). Furthermore, in a point which is relevant to philosophical divisions within psychology, Wittgenstein argues:

> It is the business of philosophy, not to resolve a contradiction by means of a mathematical or logico-mathematical discovery, but to make it possible for us to get a clear view of the state of mathematics that troubles us: the state of affairs *before* the contradiction is resolved. (And this does not mean that one is sidestepping a difficulty). (1953, §125)

Wittgenstein then proceeds to highlight the source of the difficulty which is that although we have a practice in which rules have been laid down, occasionally "things do not turn out as we had assumed" (§125). In this case, when problems arise with "the civil status of a contradiction, or its status in civil life" (§125), Wittgenstein argues: "This entanglement in our rules is what we want to understand (i.e., get a clear view of)" (§125). My conclusion is that where Wittgenstein writes about what "we" are doing and "our problems" he seems to be talking mainly to other philosophers while also trying to engage the interest of psychologists in the task of untangling similar "knots in our thinking" (1975, §2).

SHOTTER'S "SOCIAL POETICS" ACCOUNT OF WITTGENSTEIN'S METHOD(S)

In contrast, John Shotter's "social poetics" account of Wittgenstein's philosophical method (or methods) is a more radical view of the relevance of Wittgensteinian practices to psychology. In particular, Shotter (1996, 1999) builds upon a social constructionist critique of realism and an appropriation of many of Wittgenstein's remarks about philosophy that we have already examined to suggest that:

> . . . the central methodological assumption of both social constructionism and Wittgenstein's work is that we should study the continuous, contingent flow of language-intertwined interaction between people. (p. 3)

On Shotter's view, Wittgenstein offers psychologists a host of innovative methods which can be inserted into the practice of psychology to achieve what is described in the philosophical literature as an "übersicht" (Baker & Hacker, 1985), "surview" or "synoptic view" of the grammar of a particular psychological concept (or cluster of concepts). A surview is generated when we begin to examine the detail of the use of language in a particular area, assemble linguistic reminders of language-use instead of providing definitions, collect these examples into some form of "survey able" (Shotter, 1999, p. 28) whole and resist the temptation to organize or complete the detail produced on the basis of a psychological investigation or "logico-psychological" discovery (i.e., through empirical work or the creation of a new theoretical concept).

Shotter (1996, 1999) also illustrates the notion of a surview by contrasting it sharply with what is achieved in psychology by following the "way of theory". This critical account of theory in psychology extends Wittgenstein's disdain for theorizing in philosophy and concurs with specific comments by Wittgenstein about approaches to the representation of psychological concepts. For example, at one point Wittgenstein (1953) investigates whether it is possible for a person to attain "'expert judgement' about the genuineness of expressions of feeling" (p. 227). While Wittgenstein acknowledges that "correcter prognoses will generally issue from the judgments of those with a better knowledge of mankind" (p. 227), his primary aim is to dislodge the notion that there are "techniques" to be learned and a complete system to be discovered (p. 227). Instead of summarizing this expertise in terms of rules or theories, it is better to accept that even "the most general remarks yield at best what looks like the fragments of a system" (p. 228). Wittgenstein implies that a mastery of theory-based rules, concepts and categories cannot substitute for the experience of applying particular concepts and making appropriate judgements in everyday practice. Moreover, Wittgenstein's remarks provide further insights into his general criticism of inappropriate and "falsifying" accounts of psychological phenomena which are to be dismissed by "renouncing all theory" and coming to "regard what appears obviously incomplete, as something complete" (1980b, §723; 1953, p. 227).

Shotter (1999) argues that this Western "urge to theorize" manifests itself in a compulsion "to collect diverse phenomena (to do both with our world and ourselves) together within an explanatory *framework of belief*" (p. 28). According to Shotter (1996) we should not only abandon "theory-first" approaches in psychology, but also use Wittgenstein's philosophy to resist theory in other ways:

> . . . a part of Wittgenstein's philosophy has to do with trying to help us overcome this urge to turn to the "way of theory" whenever we find ourselves faced with questions about why we act as we do. To this end, Wittgenstein redescribes in a more practical way many topics and events that we are tempted to put into theoretical terms. (p. 8)

Shotter's overall aim, therefore, is to "show how the methods of philosophical investigations he outlines can also be used to great effect in our everyday affairs" (Shotter & Katz, 1996, pp. 213-214). And he provides considerable detail about ways in which we can take Wittgensteinian remarks and place them in the context of psychological debate or, alternatively, attempt to copy Wittgenstein's ability to write "poetically" in terms of "striking phrases" and "arresting moments". Shotter and Katz (1996; see also Katz & Shotter, 1996a, 1996b) offer examples of how this approach can be used to encourage trainee doctors to "hear the patient's voice" and, more generally, to develop "reflective practitioners" (Schon, 1995) who will rival those individuals who rely less critically on manuals, guidelines or a particular theoretical perspective.

Naturally, we need further illustrations of how Wittgenstein's methods are supposed to work in the practice of psychology in order to change what we do. In this respect, a good test-case of Shotter's approach might be the complicated relational-responsive practices of laughter and humour, since we are often struck by the fact that we cannot explain why a particular joke is funny or how we produce a funny line "out of thin air" in the cut and thrust of conversation. A

Wittgensteinian approach could examine how we learned our practices and discourses of laughter: for example, by examining how jokes replace more primitive expressive activities in childhood such as tickling or peek-a-boo games, perhaps recalling the childhood incomprehensibility of adults' humour, and also examining the different functions performed by laughter expressions (e.g., nervous laughter, denial, indications of evil intent, etc.). Moreover, we could expand our inquiry to investigate the similarities and differences between laughter, humour, satire, pleasure, wit, sarcasm and their related linguistic practices and particular cultural forms such as novels, comics, cartoons, and situation comedies (i.e., as they are "consumed" or used by cinema audiences, stand-up comedians, teachers, and even philosophers (see Wittgenstein, 1953, §111).

A host of issues would then be raised which, while they formed a surview of laughter practices, would not easily be captured by a general theory of humour or emotion. Engaging in this type of investigation would quickly improve an understanding of "what is involved in a group of people coming to a more articulate grasp of their practices from within their ongoing conduct of them" (Shotter & Katz, 1996, p. 219). It is also likely that individuals engaging in this type of investigation would gain a surreptitious practical mastery of the discourses involved which could then be potentially deployed, "tested" and refined in conversation. This is possibly what Shotter and Katz (1996) mean when they argue that:

> . . . what a social poetics can do for us, when put to work within our practices, is to give us a better knowledge of our 'way about' inside them, and to enable us, in their details and subtleties, to see possible new ways forward — ways that are easily obscured by the rules and principles we already have in place for their 'good ordering'. (p. 234)

This type of critical practice would therefore allow psychologists to give prominence to the discursive nature of our participation in many practices and present, for subsequent discussion, important linguistic details "which our ordinary forms of language easily make us overlook" (Wittgenstein, 1953, §132).

CENTRAL PROBLEMS WITH THE "METHODS OF SOCIAL POETICS" ACCOUNT

Despite considerable sympathy towards Shotter's account due to my own similar work to produce a Wittgenstein-inspired surview of pride, several problems need to be addressed. The central issue is the argument that the methodological similarities between Wittgenstein's philosophy and reflexive,

190

social constructionist work within psychology supports the "insertion" of a Wittgensteinian practice into psychology. Although Shotter contrasts the results of a surview with the products of the "way of theory", there seems to be no reason to think that the results of a comprehensive conceptual-discursive examination of particular cultural and linguistic practices *must* replace existing theoretical and empirical work within psychology. If the aim is to demonstrate that a surview can be regarded as providing a valuable, shared and non-theoretical resource for potential multidisciplinary investigation without necessarily including a survey of all relevant psychological theories and studies then it is reasonable. Clearly, we would not want to use a survey of psychological theories and studies as the sole basis for an understanding of the complicated practices surrounding laughter and humour.

However, it is likely that the theories and studies of psychology will be sources of confusion or "knots in our thinking" that we might want to unravel in subsequent work. This is not to deny the possibility of restricting ourselves to the attempts of ordinary people to talk about the private experiences in a way that might invite a subsequent dialogue about their uninformative or nonsensical explanations (e.g., Wittgenstein, 1953, §298). But we are really concerned with the type of "knowing our way about" that can occur in psychology once conceptual problems perhaps connected with particular theories or explanations have been disentangled, rather than the remarks of a neophyte psychologist about private and public experiences of laughter and humour. An illustration of this point is given by the fact that even Wittgenstein engaged with and criticised Freud's "explanation" of jokes in terms of unconscious causation. The aim was, as Cioffi (1998) puts in, in order to "confine Freud to a discourse for which the assent of the subject is an appropriate criterion" (p. 130; i.e., of the correctness of a psychoanalytic interpretation). Wittgenstein therefore engaged with Freud's work and, in the process, highlighted commitments that can be described as metapsychological.

In contrast, on Shotter's view becoming critical and reflexive about such aspects of our lives as humour, emotion or selfhood also involves a practice which has the aim of "sensitizing us to the fleeing and momentary events that we are 'struck by' in some way, events which are novel and unrepeatable" (Shotter & Katz, 1996, p. 215). To achieve this end, Shotter (1996) argues that psychologists can make "careful use of selected images, similes, or metaphors . . . to make reflective contemplation of their nature possible" (p. 10). However, by reducing the importance of theory and replacing it with an approach in which we collect and collate "striking examples", Shotter's approach seems to delay the development of theoretical and other advanced "abilities" such as the potential:

> To send messages; to fully understand each other; to routinely and skilfully discourse upon a subject matter; to be able to "reach out," so to

speak, from within a language-game and talk about the "contacts" one has made, and to formulate "theories" as to the nature of what is "out there": all these abilities are, or can be, later developments. (p. 9)

The account also overlooks the fact that it is possible to be truly critical of a theory or position only after its interrelated concepts, examples, and internal logic have been mastered. While it is important to reject a theory-first approach to the training of psychologists, critical work is appropriate to particular stages of an individual's "reflexive career". For example, criticism that is too sceptical, radical or early in one's training and which is not supported by a mastery of appropriate theoretical concepts and issues demonstrates an inability "to know one's way about". If adopted in a widespread manner, such a critical approach could have the unintended consequence of producing a discipline in which psychologists are able to avoid the hard work of conceptual criticism. This point is relevant to Shotter's account because it is possible that the radical practice of employing "methods of social poetics" and avoiding theory may produce practitioners without the same skills as their instructors because they have had much of the hard "disentangling" work done for them.

Although this seems to be a conservative view of Wittgenstein's remarks and methods, the aim is to show why philosophical writings such as Wittgenstein's have an enduring relevance which cannot be replaced by adopting ostensibly similar methods in psychology. Indeed, my argument is that describing Wittgenstein's philosophy as a method of "social poetics" *is* an example of a "knot in our thinking". Such remarks indicate conceptual problems that need to be worked through and shown to be problematic in order for us to demonstrate that we know our way around the discipline of psychology. Phrases such as "inserting a Wittgensteinian practice into psychology" promote confusion about the relations between philosophy and psychology because they suggest that we may take the lessons and methods of philosophical positions such as Wittgenstein's to further bolster the autonomy and reflexivity of our discipline. And although many social constructionists obviously have the skill necessary to move back-and-forth between philosophy and psychology, the radical consequence of the "method of social poetics" account may be to encourage future practitioners who are able to postpone or avoid engaging in a similar struggle.

192

Note

1. This paper is a shortened version of an argument which will be presented in a full-length form at a later date in order to address the many issues raised by radical and conservative readings of the relevance and limits of Wittgenstein's philosophy to psychology.

REFERENCES

Baker, G. P., & Hacker, P. M. S. (1985). *Wittgenstein: Rules, grammar and necessity Vol. 3.* Oxford: Blackwell

Budd, M. (1989). *Wittgenstein's philosophy of psychology.* London: Routledge

Cioffi, F. (1998). *Wittgenstein on Freud and Frazer.* Cambridge: Cambridge University Press.

Harré, R. (Ed.) (1986). *The social construction of emotions.* Oxford: Blackwell.

Harré, R., & Gillet, G. (1994). *The discursive mind.* London: Sage.

Jost, J. T. (1995). Toward a Wittgensteinian social psychology of human development. *Theory and Psychology, 5,* 5-25.

Katz, A., & Shotter, J. (1996a). Articulating practices: Methods and experiences. Resonances from within the practice: social poetics in a mentorship program. *Concepts and Transformation, 1,* 239-247.

Katz, A., & Shotter, J. (1996b). Hearing the patient's voice: Toward a "social poetics" in diagnostic interviews. *Social Science and Medicine, 43,* 919-931.

Parker, I. (Ed.) (1998). *Social constructionism, discourse and realism.* London: Sage.

Rundle, B. (1995). Analytical philosophy and psychology. In J. A. Smith, R. Harré, & L. V. Langenhove (Eds), *Rethinking psychology.* London: Sage.

Schon, D. A. (1995). *Reflective practitioner: How professionals think in action.* Aldershot: Arena.

Shotter, J. (1992). Social constructionism and realism: Adequacy or accuracy? *Theory and Psychology, 2,* 175-182.

Shotter, J. (1996). Wittgenstein in practice: from the way of theory to a social poetics. In C. W. Tolman, F. Cherry, R., van Hezewijk, & I. Lubek (Eds), *Problems of theoretical Psychology.* North York, Ontario: Captus Press.

Shotter, J. (1999). Problems with the "way of theory". In Maiers, W., Bayer, B., Esgalhado, B. D., Jorna, R., & Schraube, E. (Eds). *Challenges to theoretical psychology.* Captus: Ontario.

Shotter, J., & Katz, A. (1996). Articulating practices: Methods and experiences. Articulating a practice from within the practice itself: Establishing formative dialogues by the use of a "social poetics." *Concepts and Transformations, 2,* 213-237.

Trigg, R. (1991). Wittgenstein and social science. In A. P. Griffiths (Ed.), *Wittgenstein centenary Essays: Royal Institute of Philosophy Supplement, Vol. 28.* Cambridge: Cambridge University Press.

Wittgenstein, L. (1953). *Philosophical investigations.* (G. E. M. Anscombe, trans.). Oxford: Blackwell.

Wittgenstein, L. (1967). *Zettel.* G. E. M. Anscombe and G. H. von Wright (Eds). (G. E. M. Anscombe, trans.). Oxford: Blackwell.

Wittgenstein, L. (1974). *Philosophical grammar.* R. Rhees (Ed.). (A. Kenny, trans.). Oxford: Blackwell.

Wittgenstein, L. (1975). *Philosophical remarks.* R. Rhees (Ed.). Oxford: Blackwell.

Wittgenstein, L. (1976). *Wittgenstein's lectures on the foundations of mathematics, Cambridge, 1939: From the notes of R.G. Bosanquet, Norman Malcolm, Rush Rhees and Yorick Smythies.* C. Diamond (Ed.). Hassocks: Harvester.

Wittgenstein, L. (1979). *On certainty.* G. E. M. Anscombe and G. H. von Wright (Eds). (D. Paul & G. E. M. Anscombe, trans.). Oxford: Blackwell.

Wittgenstein, L. (1980a). *Culture and value.* G. H. von Wright (Ed.). (P. Winch, trans.). Oxford: Blackwell.

Wittgenstein, L. (1980b). *Remarks on the philosophy of psychology Vol. I.* G. E. M. Anscombe & G. H. von Wright (Eds). (G. E. Anscombe, trans.). Oxford: Blackwell.

EPISTEMOLOGICAL FRAMINGS OF MYSTICISM:
Implications for Contemporary Western Psychology

Lee Spark Jones
University of Wollongong

SUMMARY

Mysticism is characterized by the spontaneous or deliberate attainment of specialized knowledge, which challenges the parameters of positivist science by virtue of its subjective and paradoxical nature. Mysticism locates the origin of knowing in the prehension of non-sensory experience, and conceptualizes reality as flux or process. Epistemological considerations of mysticism extend traditional psychological concern with mystical experience as an object of scientific inquiry. Beyond the constraints of scientism, framings of mystical knowledge from intuitionist, radical empiricist and postmodern standpoints highlight process, plurality and paradox in epistemological formulation. In a changing climate of increasing cross-cultural and interdisciplinary influence at metatheoretical levels, mysticism provokes radical epistemological re-evaluation. This is particularly necessary wherever mainstream psychology continues to limit, misinterpret or pathologize the spectrum of human experience and knowing.

INTRODUCTION

Accounts of mystical experience, and its impact on individual and collective life, occur throughout history in the oral traditions and written records of global culture.[1] Characterized by the pursuit and attainment of knowledge derived from subjective, unitary states of consciousness (Stace, 1960), mystical knowledge has been pursued, developed and documented in association with sophisticated systems of philosophical and psychological thought (Shapiro & Walsh, 1984).

Since its inception, modern psychology has manifested its philosophical antecedents' fascination with metaphysical questions, and has attempted to substantiate mystical experience in both subjective and objective terms. However, it has also tended to marginalize philosophical and subjective exploration of mysticism, and has constrained the study of mystical experience within the bounds of positivist science.

In the ensuing discussion, I suggest that scientistic bias limits psychological investigation of experience that is not readily conceptualized and quantified within the rational-empiricist frame of orthodox science. I propose that mysticism can be framed from various metatheoretical perspectives, disrupting received theories of knowledge and inviting re-evaluation of psychology's positivist parameters. Epistemological framings of mystical experience which lie outside or at the margins of rational-empiricism are discussed from the perspectives of intuitionism, postmodernism and radical empiricism. They point to the importance of pluralistic, perspectival and process-oriented perspectives in epistemological formulation. Process philosophy is emphasized as an important vehicle for interrelating these diverse, at times contradictory, perspectives (Frankenberry, 1987). In conclusion, I consider implications for contemporary psychology as a human science with a substantial applied component.

ISSUES IN THE DEFINITION OF MYSTICISM

Formal and specific definition of mysticism has proved problematic (Woods, 1981). Mystical experience is reportedly difficult to describe in words, and is varied and wide ranging. It may occur as a spontaneous event or be approached systematically, through non-religious and religious channels. Mystic elements are found in records of religions throughout the world, for example in the indigenous spirituality of Native American and Australian Aboriginal cultures; in theistic religions like Christianity, Judaism and Islam; in pantheistic religions such as Hinduism, and in atheistic religions such as Buddhism and Taoism. Transcendent experience, such as a spontaneous feeling of oneness with nature, may also be experienced outside religious belief and nomenclature (Griffin, 1990).

In the context of contemporary psychology, definition of mysticism has been shaped by the demands of empirical research. It has philosophical foundations in William James' (1985/1902) classic exploration of religious experience, was refined by Stace (1960) and was further operationalized by more recent psychologists of religion (Spilka, Hood & Gorsuch, 1985). In an increasingly secular and empirical approach to the study of mysticism, some theorists, such as James and Jung, saw mystical experience as a natural occurrence and were interested in the psychological patterns and processes underlying its description (Broadribb, 1995). Others such as Ribot, Janet and Freud, defined mystical experience as synonymous with psychopathological states (Wulff, 1991). Such differences have also been deemed more a matter of degree than rigid distinction (Broadribb, 1995).

James saw mystical experience as characterized by an event in which "the conscious person is continuous with a wider self through which saving experiences come" (James, 1985/1902, p. 405). Stace (1960) defined the core of mysticism more specifically as "the apprehension of an ultimate non-sensuous unity in all things which entirely transcends our sensory-intellectual consciousness" (p.14). Emphasizing non-sensory based, unitary consciousness as central to mysticism, Stace maintained that hallucinations, telepathy, precognition, clairvoyance and other parapsychological phenomena are neither universal nor necessary aspects of mystical experience, although they may accompany it. He identified two basic types of mysticism: extrovertive mysticism, characterized by a sense of the life in, and unity among, all things, and introvertive mysticism, distinguished by a non-spatial, non-temporal experience of unitary consciousness devoid of content. Stace saw both as occurring within and outside religious contexts and as characterized by five qualities: noetic, ineffable, holy (although not necessarily religious), marked by positive affect, and paradoxical. Griffin's (1990) definition echoes that of Stace, emphasizing the defining element of mysticism as "an experience in which there is direct, unmediated contact with another experience" (p. 7). Smart (1965) similarly defines mysticism as "a set of experiences or, more precisely, conscious events which are not described in terms of sensory experience or mental images" (p. 75). These conceptualizations accord with the etymology of mysticism, from its Greek root meaning "to close (the lips or eyes)... keep silence" (Oxford English Dictionary, 1933, p. 816), which emphasizes closing out sensory data, or non-mediation by the senses.

Debate over the classification and definition of mystical experience underlines a difficulty in arriving at any single definition. It also may reflect a lack of distinction between content-oriented definitions, emphasizing the "what" of mystical experience, and process-oriented definitions, which emphasize the "how". Researchers have largely been concerned with the content of mysticism and related quantifiable factors, such as the categorization of experience, contextual factors and demographic data. Process-focused approaches to definition, such as Griffin's (1990, p. 75) specification of "unmediated contact" tend to have been more neglected. Such definition, which highlights the noetic quality of mystical experience and centers on the process of knowing, is particularly relevant to my discussion. Raising questions about knowledge and the nature of reality, it suggests a need for metatheoretical re-evaluation and development, as well as empirical research, in the study of mysticism.

Mysticism is interwoven with culture, into the historical fabric of individual and collective life, but the degree to which it is spoken or written about varies, depending on cultural and temporal favor (O'Brian, 1964). Mystical experience is more generally evident in Buddhist and Hindu influenced cultures, for example, where mysticism is more apparent and accessible in religious tradition, than in those western European cultures where the mystical elements of Judeo-Christian religions are obscure. In the west, mysticism was most evident in the Middle Ages in church-dominated societies, then diminished in the seventeenth century, and became almost invisible under the influence of scientific and psychological worldviews which have dominated the last century or so (Wulff, 1991).

This rise and fall in the status of mysticism is also apparent in the history of academic psychology. In the philosophical origins of the discipline, and in early interest in transcendent experience, there is recognition of subjective and esoteric experience as a valid area of psychological concern. A subjective approach to the psychological study of mysticism is found in the work of William James, the depth psychologies of Freud, Jung and others, the experimental introspection of the Dorpat school, and phenomenological, existential and humanistic psychologies (Wulff, 1991). Objective research in the sub-disciplinary fields of the psychology of religion and transpersonal psychology in particular has provided empirical support for the validity and prevalence of mystical experience, and has amassed findings on altered states of consciousness, the frequency with which mystical experiences occur, their correlation with other aspects of human behavior, their physiological substrates, and other quantifiable data (Spilka et al., 1985). However, with the dominance of positivist and reductionist trends in psychology, the study of mysticism has not featured prominently in mainstream psychology, and has been treated with disregard and even disdain. There has been little exploration of the fit between mysticism as an object of research and the metatheoretical assumptions which underlie its scientific investigation.

EPISTEMOLOGICAL FRAMINGS OF MYSTICISM

My discussion so far has reviewed the psychological study of mysticism within the epistemological framework of rational-empiricism and the constraints of positivist science. Metatheoretical consideration of mysticism provokes recognition that knowledge may be theorized and communicated in more than one way. The following discussion centers on the juxtaposition of three epistemological framings: intuitionism, postmodernism and radical empiricism. In my exploration of these perspectives, I intend the realization of a degree of epistemological flexibility that theorizes mystical knowledge in various ways, and challenges psychology's received view of knowledge. Positivist epistemology insists on sensory perception as fundamental to valid knowledge, while rejecting the possibility of multiple, contradictory theories of knowledge and the conceptualization of reality as flux. Mysticism challenges psychology to acknowledge and accommodate plural, paradoxical and process-orientated perspectives on human knowing. Such theories disrupt scientistic assumptions about the theorization of knowledge, and evoke the potential for radical reconfiguration of epistemological difference.

Mysticism as Intuitionism

Intuitionism is "a form of holistic knowing which occurs without a discernible sequence of logical stages or a specifiable basis in sense data" (Madsen, 1988, p. 36). It is often associated with idealist theories of reality and views the origin of knowledge as the knowing subject, variously described as intuition, consciousness, the Self, or a named divinity. It therefore represents a subject-subject mode of knowing which differs fundamentally from dualistic (subject-object), sensory and intellectual processes of knowing. The theoretical exposition of intuitionism is particularly developed in non-western philosophies such as Hindu and Buddhist Tantrism and Taoism (Parrinder, 1976). In contemporary western psychology, the field of transpersonal psychology has perhaps come closest to recognizing intuitionist epistemology, due to its investigation of altered states of consciousness, and subsequent exposure to related philosophies (Walsh & Vaughan, 1980). However, this theoretical work tends to lack mainstream acknowledgment.

The framing of mysticism from an intuitionist perspective is illustrated in Wilber's (1983) interpretation of mysticism as an epistemology of transcendence. Drawing on a metaphor from the writings of two medieval mystics, St. Bonaventure and Hugh of St. Victor, Wilber discusses three "eyes" (pp. 3-12) of knowledge in relation to modes of knowing found in the major schools of traditional philosophy, religion and psychology. The "eye of the flesh" (*cogitatio*) perceives the material world of space, time and objects and determines empirical fact by means of sensorimotor intelligence. The "eye of reason" (*meditatio*) regards truth as philosophic insight determined through logic. The "eye of contemplation" (*contemplatio*) finds truth in spiritual wisdom, or knowledge of transcendent or intuitive realities. This type of knowledge is entirely subjective, and difficult to define or measure. However, it is commonly acknowledged in the literature of mysticism and in everyday life (Spilka et al., 1985). Experiences such as moments of intuitive insight and apprehension of unity are commonly reported by people and described as memorable, meaningful, and provocative of change in personality and life direction (Wulff, 1991).

Wilber (1983) suggests that each of these three complementary theories of knowledge has its own validity. Each field of knowledge has its own object (sensory, mental and transcendental) and cannot be unilaterally validated by empirical or logical criteria, which apply only to the first two "eyes" respectively. Instead, each type of knowledge must be validated separately by internally meaningful components or strands, through relevant instruction, application and communication (p. 31). The validity of the "eye of contemplation" therefore is founded in proficiency in introspective practice (such as the disciplines of the Christian mystic, Hindu Tantricist or Zen *roshi*), in consequent development of specific insight, and in recognition of this insight by others, who are similarly trained.

Wilber (1983) argues that modern scientism is associated with a category error of empirical positivism, in that the justificatory criteria of material empiricist science (the "eye of the flesh") is applied inappropriately to fields of knowledge which cannot be reduced to sensory data or rational argument. However, some of the most potent questioning of this bias comes again from physical science. The idea that material substance is fixed and unchanging has for some time been dismantled by physics, calling into question modern science's enduring emphasis on establishing the facts of objective experience and prompting developments in philosophies of science which address both physical and metaphysical realities (Baker, Mos, van Rappard & Stam, 1988).

Postmodern Perspectives on Mysticism

Emerging from the deconstruction of rational-empiricism, postmodern epistemology addresses the notion of reality as continuous flux, rather than static substance as posed by post-Newtonian science. It emphasizes situated, embodied (and therefore multiple) epistemologies and the importance of practical, everyday knowledge (Kvale, 1992). From this perspective, theorization of knowledge is founded in plurality and constructivism. Kvale (1992) identifies four basic themes in postmodern epistemology: foundationlessness, fragmentariness, constructivism and neo-pragmatism. Human knowing is represented as the outcome of cognitive schemes which impose order and meaning on the continuous flux of reality. Kvale observes that here the focus of knowledge generation is shifted from attempts to describe the real as it is in itself (theoretical knowledge and knowing "that") to practical knowledge and knowing "how" (programs to collect descriptions of actions that have effectively accomplished intended ends). The test of proof by this way of thinking is not in correspondence with the real, but in whether intended ends are accomplished by designated means.

Postmodern epistemological framings of mysticism fundamentally reject the essentialist idea that mystical experience represents an immediate or direct contact with an absolute principle. Like any other experience, mystical experience and the form in which it is expressed is held to be constructed by language and belief. The primary epistemological assumption on which such framings are based is that: "There are NO pure (i.e. unmediated) experiences ... all experience is processed through, organized by, and makes itself available to us in extremely complex epistemological ways. The notion of unmediated experience seems, if not self-contradictory, at best empty" (Katz, 1978, p. 26).

Postmodern thinking challenges the orthodox epistemological standpoint that it is logically impossible for contradictory theories of knowledge to apply to human knowing. In so doing, in my view, it supports the paradoxicality of mystical knowing. Mysticism represents a mode of knowing which defies the parameters of knowledge prescribed by modernist scientific thought. In its aversion to universals and emphasis on linguistic representation, postmodern thinking also questions traditional representations of mystical knowledge. The nature of this mode of knowing remains mysterious, a matter of ongoing formulation which invites contribution from various epistemological perspectives.

Mysticism From A Radical Empiricist Perspective

In contrast to intuitionist and postmodern approaches, which recognize plurality in the theorization of knowledge, some psychological theorists have tried to address epistemological problems in the scientific study of mysticism by remaining within and extending the rational-empiricist framework. The extension of this framework hinges on the re-definition of "experience", to include types of experience that are not sensorily based. William James, for example, saw experience as "a that in the instant field of the present" consisting of qualities, intentions and relations that are in constant flux (Durant, 1961). James' radical empiricist definition of experience broadens the classical empiricist definition of experience as sensation, to include will, interest, belief, feeling and a relational aspect.

James' thinking has much in common with elements of A. N. Whitehead's (1964, 1978) process philosophy, which elaborates on a non-sensory based theory of experience. Whitehead maintained that experience consists of a stream of momentary experiences, "each of which is a process of becoming. Each momentary experience arises out of and is internally constituted by its relations to the entire past world" (Griffin, 1990, p. 15). Whitehead proposed that mystical prehension, or perception that is not mediated by the senses, constantly occurs at an unconscious level, as in prehension of one's own body cells, or in memory as the direct, unmediated perception of past experiences. Griffin offers a useful clarificatory example of the difference between mediated and unmediated perception. The perception of a tree by means of the visual system represents indirect, mediated perception. The tree is separated from the observer by a chain of psycho-physiological events. Sensory data about the tree are received by the observer, while the tree's "experience" of itself is not. The observer's prehension of his or her own brain cells, through which the data is received, represents a form of unmediated perception, constantly occurring at unconscious levels. From Whitehead's perspective, prehension is thus "the most fundamental form of perception and the basis for the internal relationship of all things" (Frankenberry, 1987, p. 165).

From this perspective, mystical experience is simply the conscious apprehension of normally unconscious, unmediated perception (Griffin, 1990). There is an interesting parallel between this conceptualization and the distinction made in mystical tradition between knowing and "unknowing" (Forman, 1990, p. 30). While mystical experience occurs and is reported within linguistically and culturally constructed contexts (and is therefore subject to cognitive construction as postmodern thinkers suggest) mystics have repeatedly stated that the experience itself constitutes "unknowing", the cessation of thought or cognitive construction. In the literature of Christian mysticism (Forman, 1990) this is referred to as "forgetting" or *vergezzen* (by the Christian mystic Eckhart, for example) or as "unknowing" (by mystics such as Pseudo-Dionysius). Mysticism also employs a "mystical language of unsaying", based in metaphor and silence, to communicate "unknowing" (Sells, 1994, p.1). Non-western psychologies, including indigenous psychologies and oriental psychologies with a strong foundation in mysticism, recognize and employ this meta-language (Heelas & Lock, 1981). Whitehead's (1978) metaphysical elaboration on James' definition of experience and his description of the prehensory process point to the relation between bodily processes and the experience of timeless unity, nothingness or unknowing that mystics describe. Thus "the felt qualities associated with religious experiencing are no more ineffable than are any other modes of experience. They contain patterns that are ready to be experienced, whether as God in the West or as Emptiness in the East" (Frankenberry, 1987, p.187).

MYSTICISM AND PROCESS

Especially in a contemporary western context, theoretical framings of mysticism appear to be ad hoc mixtures of attempts to define the content of mystical knowledge and speculation as to the process whereby such knowledge occurs, bound within positivist parameters. Process philosophy, although largely ignored in western psychological circles, potentially contributes to theorizing mystical knowing. Process is an overarching term in eastern and western philosophies which privileges change over stasis, flow over events and dynamics over essences. Process philosophies contradict realist tradition by emphasizing the flux of experience as the nature of reality. Examples include the thought of Heraclitus, Hegel, Jung and Whitehead, and Taoist philosophy. As an illustration of how process assumptions can underlie and link disparate, apparently contradictory epistemological perspectives, Frankenberry (1987) explores the importance of process in the philosophy of religion, by analyzing the interrelationship between western process philosophy in radical empiricist thought (exemplified by James, Dewey, Loomer and others), Whitehead's process metaphysics and the eastern process philosophy of Abhidharma Buddhism. Implicit in Frankenberry's analysis is the suggestion that a process approach to epistemological formulation is better suited to the metatheoretical conceptualization of mysticism than the assumptions underlying positivist psychology. There is a need to go beyond the constraints of western intellectual tradition, and the interface between eastern and western process philosophies must be explored at sophisticated levels, if subjective experience is to be theorized adequately (Hall, 1982).

As the preceding discussion has shown, mysticism may be framed from various epistemological perspectives. As Frankenberry (1987) notes, a complete epistemological formulation of mysticism is yet to be developed fully, but is supported by recognition of the importance of a process perspective. She observes:

> If sense data are not the raw stuff of experience, and actuality is about a changing, relational entity which is as much affectional as it is materially substantive, conventional modes of inquiry into the true nature of things are ultimately going to prove inadequate. There needs to be a theory of knowledge, a means of conceptualizing and knowing, a methodology which can give direct knowledge of this actuality as much as a sensory based knowledge process can give grounds for knowledge of the physical world at that level. (p. 157)

In my view, this call for epistemological development is implicit in mysticism, and particularly relevant to psychology wherever a rigid adherence to scientistic theorization of knowledge persists. Intuitionism, postmodern theory and radical empiricism all point to the insufficiency of positivist epistemology in addressing the full spectrum of human knowing.

The thinking of James, Whitehead and Wilber suggests that mystical knowledge derives from an apperceptive process which involves the coming-to-consciousness of normally unconscious, unmediated prehension of non-sensory, non-rational experience. Thus mysticism recognizes knowledge (variously described as intuition, transcendence, prehension, the cessation of thought or "unknowing") as derived from direct or non-sensory apprehension of an affective, relational and constantly fluctuating reality which underlies the sense data of the phenomenal world. It points to the inherent paradox, expressed in a great many mystical writings, of a plural and diverse world experienced as an ecstatic unity. Postmodern thinking underlines the importance of recognizing perspectival, paradoxical and pluralistic perspectives, as well as practical, utilitarian approaches to knowledge justification, in epistemological formulations of mysticism.

IMPLICATIONS FOR CONTEMPORARY WESTERN PSYCHOLOGY

The question remains as to the implications of such epistemological re-evaluation for psychology. At the level of theory, it should be evident that ongoing refinement of theoretical and metatheoretical concepts is particularly necessary where the tenor of theorization is incongruent with that which is theorized. I suggest that this is the case in mainstream psychology's response to mysticism as an object of scientistic inquiry. In addition, epistemological formulations of mysticism have important implications at the level of psychological practice.

In its close association with psychiatry, psychology has tended to treat mystical experience and related behavior as abnormal and to relegate them to levels of psychopathology or inconsequence (Neher, 1980). Individuals who experience, experiment with, or systematically induce altered states of consciousness continue to be misunderstood, ridiculed and mistreated wherever scientistic assumptions inform professional response. Professionals who adopt an open and accepting stance toward clients' altered states of awareness often meet with suspicion and discredit (Deikman, 1982). Theorist-practitioners who demonstrate acceptance of the spectrum of mystical experience may lose psychological standing. A comment such as Lundin's (1991) disparaging opinion about C. G. Jung in a standard psychological text is illustrative: "In the kindest sense, perhaps, we should consider him a mystic philosopher, rather than a psychologist" (p. 330). In contrast, Deikman (1982) suggests that western psychology must acknowledge the mystical side of those it attempts to help and that the teachings of the mystic traditions should be incorporated into psychology's approach to psychotherapy. Recognition of mysticism as a valid and distinct mode of knowing challenges psychology's metatheoretical assumptions, and invites epistemological shifts which promote a more understanding and respectful response to mystical experience in clinical practice and everyday life.

The pluralism of contemporary psychology is being increasingly recognized. Cross-cultural and interdisciplinary influence at metatheoretical levels is making itself felt, creating a more receptive climate for the radical epistemological re-evaluation mysticism provokes. Mysticism, by etymological definition, is concerned with the mysterious or unknown, the "penumbral totality" as Whitehead (1964, p.132) puts it. Similarly, at its core, epistemology is not about what is already known, but what is yet to be discovered. Epistemological theory directs the human urge to know about knowledge into hitherto unexplored dimensions. Thus metatheoretical considerations of mysticism may shed more light on the nature and process of human knowing, while also preserving its mystery.

Note

1.   Thanks to Beth Marlow, Doug Cornford and Nadia Crittenden for their helpful comments and advice.

REFERENCES

Baker, W. J., Mos, L. P., van Rappard, H., & Stam, H. J. (Eds) (1988). *Recent trends in theoretical psychology.* New York: Springer-Verlag.

Broadribb, D. (1995). *The mystical chorus: Jung and the religious dimension.* New York: Millennium Books.

Deikman, A. J. (1982). *The observing self: Mysticism and psychotherapy.* Boston: Beacon Press.

Durant, W. (1961). *The story of philosophy: The lives and opinions of the great philosophers of the western world.* NewYork: Simon and Schuster.

Forman, R. K. C. (1990). *The problem of pure consciousness: Mysticism and philosophy.* New York: Oxford University Press.

Frankenberry, N. (1987). *Religion and radical empiricism.* New York: State University of New York Press.

Griffin, D. R. (Ed.) (1990). *Sacred interconnections: Postmodern spirituality, political economy and art.* New York: State University of New York Press.

Hall, D. L. (1982). *The uncertain phoenix.* New York: Fordham University Press.

Heelas, P. & Lock, A. (1981). *Indigenous psychologies: The anthropology of the self.* London: Academic Press.

James, W. (1985/1902). *The varieties of religious experience.* Cambridge MA.: Harvard University Press.

Katz, S. T. (1978). Language, epistemology and mysticism. In S. T. Katz (Ed.), *Mysticism and philosophical analysis* (pp 22-74). New York: Oxford University Press.

Kvale, S. (Ed.) (1992). *Psychology and postmodernism.* London: Sage Publications.

Lundin, R. W. (1991). *Theories and systems of psychology.* (4th ed.). Lexington MA: D. C. Heath & Co.

Madsen, K. B. (1988). *A history of psychology in metascientific perspective.* Amsterdam: Elsevier Science Publishing.

206

Neher, A. (1980). *The psychology of transcendence*. Englewood Cliffs NJ: Prentice Hall, Inc.

O'Brian, E. (1964). *Varieties of religious experience*. New York: Holt, Rinehart and Winston. *Oxford English Dictionary*. (1933). London: Oxford University Press.

Parrinder, G. (1976). *Mysticism in the world's religions*. London: Sheldon Press.

Sells, M. A. (1994). *Mystical languages of unsaying*. Chicago: University of Chicago Press.

Shapiro, D. H., Jr. & Walsh, R. N. (Eds) (1984). *Meditation: Classic and contemporary perspectives*. New York: Aldine.

Smart, N. (1965). Interpretation and mystical experience. *Religious Studies, 1*, 75-87.

Spilka, B., Hood, R.W. & Gorsuch, R.L. (1985). *The psychology of religion: An empirical approach*. Englewood Cliffs, NJ: Prentice-Hall.

Stace, W.T. (1960). *The teachings of the mystics*. New York: Mentor.

Walsh, R. N. & Vaughan, F. (1980). *Beyond ego: Transpersonal dimensions in psychology*. Los Angeles: J. P. Tarcher, Inc.

Whitehead, A.N. (1964). *Science and philosophy*. Paterson, NJ: Littlefield, Adams and Co.

Whitehead, A.N. (1978). *Process and reality*. New York: The Free Press.

Wilber, K. (1983). *Eye to eye: The quest for the new paradigm*. Garden City, NY: Anchor Books.

Woods, R. (1981). *Understanding mysticism*. London: The Athlone Press.

Wulff, D. (1991). *The psychology of religion: Classic and contemporary views*. New York: Wiley.

IDEALIZATION IN SCIENCE:
A Methodological Reflection

Christopher Peet
University of Alberta

SUMMARY

Drawing from the example of Sigmund Koch's work, this paper examines the notion of scientific objectivity. Understanding "scientific objectivity" as a particular ideal which orients the production of scientific knowledge, I propose that scientific practitioners perform an idealization of their subject matter. This idealization is tacitly embedded within what Koch calls the "analytical pattern" of science. I speculate on the history of this embedding, sketching a route for the development of the notion of "scientific objectivity" from "pre-objective" phenomenal experience to the elaborated skillful activity of the scientific investigator. In the context of this skillful activity, idealization guides the making explicit of the tacitly experienced subject matter. It acts as a guide in the embodying of a set of values which the scientist upholds.

INTRODUCTION

This paper is guided by a particular trajectory initiated by Sigmund Koch, although it draws upon the work of both Michael Polanyi and Maurice Merleau-Ponty as well.[1] My concern is with the notion of scientific objectivity as a fundamental ideal which orients the production of scientific knowledge. I argue that the notion of objectivity performs this orienting function, in part, through suggesting to the scientific investigator a particular way of idealizing the subject matter investigated. I am using idealization in a particular sense in this article, that of a certain bodily striving to bring experience to language, a striving which, if I read Koch, Polanyi, and Merleau-Ponty correctly, lies at the heart of scientific work. This use of idealization is intended to highlight the experiential and – as embodied in the experiential – the tradition-specific historical roots of scientific objectivity, the value-ladenness of these roots, and the questionable applicability of this notion of objectivity to psychology.

In the process, I hope to raise the following questions, and to a very modest extent, address them: What kind of idealization does a scientist employ "in doing science"? What is the history of this "idealization"? How is the idealization effective? But before I move into the discussion which raises these questions, directly or by implication, some prefatory notes are requisite.

SIGMUND KOCH: FROM REFLECTION TO ANALYSIS TO CLARIFICATION

I claimed, above, this article was guided by a particular trajectory initiated by Sigmund Koch. The trajectory, in brief, begins with reflective work that becomes a deeper analysis around the relationship of method to subject matter and culminates in a clarification of this relation. The basis for the initial reflective work emerged during Koch's supervision of the six volumes of *Psychology: A study of a science* (1959a; 1962; 1963) and coheres about the fact that "psychology was unique in the extent to which its institutionalization preceded its content and its methods preceded its problems" (Koch 1959b, p. 783). Consequently, psychology's history "is very much a history of changing views, doctrines, images about what to emulate in the natural sciences – especially physics" (Koch 1959b, p. 784). What psychologists latched onto was a (mis)conception about the methodology of the natural sciences, applied to their own discipline. The error here is compound: first, in unquestioningly fixating on natural science, as if "the method" – and the success – would "automatically" transfer to psychology. And second, in getting the method wrong. Koch (1965) calls this fixation "method fetishism"; Danziger (1990), equally irreverently and appropriately, "methodolatry". Based on these insights afforded by his initial reflective work, Koch begins work at correcting this compound error. This correctional work follows a particular trajectory, shifting from reflection to analysis.

Koch analyzes the methodology of the natural sciences more thoroughly and critically than has traditionally been done by psychologists. Instead of adopting the logical or rational reconstructive fictions advanced by traditional philosophy of science, as exemplified by logical positivism, Koch looks empirically at the practice of science. In this regard, he acknowledges Polanyi (1958) as peerless, in terms of a sustained and systematic uncovering of the personal responsibility necessary at each step of the scientific research process, precluding any possible replacement of the responsibility by method, rule, or decision procedure. These practical-empirical reflections clear away some of the misconceptions about what scientific practice involves, and in so doing go some way toward clearing ground for understanding psychology as a science on its own terms; that is, in terms of its own, distinctively psychological, subject matter. Thus, in brief, the trajectory I follow is from an initial reflection on (some aspect of) scientific practice in terms of experience, to an analysis of what that practice involves, to a subsequent clarification of this practice by way of what the practice presupposes. The aspect of science on which I focus in this paper is the notion of scientific objectivity as an orienting ideal of scientific investigative practice, following the trajectory from reflection to analysis to clarification.

REFLECTING PERSONALLY ON SCIENTIFIC OBJECTIVITY

There is, of course, no shortage of critiques of scientific objectivity. Kuhn (1962) immediately comes to mind, from philosophy and history of science; there are numerous others within philosophy of science (e.g. Feyerabend, 1976). Many critiques are ideological, such as Marxist (e.g. Horkheimer & Adorno, 1972), feminist (e.g. Harding, 1986), social constructionist (e.g. Gergen, 1994; Shotter, 1993); to name only a few. The approach I am taking at present is somewhat different, and not merely because it is highly speculative, but primarily through its mode of access, which I shall dub "personal", following Polanyi's sense of the term as developed in *Personal Knowledge* (1958).

That is, I want to understand scientific objectivity not objectively, like some external "thing" I can prod from a safe distance, measure, assess, etc.; but rather personally, as a part of that same tradition which is formative of my person. I want to gain a perspective, through reflection, on that certain commitment called an "objective view" of the world which I live(d) prior to any reflection, in a sense to find the personal appeal of the notion "in me" prior to any appraisal of the notion; to find the way(s) my tradition lives me. This tentative phraseology aims to make clear that access to scientific objectivity, as a part of (my) tradition, is not restricted only to practicing scientists. I venture that even the child who learns that the sun's motion is apparent, as the earth is actually moving, has already become qualified to reflect, to the self-same extent, on "scientific objectivity" insofar as it has "transformed" their experience.

This objective may appear strange at first glance; but following Polanyi and the complementary work of Merleau-Ponty (1962), I am not taking either experience, as inarticulately but sensibly structured within the body, or language, naively. Both one's body and one's language are, as Merleau-Ponty wonderfully puts it, "pre-personal traditions", into which one is born. Becoming a person is a taking on and assuming these traditions, finding oneself "there" within them. It is "there" that we feel comfortably ourselves, not because tradition is some external "thing" or body into which "our" body, language, and self, "fits" and "feels" comfortable, but because tradition is that non- or pre-external constitutive matrix that precedes, defines, and sets the very possibility of, and hence one's sense of, "externality", "fit", "feeling", "comfort", "self", and so on. One finds oneself "there" not because tradition occupies some space which one occupies, but because one's body and language as pre-personal traditions set out an intelligible locus of spatial orientation which one takes over in the self-same acts that define one as a person.

Science stands as one of the great traditions of Europe. It can be viewed as a tradition aimed at resolving a problematic relation of knowledge to authority, which resolution is best encapsulated in the notion of scientific objectivity. The ramifications of this resolution in every sphere of life continue to the present day, of course, and have either displaced or continue to contend with other traditions – religious, philosophical, etc. – in playing an essential role in the constitution of our knowledge, practices, and our selves. Therefore to put scientific objectivity in question, is to put my self, to some degree, in question. Science and the ideal of objectivity are some of the deeper-rooted constituents of my tradition, regardless of whether I wish or desire it so; in this sense they are – to some degree – constitutive of my person, not so much "against my will", but more accurately, before my will. Questioning this is the type of reflective effort Polanyi, Merleau-Ponty, and Koch are engaged in, and what is required of psychology, if it is to transform its misconception of natural science method positively.

IDEALIZATION AND APPARENT "SIMPLICITY"

Koch (1976) points out that "It took a prolonged development of ancillary knowledge, culminating in an act of genius, to disembed the laws of such simple systems as those defined by the pendulum, the inclined plane, or the motions of falling bodies" (p. 492). This is worth pondering for some moments: the pendulum or the inclined plane; seemingly very simple dynamics involved here. Yet it took centuries, indeed, millennia, to "disembed the laws of such simple systems". Perhaps nothing testifies better to the embeddedness, in a constitutional sense, of tradition within personal experience, than the incongruity between the length of time it takes a person to learn the mechanics of such systems today, and the centuries it took in history; from the Greeks to Galileo. Obviously, the simplicity of these systems is only in retrospect!

Why are they not so simple beforehand? The clue resides, I think, in Koch's notion of "disembedding". Simple systems are embedded in the complex, ambiguous, polysemous involvements in the practically, emotionally, relationally, and epistemically jumbled opacity that mundane, ordinary experience becomes when we attempt to theorize it. To disembed distinctions, systems, and laws from this experience has been proven by history to be extraordinarily difficult. My claim is that in order to achieve this kind of disembedding, there has been a particular idealization, from experience but relying on a creative articulation of certain aspects of that experience. This creative articulation requires not only an embodied, feeling center, and a grammar (equally embodied, in a language) – both of which are intelligibly structured, as "pre-personal" traditions of body and language – but also the raising of their relation to a questionable and problematic status. To "idealize" is a bodily striving, to bring the inarticulate into language that feels appropriate as articulation of that experience.

This idealization, even before coming to be definitive of scientific objectivity, itself has a long history. To best make clear this notion of idealization, I will again cite Koch:

> What has come to be definitive of science, is a particular analytical pattern emerging first in classical modern astronomy, achieving more distinct fruition in Newtonian mechanics, and undergoing further differentiation in postclassical physics. ... [T]his pattern requires: (a) the disembedding from a domain of phenomena of a small family of "variables" which demarcate important aspects of the domain's structure, when that domain is considered as an idealized, momentary static system, and (b) that this family of variables be such, by virtue of appropriate internal relations, that it can be ordered to a mathematical or formal system capable of correctly describing changes in selected aspects of the system as a function of time and/or system changes describable as alterations of the "values" of specified variables.
> (Koch, 1976, pp. 491-2)

Rather than work through this concise and correspondingly dense description, I am concentrating only on the initial notion of "disembedding" which "this pattern requires". For my claim is that in this disembedding activity of the scientist there is already an idealization of the subject matter in a particular way, from which the remainder of Koch's description then follows. To get at this idealizing activity, I propose a speculative disentanglement of those "objective facts" usually read into "natural phenomena". In this way, the phenomenal experience prior to any ascription of objectivity is suggested, and highlights in what sense objectivity itself is an idealization from that experience. Attention to the experience highlights in what sense objectivity itself is an idealization from that experience. To do so, I first reverse Koch's sequence – from classical modern astronomy to Newtonian mechanics to postclassical physics – which brings us to pre-classical astronomy.

Reflection on astronomy outlines the "naive" phenomenal experience of "the stars", and demands imaginative co-operation in order to work one's way "under the history", and to make it "personal".

SPECULATION: ON THE TACIT, THE EXPLICIT, AND IDEALIZING

The stars, or "the heavens", are that which is the furthest away from us, in the ordinary sense of distant, in fact unreachably distant. The expanse of space in which the stars shine suggests an infinity, within which the finitude of distances situates itself. These inconceivable distances enable consistent and reliable measures over time. Landmarks erode, rivers change course, lakes dry out ... but the stars are always there, their positions gaugable on any clear night. Their positions are impervious to interference on the part of people, too; nothing we ever do could affect "the stars in their courses". Mythologies and cosmologies reflect this indifference and independence: the heavens have precedence over earthly things. Practically, this timelessness dovetails with the consistency of measures, as Greek astronomers could use Egyptian records over a thousand years old, but still approximately accurate. And further, this consistency was not only over time, but bore out an order in the stars, a non-human order revealed in the patterns of the zodiac, the cycle of the seasons, the equinox, the solstice. These various characteristics – of distance, of measure, of timelessness, of precedence (both of temporality and of significance), of independence from this-worldly matters (including human), and of order – taken together, underwrite a possible story of a cosmos utterly outside and unaffected by human affairs, which the human world of striving and doing, thinking and making, is "thrown up against". That is, these characteristics underwrite a possible story of the cosmos which within the European tradition has become definitive for "scientific objectivity". But there are numerous other characteristics derivable from the phenomenal experience of the heavens, as other traditions – Chinese, Arab, Mayan – bear out. And, these other civilizations which conceived of the stars in similar terms did not derive a notion of objectivity in the scientific sense, as Europe did. To put it differently, that these characteristics were present tacitly in the phenomenal experience of the stars, is not enough to determine their explicit characterization, and certainly not enough to explain why some of these characteristics become singled out – idealized – and not others. What else is required?

To continue this speculative reading, it would seem that also required is some sophistication in symbolic ordering in a formal sense, so as to enable communication, preservation, comparison, and so on; this in turn again presupposes some civilization to support these knowledge-related practices.

   Symbolic ordering and civilization combine to make for traditions of articulation which make explicit certain features implicit in experience, and in turn build on, elaborate, and revise these articulations further (see Cassirer 1953). But again, none of these necessities are in themselves sufficient; nonwestern civilizations display these features but did not develop a comparable notion of scientific objectivity. That is, without a deeper understanding of the transformations wrought upon tacit experience (in this case, of "the heavens"), the ability of historical analysis to "explain" particular historical outcomes will prove inadequate. These transformations wrought upon experience must devolve upon some personal center, some human agent; but as I have been at pains to keep in the forefront throughout the discussion so far, this personal center is always and necessarily constituted, in its very assumption or manifestation of its agentic acts, by pre-personal traditions. The transformations wrought upon tacit experience which bring the experience to a particular articulation should be conceived as neither entire arbitrary nor creation ex nihilo. These extremes either ignore history, as manifest in tradition, or experience, as manifest in the person. To get at these transformations of experience, then, requires historical analysis but also a penetration into that which makes some particular transformation appealing in its implications, whether cognitively, morally, politically, and so on.[2] Ultimately, the appeal would have to be found in terms of orientations to what is good, or desirable, or ideal – the tack I have adopted in this paper – and these find their best expressions in terms of particular values, to which I return below.

   At this point in the speculation, the notion of idealization becomes necessary. It can be defined as that which guides the transformations wrought upon experience in making the tacit explicit, or in different words, as that economy of the dynamic between tacit experience and making explicit, an economy configured in the particular language of a particular history. For the meaning of the experience – in this case, of "the heavens" – is neither reducible to some ahistorical, unproblematic direct perception of a stimulus, as traditional accounts of science would have it, nor is it entirely constructed in some arbitrary conventions of discourse, but it takes place in that mysterious and irreducible dynamic between the tacit and the explicit, between body and language. In making explicit certain characterizations implicit in the phenomenal experience of the stars, an idealization polarizes the possibilities in experience into a certain configuration. Certain possibilities are privileged in such a configuring, while others are ignored or downplayed. The idealization acts in a sense like a Gestalt principle, ordering the parts into some particular whole, which makes sense of those parts integrated in some singular, particular fashion. The ever more sophisticated idealizations employed by physics, then, are ever more inclusive reductions of the totality and complexity of phenomena implicit in our experience of the cosmos. Idealization capitalizes on the interplay between tacit possibilities and explicit realizations in "acts of disembedding" by the scientist, skillful acts which integrate the accumulated knowledge of a tradition into the scientist's experience and then configures the subject matter under study, creatively, into a new light or meaning.

VALUES, SCIENTIFIC OBJECTIVITY, AND IMPLICATIONS

If we follow this reasoning and feel the speculation to be plausible thus far, the question that emerges at this point is: What guides this particular economy of idealization, this skilful utilization of the tradition? For the creative work here, is performed primarily tacitly; a mostly inarticulate skill of selecting and discarding, emphasizing and ignoring, that in contrast to claims from traditional views of science and to still-dominant views of science in psychology, cannot itself be replaced by a formal rule or method. If this creative work takes place both tacitly, in the body, and explicitly, in language, personal experience has to be understood nonreductively. That is, it cannot be understood by way of a reduction to a set of rules, propositions, or methods, or to social conventions of the time – though to be sure these all play some part – but by understanding the situation of personal experience both historically in relation to traditions, and personally, in relation to feeling, values, language, to name only some. The attempt to bring felt, bodily experience (which the scientist knows intimately, but inarticulately) to language needs a far richer exploration than rules of method. The notion of method substituting for this experience merely redescribes the problem, for any rule must be applied and this application presupposes an embodied involvement. Any formulation of method or rule relies, whether this is admitted or not, on some ascription of experiential application of the rule which is therefore not further reducible to a further rule. Rules and method do not ensure scientific objectivity. By the same logic, the guides of the creative work of the scientist appear as those values and beliefs, perhaps themselves as inarticulate as the skillful act of the scientist, embedded in the scientist's person and tradition. These are the values by which the scientist lives. Scientific objectivity must be understood, both historically and personally, in terms of the values which appeal to experience in tradition-specific ways.

Applying this line of reasoning with its concluding emphasis on values to the case at hand, what should be revealing here is the uncovering of the rootedness of "scientific objectivity" in the pre-scientific astronomic experience, and further the tradition-specific values which came to be implicit in the subsequent understanding of "scientific objectivity" as an ideal. Reminding ourselves of Koch's characterization of the application of this "idealized domain", that the domain "can be ordered" either formally or mathematically, and its behavior and behavioral changes over time, precisely described, and rendered predictable, what values emerge as implicit in the transition from pre-idealized experience to an ideal of scientific objectivity? I highlight five points drawn from my above speculative description of pre-classical astronomy's "phenomenal experience of the stars".

First: the reliability of measures over time which the stars afforded, is converted into control on the part of the scientist. Rather than relying on "favorable conditions", such as a good vantage point and a clear sky, the scientist can create and manipulate the conditions. While the scientist still enters the now-idealized domain "on its terms", he or she knows, understands, describes, predicts, and controls those terms. The scientist in submitting to the terms of the domain simultaneously transforms his or her relationship to the domain into a relationship of instrumental value.

Second: the order displayed in the stars – a non-human order, timeless and independent of the human world – transformed into formal, systematic relationships of an ideal domain, come to be understood as knowledge of laws and truth independent of human making or thought, the reality underlying appearances and mere opinions; knowledge of this order lays claim to truth.

Third: the indifference and independence of the stars translates into an idealized domain that operates neutrally and impartially. Human involvement within this domain, e.g. an instrumental manipulation, disturbs the system but not its neutrality. Knowledge gained here is not only true, but applicable to all and any, and thus implies egalitarian value as the neutrality extends both ways: there is in principle no innate privilege accorded the knowers.

Fourth: as independent, the idealized system should also be accessible in principle to all and any. This accessibility argues for a bypassing of authority. As anti-authoritarian and anti-dogmatic, it has the value of supporting a freedom of access, not only for scientists in particular, but for all and any to be "enlightened" by knowledge. Objectivity argues, in political terms, for liberty.

Fifth: although independent of the human domain, that humans recognize its order, and that this recognition requires a skillful, creative activity of idealizing by a knower, combined with a demand for accessibility by all (in principle), leads not only to an intrinsically generated procedure of self-verification (i.e. replicability: description of the system, such as with a scientific finding, is repeatable) and further arrogates to itself a notion of a self-perpetuating accumulation of knowledge. It holds the promise, as an ideal, of knowledge as progressively freeing us from the ignorance, superstition, and suffering of the present, and thus has emancipatory appeal.

These values (instrumental control, truth, egalitarianism, liberty, progress, and emancipation) as transpositions of certain characteristics of the phenomenal experience of the stars (as distant, timeless, independent, orderly) are, I argue, tacit guides of the idealizing activity which is a crucial component of scientific investigation. They act as the tacit supports of what adherents of the scientific

216

tradition mean when they appeal to "scientific objectivity". A cursory look at these values embedded in scientific objectivity as an ideal confirms the historical specificity of the emergence of the ideal, in their being fundamental values of the Enlightenment, shaped in the confrontation with the dogmatic authority of the Church and a Church-supported Aristotelianism. As such, these values are embedded in scientific practices and continue to inform and orient notions we have today of truth, democracy, liberty, progress, etc. But, and here I remind the reader of those other ideological critiques of science which are also prevalent today, it is obvious that science as a widespread institutional practice has not obtained all the desired effects of realizing those values. In fact, on numerous occasions science has effectively realized the opposite. This being the case, not only does it appear incumbent to re-examine our scientific practices, but also, before applying these wholesale to psychology, acknowledge that the history and subject matter of psychology as a scientific discipline is radically different from that of the natural sciences.

The idealizations implicit in natural science practice as transposed from the ancients' experience of the heavens, may prove of even less applicability for deriving scientifically objective psychological knowledge than the myths and metaphysics of those self-same ancients. Consequently we had best ask, and in this the ground-breaking and complementary work of Koch, Polanyi, and Merleau-Ponty can serve as "idealized" guides, what kind of idealizations should psychology consider that are appropriate to its subject matter, and for its methodology; guided by what values, and to what end? For we cannot rely on rules or method to ensure scientific objectivity, but appear instead to need to engage in critical reflective work that orients us to our values, our history, and ultimately to our own personal experience – even if this experience is mostly inarticulate and grounded in traditions which precede us.

Notes

1.   I would like to thank the Social Sciences and Humanities Research Council (SSHRC) of Canada for their funding support (a doctoral fellowship grant, #752-99-1198). Also, for comments and support, thanks for Natalia Shostack, Leo Mos, and Don Kuiken, and to the weekly Theoretical Seminar at the Center for Advanced Study in Theoretical Psychology at the University of Alberta.

2.   The best example of a type of historical analysis which sustains this as an explicit theme is Charles Taylor's *Sources of the Self* (1989). In this regard see especially Ch. 12, "A digression on historical explanation".

REFERENCES

Cassirer, E. (1953). *Philosophy of symbolic forms. Vols.1-3.* Translated by R. Mannheim. New Haven CT: Yale University Press.

Danziger, K. (1990). *Constructing the subject: Historical origins of psychological research.* Cambridge: Cambridge University Press.

Feyerabend, P. (1976). *Against method.* New York: Humanities Press.

Gergen, K. (1994). *Realities and relationships: Soundings in social construction.* Cambridge & London: Harvard University Press.

Harding, S. (1986). *The science question in feminism.* Ithaca: Cornell University Press.

Horkheimer, M., & Adorno, T. (1972). *Dialectic of enlightenment.* Translated by J. Cumming. New York: Seabury.

Koch, S. (Ed.). (1959a). *Psychology: A study of a science. Study I: Conceptual and Systematic. Vols. 1-3.* New York: McGraw-Hill.

Koch, S. (1959b). *Epilogue.* In S. Koch (Ed.), (1959a), pp. 729-788.

Koch, S. (Ed.). (1962). *Psychology: A study of a science. Study II: Empirical substructure and relations with other sciences. Vol. 4.* New York: McGraw-Hill.

Koch, S. (Ed.). (1963*). Psychology: A study of a science. Study III: Empirical substructure and relations with other sciences. Vols. 5-6.* New York: McGraw-Hill.

Koch, S. (1965). The allures of meaning in modern psychology. In R. Farson (Ed.), *Science and human affairs* (pp. 55-82*).* Palo Alto, CA: Science & Behavior Books.

Koch, S. (1976). Language communities, search cells, and the psychological studies. In W. J. Arnold (Ed.). *Nebraska Symposium on Motivation, 1975.Vol. 23:* 447-559. Lincoln: University of Nebraska Press.

Kuhn, T. (1962). *The structure of scientific revolutions.* Chicago: University of Chicago Press.

Merleau-Ponty, M. (1962). *Phenomenology of perception.* Translated by C. Smith. London: Routledge & Kegan Paul. (Originally published in 1945.)

Polanyi, M. (1958). *Personal knowledge: Towards a post-critical philosophy.* Chicago: University of Chicago Press.

Shotter, J. (1993). *Conversational realities.* London: Sage.

Taylor, C. (1989). *Sources of the self: The making of the modern identity.* Cambridge: Harvard University Press.

STRATIFICATION IN EXPLANATION

Hans van Rappard
Free University of Amsterdam

SUMMARY

Over the past few ISTP conferences I have presented a number of research notes aimed at the explication of the concept of psychological stratification-levels. The results suggest two points. The first is that levels may be construed in terms of the constraints imposed by research designs or theoretical formulations on the behavioral scope, i.e, the range of behaviors open to the subjects concerned. The second point holds that scope may be explicated in terms of contexts, as used in intensional logic. Taken together, these points entail that low-high levels may be approached as few-many contexts.

INTRODUCTION

A problem in theoretical psychology is the human penchant to transcend the given context. Because of this the explanation of behavior tends to require that a plurality of contexts be taken into account. Throughout the history of the discipline, psychologists have tried to reduce the number of relevant contexts, which often gave rise to alternative approaches to explanation. The paper analyses the causal-mechanistic and teleological explanation-types in terms of their relative scope, thus placing them in the "stratification of explanation".

Over the past few ISTP-conferences I have presented a number of research notes aimed at the explication of the concept of psychological level of stratification. Many authors, notably in cognitive psychology but in other fields too, happily talk about levels, or levels of description or explanation without giving so much as a clue as to what they have in mind. In many case "levels" seem

220

little more than a useful means to silence opponents by gratuitously pointing out that she or he just is not on the same level as the speaker. In many other cases (Dennett among others) the level-concept is used in a rather general way, which is fine in the particular context the author is concerned with but which leaves a lot to be desired once you begin to wonder what exactly is meant, or how you could possibly use the concept yourself.

The results of earlier papers suggest the following: The basic idea is that psychological levels may be construed in terms of the degree of constraint on the *behavioral system*, that is, the interaction between (research) subject and environment. With the possible exception of qualitative research, any scientific investigation imposes constraints on the behavioral system by means of its research design and the theoretical formulation of the problem under study. Constraints are imposed in order to control the variables which are irrelevant to the purpose of the particular research. In other words, the range of possible behaviors open to the subject is restricted, and this means that what I have called the *scope* of the behavioral system is narrowed.

What this amounts to in common sense terms is that levels can be approached in terms of the relative amount of elbow room, that is, the behavioral options or alternatives accorded by psychological theories, methods, and research designs. Orthodox behavioristic work tends to leave us with little elbow room but this will be different in theories in which one or another kind of meaning features prominently. Therefore, behavioristic approaches must generally be called "low-level", whereas a high alloy of meaning tends to raise the level of theorizing considerably. This would seem to fit in with our intuitive understanding of levels: many behavioral constraints make for little freedom and hence low-level psychology, whereas aproaches characterized by relatively few constraints leave the subject with rather a lot of space to manoeuvre and are therefore assigned to a high level.

To return to more formal terminology: the constraints entailed by a particular method, design, or theory are geared to reducing the number of behavioral alternatives, or the scope that was just mentioned. It can therefore be said that the scope of a psychological approach designates its level. In other words, low-to-high level may be construed as narrow-to-wide scope. But what exactly is meant by a narrow or wide scope?

Elsewhere (Van Rappard, 1996) I have argued that the scope-concept may be explicated in terms of *contexts* as used in intensional logic. Intensional logic basically holds that expressions may have different extensions in different contexts. In different contexts a person may be a friend, husband, lover, senior vice president, father, commanding officer, etc. By context is meant the here-and-now on which the truth of a sentence depends. For instance, the sentence "it is raining" will be true in a given context if it is indeed raining in that context. But the sentence "it rained" refers to a moment in time before the "now" provided by the context in which it is uttered and so requires not one but two contexts. And the sentence "perhaps it is raining" introduces a conceivable or possible state of affairs, which may not be present in the given context at all and even be unlikely to materialize shortly. Now "rain" is a simple case but often the number of possible contexts may be quite large: just think of all the dreaded, or wished for "possible contexts" that therapists have to deal with. Hence, in interpreting a sentence in any given context, it is often necessary to take other contexts in consideration (Gamut, 1991, 2, pp. 13-14).

LEVELS AND CONTEXTS

What was said above about levels and contexts can be fleshed out by means of the following example: Working on a theory of action identification Vallacher & Wegner (1987, p. 4) wrote,

> [o]ne sees if someone is home by pushing a doorbell, and one pushes a doorbell by moving a finger. Although these three act identities all pertain to the same act, they exist at different levels ... "Seeing if someone is home" occupies the highest level, "pushing a doorbell" the next highest, and "moving a finger" the lowest level.

For present purposes it is important to see that the probability that I move my finger in order to see if, say, "Jane is home" is lower than the probability that I do so in order to push a doorbell. This means that "seeing if Jane is home" has a wider scope than the description of that act as "moving a finger", because the former entails more contexts, that is, more possible, or alternative states of the world. It would not make sense to say that I am seeing if Jane is home if I were married to Jane but things would be different if Jane had filed for divorce and put a new lock on the door. And we would probably be surprised if the milkman said that he was seeing if Jane, rather than Mrs. Smith were home. In short, in some contexts "I am seeing if Jane is home" is true but in many others it is not. In order to decide this it may be necessary to take many contexts into consideration.

But now you may ask, what then, is the difference with the identification of "I am moving a finger"? Finger-moving is a highly constrained identification of a particular act, which, as argued earlier, because of these constraints entails few contexts. At the same time however, this low-level act entails many contexts in the sense that it can be identified across very many contexts. That is, in many different "here-and-nows" it can easily be decided whether or not a particular finger is moved. "I move a finger" is just as truth-functional as the sentence "it rains".

However, turning to the sentence "I am seeing if Jane is home" it will be realized that this high-level sentence, by virtue of its being unconstrained, *also* entails many contexts: Yet it can *not* be easily identified across many contexts. As mentioned, we may have to take into consideration quite a few contexts if we are to decide if someone is indeed looking if Jane is home. So, in both low-level and high-level sentences many contexts seem to be involved and we may therefore wonder if there might be something wrong with our use of context?

The difficulty can be sorted out, I think, by distinguishing between two different kinds of contexts: "I move a finger" can be identified across many contexts but, in contradistinction to the "looking if Jane is home" sentence, these contexts are all *identical*. That is, they are identical as far as a particular action is conceived as moving-a-finger. Identifying or conceiving an act as moving-a-finger entails that it is truth-functional, or, in the present terminology, mono-contextual (cf. "it is raining"). In such cases, only one context is needed in that all relevant context are identical because they are determined by the simple question "is, or is not the finger moved?"

The "looking-if..." sentence on the other hand, needs for its identification many different contexts, as was demonstrated by the example. But calling these contexts "different" is not enough to bring out their specific nature. It is important to understand from the example that the contexts mentioned all concern *alternative* contexts. Suppose that a particular act may easily be identified as "moving a finger", and also fairly unproblematically as "pushing a doorbell", then it may nevertheless require that we consider many alternative contexts if we are to reach the conclusion that X was, or was not looking if Jane was home.

LEVEL, SCOPE, AND CONTEXT

Let me briefly summarize what has so far been argued: Firstly, the level of a psychological theory or research formulation can be construed in terms of its scope, that is, its degree of constraint. In other words, the spectrum of low-to-high levels may be understood as many-to-few constraints, or narrow-to-wide scope, respectively. Secondly, since scope allows explication in terms of contexts – alternative contexts, that is – narrow-to-wide scope may be conceived as few-to-many alternative contexts. Putting this jargon as simply as possible, the entire scheme boils down to the view that what we intuitively tend to call *high-level* psychological theories because they allow many behavioral options, are characterized by a *wide scope*, which entails *many alternative contexts*.

It bears repetition that the contexts we are concerned with are called "alternative" contexts because, as the "Jane-example" points out, they typically entail behavioral alternatives. In an earlier paper (Van Rappard, 1999) I have elaborated the view that problem solving and decision making may also be understood in terms of behavioral alternatives, or, to use the proper terminology, paths to the goal. For instance, in problem solving the search-space describes the alternative paths to the goal that are open to the problem solver.

A paths-to-the-goal analysis of Hull's and Tolman's views on place versus response learning, illustrates these issues. Although the example is very simple the analysis demonstrates that the scope of Tolman's theory was wider than Hull's because, in contradistinction to the former, Hull's mechanism allowed his robo-rats not one single alternative path to the food box. Tolman's cognitive map of the maze, however, did allow such alternatives, even if not too many.

Hull and Tolman are also relevant to the present paper because their work features different types of explanation, which, using the terminology of Sam Rakover (1997) may be called, causal-mechanistic and noncausal-mechanistic, respectively. In the rest of the paper I will argue that these types entail different levels and, more precisely, that causal-mechanistic explanation must be placed at the bottom-end of the stratification scheme, whereas the second type may be placed closer to the top. In view of the proposed level=scope=alternative-contexts approach, the argument will follow the simple strategy of describing causal and noncausal-mechanistic explanation in terms of the alternative contexts implied by each type.

I will turn first to the causal-mechanistic type of explanation. Just now I have referred to a paths-to-the-goal analysis of a Hullian learning experiment, which demonstrated that this behavioristic approach did not allow of any alternative paths or contexts and hence may be called, mono-contextual. Also, Hull was called a mechanicist. Does this mean that mechanicistic approaches are generally mono-contextual and should therefore be assigned a low-level position?

Rakover (1997), having described the basic idea of Hempel's neo-Humean D-N model of explanation, writes,

> [Its] requirements ensure that the explanation will be based on empirical observations on the one hand, and on rational and justified rules of inference on the other. The universal law of nature must be based on empirical observations, but these observations must be *independent* of the phenomenon for whose explanation the universal law has been invoked (p. 51).

In this quotation the word "independent" should be stressed. It points out that, as every freshman is supposed to know, in causal explanation cause and effect must be defined independently of each other. In this, I think, an essential aspect can be seen of what I have called, mono-contextualization. Along with their being contingently connected, discrete units, the logical independence of cause and effect ensures that they cannot mutually define each other. So, their mono-contextuality is safeguarded. Ideally, the conditions of causal explanation are as mono-contextual as the sentences "it is raining" or "I move a finger". All obtain across a multitude of *identical* contexts. But the logical independence of cause and effect not only prevents these conditions from entailing each other but, by virtue of this, also precludes alternative contexts. This may be seen in the noncausal-mechanistic type of teleological explanation to which we now turn.

The second main category of explanation types, which Rakover called noncausal-mechanistic is fairly wide. In this account I will ignore the various fine-grained distinctions and focus on teleological explanation, which, I expect, will intuitively be felt to be the highest-level type of explanation. Incidentally, an often mentioned third explanation-category is Functional explanation. But this category turns out to be a rather wide sort of in-between category, at the top bordering on teleological, and at the bottom on causal-mechanistic explanation. Various authors therefore distinguish between Teleo- and Turing-functionalism (Looren de Jong, 1997). Because of its fuzzy in-between nature I will also ignore this category and its sub-divisions. Going into them would not add anything fundamental to my treatment of stratification in explanation.

CONCLUSION

Given what has already been said it will not come as a surprise when I say that in the final section of this paper I will argue that teleological explanation is multi-contextual. Please recall that here as well as with regard to mono-contextual causal explanation "context" refers strictly to alternative contexts.

Now – and this, too, is basic knowledge that the average freshman is supposed to have available – the picture that is usually sketched of teleological explanation tends to be the opposite of causal explanation. The basic difference concerns exactly the points referred to by Rakover: the discreteness and the contingency, that is, the logical independence of the conditions of causal explanations. This independence is completely lacking in their teleological counterparts. In his *The Explanation of Behaviour* (1964), Taylor has argued that teleological explanations cannot meet the Humean and even atomistic requirement that the conditions involved be separately identifiable because they are

> connected with some form of holism ... The first term of a teleological correlation violates the stringent [ie Humean: HvR] requirement since it identifies the antecedent condition of the event to be accounted for, B, as a state of affairs in which B will lead to G. Thus the antecedent is identified in terms of its law-like connexions with two other events, B and G, i.e., as

that state of affairs in which, when B occurs, G will follow. (p. 12)

The antecedent, in other words, is identified not separately but, on the contrary, with reference to other states of affairs – and this is of course a mortal sin to the heirs of the Humean tradition.

Taylor's fairly abstract reasoning may be fleshed out by returning to our Jane-example. The teleological explanation of the question "why is X pushing a doorbell?" by "because X is looking if Jane is home", assumes that X expects his bell-pushing (B) to take him to the desired goal of knowing if Jane is home (G). In other words, X expects that, as put by Taylor, "when B (bell-pushing) occurs, G (the goal of knowing if Jane is home) will follow". Moreover, given this expectation (or wish, hope, etc.) the given context is transcended and so the explanation requires for its verification that a number of alternative contexts be taken into consideration. It is not difficult to see that these contexts are impossible to determine in isolation. The possible alternative context that, say, X is still officially married to Jane but that she has thrown him out and put a new lock on the door, is meaningless if taken separately from X's wish to see if his not-so-loving spouse will let him in. But X may be cheating and his real reason for pushing the doorbell may be his desire to scout the house with a view to a possible burglary. That would be yet another alternative context but again, it would not make sense if X weren't pushing the doorbell of Jane's house. The alternative contexts – which in this case may perhaps also be called initial conditions – cannot be defined independently of the goal which is used to explain X's doorbell-pushing behavior. Incidentally, this example demonstrates that, as has been argued by many authors, teleological explanations entail a plurality of intial conditions (cf. Valentine, 1992). This is so because by pursuing a certain desired goal, the behavior cannot but transcend the given context and therefore cannot be conceived separately from the alternative contexts that are entailed.

To sum up: I have offered some arguments for the proposition that teleological explanations entail more alternative contexts and thus a wider scope than causal-mechanistic explanations. The former may therefore be placed at a higher stratification level.   A similar result was achieved by a paths-to-the-goal analysis of an experiment conducted by both Hull and Tolman, which was briefly mentioned above. Indeed, as Rakover wrote,

[T]he experimental controversy between Hull's causal mechanistic approach and Tolman's teleological approach to the question of place versus response learning was about the metatheoretical question of the appropriate model of explanation.
(Rakover, 1997, p. 65)

REFERENCES

Gamut, L.T.F. (1991). *Logic, language, and meaning* (2 Vols). Chicago: University of Chicago Press.

Looren de Jong, H. (1997). Some remarks on a relational concept of mind. *Theory & Psychology, 7,* 147-172.

Rakover, S.S. (1997). Can psychology provide a coherent account of human behavior? A proposed multiexplanation model. *Behavior and Philosophy, 25,* 43-75.

Rappard, J.F.H. van (1996). Level, scope, and context: An approach to stratification. In C. Tolman, F. Cherry, R. van Hezewijk & I. Lubek (Eds) *Problems of theoretical psychology.* Toronto: Captus Press.

Rappard, J.F.H. van (1999). Scoping up scope: Steps towards level assessment. In W. Maiers, B. Bayer, B. Duarte Esgalhado, R. Jorna & E. Schraube (Eds) *Challenges to theoretical psychology.* Toronto: Captus Press.

Taylor, C. (1964). *The explanation of behaviour.* London: Routledge & Kegan Paul.

Valentine, E.R. (1992). *Conceptual issues in psychology.* London: Routledge.

Vallacher, R.R. & Wegner, D.M. (1987). What do people think they are doing? Action identification and human behavior. *Psychological Review, 94,* 3-15.

THE WITHERING OF THEORY IN MAINSTREAM SOCIAL PSYCHOLOGY:
Whither Our Next Theoretical Turn?

Ian Lubek, Mark Ferris*, Angela Febbraro**, Natasha Bauer***, Brian Ross***, Heather Thoms-Chesley, Sue Edmonds, and Michael Andrews
*University of Guelph; *University of Western Ontario; **Wilfrid Laurier University; ***York University*

SUMMARY

We first describe cases where critical theoretical social psychological ideas do not reach their primary intended audiences, through processes of gatekeeping and invisibilization. Scanning eight major social psychology journals at 10-year intervals from 1947 to 1997, we noted that only limited space had been allotted, about 10.8%, for publishing non-empirical articles– those not reporting new data, two thirds of which were "theoretical". This is contrasted with the rate of 26.3 % senior-authored non-empirical journal article production, as seen in the career-long publication outputs of a sample of 338 social psychologists trained (1949-1974) at University of Michigan. Women were seemingly less successful than men in placing their non-empirical work (as compared to empirical) in the eight prestigious social psychology journals. As mainstream journal space seemingly withers away, we may ask whither social psychologists may turn to publish their non-empirical/theoretical articles, especially when critical positions are taken. If social psychologists must turn away from their own journals for theoretical ideas, what long term effects will this have for the overall encouragement, mentoring, and ongoing struggle for visibility, of writings about theory?

INTRODUCTION

Why does it appear so difficult to find challenging theoretical articles *published* in mainstream social psychology journals at a time when authors have increasingly *produced* such work? To partially answer this question, we have begun examining various processes of gatekeeping (Lubek & Apfelbaum, 1987) and invisibilization that may be hindering more ready access to social psychological theoretical work.[1] The invisibility and invisibilization of ideas may involve a complex set of overlapping processes, some of which are "active" and "voluntary", as Lubek et al (1998, p. 93) suggested. One simple form of invisibility of ideas may have to do with (i) *unavailability* or "a lack of accessibility to a set of ideas, a publication, a translated version, or an inclusive professional publication indicator such as *Psychological Abstracts*". Other processes may involve the author's actions:

> (ii) *voluntary self-invisibilization* may involve a choice not to submit ideas to particular outlets viewed as not reflecting the author's concerns, perspective, paradigm, or primary intended audience; (iii) *not-so-voluntary self-invisibilization* may involve an (almost "conditioned") avoidance response (Lubek & Apfelbaum, 1987) or withholding of submissions due to prior aversive rejections or blockages… (1998, p.93)

Examples may also show the more active participation by editorial decision-makers concerning the appearance and circulation of theoretical ideas:

> (iv) *invisibilization* is an *active* process which results in the blockage of ideas from their intended readers through gatekeeping procedures… (Lubek, 1995); … (v) *re-visibilization* involves active efforts to promote and disseminate ideas to a community, and to resist or undo the invisibilizing effects of (i) to (iv) above…. (1998, p. 93)

Let us first examine some anecdotal evidence of invisibilization related to theoretical and critical work in social psychology.

Editorial Displacements of Billig's (1994) and Apfelbaum's (1997) Theoretical Critiques

A reading of the two published versions of a paper by Michael Billig (1994, 1998) along with the accompanying contextualizations (Spears, 1994; Ussher, 1994; Stringer, 1994) offer a partial account of how the *European Journal of Social Psychology* had earlier rejected it. Billig had examined issues of that journal and suggested that its pages were "depopulate" or "devoid of individual characters" (Billig, 1994, p. 309); he also indicated that this situation needed remedying. Since the paper was refused publication by the very journal whose practices were being critically analysed , that journal's readership – the social psychologists presumably doing the depopulating – would never directly be confronted by Billig's arguments (Lubek et al, 1998).[2] Rather, two somewhat different audiences would learn about depopulating social psychology.

A second case history of invisibilization may also be cited in the treatment afforded by another European social psychology journal to a critical, feminist article written by Erika Apfelbaum (Lubek et al, 1998; Lubek 2000a).[3] After initial suggestions of rejection by the editor, the article was eventually banished to the back of the issue, placed by itself into a section called "Debates and Counterpoints" (specially created for this article), stripped of its title in the table of contents, and then finally had both of its abstracts – French and English – removed. This latter action effectively invisibilized it for all those searching the literature using such professional bibliographic search tools as the various paperbound, on line or CD-ROM versions of *Psychological Abstracts* (see Lubek, 2000a, for a longer discussion of the problems of "missing abstracts").

MICHIGAN MENTORED MEN AND WOMEN: Missing the Mainstream Messages

We may now turn from these two anecdotal illustrations to an argument based upon the "triumph of the aggregate" (Danziger, 1990), that is, to a more systematic treatment of the tension between the *increasing production* by authors of critical and/or theoretical articles and the *decreasing reception, dissemination and visibilizing* of this work within mainstream social psychology's journals. We may examine, using both qualitative and quantitative indicators, the openness of the major journals to a large sample of theoretical production from a large number of social psychologists. Previous research traced the career-long publication patterns of all 338 social psychology PhDs trained at the University of Michigan between 1949 and 1974 (Febbraro et al, 1996). Ross et al (1996) and Febbraro et al (1999) examined and evaluated almost 3000 senior-authored journal articles written by these social psychologists, only 53 of whom (15.7%) were women. We judged as "empirical" all those articles generating new data and found overall that 26.3% were "non-empirical" articles, producing no new data. About two thirds of these non-empirical articles were reliably judged to be either "theoretical" or "meta-theoretical",[4] with the remainder dealing with methodology, statistics, design, reviews, and meta-analyses. In these earlier studies, Ross et al (1996) and Febbraro et al (1999) had examined the various linkages between these social

230

psychologists' publication patterns, the "seasons for theory", and their formative experiences when being mentored.[5]

In exploring research strategies and publication practices, Angela Febbraro (1997) had matched the 53 women Michigan PhDs to 53 male colleagues who had been supervised by the same mentors at the same time, and interviewed in depth almost half. Some of their reflections have in turn informed the current study, along with our ongoing interest in processes of journal gatekeeping (Lubek & Apfelbaum, 1987) and invisibilization, especially for critical and/or feminist work (Lubek et al, 1998; Lubek, 2000a).

Historically, social psychologists, especially those claiming heritage in the Lewinian tradition, have faced identity issues involving juggling of, and finding a balance among, three aspects of their field: theorizing, data-gathering and applied practice (Lubek, 2000b). The Michigan sample of men and women in fact followed differing careers after their PhDs and had different publication patterns and strategies within both academia and applied practice areas. As Febbraro et al (1996) indicated, about two thirds of the 53 Michigan women pursued academic careers after their PhDs; half reaching the rank of full professor. In comparison, about 80% of the 53 "matched men" pursued academic careers after graduating, and three quarters reached full-professor status. In applied areas, about one third of the women pursued careers primarily in clinical private practice (with many in fact receiving additional clinical training after their PhDs). While about 40% of the matched men were also engaged in applied activities, but this was often in addition to their academic careers, especially in the areas of independent consulting (e.g., market research, statistical analysis, organizational development).

In terms of balancing empirical research with theorizing, Ross et al (1996) found more theorizing appearing *later* in their careers. As one of the women interviewed by Febbraro (1997) pointed out:

> Well, I certainly think that it takes a while in one's career to feel... the self-assurance to be able to do a straight theoretical piece, or even to emphasize theory. I mean I can remember when, as a very young scholar... presenting at meetings ... but being very nervous about presenting anything but just a very carefully designed and argued data [set]... and you'ld barely take off with any generalizations at all. And as you grow in the field, and in your own self-confidence, I'm sure that... the balance shifts quite dramatically toward being more willing to speculate, and generalize from your data, and not feel so restricted. So yes, I think... that has happened in my career [and]... something that I've observed generally in people's careers.

After specific training to become a social psychologist, how does one communicate ideas and maintain intellectual (and hierarchical) bonds with relevant other members of the paradigmatic community?[6] Who should be the prime audience for these social psychological ideas concerning both new data and theorizing? Many of the women social psychologists (and a few of the men) reported their reasons for *not* sending their studies to the major social psychology journals aimed at their colleagues. Rather they seemed more autonomous and did not always follow the set strategies of their male colleagues or mentors for gaining tenure, promotion and disciplinary visibility. Thus one of the women reported:

> In the last 20 years, I've been fairly disappointed in the field... I could go through journals... through [the *Journal of*] *Personality and Social [Psychology]* for 6 months and find only two articles that had any interest for me at all... and even just intriguing ideas.... it just didn't...have it for me. It seemed so close to the data, and so uninteresting. But the women's movement came along...and was full of wonderful content. And I shifted my orientation... and started publishing in other areas... in different... journals... in feminist journals like... *Psych[ology] of Women Quarterly*...and so forth.

Another woman confided:

> I have published a lot of chapters in books, rather than in peer-reviewed journals.... Some of it's ideological... There are so many special journals now, and often they have a theoretical orientation or a methodological orientation. So that if you want to target that particular publication, you have to toe the line.

Still another had said:

> More of my stuff has been published in books than in journals.... I hate the review process for journals.... I do a lot of invited chapters. But when I have published in journals it's ... a lot in the feminist, but not a lot in the mainstream [psychology journals]. And I think that is a result of the kind of research that I do now..... I haven't published in JPSP [*Journal of Personality and Social Psychology*] at all, the primary journal of the field, because I'm not willing to do the research that they publish.

Many of the Michigan PhD's theoretical papers did not just represent reviews of theory and meta-theory but in fact involved critique of theory and the description of alternative theories, such as feminism. Given this turn among the authors of theoretical texts, let us look more systematically at the dissemination of these ideas: Are the journals aimed at social psychological readers (and their editors) open to such critical and/or theoretical work?

Receptivity to Theory of Mainstream Social Psychology Journals: "I Don't Want to Hear it!"

Some of the Michigan social psychologists had talked of purposefully avoiding mainstream journals for their work; and the anecdotal case studies of Billig and of Apfelbaum provided examples of non-voluntary displacements of the work of critical theoretical social psychological authors. Let us examine the various gatekeeping and/or invisibilizing mechanisms facing social psychologists trying to access their professionally relevant audience, especially with theoretical ideas. At the same time, we shall also question whether a possible gender difference occurs in terms of access to mainstream journal pages for theoretical articles.[7] Will men and women social psychologists in fact have identical experiences in bringing their non-empirical and theoretical work into the mainstream social psychology journals?

Two of the co-authors examined, at 10-year intervals beginning in 1937, the openness of eight mainstream social psychology journals to the non-empirical research of men and women.[8] (As reported earlier, about two thirds of these non-empirical articles may be reliably classified as "theoretical"/ "meta-theoretical".)

For the eight mainstream social psychology journals overall, almost 88% of the articles published for professional social psychologists were empirical, data-generating articles.[9] The men's senior-authored articles sampled each decade seemed more prominent than women's contributions, although women were increasingly joining the ranks of social psychology in the five decades after World War II.

We found that only 10.8% overall of the nearly 2600 articles in these major eight social psychology journals (sampled at 10-year intervals), were non-empirical. Women's non-empirical contributions were relatively much smaller than the men's, averaging about 1.3% of all those journals' published articles, compared to men's non-empirical contributions averaging 8.9%. Given the small place devoted to such articles overall and a gender ratio of almost 7 to 1, one working hypothesis from this partial sampling technique might be that if you have things both social-psychological and non-empirical/ theoretical to say, the mainstream journals may not be very open to these ideas, especially if you're a woman author.

THE TENSION BETWEEN THOSE WHO *WRITE*, AND THOSE WHO *PUBLISH*, THEORETICAL ARTICLES FOR SOCIAL PSYCHOLOGISTS

The low proportions[10] of mainstream journal space devoted to non-empirical publications by men and women may nonetheless serve as an indicator of the permeability to critical/theoretical articles *which have already been accepted* by the mainstream editorial process. But does this accurately reflect the *actual production* of social psychological empirical and non-empirical-theoretical work? To address this, we now looked at the *total* productivity, decade by decade (1949-1997), of all 285 men and 53 women Michigan-trained social psychologists. When we looked at mean percentage per decade of their own output which appeared in the primary eight social psychology journals, we noted that for their *empirical articles,* the men had published 38.4% of their output in those journals, while women had 28.2%. In addition, we looked at contributions to three important American Psychological Association (APA) journals which also provided important "visibility sites" for social psychologists. *American Psychologist*, *Psychological Review* and *Psychological Bulletin*. Finally, we looked at the applied, social problem-centred *Journal of Social Issues* (published by APA`s Division 9 , SPSSI) . Men had an additional 2.2% of their empirical work appearing in these four journals, while women had an additional 1.6%, but solely confined to *Journal of Social Issues.*

Nonetheless, while men and women social psychologists had each managed to place a good proportion (40% vs 30%) of their *empirical* writings in these journals visible to social psychologists, they would not have the same success rates in publishing their non-empirical, theoretical work. Where should these articles appear in order to enhance the visibility of these ideas (especially if they are critical and/or feminist, as in the cases of Billig and Apfelbaum)?

Overall, for our Michigan sample, all of whom were now between 25 and 50 years beyond their PhDs, , there had been over time an increasing proportion of their output devoted to *non-empirical* work, such that by the 1990s, 50% of the production of both the men and women was now non-empirical! But how will all this work become visible to their peers, if we recall the low rates of acceptance (less than 11%) of non-empirical work in the eight mainstream social psychology journals?

Men in fact were able to publish modest quantities of their non-empirical work in these mainstream journals – about 10.2% each decade of their production, compared to 4.6% for women. And the men did even better with the three APA journals with an additional 21.6% of their total decadal output appearing there, compare to 15.6% for women. Men additionally placed 8.2% of their non-empirical work in *Journal of Social Issues* while women placed 5.0% there. In

234

these 12 journals, the men therefore were able to place 40% of their non-empirical output, while women placed 25.2%. Broken down by decades, the women in fact had *no success* with any of these 12 outlets in the 1950s and 60s, and only with the *Journal of Social Issues* in the 1970s. In the 1980s, they published half their non-empirical articles in the 3 APA journals and *Journal of Social Issues*. In the 1990s, and *for the very first time*, they managed to publish 23% of their non-empirical articles in the eight mainstream social psychology journals!

Some of these seemingly different gender patterns may well have to do with voluntary individual strategies towards social psychology, its mainstream or malestream ideas, and its publication practices, as indicated in some of Febbraro's (1997) interviews. But some of this may also be due to involuntary invisibilizations, whereby disciplinary gatekeepers of the mainstream still show a 90% preference for things empirical., and relatively little interest for theoretical papers, authored by women.[11]

Who then is paying attention to the theory, meta-theory and critique – feminist and other – produced by social psychologists? Perhaps as far as "theoretical" social psychological ideas are concerned, the mainstream journals have seen a withering up of interest and must be largely bypassed by authors of theoretical papers. Whither, therefore, can social psychologists turn to publish their non-empirical, theoretical articles – especially when critical of mainstream positions – in order to reach a relevant , and possibly even attentive, audience of their fellow social psychologists? And if social psychologists must turn away from their own journals for theoretical ideas, what effect will this have in the long run for the overall encouragement, mentoring and continued visibility, of writings about theory and their place within social psychology's delicate balancing act between theory, data and practice?

Notes

1.   The work reported here was part of a larger ongoing project supported by a grant from the Social Sciences and Humanities Research Council of Canada to IL and NB, and an RAB-SSHRC travel grant from the University of Guelph to IL. Daryl Samotowka, Mary Ann Hartt, Sarah Brown and Amy Brown have also contributed to the building of our Michigan database. Portions of this paper were prepared while IL visited the GEDISST, IRESCO, CNRS, Paris, France, University of Western Sydney and University of New South Wales. Data reported here borrow most heavily on the quantitative archival work of MF and from the doctoral research of AF (Febbraro, 1997).

2.   The journal's reviewer was reportedly "embarrassed" by portions of Billig's paper (Billig, 1998, p. 127; p. 144) and concluded that the paper should not be accepted by the journal and "that its publication anywhere else would be ill-advised as likely to hurt the reputation of the author" (p. 146).

3.   Here, the male editor of this French social psychology journal tried to overrule the decisions made by the issue's two feminist guest editors and their reviewers to prominently feature Apfelbaum's (1997) critical article entitled "Social psychology under women's scrutiny: on not thinking about domination relations".

4.   Throughout this article, in referring to "theoretical" or "theory" articles, we also include those categorized as "meta-theoretical".

5.   Ross et al (1996) examined the relationship between these social psychologists' productivity and the "seasons for theory", both the development of theoretical writing within their career-span and across changing socio-historical periods such as the 1960s. Febbraro et al (1999) also asked about the process of mentoring of these men and women and attempted to assess the degree of either modelling of, or independence from, the theorizing of their male and female mentors.

6.   In an academic world of "publish or perish", the presence or absence of such publications in quantity – often with a rider that they be in highly respected, peer-reviewed journals, is also linked to career progress– hiring, tenure, promotion (Lubek, 1980; 1995; Lubek et al, 1998).

7.   Febbraro et al (1996) noted that women had been increasingly joining the *applied* social psychology division of the American Psychological Association (Division 9 or SPSSI) although they were not being granted honorific status as Fellows at the same rate as their male colleagues. To a lesser degree, women were also entering *experimental* social psychology, or Division 8, with even a lesser rate of becoming Fellows. This increasing presence of women within social psychology came at a time when social psychology *itself* was becoming a diminishing part of the psychological scene.

8.   The entire annual volumes for 1937, 1947....1987, 1997 were examined, for every journal publishing at that time. The eight journals were: *Journal of Personality and Social Psychology* (and its predecessor the *Journal of Abnormal and Social Psychology*), *Journal of Experimental Social Psychology, Personality and Social Psychology Bulletin, Journal of Social Psychology, European Journal of Social Psychology, Human Relations, Social Psychology Quarterly (Sociometry),* and the *British Journal of [Clinical and] Social Psychology.* We report all studies where we were able to discern and confirm the gender of the senior author.

9.   Only once, in 1947, did the percentage dip below the level of 80% (to 68%).

10.   Our descriptions above must remain tentative, resting on percentages of one sampled year each decade, and without benefit of statistical tests for trends and differences.

11.   We have begun to look at alternative outlets for non-empirical/theoretical work. In the 1970s, the *Journal for the Theory of Social Behaviour* was started, and joined a decade ago by *Theory & Psychology* and *Feminism & Psychology*. But see Lubek (2000a) for differential visibilization policies of the latter two, both published by Sage. For the years 1987 and 1997, these three journals published 17 empirical articles (1 by a man, and 14 by women) and 119 non-empirical articles– 59% by men, 32% by women (with 9% gender-unclassified senior authors).

REFERENCES

Apfelbaum, E. (1997) Contrepoints et debats: La psychologie sociale à l'épreuve des femmes: l'impensé des rapports de domination. [Counterpoints and debates: Social psychology as challenged by women: The ignored concerning relations of domination] *Revue Internationale de Psychologie Sociale/International Review of Social Psychology* , *10*, (2), 153- 169

Billig, M. (1994). Repopulating the depopulated pages of social psychology. *Theory & Psychology, 4* (3), 307-335.

Billig, M. (1998). Repopulating social psychology texts: Disembodied "subjects" and embodied subjectivity. In B. M. Bayer & J. Shotter (Eds) *Reconstructing the psychological subject* (pp. 126-152). London: Sage.

Danziger, K. (1990). *Constructing the subject. Historical origins of psychological research.* New York: Cambridge University Press.

Febbraro, A. (1997). Gender, mentoring, and research practices: Social psychologists trained at the University of Michigan, 1949-1974. Doctoral Dissertation, University of Guelph.

Febbraro, A. , Lubek, I., Bauer, N., Ross, B., Thoms, H., Brown, S. & Hartt, M.A. (1996). Incidence du genre et du mentor sur la production scientifique et la carrière des psychologues: La perspective de la psychosociologie de la science. (trans. N. Apfelbaum-Lubek). [Gender differences, mentors, scientific productivity and careers among psychologists: The perspective from the social psychology of science.] *Cahiers du GEDISST, 16,* 123-160.

Febbraro, A., Ross, B., Thoms-Chesley, H., Bauer, N., & Lubek, I.(1999). Inter-generational theory generation and gender. In W. Maiers, B. Bayer, B. Duarte Esgalhado, R. Jorna & E. Schraube. (Eds) *Challenges to theoretical psychology,* (pp. 109-118). Toronto: Captus Press.

Lubek, I. (1980). The psychological establishment: Pressures to preserve paradigms, publish rather than perish, win funds and influence students. In K. Larsen (Ed.) *Social psychology: Crisis or failure?* (pp. 129-157). Monmouth, Ore: Institute for Theoretical History.

Lubek, I. (1995). A "social psychology of science" approach towards an inter-personal history of social psychology. In H.-P. Brauns, S. Jaeger, L. Sprung & I. Staeuble (Eds) *Psychologie im soziokulturellen Wandel-Kontinuitäten und Diskontinuitäten.* (pp. 98-114). Frankfurt: Peter Lang.

Lubek, I. (2000a). Revisibilizing Erika Apfelbaum's (1979) "lost chapter": A case study in the invisibilizing of women's work in social psychology. Unpublished paper, University of Guelph, Guelph, Canada.

Lubek, I. (2000b). Understanding and using the history of Social Psychology. *Journal of the History of the Behavioral Sciences, 36*, (4),

Lubek, I. & Apfelbaum, E. (1987). Neo-behaviorism and the Garcia effect: A social psychology of science approach to the history of a paradigm clash. In M. Ash and W. Woodward (Eds). *Psychology in twentieth century thought and society.* Cambridge: Cambridge University Press, pp. 59-91.(Reprinted, 1989).

Lubek, I., Febbraro, A., Ferris, M., Bauer, N. Samotowka, D., Edmonds , S., Ross, B. & Thoms-Chesley, H. (1998) Historiographical invisibility and invisibilizations: Examples from the history of social psychology. In J. Good (Ed.) *European Society for the History of the Human Sciences: Proceedings of the XVIIth annual conference.* (pp 93-100). Durham: Centre for the History of the Human Sciences.

Ross, B., Febbraro, A., Thoms-Chesley, H., Bauer, N., & Lubek, I. (1996). Is there a season for theory? Patterns of theoretical, methodological and empirical writings of a sample of men and women social psychologists over the lengths of their careers. In C. Tolman, F. Cherry, R. van Hezewijk & I. Lubek (Eds). *Problems of theoretical psychology* (pp. 228-241). Toronto: Captus Press.

Spears, R. (1994). Why "depopulation" should not (necessarily) be taken personally. *Theory & Psychology, 4* (3), 336-344.

Stringer, P. (1994). A letter to Michael Billig. *Theory & Psychology, 4* (3), 353-362.

Ussher, J. M. (1994). Sexing the phallocentric pages of psychology: Repopulation is not enough. *Theory & Psychology, 4* (3), 345-352.

V SUBJECTIVITY AND DEVELOPMENT

BEING CLICHED:
Women's Talk and Feminine Subjectivities

Niamh Stephenson
University of Western Sydney, Nepean

SUMMARY

In this chapter, I discuss ways of theorising the relationship between women's subjectivities and social practices of talk. I draw on sexual difference feminism (e.g. Irigaray, 1977; Irigaray 1985a; Irigaray 1985b; Irigaray, 1993) to argue for the need to move beyond phallocentric accounts of women's subjectivities, and to theorise power relations as intrinsic to social practices of talk (rather than describing the operation of power as disruptive of ordinary conversation). This approach to power offers a critique of many claims to equality between the sexes, on the basis that such claims perpetuate phallocentric versions of subjectivity. But here, I draw on a notion of "fictional equality" (Sennett, 1976), arguing that particular conventions which involve acting *as if* equality existed can be thought to result in the subversion of phallocentric subjectivities. This is because conventions of talk in which the subject is constituted as self-distanced might undermine the unitary, self-knowing attributes of phallocentric subjectivity. My argument begins with, and progresses through a discussion of one particular account of a young woman talking to a man on a bus.

MEMORY-WORK

Maria
> She was about 19 or 20 and was at university. She was travelling into the city on a bus and was about half way there when the old man next to her remarked on the female bus driver. He said how marvelous it was these days that women

were now capable of doing such things. She replied saying that women have been capable of many things but it is only now that they are allowed to do some of them. They got into a conversation about women's roles and he seemed to be of the mind that the roles performed by the sexes were grounded in nature. She gave a few cross-cultural examples which she had learned in her studies. He seemed surprised by this information and appeared to take it in. The conversation was friendly, both of them learning from each other. When the bus got to its final stop, they both thanked each other for the conversation saying how much they both enjoyed it - there was a genuine mutual appreciation for what had passed. A woman also getting off the bus said "I think we all enjoyed that conversation". Another lady said something similar, and she (Maria) said that she should have joined in. The woman said that she (Maria) seemed to be doing well enough on her own. People were smiling at both of them as they got off the bus - she went away feeling very good about the conversation she'd had, feeling like she really got someone to understand something and at the same time learned another's perspective.

This is an account of a "good conversation", produced for a memory-work group which met monthly for about a year, to discuss the topic of women's conversation (Stephenson, 1997). The rationale for this research arose, initially, from a particular understanding of subjectivity as constituted in intersubjective communication. This understanding can be traced from Mead's (1964, 1981) symbolic interactionism through to contemporary social constructionist psychology. For example, Harré contends that "[p]eople and their modes of talk are made by and for social orders, and social orders are people in conversation" (1983, p. 65). What happens, I ask, if we question the universalising tendency for "people" to mean "men", and if we seek to understand the relationship between women's subject-ivities, talk and the socio-symbolic order?

I address this question by drawing on women's experiences of conversation, as these experiences were written, related, debated and problematised through the process of memory-work (Haug, 1987; Crawford et al.; 1992, Stephenson, Kippax and Crawford, 1996). Very briefly, memory work involves writing accounts of particular events, and reading and analysing them as a group. In the group discussions about the memories, participants read "against the grain". Instead of accepting the memory as a true account, the idea is to question how it is that particular interpretations are possible. The analysis of the memories began in the group meetings, and developed as I wrote about the meetings. Whilst I am indebted to the group for many ideas, it would be unfair to claim that the concerns raised in this chapter are representative of the group.

Memory-work offers a way of theorising experience and subjectivity. Theory-driven explanations of experience can overlook the complexities and contradictions within experiences of talk. Grounding the analysis in women's conversation is an attempt to attend to these contradictions. The meaning of any given experience can always be contested (a process which is encouraged in memory-work). Here, experience is not approached as the bedrock of subjectivity, rather it is framed as the problem to be addressed (Scott, 1993). I read these memories and discussions as residues of the processes through which women's subjectivities are currently being constituted and lived in Sydney, Australia.

The question arises, why analyse women's talk through memory-work - as opposed to, say, doing a linguistic analysis of talk in "naturalistic" settings (e.g. Lakoff, 1973; Lakoff, 1975). Feminist linguists and socio-linguists have usefully highlighted the double bind which positions women as speakers. Lakoff puts it in the following terms: "[Women's] language works against treatment of women as serious persons with individual views" (1973, p. 45). "A woman is damned if she does and damned is she doesn't ... whichever course the woman takes - to speak women's language or not to - she will not be a respected" member of society (quoted by Crawford, 1995, p. 45-6). However, Lakoff does less in the way of addressing how women live conversation and how women are produced as particular kinds of subjects through practices of talk.

In analysing memories of past conversations, together with discussions about those memories, I am not seeking more or less true accounts of past events, nor am I attempting to outline the truth of women's lived experience and feminine subjectivities. Instead, these texts are treated as traces of the processes through which subjectivities are formed. Like subjectivity, the meaning of these processes is neither fixed nor unitary.

THEORISING WOMEN'S PLEASURE

Maria's memory about "a good conversation" is of interest for three, not unrelated, reasons. Firstly, Maria is a woman in public and this is one of the few accounts of a conversation in the public realm produced over the course of our meetings. The public and private domains are marked by sex. Historically, the increased separation of public power and private power has been concomitant with women's exclusion from public power (Hall, 1985). The apparent ease of the conversation between Maria and the man can be read as evidence of the fact that things have or can be changed and women can occupy a place in the public realm. In this sense, the memory can be read as an account of subversion of the sexing of the public/private dichotomy.

Secondly, the specific account of what constitutes a good conversation is of interest: a person marveling, giving information, surprise, being friendly, the participants "learning from each other", "genuine mutual appreciation", an encouraging audience, getting "someone to understand something and at the same time learning from another's perspective". Much of this description highlights the way in which the conversation is being characterised as an exchange. But what exactly is being exchanged? Although the man appears interested in what "she learned in her studies" about "women's roles", there is no description of what it might be that Maria gathers from him. We could read it in terms of recognition: what Maria gathers on this journey through public space is that she is capable of gaining the man's recognition of women's place in the public realm, and of using it as a basis for mutual understanding. In this reading, the memory concludes with what Maria learns - she can get recognition from "another's perspective"; in so doing, Maria transcends the double bind which positions women as speakers (as articulated by Lakoff). It follows that Maria's memory can be read as affirming a social constructionist approach to subjectivity; in both this reading of the memory and social constructionist psychology power relations aren't so much ignored, as characterised as extrinsic to the exchange of communication (Joas, 1985, Stephenson, in press).

A third reason for my interest in Maria's memory is that the meaning of the memory was hotly contested in the group. There was considerable resistance to the kind of reading outlined above. In the group discussion, it was implied that perhaps Maria misread the entire situation. Maybe the recognition Maria was getting was from a man who was simply enjoying the company and attentions of a young woman, the topic under discussion being of little relevance to him. It wasn't as if he was going to walk away from the bus actually contemplating what Maria had "learned in her studies". Implicitly, Maria is being accused of suffering from false consciousness - if only Maria had been more aware of the potential for the old man to be condescending she would have written a very different version of the memory. Maria didn't disagree entirely. The conversation was a good one from her point of view, partly because she enjoyed talking to an older man, he too could well have liked talking to a young woman regardless of what she was saying. But this didn't undermine the fact that it was a good conversation. She insisted that he was interested in the subject matter; all right, the man didn't wholeheartedly agree with every word she'd said, but she wouldn't expect as much. What she thought was special, was the fact that they had talked about such a potentially contentious issue in a friendly way. The *manner* of their talk was unexpected. Maria resisted the idea that she was being patronised by the man. This was, in turn, read as her unwillingness to entertain the notion that the good is haunted by the spectre of the bad, a rigid defense. Once framed this way, Maria's position is invalidated on the basis of her failure to take on the notion that the meaning of experience cannot be fixed. Rather than try to establish whether Maria's interpretation and defense are correct, I want to take another approach. This involves returning to the specificities of Maria's account of a "good conversation" (details which received little attention in the group discussion). The problem begins to crystallise. Pointing towards the ambiguity of the meaning of talk, and understanding the power relations which position women as ineffective speakers, are crucial strategies in a feminist analysis of talk (e.g. Crawford, 1995). Yet, we need to attend to the specificity of *particular* interpretations of conversation, and to be able to do so in a way which does not result in simply writing them off, on the basis of (an implied) false consciousness. The problem isn't the tension in the group *per se*, it is what is being excluded by the conflicting interpretations of the memory. By critiquing the lack of ambiguity in Maria's own interpretation, the group managed to avoid a discussion about the possibility of women's talk in the public realm being subversive or pleasurable.

QUESTIONING EQUALITY

Maria's insistence on a "genuine mutual appreciation" between herself and the old man shores up a notion of conversation as an exchange between two, already existing, subjects. They exist prior to the conversation in the sense that each can appreciate something about the other. Further, in the first reading of the memory, Maria and the old man are cast as potentially equal in their capacity to hold forth in this public situation, talking with a stranger on a bus. The audience of "women" and "ladies" echoes this reading, with comments along the lines of Maria "was doing well enough on her own". The scepticism, voiced in the group, about this idea of talk as an exchange between equal individuals can be understood against a backdrop of feminist thought and research on speaking positions and the notion of communication itself.

A concern with inequalities in language and talk is central to sexual difference feminist thought (e.g. Irigaray, 1985a). To speak is to enter into the symbolic order, a field through which subjectivity is constituted. Although there are both masculine and feminine points of identification in the symbolic order, both forms of subjectivity are phallocentric, relating to masculine fantasies. This is because language acts as a lens through which one sex can be imagined, and the other is rendered as a lack. Irigaray argues that "all Western discourse presents a certain isomorphism with the masculine sex: the privilege of unity, form of the self, of the visible, of the specularisable" (1977, p. 64). So the subjects of this symbolic order are phallocentric subjects - regardless of whether masculine or feminine positions are lived by a man or a woman. The feminine term remains outside, an excess which disrupts the symbolic order.

Irigaray's work counters attempts to define "woman" in terms of a singular identity, or subjectivity. Instead of asking "What is woman?" she argues that we need to "[repeat/interpret] the way in which, within discourse, the feminine finds itself defined as lack, deficiency"; we need to "signify that with respect to this logic a *disruptive excess* is possible on the feminine side" (1985a, p. 78). Sexual difference feminism offers a critique of explanations of women's subjectivity which entail splitting the good feminine aspects of subjectivity from the bad masculine aspects (cf. Kristeva, 1986). Hence, this approach allows discussion of women's own complicity

246

in structures and social practices which work to deny feminine autonomy, specificity and subjectivity (Rose, 1986). It has implications for how we consider both the processes of communication and the subjects who are constituted through it, or excluded from it. The analysis of phallocentrism afforded insight into many of the memories produced over the course of our meetings - particularly accounts of times when women appeared to use "shared rational means" of discussing differences, only to find our words dismissed (Stephenson, 1997).

Stressing the inherent ambiguity of conversation, Ien Ang writes "if meaning is never given and natural but always constructed and arbitrary, then it makes no sense to prioritize meaningfulness over meaninglessness ... failure to communicate should be considered 'normal' in a cultural universe where commonality of meaning cannot be taken for granted" (1994, p. 198).

Read in the light of this interest in the failure and nonsense of communication, it can be argued that Maria's defence of her interpretation of the memory shores up a phallocentric notion of communication. That is, because the equality of communication described in the memory exists within the symbolic realm, the feminine term is excluded, so this version of "equality" is to be deconstructed rather than celebrated.

This theoretical critique of "equality" highlights the problem of the rigidity of Maria's interpretation. But the argument that I have just outlined does less in the way of addressing why this particular account of a good conversation gave rise to tension and defense. I want to retain the emphasis on communication as ambiguous, but also to take account of the way in which theory can slide into ideology and become the basis of accusations of false consciousness. What am I trying to protect, I wonder? Is it an innocence in the way Maria happily uses "what she'd learnt in her studies", seemingly blissfully unaware of the misreadings she might be affording and the difficulties against which she might be defending? Or, is it the ways in which theory can be wielded to occlude the experiences we need to understand? What is of interest in this case is that Maria, a young woman, is being knowledgeable in public. At this point I want to look at the memory in terms of the possibilities that this story reveals about women speaking in the public realm, possibilities which were overlooked in the group discussion.

PUBLIC SPEAKING

The counter reading of Maria's memory can be recast as a rejection of the seemingly oblivious pleasure afforded by entering into a social convention, "talking to strangers". A young woman naïvely "informs" an old man about something he seems bound to resist. Although other memories produced in relation to this cue "a good conversation" were accounts in the private realm, they also evoked clichéd modes of talk. For example, one was a tale of the space to which relationships between women are relegated in heterosexual relationships, a story about the understanding and comfort women can offer each other amid situations of (heterosexual) love and loss. Another member of the group wrote about drawing on a social convention, talking about books, as a way of talking to someone whose company she thought she could never enjoy (Stephenson, 1997). In her introduction to memory-work, Haug (1987) characterises clichéd forms of expression as smoothing over the need to explain women's appropriation of "difficult realities". As memory-workers we had learnt to approach clichés as concealing the salient details of women's lives; clichés, we thought, covered over the gap between women's lives and phallocentric notions of "woman". They were the stuff of deconstruction and as a group we were beginning to feel adept at it. Yet in our "good conversation" memories we were confronted with our own enjoyment, not just of clichéd ways of expressing ourselves, but of clichéd ways of being. If our pleasure was clichéd, was it simply a dupe serving to obscure the process of our subordination?

What is the good of being clichéd then? Walkerdine (1990), commenting on Janice Radway's research on women and romance fiction, argues against approaching romance as an ideology to be transcended. This is because particular fantasies played out in romance fiction are integral to "the material *and* psychic reality of [readers'] servitude and the pain of their longing for something else" (p. 200). It is impossible to demarcate between "actual experience" and "fantasy" and it is not my intention to do so. Rather, I find it useful to approach our talk of clichés as talk of the lived experience of fantasy. With regard to Maria's memory this leads to a discussion of discourses of conversation pertaining to the public realm, and the ways in which women are (or are not) excluded by them. We can return to the memory, reading it in terms of a fantasised or fictional equality.

What might be entailed in such a fantasy? In *The Fall of Public Man*, Richard Sennett (1976) argues that the value of conventions enabling participation in the public realm is that they have provided a release from consideration of the relationship between one's actions and oneself, or one's true self. Sennett examines how talk between people (men) of different origins and classes took place in the coffeehouses of Paris and London in the late seventeenth and early eighteenth centuries. Men went to these places for information. So that conversation could flow, coffeehouse talk "was governed by a cardinal rule: in order for information to be as full as possible, distinctions of rank were temporarily suspended; anyone sitting in the coffeehouse had a right to talk to anyone else" (1976, p. 81). Talk was premised on the fiction that participants were equal. This fiction was possible, according to Sennett, because of an understanding of speech which was pervasive in the theatre of the day. Audiences did not read a play as representing reality, rather as creating a version of "reality through its conventions" (p. 79). In both the theatre and in coffeehouses, the meaning of a speaker's words was treated as self-evident (rather than hidden); "[t]o speak was to make a strong, effective, above all self-contained statement" (p. 79). Conversation between strangers involved a kind of self-distance; one's words were not evaluated in terms of one's identity or social positioning.

Sennett contends that sincere expression of one's true self is the antithesis of sociability in the public realm. Social conventions he argues, "are rules for behaviour at a distance from the immediate desires of the self", they are about being expressive rather than expressing oneself (1976, p. 266). If the public realm privileges masculine speaking positions, it is likely that the kind of self-distance to which Sennett refers is a luxury more often afforded to men. However, the kind of speaking position outlined by Sennett can subvert phallocentric masculinity (i.e. rational, unitary, autonomous subjectivity). "Being expressive" does not position the speaker as the originator of social conventions, nor are social conventions evaluated in terms of their capacity to reflect or represent the speaker. This approach to talk in the public realm counters the impulse to read the "fictional equality" of such a convention as meaningless or empty. Because the subject of clichéd conventions is a self-distanced subject, such conventions can be understood as constitutive of otherness, of non-unitary subjectivity - as opposed to failed or ideologically suspect subjectivity.

THE OTHERNESS OF "FICTIONAL EQUALITY"

Maria's defense of her memory was read in the group as a claim to true self-knowledge, an attempt to represent feminine subjectivity as singular, something which can be captured and accurately represented ("this is what really happened and who I really am"). But the counter-claim only reproduces the problem. By suggesting that Maria is defending against unspoken anxieties and shoring up phallocentric fantasies ("that's not who Maria really is"), Maria is still positioned within a discourse about the truth of women - in this case just as a failure. In contrast, if we approach clichéd conventions as affording self-distance, we are reminded that we can read the memory as an account of a moment in time. This is not the be all and end all of Maria. Ceasing to read the speaking subject in terms of the question of authenticity of subjectivity encourages multiple interpretations of the memory. But I want to return to consider what might be "good" about the memory, what might afford the pleasure in this account.

Maria can be read as potentially capable of challenging the man's position on the "natural" grounding of men and women's roles. The discussion between the man and the young woman is enabled by the convention of "talking to strangers on a bus". In this convention we would expect the flow of talk to be maintained - rather than expect the conversation to become an exercise in persuasion. Maintaining the flow of talk involves excluding difference, imposing a fictional equality between speakers. This kind of exclusion can feed into a fantasy of equality making sexual difference harder to acknowledge and discuss. Yet, entering into a fictional equality can also enable the proliferation of difference in at least two ways. Firstly, it allows both Maria and the man to recognise each other as different. Secondly, it allows Maria to recognise *herself* as different, to be "indefinitely other in herself" (Irigaray, 1985a, p. 28). It is this kind of fluidity, the otherness of subjectivity, which Irigaray foregrounds as potentially disrupting the unitary, static notions of masculinity and femininity entailed in the symbolic order. In Maria's memory, the notion of being "other in herself" is evoked in the surprise of the unexpected friendliness and appreciation which characterises her conversation with the old man. It also provides a way of re-thinking self-distance. In Sennett's own articulation self-distance is characterised as something a rational, unitary subject can do. Whereas here, self-distance is a doing, through which rational, unitary subjectivity is subverted.

CONCLUSION

The pleasure of Maria's conversation can be understood as produced in the tension between two modes of talk. On the one hand, because she is a woman talking about women she is vulnerable to being read as if she is speaking the truth of women, and to being patronised. On the other, she is participating in the convention of talking to strangers. Because ostensibly this convention dispenses with notions of true selves, conferring the status of "other" on all involved, it can undermine positions of authority and self-knowledge. Maria can be read as subverting masculine autonomy (in the sense that she counters the man's initial comments). But, more importantly, she realises the malleability of social conventions in that she is a woman speaking and being heard in public. The ambiguity remains. I suggest that it is because of (rather than in spite of) the fact that she risks being positioned as other in relation to phallocentric notions of subjectivity that the experience is remembered as pleasurable (Stephenson, in press).

So, when we consider social conventions of speech entailed in the public realm as sites for the production of women's subjectivities, particular moments of conversation can be read as potentially enabling self-distance, a way of becoming other in and to ourselves (Sennett, 1976). However, the resulting experiences of freedom (freedom from the notion of a true self) are still underpinned by a tension; i.e. the tension between the proliferation and obliteration of difference upon entering into social conventions. Maria's memory can be read as suggesting the malleability of clichéd conventions, conventions which women often experience as restrictive. But clichéd ways of being can also be the means through which women experience pleasure in talk, indulge in improper fantasies and experience ourselves as other in and to ourselves.

250

REFERENCES

Ang, I. (1994). In the realm of uncertainty: The global village and capitalist postmodernity. In D. Crowley & D. Mitchell (Eds), *Communication theory today* (pp. 193-213). Oxford: Polity Press.

Crawford, J., Kippax, S., Onyx, J., Gault, U., & Benton, P. (1992). *Emotion and gender: Constructing meaning from memory*. London: Sage.

Crawford, M. (1995). *Talking difference: On gender and language*. London: Sage.

Hall, C. (1985). Private persons versus public someones: Class, gender and politics in England, 1780-1850. In C. Steedman, C. Urwin & V. Walkerdine (Eds), *Language, gender and childhood* (pp. 10-33). London: Routledge, Kegan & Paul.

Harré, R. (1983). *Personal being: A theory for individual psychology*. Oxford: Basil Blackwell.

Haug, F. (Ed.). (1987) *Female sexualization: A collective work of memory* (E. Carter, Trans.). London: Verso.

Irigaray, L. (1977). Women's exile. *Ideology and Consciousness, 1,* 62-76.

Irigaray, L. (1985a). *This sex which is not one* (C. Porter with C. Burke, Trans.). Ithaca: Cornell University Press.

Irigaray, L. (1985b). *Speculum of the other woman* (G. Gill, Trans.). Ithaca: Cornell University Press.

Irigaray, L. (1993). *Sexes and genealogies* (G. Gill, Trans.). New York: Columbia University Press.

Joas, H. (1985). *G. H. Mead: A contemporary re-examination of his thought* (R. Meyer, Trans.). Cambridge: Polity Press.

Kristeva, J. (1986). Women's time. In T. Moi (Ed.), *The Kristeva reader* (pp. 187-213). Oxford: Basil Blackwell.

Lakoff, R. (1973). Language and woman's place. *Language in Society, 2,* 45-79.

Lakoff, R. (1975). *Language and woman's place*. New York: Harper and Row.

Mead, G. H. (1964). *Selected writings of George Herbert Mead* (A. J. Reck, Ed.). Chicago: The University of Chicago Press.

Mead, G. H. (1981). *On social psychology* (A. Strauss, Ed.). Chicago: The University of Chicago Press.

Rose, J. (1986). *Sexuality in the field of vision*. London: Verso.

Scott, J. (1993). The evidence of experience. In H. Abelove, M.A. Barale, & D.M. Halperin (Eds), *The lesbian and gay studies reader* (pp. 397-415). London: Routledge.

Sennett, R. (1976). *The fall of public man*. Cambridge: Cambridge University Press.

Stephenson, N. (1997). *Strange expressions: Remembering women's conversation*. Unpublished PhD thesis, Maquarie University, Sydney.

Stephenson, N. (in press). 'Speaking as a woman': Subjectivities and social practices of talk. *Australian Psychologist.*

Stephenson, N., Kippax, S., & Crawford, J. (1996). You and me and she: Memory-work and the construction of self. In S. Wilkinson (Ed.), *Feminist social psychologies: International perspectives* (pp. 182-200). Buckingham: Open University Press.

Walkerdine, V. (1990). *Schoolgirl fictions*. London: Verso.

INDIVIDUAL RESPONSIBILITY AND SOCIETY:
A Subject Science Approach

Ute Osterkamp
Free University of Berlin

SUMMARY

This article questions the prevailing individualized notions of subjectivity, individuality and responsibility and points to their function in justifying restrictive conditions by reversing the causes and the consequences of suppression. It advances the notion of "meta-subjectivity" referring to the specific human potentiality of consciously influencing the conditions influencing us – only to be realized on a meta-individual level and necessarily implying our responsibility for societal development and thus also for the situation and behavior of others. This is elucidated using approaches explicitly criticizing traditional psychology's individualism while replacing it by a more societal approach and showing how such approaches relapse into individualism when they ignore specific human "meta-subjectivity" and along with it the manifold obstacles to realizing it.

INTRODUCTION: THE SOCIETAL NATURE OF HUMANKIND AS A PRECONDITION FOR GRASPING SUPPRESSION

In the last two decades traditional psychology's fixation on the individual and its neglect of societal circumstances has been criticized "radically" especially by other social sciences. Since these shortcomings are usually attributed to psychology focusing on individuals' "nature" as an explanation of their behavior, the abandonment of this notion seems to break this impasse. However it more often than not results in the biological reductionism merely being replaced by a sociological one. Both camps, the criticized and the criticizing differ from each other merely in their holding opposite positions within the shared dualism of nature and individual, on the one hand, and culture and society on the other. Such a dualism, however, irrespective of the position chosen and one's own possibly progressive intentions, functions to vindicate people's estrangement - their expropriation from the means to influence the circumstances of their lives consciously, i.e. in accord with their own needs and hopes.

In contrast to such controversies of whether human behavior is determined by nature or society, Critical Psychology as founded by Klaus Holzkamp, started from the conviction that such questions are put in a way which rather obscures problems than helps to clarify them. Admittedly the term "human nature" is generally used by psychology to explain people's different access to societal possibilities by alleged biological differences. But simply dropping this term obviously doesn't solve the problem but, on the contrary, silently presumes infinite adaptability is human nature and merely deprives us of the means to conceive suppression as well as its objective function and subjective costs. In our view, the potentially reactionary implications of the term "human nature" can only be countered if we don't use it to explain individuals' different social positions or personal behavior as an expression of their different nature, but tackle it on a meta-individual, i.e. phylogenetic level as a specific potentiality which applies to all human beings alike and differentiates them from all other species. This does not imply, as might be assumed, hailing humankind as the crowning of Creation, but rather recognizing the specific human form of suppression as well the manifold forms of its ideological disguise.

The species specific quality of human beings, however, is, as is suggested by our analyses of phylogenesis, their "societal nature", i.e. their relative freedom of behavior from external or internal compulsions. In contrast to all other species, people don't characteristically act under the pressure of circumstances and/or their own neediness but are able to create the conditions of their lives in accord with their needs and desires which themselves will retroactively develop and differentiate in this process of individual self-extension into the external/societal world. The processes of world-creation and self-creation are thus one and the same process. People's societal nature as their potential power of determining the conditions they are dependent on, however, can only be realized by overcoming their individual limits in cooperation with others under the shared goal of improving common life conditions.

The extension of one's own potentialities in cooperation with others, however, applies only to conditions of equal access to societal potentialities. In societies where the majority's influence on the conditions of their existence is systematically curtailed, other people appears less as a precondition of one's own potentialities, but are rather judged according to the personal advantages or disadvantages to be expected from them and/or seen as competitors for scarce resources. This competition turns out to be the most powerful tool of undermining any resistance and is therefore not left to chance or pressure of circumstances, but additionally reinforced. A most effective means to this end is the reversal of causes and consequences of suppression by individualizing and personalizing the problems, i.e. blaming people for the effects suppression has on them – according to Marx and Engels the essence of the bourgeois' duplicity and hypocrisy (cf. Osterkamp, 1999a).

In a similar vein, Elaine Scarry (1985) talks of projecting out our needs and capabilities into the external world where they are objectified, made social, placed in a universal exchange, freed from their privacy and their confinement to ourselves. What differentiates the human species from other creatures is, she notes, neither the natural acuity of our sentience nor the natural frailty of the organic tissue in which it resides but instead the fact that our sentience is objectified in artifacts and is thus fundamentally transformed to be communicable and endlessly sharable. Freeing our sentience of its embodiedness in a process of self-transformation makes, as Scarry points out, both the external world sentient, compassionate and attentive to us as well turns our body itself into an artifact. She talks in this connection of "tiers of projected embodiedness" or "layers of objectification" which separate us from the state of objectlessness, i.e. the immediate experience of our physical vulnerability.

In class societies, however, the inextricable connection of world- and self-creation is, as Scarry puts it, structurally dissolved. Those who are exhaustingly engaged in acts of artifice are largely exiled from the realm of self-artifice. All their psychic states are, as she depicts, nearly without objectification, and all their life activities stand in the vicinity of physical pain. Thus, Scarry sums up, two kinds of people are created – those who suffer, desire, and risk in their bodies and those who suffer in "their" artifice: While the capitalist suffers in his money, the worker suffers in his very existence. But not just suffering, but all forms of consciousness are, as Scarry emphasizes, involved in the difference between belonging to those who are largely disembodied or belonging to those who remain radically embodied. The objective difference of self-extension into the external world in liberating from the body's immediate demands by realizing/objectifying them, in turn, carries with it, as Scarry puts it, differences in the capacity for new forms of self-extension which, however, usually appear as personal differences in ambition, talent, style, professionalism etc.

INDIVIDUAL SUBJECTIVITY AS A META-SUBJECTIVE PROCESS

Klaus Holzkamp (1983, 1996) suggests the term "meta-subjectivity" to facilitate tackling the fundamental unity of world- and self-creation in social science. This term entails a fundamental change in psychology's orientation: the individuals are no longer the object of research (to perfect their controllability and usability) but rather the subjective import and impact of societal conditions are to be examined which make it appear a matter of course that people are viewed as a problem instead of their being enabled to recognize the societal context of their difficulties and conflicts (and the social context needs to be highlighted if people are to tackle their problems in a way that solves them rather than making them worse).

To conceptualise this difference, Klaus Holzkamp distinguishes a mere subject-orientation from a subject science approach. While the subject-orientation tries to get as much information about the individuals as possible in order to perfect control over them, a subject science approach is engaged in widening individuals' influence on the conditions they are dependent on – a process simultaneously revealing the manifold obstacles hampering such attempts. Similarly to a subject-orientation, a subject science approach also starts from people's immediate experiences; yet it is not content with merely describing, labelling, and statistically categorising them but views the individual experience only as the indispensable starting point for actual scientific research – replacing the descriptive access by a constructive one through penetrating outer appearances and revealing their societal context and interdependence.

Since our potential power over the conditions we are dependent on is to be realized only together with others, the term "meta-subjectivity" doesn't entail merely a widened perspective on life but implies a more comprehensive notion of responsibility. Having influence on the conditions of one's life necessarily entails being responsible for them and thus also responsible for the others' situation and behavior affected by the conditions we support, whether we want to or not. Or put in another way, from the subject's position: ignoring the preconditions of others' behavior is grounded in our defensive tendency to protect our good conscience while leaving others to their fate.

The notion of "meta-subjectivity" hence does not at all negate our individuality and/or responsibility for our personal behavior altogether, as it might seem at first sight, but merely clears up and creates the preconditions enabling us to realise our "societal nature" and subjectivity. In contrast with that, ignoring how behavior is mediated by societal conditions, means reducing individual responsibility to self-discipline but denying the individuals the basis for realising the "morals" they are asked to practice; the inherently preprogrammed failure functions to convince them both of their own inferiority and to morally legitimate given power relations.

Disregarding or ignoring the societal mediation of people's behavior is substantiated by an abstract moral system confirming the usual reversal of causes and consequences of suppression – an ideological mainstay of each power structure. Hence, if we want to resist this ideological mechanism, we have to make a radical break with concentrating on the manifestation of societal restrictions in people's behavior and instead examine these restrictions themselves as well as the manifold modes of their ideological vindication.

The prescriptive notion of morality as an external standard (systematically ignoring its own historic-societal context and function) embodies the notorious dualism of egotism and altruism as an indubitable reality. Taking into account the others' interests is in this view not seen as realizing one's own subjectivity but a moral commandment necessarily contrary to our own interest, with the only topic of disagreement being the question of how far such a self-castigation should go. While some scholars (for instance Zygmunt Bauman, 1989) seem to view self-sacrifice as the paragon of morality, others evidently prefer a more moderate notion; Mordecai Nisan (1986), for example, advances his model of moral balance tolerating moral lapses as long the overall balance is biased to the good. The other's welfare is apparently of no interest as such, but merely a means to achieve better grades in morality.

The predominance of a notion of "subjectivity" bound to the individual is surely explained to a large extent by the fact that we have been so indoctrinated with the idea that we can hardly imagine an alternative except as abandoning the idea of individuality and a person's uniqueness altogether. But apart from such an ideological impact, we evidently cling to the narrow notion of subjectivity on our own (defensive) behalf since we are not merely suffering suppressive conditions but are always tied to them and part of them. Hence, questioning suppressive structures always requires, if not merely to serve appellative or ideological functions, examining our own share in them. However, the fact that we don't merely suffer suppression (or fight against it in the name of others) but actively practice it and profit from it, is a reality we rather prefer to ignore – and have good reasons for doing so as long as the structurally imposed complicity is not grasped as a particular humiliating and disarming form of our own suppression, but misunderstood as an expression of our personal lust for power. The denial of the suppressive character of one's own behavior, however, is itself an aspect of suppression and essential for it functioning efficiently: Becoming aware of the suppressive character of one's own behavior – actually based in our compliance with restrictive structures – makes it problematic to see conformity to the norms as a virtue. Where suffering suppression can be meliorated by transposing it into the "virtue" of modesty, humility etc., others accusing me of suppression can only be met by either denial or willingness to change. Since change always involves questioning given normality and thus conflict, the tendency is to deny and indeed to see the accusation as suppressive in itself – thus confirming the general reversal of causes and consequences of suppression through one's own behavior.

AGENCY AS A DETERMINANT OF THE SOCIETAL CONDITIONS OF OUR LIVES: Toward the Overcoming of Dualistic Thinking

Since the individualized concept of subjectivity and responsibility represents a slave- or slaveholder-morality rather than a universal one, alternatives can only become visible when we turn to the power structures and their impact on our "personal" behavior, which "scientific" discussion too usually passes over in silence. Above all, this implies dealing with our own entanglement with suppressive conditions – including the manifold "good reasons" better to remain ignorant of them. As long, however, as we avoid doing so we will – despite all possible progressive intentions – defend the conditions enforcing such a defensive behavior on us and relapse into the personalizing way of thinking with the usual reversal of causes and consequences of suppression in its wake.

In order to make these statements more convincing, I shall try to illustrate them using some examples from emotion research. This seems apposite since in the last two decades it is precisely here that many interesting approaches have been developed as a critique of traditional psychology's "worldlessness" and its dualistic notions, particularly the contrast between emotion and cognition which is then sought to be overcome by stressing the cognitive quality of emotions too. Thus, for example Richard S. Lazarus (cf. 1977, 1990) imparts (though rather in passing) the most crucial insight that emotional appraisals are usually blended with people's actions and only become an "outstanding" problem if their objectification is being hampered. This corresponds in a way with Freud's (1915/1981) differentiation between the "idea" and the "amount" of an "affect" which disintegrates if the critically evaluated object, for instance the father, is not allowed to be objectified or named. Lazarus, however, questions as little as Freud does "authorities" who cannot afford to be evaluated by those they govern. Instead, he too narrows his interest down to individual attempts of coping with such a de-objectified arousal. This is, as he states, possible by "re-appraising" the situation, or by directly controlling the arousal by using tranquilizers, relaxation exercises, drugs etc. He praises the subjective capacity of such a re-appraisal and "calming down" as an expression of individuals' personal autonomy which, however, can, as he simultaneously warns, go too far, become pathological and result in a total loss of reality or of one's own identity.

The cognitive approach to emotions is radicalized in social constructionist theory in so far as it largely ignores if not denies the "embodiment" of emotions altogether. Such a denial of emotions' physical substantiality, however, not only makes suppression unconceivable but presupposes it implicitly as a matter of course. Claire Armon-Jones (1986), for example, advances the idea of emotions as social prescriptions and consistently discusses them only from the perspective of their social usability; according to her, the main function of emotions is to stabilize given power-structures by ensuring individuals' loyalty and mutually moral surveillance. Owing to this, emotions like guilt and shame rank high and are largely identified with individuals' morality. The question of what subjective meaning a particular emotion as well as their "prescription" have, does not arise. The "radical" social constructionist version of emotions as merely created by their naming is usually compensated for by a general willingness to compromise. Thus, Armon-Jones, too, concedes that there may be some "natural" emotions though she herself is mainly interested in the prescribed ones which, as she admits, might yet be substantiated by natural ones – the inborn fear of big animals, for example, may be transformed into the respect for authorities, as she explains.

Though social constructionist theory surely doesn't deny suppression it evidently holds that it can be ignored as a limited problem which, in any case, has nothing to do with one's own thinking. Thus, for example, Armon-Jones answers an anticipated criticism of social constructionism neglecting suppression by stating that emotions can only be suppressed if they had been constituted first, and therefore it is better to concentrate initially on how they are produced. This way of arguing basically excludes the possibility of people's "emotionality" or irrationality as being produced to justify their suppression. Such a customary first-then-logic or either-or-arguing, however, tends to end up in the common compromise of "humanizing" suppression by closing one's eyes to its effects. Here too, we find Freud once again advancing a more dialectic view and overcoming the simple dualism of emotions as either socially constructed or biologically grounded when he at least partially indicates (and simultaneously veils) the production of people's instinctiveness by denying them the means to realize their desires as prerequisite of their development. The most effective means of warding off people's aggressions caused by their exclusion from societal potentialities, he notes, is to transform them into feelings of shame and guilt about one's own moral insufficiency.

From a meta-subjective perspective which aims not at increasing society's influence on people but people's influence on society, the question would less be whether and what emotions are natural or cultural, whether they occur in animals too or only in people, but under what conditions, for instance, our anger amounts to a "bestial rage" or "blind hatred" so that we remain controlled by it and thereby also by the conditions which give rise and reason to it.

The criticism of social constructionist theory usually does not refer to narrowing its interest in people to their societal usability and emotional manipuability, but only to the futility of such attempts. Thus, for instance, John D. Greenwood (1994) puts forward the argument that the social quality of emotions doesn´t result from their prescription, but is immanent to them; naming them doesn´t bring them into being, he argues, but, on the contrary, emotion words will only make sense if they describe some subjective reality, and the content of the word "shame" can only be grasped when people have already experienced it. In his further explanations, however, he himself reduces emotions to a kind of social cement and a tool to "shame" people via the threat of their possible exclusion. According to him, specific human emotions are those concerned with our social reputation as, for instance, shame, guilt, pride, envy, jealousy etc., i.e. emotions which indicate rather inhuman conditions from a subject's standpoint where people´s acceptance is not a matter of course but always has to be proven anew.

The danger of merely reproducing common sense in academic thought instead of surmounting it because we lack the "appropriate means to see what is ongoing before our eyes", as Scarry puts it, becomes apparent in Robert C. Solomon's (1984, 1993) work, too. Since he regards psychology's "individualism" and "physiologism" as the essential source of its insufficiency, he tries to overcome it by denying that the physiological dimension of emotions has any import for understanding emotions at all. Emotions are, he states, judgements differing from normal ones only by their heat and hastiness. In contrast to mere "feelings" (like pain) referring to nothing else but to themselves, emotions are, he emphasizes, only to be recognized by their relatedness to the external world which they reflect the subjective meaning of. Since, however, Solomon too evidently views societal conditions in the final analysis as outside of people's influence, in the final analysis, he likewise turns emotional appraisals against individuals themselves by dismissing all emotions as "inappropriate" which could provoke conflicts. Contrary to feelings like pain (which merely happen to us) emotions are, he argues, judgements made by us and so we are inherently accountable for them: In order to change our emotions, we would simply have to change our appraisals embodied in them. The subjective costs of such an imposed re-appraisal or self-denial, vividly depicted by Freud and at least hinted at by Lazarus, remain invisible. Though he explicitly states that emotions will only be understood by the external objects or events they refer to, in his further explanations this insight is lost again. Thus, for example, he suddenly assumes a striving for self-esteem as a final "motive" of all emotions and hence relapses into exactly that same essentialist view he rightly criticizes psychology for. Instead of inquiring into the particular circumstances which render "self-esteem" as a problem engaging all our concern, he then tackles the academic question of whether this "motive" will apply to all emotions alike or not. A similar move away from his premises can be noted when he – despite his statement that emotions can only be understood by their objectification – doesn´t inquire into the causes and processes of their de-objectivation but ponders instead about the abstract "problem" of whether Freud's "free floating anxiety" is to be categorized as a feeling or an emotion.

SOCIETAL DEMORALIZATION: An Essential Means of Undermining Personal Integrity and Subjectivity

A radical break with the individualizing/personalizing notions of subjectivity, responsibility and morality has been made, as far as I can see, only by those who had survived German extermination camps. Since they had experienced the inhumanity of fascist normality uncushioned by any of the usual privileges or chances to overlook it (in that it merely seemed to affect some distant others), they took quite "naturally" the subject standpoint – pointing to the societal causes of their suffering.

The omnipotence of the fascist brutality in the camps as well as the impossibility of ignoring the potentially fatal consequences of being unable to help others, evidently made ineffective the usual attempts at asserting one's own "innocence" or consoling oneself about one's own demoralization by pointing to the even greater corruption of others. Refraining from every attempt (anyway futile in their particular situation) to maintain the semblance of morality, evidently gave the "survivors" the "inner" independence to grasp the conditions of their own demoralization as well as the societal function it serves. With that, they quasi re-reversed the "normal" reversal of causes and consequences of suppression, i.e. viewed their "immorality" not as a personal failure and something to be hidden in shame, but as the most inhuman crime done to them – depriving them of any self-respect and resistance.

Thus, for example, Jean Améry (1988), Imre Kertész (1997) and Primo Levi (1993), who all had survived Auschwitz and other death camps, on the one hand, decisively rejected all "excuses" for their actual behavior, but, on the other hand, also all attempts (how ever sympathetically or emphathetically advanced) to judge it from an external standpoint; instead they demanded a thorough inquiry into the fascist strategies of demoralizing their "objects" and especially into their "normal" embedding and pre-stages (generally accepted if not welcomed by the German majority).

The survivors' insight into the inhumanity of a "normality" they had systematically been excluded from and thus perforce gained a certain "distance" to, was not grasped by the majority as a chance to understand the mechanisms of their own demoralization, i.e. of how they had been made to comply with the fascist system and turn a blind eye to what it meant for those defined as "enemies". Instead, each questioning of normality (and the majority's acquiescence in it) was rather perceived as an attack on the majority's "innocence", which they claimed they had kept untarnished despite their complicity with the fascist system. This denial of one's own active entanglement in the fascist system and hence co-accountability for its crimes was not left to chance but systematically guided (if not prescribed) by the official way of "coming to terms with the past". For this purpose, fascism had to be personalized, narrowed down or projected onto some exceptionally "inhumane" persons or groups so far beyond everyday normality as to make the latter free of all suspicion and remove any need for self-scrutiny. This self-assuring attitude and denial of any criticism, however, largely hampered, as Améry notes, endeavors towards grasping the past – a past shared both by the German majority as well the persecuted groups, despite their radically contrary positions within it. The refusal to deal with the past and take responsibility for it by searching for an understanding of how it could have happened, condemned the "survivors" to the same isolation they had already suffered from under fascism – according to Améry, the worst aspect of their situation; it was combined with "blaming the victims" for failing to overcome their "resentments" which in its final analysis meant, as Améry states, being blamed for having survived and bothering the majority with their (the "survivors'") personal incapacity of coming to terms with what "simply happened to them". However, it was, Améry points out (and surely still is), precisely the majority's rejection of dealing with their own share in the fascist past which nailed them to their suffering and robbed them of any possibility to rid themselves of it.

Similarly to the German majority and its political representatives, social sciences too lost interest in the survivors' reports once they were no longer confined to portraying their past as artistically or emotional as possible but became "political", i.e. pointed to their preconditions within accepted normality (cf. Peitsch, 1990). If, however, social (power)structures are not to be questioned, those suffering from them have to be silenced. Améry (1988) for example, pours scorn on the services of psychology in particular through the invention of the "KZ-syndrome", pathologizing the "survivors" for their "abnormal" obsession with the past. Such a victimization, however, cheats the "survivors", as Améry makes clear, out of any chance of "productively" overcoming their sufferings by objectifying them, i.e. clarifying and overcoming their societal causes – thus regaining their own "agency" and subjectivity in a process of humanizing the world. But for the majority too, refusal to accept the insights of former extermination camp prisoners into the inhumanity of our "normality" has its price; it confirms the circle of our own disempowerment and its implicit asociality mutually supporting themselves in binding us to the conditions of our own powerlessness and humiliation.

CURRENT RESEARCH AND OUTLOOK

Most recently, Lenora Fulani (1998) has (with reference to Fred Newman and Lois Holzman) discussed the inherent "authoritarianism" and "judgementalism" permeating moral philosophy and moral development research; she too questions morality as an external standard people have to live up to which, as she likewise points out, actually tends to hinder rather than encourage individual morality. Consequently, she rejects the manifold attempts to save the prevailing moral system by modifying it. In the course of her argument, she also challenges Gilligan´s suggestion of correcting the prevailing orientation on "justice" by introducing greater consideration of the care-dimension. Rather than clinging to the idea of morality as an abstract system codifying our lives in one way or other we should, she suggests, concentrate on the actual "morality-making" as it "occurs in the everyday, moment-to-moment, continuous meaning-making activity of human beings engaged in living their lives" (p.149). From such a "activist perspective" the actual question to deal with would be "how do we help support people to transform the circumstances that determine us?" (p.154).

This notion has much in common with the view I tried to explain here. Since, however, Fulani, does not inquire closer into the societal production and function of individuals´ demoralization, she herself remains "abstract" and runs the risk of simply duplicating reality, i.e. confirming given power structures - which can only be overcome if we consider the fact that they are not merely imposed on us but that we are also profiting from them and supporting them. Thus, for instance, Fulani attacks the "authoritarian reification of the morality-making activity" as a "non-changing ideal...to which we must strive and by which we are judged"; and she likewise points to the disempowering effects of given morality and how it hinders people from participating "in creating developmental environments, thereby developing themselves in all ways, including what we might identify as morally" (p.150). However, when she advances her own view of a morality as emerging from our everyday activities, she tacitly ignores the fact that we are already "participating" and that a main task of critical psychology is hence to analyze the concrete ways in which it happens as well as the preconditions, implications, and consequences such a "participation" has. This entails the necessity of inquiring into the manifold modes of guarding against the potentially "revolutionary" insights into our entanglement with the suppression of others we are in many ways made to deny and which, in turn, will secure our loyalty with given power structures as long as it remains denied. Ignoring the suppressive character of our own behavior, however, means contributing to the societal "unconsciousness" indispensable for power structures. From a subject science point of view, therefore, inferring morality from people´s factual behavior will scarcely suffice. To overcome the dominant morality and its demoralizing effects, rather an even higher "abstraction" is required, a kind of "meta-subjectivity" (Holzkamp, 1996), i.e. an attitude not only defensively concerned with our own moral unassailability or with the - lesser - morality of others as its foil, but which takes responsibility too for the others' moral integrity by exposing and overcoming the societal structures and mechanisms of their demoralization. This, however, will only be possible if we do not try to hide our own demoralization but grasp it as an expression of inhuman conditions to be overcome as soon as possible.

REFERENCES

Améry, J. (1988). Ressentiments. In J. Améry *Jenseits von Schuld und Sühne. Bewältigungsversuche eines Überwältigten* (pp. 81-101). Stuttgart: Klett-Cotta.

Armon-Jones, C. (1986). The social function of emotion. In R. Harré (Ed.), *The social construction of emotion* (57-82). Oxford: Blackwell.

Bauman, Z. (1989). *Modernity and the Holocaust*. Ithaca NY: Cornell University Press.

Freud, S. (1981/1915). Instincts and their vicissitudes. In J. Strachey, *The standard edition of the complete psychological works of Sigmund Freud*. (Vol. XIV, pp.105-140). London: Hogarth Press.

Fulani, L. (1998). Moving beyond morality and identity. In Burman, E. (Ed.), *Deconstructing feminist psychology* (pp. 140-158). London: Sage.

Greenwood, J. D. (1994). *Realism, identity and emotion: Reclaiming social psychology*. London: Sage.

Holzkamp, K. (1983). *Grundlegung der Psychologie*. Frankfurt/M.: Campus.

Holzkamp, K. (1996). Psychologie. Selbstverständigung über Handlungsbegründungen alltäglicher Lebensführung. *Forum Kritische Psychologie 36*, 7-112.

Kertész, I. (1997). *Galeerentagebuch*. Reinbek: Rohwohlt.

Lazarus, R.S. (1977). Cognitive and coping processes in emotion. In A. Monat, & R.S. Lazarus (Eds) *Stress and coping. An anthology* (pp.145-158). New York: Columbia University Press

Lazarus, R.S. (1990). Constructs of the mind in adaptation. In N.L. Stein, B. Leventhal & T. Trabasso (Eds), *Psychological and biological approaches to emotion* (pp. 3-19). Hillsdale NJ: Erlbaum.

Levi, P. (1993). *Die Untergegangenen und die Geretteten*. München: dtv, 1993, pp.33-69

Nisan, M. (1986). Die moralische Bilanz. Ein Modell moralischen Entscheidens. In W. Edelstein and G. Nunner-Winkler (Hrsg.), *Zur Bestimmung der Moral* (pp. 347-376). Frankfurt/M.: Suhrkamp

Osterkamp, U. (1999a). Gefühle/Emotionen. In *Historisch-Kritisches Wörterbuch des Marxismus* Vol. 4, (pp. 1329-1347). Argument: Hamburg

Osterkamp, U. (1999b). Reflections on emotionality, morality, subjectivity and power. Paper presented at the Millennium World Conference on Critical Psychology, Sydney, April/May.

Peitsch, H. (1990). *"Deutschlands Gedächtnis an seine dunkelste Zeit". Zur Funktion der Autobiographik in den Westzonen Deutschlands und den Westsektoren von Berlin 1945 bis 1949*. Berlin: Sigma

Scarry, E. (1985). *The body in pain: The making and unmaking of the world.* Oxford: Oxford University Press

Solomon, R.C. (1984). Getting angry. The Jamesian theory of emotion in anthropology. In R. A. Shweder & R. A. LeVine (Eds), *Culture theory: Essays on mind, self, and emotion* (pp. 238-254). Cambridge: Cambridge University Press.

Solomon, R.C. (1993). The philosophy of emotions. In M. Lewis & J. M. Haviland (Eds), *Handbook of emotion* (pp.3-14). New York: Guilford Press.

MODELS OF THE LIFE-SPAN FOR AN AGEING SOCIETY

Rosemary Leonard and Ailsa Burns
University of Western Sydney, Nepean; and Macquarie University

SUMMARY

The panic surrounding the "greying" of western societies reflects an unnecessarily negative view of older people. This paper examines how models of the life-span can either encourage panic or assist us to construct a society with a positive attitude to the contribution of its older people. The paper contrasts "rise and fall" models, which include most physiological and cognitive theories, with "progress" models such as stage or life course theories. In particular it is argued that life course approaches with the addition of a political-economy perspective are promising in that they reposition older people individually and collectively as active contributing creators of their own quality of life.

INTRODUCTION

The panic surrounding the demographic trend for western societies to have a larger proportion of older people reflects an unnecessarily negative view of older people as helpless dependents using up vast quantities of resources for no benefit to younger society. This paper examines how models of the life-span can either encourage panic or assist us to construct a society which recognises the current contribution of its older people and allows that contribution to increase.

The topic "Models of the life-span for an ageing society" implies the question, "How can we best model the life-span given that in most western societies people are living longer?" The question itself contains assumptions which are inconsistent with the positivist search for an underlying explanatory law.

It implies that there is not just one correct way to understand the life-span, for if there were presumably it would be correct regardless of whether society is ageing or not. The assumption of many possible models is not just a reflection of the many ways that lives are being lived (eg career woman in the city versus Aboriginal woman in a desert settlement). Such variations in life-span are the information which the model must represent. One criterion for identifying a satisfactory model could be its ability to deal with diversity.

If the search for a best model is not just a question of correctness, then it is part of the political or moral domain. It implies that our choice of model has implications for the welfare of people within the society. One way to understand the importance of our models is through Harré's (1983) work on personal being. Harré argues that what distinguishes people from non-people is that we have theories about the self. These theories are acquired from the society we live in and tell us how to be a person. There may be a variety of ways that are prescribed by particular cultures but the range will not be huge. Humans follow the prescriptions so that they become people within a society. From this perspective, models of the lifespan can then be seen as theories of the self which are adopted in the process of becoming a person within a society. A model that is widely adopted defines the type of people we are. What we need to understand are the effects on the creation of persons when we promote one particular model rather than another. Ultimately the question of which is the "best" model can only be answered through wider debate about values and the types of people we wish to create in our society.

"RISE AND FALL" MODELS

Rise and fall models assume a steady increase in almost all physical and cognitive abilities throughout childhood, adolescence, and young adulthood, followed by stability though middle-age and then a gradual decline in all functioning. The endpoint of the fall of later life corresponds to the infantilising of older people critiqued by Hockey and James (1993). The model is well represented in the writings of gerontologists, economists and health service professionals (Clare and Tulpule, 1994: McCallum and Geiselhart, 1996).

One example of a rise and fall model is *disengagement theory* which asserts that there is a process of gradual withdrawal from society. This idea is based in functionalism, and the disengagement is taken to be natural, inevitable and beneficial. Thus for the frail aged confined to a nursing home, it has been thought natural to withdraw from the present into a state of reminiscence about the past, leading to further social isolation. Sargent (1999) objects to disengagement theory because withdrawal and isolation may well be forced on some older people by society's devaluation of them and policy towards them.

Further, the extent to which the rise and fall model is the dominant model of ageing in society is reflected in everyday discourses (for example, we speak of older people as "over the hill" or "past it"); and the acquisition of any condition associated with ageing may be treated as a sign that all mental and physical functions are deteriorating. The rise and fall model fits our everyday experience that those at the bottom, young children and older people, are less valued than those at midlife who are "at their peak" and those "on the way up" are more valued than those "on the way down." These discourses include a moral imperative for the ageing individual to slow down the inevitable decline into dependence.

This moral imperative is reflected in *activity theory* which holds that continued activity is characteristic of older people and beneficial to them. Sargent (1999) argues that this inspires judgmental exhortations to "cope" on below poverty-line income or by means of entrepreneurial ventures taken up in later life. This implies that those who do not manage have personally failed. Also, the moral imperative can lead people to relinquish their independence to the advice of doctors, and other medical personnel who offer chemical, surgical and other interventions.

An easy outcome of the assumption of a rise and fall model of the life-span, therefore, is that ageing itself becomes seen as undesirable and therefore open to medical intervention. In our present society more and more issues are becoming medicalised, as the medical profession takes up a powerful role in determining normality (Russell & Schofield, 1986). One result of medicalisation is that when health issues associated with aging are studied the emphasis is often on the delaying of the "downward slide" of ageing by artificially maintaining youth. For example the menopause industry encourages women to avoid, at considerable expense, a normal aspect of ageing. Further McCallum and Geiselhart (1996) highlight the way in which expensive, and often inappropriate, publicly funded interventions for older people lead them to be seen as greedy burdens on the taxpayer. In contrast, little attention is given to those conditions which older women most need help with in order to live full lives. When ageing itself becomes viewed as a medical condition in need of treatment there is no room for the possibility of new opportunities or personal growth.

Perhaps the most problematic aspect of rise and fall models is their failure to account for the empirical evidence that many people express high levels of life satisfaction with their later years (e.g. Ryff 1982; Brandstadter & Greve, 1994; Reker & Wong, 1991; Carstensen, 1992). This so-called paradox of aging (Carstensen, 1992) may be a result of what Dannefer (1984) has called the ontogenetic fallacy. This involves interpreting patterns that are common in a particular time and place as a universal psychological developmental process. In looking at retirement and later life, the ontogenetic fallacy has involved an uncritical assumption that work and family roles are what all of adult life is about.

It follows logically then that when these roles are removed - by retirement and by children growing up - there is very little left. From this point of view the best that the older person can do in this situation is either to struggle against absence, or to accept it. If, however, the work and family are not central to all times of life, it becomes possible to look at the "presences" rather than the "absences" of later life.

If ideology is understood as the system of values, beliefs and behaviours which maintain a particular structure of power (Sloan, 1999; Augoustinos & Walker, 1995) then the taken-for-granted nature of rise and fall models, despite ample contrary evidence, and their role in maintaining medical dominance reveals them to be ideological in nature. The role of psychology then should not be to support such ideology with notions such as activity or disengagement theory but to reveal its ideological nature and to undermine its power by offering alternative models.

STAGE MODELS

Stage models are less panic inducing than rise and fall models. Stage models of the life-span (Freud's, Piaget's and Erikson's being the most well-known) all assume progress conditional on the resolution of the issues, emotional, cognitive or behavioural, raised by a particular stage. Even those theories of personality development which include later life (Erikson, 1980; Levinson, Darrow, Levinson, & McKee, 1978) often describe the development of the self in terms of apparently biologically predetermined stages. While there is empirical evidence that the stages described by these researchers fit the experiences of certain groups of North American males, many women feel a lack of identification with those stages and there has been strong critique of both the concept of stages and the content of them.

First, the concept of a stage is that at a particular age one needs to complete a particular developmental task or one cannot move on to the next stage. The order is immutable. Further, if a person does not complete a task at the appropriate age then there is the implication of retarded development. There are a range of criticisms of the concept of stages. Some researchers (eg Arber & Ginn, 1995; Hockey & James, 1993) are critical of the way in which stage approaches claim to define normality. They emphasise the role of the social environment, as set by the cultural-historical context, in limiting what is considered a normal progression. Others stress the possibility of equifinality which is achieving the same developmental level by different routes (eg Valsiner, 1985). Even if stages were appropriate for early life, it is doubtful that that they would apply to later life as people have the opportunity to become more diverse as their lives continue; changes that Luszcz (1999) refers to the multi-dimensionality and multidirectionality of later life.

Those who are critical of the content of the stages described by Erikson and other personality development researchers point to some obvious ways in which those life stages do not apply to women or to men from other cultures (Hassan & Bar-Yam, 1987). For example Erikson's stage of generativity, concern for providing something for the next generation, is supposed to occur in the forties or fifties, that is, after most women have completed their childrearing. Most problematic for an ageing society is the paucity of stages described for the period after mid-life. For example, Erikson describes seven stages up to the age of fifty but only one for the following thirty years. We can ask whether this is because his "participants" have a theory of self which does not develop after fifty or whether Erikson did not look for signs of development.

Although problems of the number and nature of stages may be overcome by further research into the stages of the second half of life, the further criticisms of the whole concept of the universal and invariant stages are more difficult to overcome. Even if further research were to identify valid stage descriptions of current lives there is the political or moral question of the type of people such theories create. The person is disempowered by such theories because life is thereby predetermined and there is no clear role for personal agency in resolving the dilemmas of their current stage. According to Harré (1983) this problem arises because the dilemmas are presented as a conflict of sub-personal elements such as unconscious drives. An image is conjured of the person as rather like a football ground being churned up by the struggles of opposing teams but unable to influence the outcome.

While these criticisms are severe and cannot be discounted, some researchers, minimising the emphasis on stages, have found the idea of Erikson's life tasks useful. For example, McAdams (1985) argues that the life task of establishing one's identity, which Erikson fits into early adulthood, is one which might be of central interest at that age but is relevant throughout the life-course. If we remove the strict order and ages from stage theory we still have the notion of personal development tasks. Some personal development tasks will be structured by society for very specific ages (eg matriculation examinations) while others have a slightly wider age range (eg motherhood) and yet other tasks can be taken on at any age (eg becoming more assertive). Even within the one event, the nature of the task will vary from person to person (eg motherhood may mean coping with social isolation, excessive physical contact, sleeplessness, responsibility etc which will vary in the degree to which they are experienced as problematic). The idea that people can develop through engaging with personal challenges may be worth salvaging. If the dominant theory of the person allowed people to choose challenges throughout the lifespan and grow through engagement with them then increased longevity would be valued for the opportunity for increased growth.

POLITICAL ECONOMY MODEL

The political economy model of ageing emphasises the ways that "[t]he structure and operations of major social institutions shape the subjective experience and objective conditions of older persons" (Estes, 1991). It is critical of other gerontological perspectives on two main counts. One is that they take for granted existing structural arrangements and the importance of the market in distributing rewards in society. The other is that they explain dependency of some older people as a result of their individual life choices in their work and behaviour.

The broad brush of the political economy perspective has enabled the exposure of the role of transnational companies in industries related to ageing. For example the political economy analysis reveals that pharmaceutical companies will be economically motivated to develop and promote "cures" for minor ailments which almost everybody suffers from rather than cures for severe conditions which cause real suffering to relatively few. Since most people in western countries are lucky enough to age, the identification of any aspect of ageing, from wrinkles to menopause, as in need of a "cure" is likely to be lucrative. Similarly a whole range of other industries and professions benefit from the medicalisation of ageing. The political economy model, therefore, shows that there are powerful interest groups who benefit from the promotion of rise and fall models of the lifecourse.

In the broad brush of the political economy model, small groups and individuals are not seen as significant causal agents. This can be seen as an advantage to the extent that it avoids a "blame the victim" mentality but also as a disadvantage in that it ignores our agency in shaping our lives by interacting with current structures and perhaps changing them (Sargent, 1999). As with all theories, the widespread adoption of a political economy model would lead to people creating themselves into a particular type of person. The type of persons that are created if we adopt the political-economy model are ones who are aware of the interplay of powerful economic interests and would not blame individuals for their disadvantage, but would not have a theory of self that allowed them to try to change the situation. Many might become cynical or depressed.

LIFE-COURSE MODELS

Life course models offer considerable promise for a positive approach to ageing. These models, consistent with personological and feminist approaches, value the integrity of the whole person with a past, present and future. Research from a life course perspective emphasises the path through life of people within their social and historical context. That is, it considers both the intra-personal factors such as people's interests and anxieties and also the external factors such as social expectations or access to resources which shape a life path that maintains some coherence and yet is open to change.

The life-story line is a concept borrowed from narrative theory which is used by a number of researchers for understanding coherence through the life course (eg Gergen, 1990; McAdams, 1985; Helson and Picano, 1990). We choose, create and at times revise our life stories and it is these stories which both direct our future choices and goals and make sense of past experiences. Out of the stream of everyday life, certain events are labelled as important because they contribute to the plot: others are seen as trivial.

Life-story writing, however, is not a purely individual activity. The social environment, as set by the cultural-historical context, defines what constitutes a normal story. In each society there will be a dominant plot for each gender, which most people will approximate, and a few alternative plots. For example, the dominant story-line for women in many western countries is for them to finish their education, work, marry, have children, and return to the workforce part-time and then later full-time. Of course not all women follow the dominant story-line. They may follow one of the alternative plots on offer, such as "career woman" or "single mother on pension". Even those who choose totally idiosyncratic life-stories may nevertheless use the dominant stories as reference points against which decisions are made.

As Gergen (1990) points out, the storyline after midlife is usually depicted as one of loss as children leave home, then follow the losses of fertility, work, husband, health, independence and finally life itself. Such a negative story-line does not encourage women to think about their futures, and discourages planning for a better alternative (Leonard, 1999). Yet many of these so called losses can be a source of new-found freedom and energy and many women express surprise at their enjoyment of life in their sixties and seventies. With a life course approach there is no paradox involved in addressing the "presences" of later life which have been identified by a range of researchers, for example the greater interiority after midlife, as Neugarten (1977) proposed; the contentment in the here and now, proposed by Ryff (1982) and Carstensen (1992); or Reker and Wong's (1988) notion of increase in collectivism in later life.

Unlike most life-event research, life course models do not make assumptions about what is important but elicit from the participants, which events are of significance for them. Life course approaches allow people to be active in the construction of their identities while taking into account the opportunities and constraints of the particular historical time and "life space" (Richards & Larson, 1989, Stewart & Malley, 1989). What is relevant is the conditions that may enhance or diminish potential for personal growth and fulfilment. No doubt some conditions facilitating personal growth and fulfilment do decrease with age. Others such as "lived experience" will increase hence the model allows for the multidimensionality and multidirectionality of later life (Luszcz, 1999). Some increases may occur through the taking of personal challenges as suggested in the section on stage theory.

Again the question needs to be asked about the type of people we will become if this theory of the self were widely adopted. Key characteristics could be that people would become protagonists in their own story line (not mothers, daughters, wives); able to be consciously planful; looking to identify the constraints and opportunities of their present life space; and focusing on their unique experience.

CONCLUSION

Any society, but an ageing society in particular, will be the poorer for the loss of the potential contribution of its older people. Those models of the life-span which see ageing as "all downhill" not only serve dominant ideological interests by creating people who use that as their personal theory of the self thereby becoming as useless as that model depicts. Stage, political economy and life course models all present more positve alternatives. The notion of growth through the resolution of life challenges is an idea from stage theories which is potentially empowering and could be a worthwhile incorporation into a life course approach. Life-course models have the greatest flexibility and the strongest emphasis on personal agency. By focusing on subjective perceptions, however, they risk conceptualising ageing as an individual concern and underplaying the common experiences and challenges and pressures exerted by larger economic forces. The addition of the political-economy perspective on ageing may be an essential ingredient to ensure that older people do not consider ageing to be their individual problem. On its own the political economy model of ageing offers little opportunity for an individual or small group to implement change. However, the life-course and political economy models together reposition older people individually and collectively as active contributing creators of their own quality of life. It is only by fully engaging with its older people that a society can stop seeing them as the problem and suggest ways of exploring the opportunities to work together to replace dependence with inter-dependence.

REFERENCES

Arber, S. & Ginn, J. (1995). *Connecting gender and ageing*. Buckingham: Open University Press.
Augoustinos, M. & Walker, I. (1995). *Social cognition : An integrated introduction*. London: Sage.

Brandstadter, J. & Greve, R. (1994). The aging self: Stabilising the protective processes. *Developmental Review, 14,* 52-80.

Carstensen, L. (1992). Social and emotional patterns in adulthood: Support for socio-emotional selectivity theory. *Psychology and Aging, 7,* 331-338.

Clare, R. and Tulpule, A. (1994). *Australia's ageing society.* EPAC Background Paper No 37, Economic Planning and Advisory Council, Canberra.

Dannefer, D. (1984). Adult development and social theory: A paradigmatic reappraisal. *American Sociological Review, 49,* 100-16.

Erikson, E.H. (1980). *Identity and the life cycle.* New York: Norton.

Estes, C.L. (1991). The new political economy of aging: Introduction and critique. In M. Minkler & C.L. Estes (Eds) *Critical perspectives on aging: The political and moral economy of growing old.* New York: Baywood.

Gergen, M. (1990). Finished at 40: Women's development within the patriarchy. *Psychology of Women Quarterly, 14,* 471-493.

Harré, R. (1983). *Personal being.* Oxford: Basil Blackwell.

Hassan, A. B. & Bar-Yam, M. (1987). Interpersonal development across the life span: Communion and its interaction with agency in psychological development. *Contributions to Human Development, 18,* 102-128.

Helson R. & Picano, J. (1990). Is the traditional role bad for women? *Journal of Personality and Social Psychology, 59,* 311-320.

Hockey, J. & James, A. (1993). *Growing up and growing old: Ageing and dependency in the life course.* London: Sage.

Leonard, R. (1999). Empowerment through the life course approach. In Onyx, J. Leonard, R. & Reed, R. (Eds) *Revisioning aging: The empowerment of older women.* New York: Peter Lang.

Levinson, D.J, Darrow, C.N., Levinson, M.H., & McKee, B. (1978). *The seasons of a man's life.* New York: Knopf.

Luszcz, M. (1999). Ageing: Cognitive and developmental perspectives. Keynote address to 34th Annual Conference of the Australian Psychological Society, Hobart, October.

McAdams, D.P. (1985). *Power, intimacy, and the life story.* Homewood, Illinios: The Dorsey Press.

McCallum, J. & Geiselhart, K. (1996). *Australia's new aged.* Sydney: Allen & Unwin.

Neugarten, B. (1977). Personality and aging. In J.Birren & K.W. Schaie (Eds) *Handbook of the psychology of aging* (pp.626-49). New York: Van Nostrand-Reinhold.

Reker, G. & Wong, P. (1988). Aging as an individual process: Towards a theory of personal meaning. In J. Birren & V. Bengston (Eds.) *Emergent theories of aging* (pp.214-46). New York: Springer

Richards, M.. & Larson, R. (1989). The life space and socialization of the self: Sex differences in the young adolescent. *Journal of Youth and Adolescence, 18(6),* 617-626.

Russell, C. & Schofield, T. (1986). *Where it hurts: A sociology of health for health workers.* Sydney: Allen & Unwin.

Ryff, C. (1982). Self-perceived change in adulthood and aging. *Journal of Personality and Social Psychology,* 42, 108-15.

Sargent, M. (1999). Not gerontology, but - . In Onyx, J., Leonard, R. & Reed, R. (Eds) *Revisioning aging: The empowerment of older women.* New York: Peter Lang.

Sloan, T. (1999). Ideology critique in theory and practice. Paper presented at the International Society for Theoretical Psychology Conference, Sydney, April.

Stewart, A.J. & Malley, J.E. (1989). Case studies of agency and communion in women's lives. In R.K. Urger (Ed.) *Representations: Social constructions of gender.* Amityville, NY: Baywood Publishing Co.

Valsiner, J. (1985). *The role of the individual subject in scientific psychology.* New York: Plenum.

PSYCHOLOGICAL THEORISING IN TRANSDISCIPLINARY PERSPECTIVE

Wolfgang Maiers
Free University of Berlin

SUMMARY

The call for interdisciplinarity within psychology appears to be an ambivalent one. The integration of investigative practices and knowledge from other academic realms into psychology has recurrently been tantamount to sacrificing an independent understanding of the psychological. It is not only with respect to the (wishful) emulation of physics or to the advance of computer-scientific metaphors, with the cognitive turn, that psychology's history can be written as the history of an "imitative science". The same holds true for alternative designs of psychology as an interpretative investigation in strict analogy to the hermeneutics of textual material. Interdisciplinarity raises issues of the possible unity of the sciences and of how this relates to reality. The scientific program of materialist dialectics, while facing up to the philosophical problem of realism, opens a new perspective for an explanatory understanding of the totality of nature and society that does not concern itself with disciplinary entrenchments. In this vein, Critical Psychology builds its own specifically psychological conceptual and methodological system within a truly "transdisciplinary" framework.

INTRODUCTION

The history of the sciences can be marked by two opposite tendencies: The exponential growth of knowledge, with its increasing specialisation of technical terminology and of research methods, means that the differentiation of traditional disciplines since the last century persists to date. This effects, second, a necessity for integration through cross-disciplinary communication and cooperative knowledge production.

In distinction to mere *pluri-* or *multidisciplinarity*, where a shared theme is explored from different angles without touching upon the customary configuration of disciplines and theoretical discourses, I shall confine *interdisciplinarity* to a stage of development where problems can be conceptualised only within a framework able to comprehend distinct, however connected domains of world knowledge. Interdisciplinarity is dependent on elaborating a unique methodology and meta-theory which includes the explicit formulation of a new consistent terminology. Such concerted efforts may eventually lead to the institutionalisation of new research directions that extend beyond any given disciplinary order. Quantum chemistry is but one eminent example of qualitative leaps in the progression of basic scientific knowledge ensuing from successful interdisciplinary cooperation. The social sciences have increasingly been included since global problems of humankind came to the fore that required an understanding of the interactions of natural, material-technical and societal processes. Hence, in the current fragmented landscape of diverse scientific endeavours, the boundaries and transitions between disciplines attract growing epistemological attention, and interdisciplinarity is welcomed as a taken for granted value. Indeed it can stand for a form of scientific practice in which, on the premise of a recognition of established disciplinary standards of cognition, the unity of sciences is being realised.

Interdisciplinary practice rests on disciplinarity. One should bear in mind, though, that the current demarcations of the sciences are not least the result of the contingencies of historical development and hence, in principle, open to reconsideration and change. As a matter of fact, certain practical and theoretical difficulties of interdisciplinary cooperation are rooted in foundational problems of traditional academic organisation. To these historical burdens belong the perennial debates on the heterogeneity of scientific cultures: the "clash between the faculties". The dialectics of disciplinarity and interdisciplinarity is to be investigated not least in regard of the issue of the unity and differences between the natural, social, and cultural sciences as to their linguistic devices, methods, thought forms and communicative modes as well as to the degree to which they express societal interests.

In the following, I shall not so much concern myself with scrutinising successful cases of psychology's interdisciplinary cooperation as direct my focus primarily to its notoriously uncertain disciplinary status within a division of labour in the human studies that is everything but an unproblematic "multi-perspectival" mapping of a multi-dimensional objectivity. Does perhaps the call for interdisciplinarity stem from the need to compensate for structural distortions in the human-scientific representations of reality?

PSYCHOLOGY'S IMPASSE AND PSEUDO-INTERDISCIPLINARITY

An historical explication for the problematic shaping of psychology as an academic discipline would go beyond the scope of this paper. Let me therefore turn directly to contemporary *nomological psychology*. It provides a meta-language and a standard setting of experimental and statistical research to which all "proper" psychological hypotheses need to be adjusted by expressing them as statements about contingent empirical relationships between independent and dependent variables. Concerning the particular kind and contents of theorising, the *variable-psychological* conceptual frame leaves considerable degrees of freedom: (seemingly) exact methodological prescriptions are paralleled by a vast indeterminacy as to how to unterstand the variables and resulting findings. Taking a *methodological individualism* and a system of *timeless mental categories* as a starting point, the *connection between subjectivity and societability* does not even come to mind as a germane psychological question.

If proponents of mainstream psychology are sensitive to this problem at all, they usually retreat to some necessary division of scientific labour: Societal, historical facts, they argue, do not fall in the competence of psychology, but are the exclusive province of economy, sociology, political studies etc. For such non-psychological facts to be taken into account as background variables, they first have to be translated (via operationalisation) into the nomothetic language of variables. Psychology's concept of "environment" grasps human living conditions only as immediate causes or effects of individual activities. All connections between the individual and the societal reproduction process exceeding the limits of inter-individual interactions or individual lives are shut out. Due to the indifference to historical-societal structures, the psychological lawful relations by which behavior is linked to antecedents are hypostatised as *ahistorical* invariables. Misrepresenting the individuals as self-contained behavioral units in an environment deprived of all concrete meaning, the subject- and world-distorting variable-scheme is the most unveiled expression of what inheres in bourgeois psychology in general: a phantasm of the "abstract-isolated human individual" (Marx).

The encapsulation of individuals and their subjectivity in the immediacy of the circumstances of their lives marks the essence of a specifically psychological view in the overarching organisation of segmented human studies. Definitions of the individual on the one hand and of the societal, on the other, are torn apart in separate terminological reference systems, unable later to be rejoined coherently. Traditional psychology and sociology alike prove unable to explain through which characteristics of individual subjectivity human beings are designed to participate in the societal production of their living conditions. This constitutional blindness puts on the agenda an *interdisciplinary re-connection* of the individual subjective and the societal aspects of human life activity.

One way to achieve this is the common practice to qualify psychological laws by considering, ex post facto, sociological, economic etc. variables. While such multifactorial thinking is easily hailed as a *context-sensitisation* of psychology, it is in fact inadequate as it does not affect the core of psychological statements as such. Additive syntheses accomplish only an indifferent conglomeration of co-existing variables with each contributing some amount of influence to human psychology. Heterogeneous ways of looking and technical languages are thus combined in some naive theoretical syncretism.

Besides this eclecticism there is a second kind of an allegedly "interdisciplinary" transfer of knowledge, which I should like to label *reductionist foundation:* the naturalistic attempt, that is, to frame psychological statements in terms borrowed from other sciences. A kind of reductionism prevails here that presupposes human life as an unconscious, naturelike process. Psychology is peculiar in that ever since its institutional inception it has primarily adopted its technical language and the related methodological principles from the natural and exact sciences and, via this transplantation, has achieved its identity as an acknowledged mature academic discipline within the established ensemble of sciences. On closer scrutiny, this emulation turns out to be a wishful imitation, to some extent even a travesty of natural scientific experimentation, measuring procedures, and theorisation (Maiers, 1988). This "as-if" both fosters and conceals the lack of a genuine scientific discourse based upon a consistent and unifying definition of psychology's unique subject matter.

Let me point at just two examples: The behaviorist paradigm of classical conditioning introduced Pavlov's unconditioned/conditioned reflex (and supplementary concepts) as an omnibus principle of psychological explanation largely ignorant of the underlying "theory of higher nervous activity". Untouched by the finding that in all relevant applications of classical conditioning to human beings the hypothetical association processes involve a minimal awareness of the person, calling for explanation beyond the usual mechanistic account in terms of inter-stimulus contiguity, the pseudo-physiological stimulus-response language of behaviorism has successfully offered a rhetoric which feigns a causal (qua physiological) foundation of psychological constructions and hence lends them a status of serious science.

In the mid-fifties information theory suggested itself as a new model science (not only) for psychology that permitted a scientifically rigorous study of complex mental phenomena. Cognitivism replaced the stimulus-response terminology with computer-scientific metaphors such as input, encoding, storage, that have since pervaded psychological theorisation even outside the domain of cognition. When, e.g., the "optimisation of neuronal networks" is circumscribed as "learning of the system", one may regard such wording as unproblematic as long as one keeps aware that it ascribes properties and activities to the system which are specific to human beings or, at most, organisms. However, it is anything but evident, when psychology – unmindful of the fallacious system-actor contamination – derives from such analogies a new connectionist theory of human learning, without going into the specific nature of the latter.

While "physiologising" is tantamount to illegitimately *universalising a specific conceptual level* that reflects a specific qualitative level of the organisation of matter, the modeling on system and information theory rather comes to *mystifying a special abstraction*. Undoubtedly, their schemata accomplish a quantitative description of structures and functions of a broad class of processes of intra- and inter-systemic reciprocal actions in qualitatively distinct unorganic and organic systems. By the same token, however, they disregard the concrete characters of these diverse processes of reflection and regulation as well as their mutual transformations. By abstracting from – i.e., ignoring – the abstract character of these notions, the analytically extracted aspects are accredited with an autonomous order and potency – fitting with what Marx criticised in Hegel's work as "fantastic abstraction". Integrating knowledge by employing cybernetic, information theoretical, etc. conceptual systems as universal (meta-)theoretical frames runs into a sacrifice of psychology proper (Leontiev, 1978, chap. 2).

The ultimate reason for its "imitative science" character lies in traditional psychology's failure to recognise human consciousness as a medium of the practical interaction of corporeal subjects with the historically produced, super-individual system of natural and social meaning structures. Because of this "subject-" and "world-lessness" – as related aspects of one and the same constitutive solipsism – psychology misses opportunities to articulate, let alone to answer, those "psychological" questions that are posed specifically to it both from within academe and from ordinary societal practice.

On the one hand, the essential nature of psychology's subject matter appears to lie, quite obviously, in our *immediate experience* of the world and ourselves. On the other hand, this very experience is suspected of being inaccessible to scientific analysis since it is given only to "me", not intersubjectively. This *privacy* is, however, an *artefact* – a consequence of approaching the experiential "immediacy", the "phenomenal givenness" of human experience, from a third person observational base (as defined by positivistic criteria of scientific objectivity). As long as researchers mean to observe "the other ones" in an allegedly natural scientific perspective from an aloof standpoint and hence exclude their own experience as a medium of interpersonal communication from the scientific analysis, the (naturally differing) experience of people of their common world dissolves as a shared reference base. The "other ones" seem to remain directly observable only with respect to their "organismic responsiveness".

Banishing their subjectivity into a "black box", one can only speculate about what is going on under other people's skin.

The most radical conclusion was drawn by the behaviorists, who substituted their physicalist terminology for a theoretical description of conscious, subjective, or mental states and events. Stimulus patterns were not accounted for as segments relating to a world out there, independent of the theoretical focus and experimental design, but only inasmuch as they affected the subjects some way or another. Their responses were not recognised as a possibility for individuals to grasp and alter reality, but only as effects of the (experimental) conditions.

Cognitivism puts the world in which we live even more backstage. Its concept of input is void of any direct external reference: Hiding behind it, is an agent not represented in the information processing system, namely the "user" who feeds the system with data. What exactly causes (rather: leads the user to) this or that particular input can in principle not be discussed within the model. Cognitivist theories move, so to speak, in a virtual space – an immanence of mental acts mediated by symbols of a program language – where no real subjective actions and experiences in the objective "tangible" world occur.

Owing to their common subjectivistic presuppositions, neither S-R psychology nor cognitivism are able to provide a satisfactory answer to the plain question of how we human beings can possibly *communicate* with the world (as a *world-for-us*).

EVOLUTIONARY PSYCHOLOGY AND THE LINGUISTIC TURN: Psychology Astray

What does such a "preparadigmatic" disciplinary status of psychology imply for its interdisciplinary orientation? I have already mentioned the naturalistic reductionism that persists in the mainstream as the dominant consequence of its readiness to found psychological principles anew on the grounds of some other reference discipline. *Biologism* has always been among the favorite forms of this kind of "interdisciplinarity". Since the 1970s, one prominent example of a comprehensive biologistic approach has been sociobiology. Today the appeal to biology as ultimate explanation is topical in a form that dissociates itself from sociobiology, and claims instead to offer a new approach named *Evolutionary Psychology* (see, e.g. Tooby & Cosmides, 1992).[1] Scientifically, it sets the task of achieving unity for the sciences – in actual fact the social sciences – under the tutelage of biology. The political objective is to offer guidance in matters of social concern through scientific definitions of a universal human nature. Neither aim is new. As for the first project, let me just point to the available philosophy and history of science literature providing evidence that the world of science is one in which the boundaries between the biological and the social are *permeable* (Maiers, 1988). This includes a critical interrogation of the traditional reading of a society-/culture-free epistemological status for the natural sciences. Tooby and Cosmides, by contrast, insist on a dichotomy between social- or cultural-scientific explications of the human psychological architecture, which they deem basically flawed, and biology as providing truthful, methodologically disinterested and impersonal accounts.

That the "new" evolutionary psychology is more or less modeled on the old sociobiology, is manifested in Tooby and Cosmides' claim that evolutionary theory explains, through individual psychology, the whole range of societal/cultural practices. Rarely does evolutionary psychology present itself so obviously as ideological as in the words of Laura Betzig, editor of *Human Nature*, in which human agency is bluntly granted to genes:

> From pregnancy complications, to the stress response, to the beauty in symmetry, to the attraction of money, to the historical tendency of the rich to favor first born sons, everything we think, feel and do might be better understood as a means to the spread of our own – or of our ancestors' genes. (cited in Rose, 1998, p.1)

As Rose (1998, p. 6) puts it, "Evolutionary psychology is merely Social Darwinism in fancy new clothes". It shares "a good deal of the pick and mix culture of postmodernity" and yet clearly purports a biological determinism – "this time drawing cultural strength from the powercharged discourse of the new genetics".

A consistent evolution-theoretical approach can neither historically nor systematically be held responsible for the continuing hold of naturalism in terms of a survivalist adaptivism on psychology (Maiers 1988). And, as Rose (1998, pp. 9f.) rightly underlines, the strongest genetic determinist claims about behavior do not for the most part come from molecular biologists. Rather, they are being made by psychologists, psychiatrists, philosophers, sociologists etc. who seem to expect from biology a new scientific footing on which to put their own disciplines.

The *functional autonomy of human activity* from strict genetic determination, however, requires special tools of analysis. This becomes especially evident *historically*, hence a word about anthropogenesis is appropriate. Socio-economic, technological, cultural, and mental changes have taken place throughout the tens of thousands of years of human social history without any significant parallel genetic transformations. The same genotype evidently supports a huge variety of life activities. It functions as a general substratum that provides the human race whith the maximum capacity for adjustment through learning. By virtue of evolutionary principles, the determining role of biology has been transformed into the paradoxical force of a specifically human biology which transcends itself in allowing extra-biological influences on activity by exposing the individual to the world via social and technological mediations (Ratner, 1998, p. 103). Just as biology's unique properties cannot be reduced to combinations of physical and chemical matter from which they have emerged, so human sociability represents a new level, higher than that of the species-specific biological make-up. While the "human surpassing of evolution exemplifies the higher level dialectical *Aufhebung* of lower processes" (Ratner, 1998, p. 99), the evolutionary psychological concept of evolution and hence of human nature is, by contrast, deeply ahistorical.

Another kind of naturalist reductionism can be found in the study of the intricate mind-brain problem, where it is classical physiological determinism particular in the new face of cognitive neuroscience that is widely evidenced. Rejecting both vulgar materialism, which explains consciousness as nothing but neurophysiological processes without any emergent properties of its own, and dualism, which severs the mind from the brain, the mind-brain relationship could be more fruitfully understood in terms of a *dialectical monism* – a developmental unitary account of the material universe which acknowledges

> consciousness as a new form or organisation of brain functions which possesses unique "macro-properties" and laws which are ... "recognised to be real and causal in their own right, as subjectively experienced, and to be of very different quality from the neural, molecular, and other material components of which they are built" (Sperry, 1980) (Ratner, 1998, p. 102)

One might be led to believe that it is the chief aim of interdisciplinarity to avoid any unfounded prevalence of specific disciplinary perspectives and to acknowledge instead the *multiperspectivity* in which the multi-faceted nature of psychological phenomena emerges. This consideration ignores, however, that often such openness to the plurality of disciplinary views has led straightaway to reductionism due to the omission of analysing the multileveled relationship – here between psychology and biology, in which biology serves as a necessary substructure but does not causally direct (predict) the phenotypic performance of any of the psychological activities. Biologism can therefore be aptly summarised as a pseudo-scientific, ideological extension of biology's explanatory empire of organismic structures and adaptive functions to the qualitatively distinct societal level.

Naturalism in the shape of some "psychobiologism" is, however, not the only possible consequence of psychology's worldlessness. The individual-society relationship can also get lost in social-theoretically informed "interdisciplinary" positions. Such orientations, claiming to overcome the scientistic naturalisation of subjectivity, are not in themselves protected against the pitfall of leaning on some model science and losing out of sight the specificity of psychological phenomena. For example, historical materialism based investigations of the historical constitution of subjectivity have proven liable to slip into a kind of sociologism or economism asserting that individuality might be penetrated on the basis of a sufficient concretisation of political-economic analysis. In the (broadly speaking) postmodernist currents of the 1980s, drawing on some brand and combination of social constructionism, (analytic) philosophy of language, post-structuralist thinking, cultural perspectivism and so forth, this reduction of individual subjects to mere functions of societal structures and processes recurs in an "objectivism of the cultural". It strikes me that various versions, introducing into their theorisation more and more guiding analogies such as drama, or text, from cultural perfomances like theatre, literature, etc., not only (justly) deconstruct abstract universalist and individualistic notions of the subjective. Rather, they tend to limit, distort or abandon altogether the practical-experiential side of subjectivity that does not exist apart from sensuous-real individuals acting in a real world. The coincidence with the traditional structuralist (namely Althusserian) elevation of the historical process over its actual participants goes along with a characteristic shift in perspective: At work is, so to speak, an "idealism of language".

Let me take a closer look at the new emphasis in psychology on the linguistic fabric of the human world as a further step along the lines of the *interpretive (hermeneutic) turn*. That "the symbolic and semiotic systems ... mediate between the individual, the social and the historical" (Brockmeier, 1997, p. 7), and that "in particular, narrative discourse plays a crucial role in what we conceive of, and construct as, our reality" (p. 4) is beyond dispute. I wonder, however, whether there is not more at stake if literary criticism, narratology, semiotics, and hermeneutics take on the function of models for the methodological and epistemological design of psychology. My suspicion is aroused by claims that over-emphasise the relative independence and self-referentiality of symbol systems or even flatly deny that symbolisms *represent* something beyond themselves which pervades and defines their structures and meanings.

It can hardly be denied, "that life and story are internally related, that the meaning of life cannot be determined outside the stories told about it" (Brockmeier, 1997, p. 13). Less evident, however, would be a view that "human life is not only interpreted in stories but *is* itself a process of narrative interpretation." (p. 13, emphasis added). In a strict sense this amounts to saying that narratives constitute the realities of life in the first place as a meaningful coherent nexus. The argumentation is less straightforward, however. Brockmeier concedes in passing (p. 11) some "material reality prior to, and independent of, human discourse and thought". Soothing the irritation of "realists", this indicates an awareness of the tensions that exist within the tripartite relationship between the preexisting order of things and events in the world, our practical experiences, and our narratives. Disappointingly, though, the author nowhere elaborates on this issue. Instead he maintains that it is through their stories that humans construct their world and themselves, distancing himself from what he (together with Harré) has elsewhere called the "representation fallacy" (Brockmeier, 1997, 273f).

Whether in the above case a hard-line social constructionism is indicated or not, to view reality as nothing more than a function of how it is presented in discourse or narratives would appear to me as a predication upon truly idealist premises, leading psychology into the paradoxes of a (self-refuting) *relativism*.

CLOSING THE DIVIDES: Toward Transdisciplinarity

At first glance, the call for interdisciplinarity within psychology appears to indicate an overdue integration of relevant investigative practices and knowledge from other academic realms into psychology. On closer inspection it often turns out to be a scientific foundation of the psychological not of psychology's own making – a reductionist modeling by which "indigenous" problems, conceptualisations, and methodological principles get lost. We are still confronted with the unsettled problem of founding a psychology that is committed to the experiential standpoint of human agents, without being trapped in the illusions of psychologism. What conceptual and methodological basis is required in order to establish a non-reductionist relationship between psychology and its neighbouring academic disciplines?

The above antinomies of traditional psychology can be traced back to its theoretical dissolution of the nexus between the subjects' (mental) life activities and the surrounding world in its independent objective structure. We have to close the *artificial divide* between those aspects of the world that affect the experiencing individual and the objectivity behind them, which is mistaken to be an external – physical, economic, technical, etc. – reality outside the reach of psychology. The world is always already a humanised world: As an historically produced configuration of material objects, systems of iconic and discursive symbols and related forms of practice, cognition, and social intercourse, the world is *meaningful* before each individual can practically and theoretically appropriate it.

Objective societal meanings represent generalised possibilities for action to which individual members of society relate one way or another according to their needs and situation (as experienced). The point of a truly *subject-scientific*, *individuo-centred perspective* of "subjective grounds for action" in their objective "premises" (as provided by the circumstances of life) is that it ensues from the recognition of the economic mode of the societal life process through which the individual maintenance of life is mediated.

Understanding human agency also requires that we replace the old-established psychological *dichotomy of naturalness and societability* with a concept of human subjectivity as a differentiated fabric of natural and societal determinants (Maiers, 1999). To find theoretical unity beyond superficial multifactorial syntheses with their arbitrary eclectic blends of heterogeneous theory fragments, calls for *mediation* through a *genetic* method that reveals the interrelations and concrete transformations of the *distinctive qualities and forms of motion of matter*. In our particular case, this means reconstructing the natural-historical genesis and social-historical development of human consciousness, based upon a comprehensive explanation of the preceding evolution of infra-human psychic life processes. Via this analysis it is possible to derive an adequate place in the architecture of human subjectivity for different mental phenomena like emotionality, motivation etc. as particular developmental forms of psychic reflection – and thus to escape abstract-general misrepresentations of human consciousness. The psychological subject matter is no longer decomposed in abstract functional aspects, each assigned to exclusive subdisciplines, theoretical descriptions and methodical procedures. Reductionism – as the failure to hit the human specificity of the psychical – and eclecticism – as the inability of comprehensive, integrative conceptualisation – are, as Leontiev (1978) rightly remarks, just two manifestations of the same basic lack of historical analysis.

This guideline is revealing with respect to our topic of *interdisciplinarity*. It can only be followed, if one throws over the traditional bounds of psychology and systematically draws on the empirical material and accumulated theoretical knowledge from the biological, anthropological, economic, historical etc. studies that are fundamental for understanding the origins and development of the reflexive world- and self-experience of human subjects. Building a rigorously, if differently, scientific, i.e. radically "subject-scientific", psychology is based upon an explanatory understanding of the totality of nature and society that cannot be limited by disciplinary entrenchments.

Taking it seriously, the claim for interdisciplinarity raises the issues of the connections between various disciplinary perspectives and so about the possible *unity of sciences* – which should not be confounded with reductionist programmes for a "uniform science" as exemplified in the late physicalist movement. By necessity this leads to the fundamental issue whether and how this *reflects* an objectively existing structure of reality. Skepticist conclusions from the – unquestionable – constructivity, openness, and often incommensurability of historically and contextually bound knowledge that underly agnostic denials of an objective reality, are often due to a biased understanding of reflection as something being untouched by the relativity of cognitive perspectives from different societal locations. They thereby remain completely caught up in exactly the *predialectical "correspondence theory"* of cognition, which they believe to have escaped. This epistemological model of a mechanistic "mirroring" of reality, however, is outdated in the light of the materialist philosophy of practice that entails an entirely new conception of reality and of knowing. The scientific program of materialist dialectics, while facing up to the philosophical problem of realism, provides for a *radically interdisciplinary episteme*. Neither disregarding nor reifying the conventional departmentalisation of academic labour, its type of scientific rationality offers a new perspective for the *integration of natural and social sciences* through the *historicisation* of all forms of being and thinking. In its integrative world-view, nature, society and human consciousness are related to one another as particular differentiations within a *monism of matter*, that exist through movement, development, history. This epistemological rationale for a unified science has been corroborated by the "spontaneous-dialectical" tendency of contemporary sciences to raise "nature" to a category of the social and cultural-historical studies and to incorporate "historicity" as a constitutive dimension for natural scientific knowledge production.

Viewed in historical perspective, the task seems clear: Recognising the historically grown multitude of special fields *and* following the regulative idea of the unity of sciences, a perspective of an innovative culture of a *transdisciplinary* production of knowledge is to be opened up. Transdisciplinarity comes into existence when research is based upon a shared axiomatic, a mutual pervasion of disciplinary epistemologies, a clustering of inter-disciplinary problem solutions that draws on a unified pool of theories.

Within the ontological and epistemological framework of dialectic and historical materialism, Critical Psychology aims at overcoming the idealist dualism of humans as either natural or cultural beings, and at realising the concrete unity of natural- and social scientific knowledge in the human sciences. With its strictly interdisciplinary episteme, Critical Psychology contributes to a prospect of unified science and transdisciplinarity of human cognition.

Note

1.   The following argumentation draws inspiration from a draft survey on Evolutionary Psychology by Hilary Rose (1998) to appear in Rose, H. & Rose, S.(Eds) *Alas poor Darwin.*

REFERENCES

Brockmeier, J. (1997). Narrative realities, human possibilities. In Brockmeier, J. (Ed.) *Narrative realities:Perspectives on the self*, 4-17. Vienna: Internationales Forschungszentrum Kulturwissenschaften.

Brockmeier, J. & Harré, R. (1997). Narrative: Problems and promises of an alternative paradigm. *Research on Language and Social Interaction, 30*(4), 263-283.

Leontiev, A.N. (1978). *Activity, consciousness, and personality*. Englewood Cliffs, NJ: Prentice-Hall

Maiers, W. (1988). Has psychology exaggerated its 'natural scientific character'? Remarks concerning an empirical topic and a methodological desideratum of 'theoretical psychology'. In W. J. Baker, L. P. Mos, H. van Rappard & H.J. Stam (Eds) *Recent trends in theoretical psychology* (pp. 133-143). New York/Heidelberg/Berlin: Springer.

Maiers, W. (1999). Critical Psychology — an unfinished modern project. In W. Maiers, B. Bayer, B. D. Esgalhado, R. Jorna & E. Schraube (Eds) *Challenges to theoretical psychology* (pp. 457-466). North York: Captus Press.

Ratner, C. (1988). Psychology's relation to biology: qualitatively distinct levels. In W. J. Baker, L. P. Mos, H. van Rappard & H.J. Stam (Eds) *Recent trends in theoretical psychology* (pp. 95-105). New York/Heidelberg/Berlin: Springer.

Rose, H. (1998). *Evolutionary psychology: Social Darwinism and the standard social science model*. Unpublished MS.

Tooby, J. & Cosmides, L. (1992). Psychological foundations of culture. In J. Barkow, L. Cosmides & J. Tooby (Eds) *The adapted mind: Evolutionary psychology and the generation of culture* (pp. 19-136). New York: Oxford University Press.

REINTEGRATING SENSE INTO SUBJECTIFICATION

Martin Hildebrand-Nilshon, Johanna Motzkau, and Dimitris Papadopoulos
Free University of Berlin

SUMMARY

Subjectification displays the specific processes forming individual existence in the multiple interrelations between persons and their surroundings. In this sense subjectification corresponds to the idea of an individual as the intersection of the production of meaning and the efficacy of power. In this paper we want to assert that subjectification is more than the mere positioning of the individual between tangents of meaning and practice; it also entails the necessity of creating sense through the subjective reorganization of the conduct of self and of others. The driving force of this movement emerges from the political and social affinities realized by the participating subjects. In our paper we also wish to argue for the historical specificity of such a conception. That is, the notion of an individual both dialogical and self-reflective, although represented by alternative psychologies as the key presupposition for a critical stance in psychology, seems to reflect primarily the dominant postindustrial realities of North Atlantic countries. Finally we offer an insight into some of the central aspects of current socioeconomic reasoning in psychological theories.

INTRODUCTION

First of all we would like to outline our insights into subjectification in order to create a common basis for understanding. The process of subjectification comprises all the ways in which a person transforms him or herself into a subject (Hildebrand-Nilshon and Papadopoulos, 1998; Foucault, 1982). The concept of subjectification bifurcates into two ideas. First, it is a mode of power which could be described as a governing technique of the self-enterprising individual (Foucault, 1984). Secondly, it is the possibility of self-articulation. Its power is efficacious as a communicative, intersubjective practice based on existing societal constraints and conditions, and thus functioning according to present or future actions that aim to promote or to nullify possible relationships to others. Governing action is divided into both acting upon others and acting upon the self, and in this sense it could be understood as the various social rationalities and practices in which individuals employ strategies for their subjectification (as the "conduct of conduct"; cf. Rose, 1996). We will enlarge on the inevitability of this process, after showing the implicit efficacy of sense.

Prevailing critical theorization purports to help elucidate the opaque concepts of identity and subject with the intention of revealing the mechanisms which subjugate individuals within the insidious power of discourses. Meanwhile the number of deconstructions is exponentially increasing and very soon even the word "subjectification" will be passé. To forestall this development we would like to closely examine some of the salient ideas produced in these discussions in order to point out their inadequacies. There is one aspect common to all of these critical theories: They all concern the question of speech and self-enunciation. Subjectification is depicted as primarily the creation of the self by the self, and thereby as its positioning within discourses. Obviously speech seems to display a basic mode of the subtle process of subjectification. For the time being we would like to refer to subjectification as the constitution of subjects by saying "I". We will enlarge this definition later, after we have made sense of its place in the concept of subjectification.

RECONSIDERING SENSE

Sense is the sphere we enter every time we speak. It is implicit in speech. It is therefore impossible to enunciate the sense of what one is simultaneously saying. However, it is possible to talk about the sense of what one was saying before. But while doing so, a new sentence is produced, implying its own sense, which is – again – not simultaneously uttered. Thus the sense of this new sentence is again disguised, and exists implicitly (Deleuze, 1969). One could extend this series of quasi-explanations infinitely because, as we will show, sense inhabits a sphere beyond words, even though it motivates them in a special way.

At first glance this looks like semantics, but sense is more than a functional device of logic. We would like to visualize its efficacy as a whole and illuminate the consequences this has for the concept of subjectification. In short, we would like to cultivate the "ability to not-understand" (Deleuze, 1987, p. 169).

By no means does sense have to be brought into existence as such, because it never vanished nor was it destroyed. It is merely concealed by the epiphany of the absolute power with which logic is endowed. Referring to subjectification as the constitution of the ones who say "I", sense must be made completely intelligible again, because it portrays a basic, even an indispensable part of subjective existence.

Speech, and consequently the "saying-of-I" presupposes the existence of sense. The words used to form a sentence should be taken as "names" for things and facts. They are bound to the rules of logic which ensure the formal function of speech. As opposed to this, sense even exists in the absence of speech and independent from those "names". Sense is their presupposition and inscription, even though it appears to be produced and reproduced while individuals speak. Sense lingers between speech and things, being the definition of their difference, embodying their connectedness as their line of demarcation (Haraway, 1985). Sense is indifferent towards the effect of contrasts and contradictions, because these are characteristics of syntax and grammar which do not affect sense. Within sense, "contradictions" coexist. Furthermore sense persists in contradictory meanings. "True/False" equally contain sense, and consequently do not exclude each other. Sense has to be taken as a doubling that simultaneously spreads in two directions: the inert promotion of divergence on one hand, and the annulling of exclusiveness on the other hand.

With respect to sense, speech obviously loses all its correspondence to the signified, and relates exclusively to the expression, which comprises the "self-articulation" of the subject. Sense inhabits the expression, insists on the expressed which is the inevitable part of speech, while it exists independently from it. Herein the subject constitutes itself, creates its sense. In this sphere affinities come into effect, and desires break loose which force the individual to enter the reciprocal interplay with the other. Simultaneously this is the place where thinking affects itself (Deleuze, 1987, p. 167). The contradiction-free sphere of sense, beyond categorization, enables thinking to intrude into the impossible, to think its own unthought. This is the "drawing in of sense", the dynamic which necessitates that individuals repeatedly inscribe themselves into the creation of sense, and relations to others. This is the sublime and subtle background of "saying-I", this is the enrichment with which we would like to complete the notion of subjectification.

To avoid misunderstanding at this point: We do not claim that subject and object coincide, or that things are exposed to the creative arbitrariness of the subject. Nor do we want to abolish logic, whose rules are indispensable for the formal functioning of speech. We just want to recapture the possibility of discussing the relation: subject, signifier, signified while referring to the ambiguous, non-categorical character of expression and therefore uncovering sense (Walkerdine, 1988, p. 12 ff.).

It is now possible to point out an inconsistency, which could potentially infect theoretical thinking. Traditionally sense is something thought of as subordinate to logic. It serves as a characteristic of utterances. In this concept, sense obviously covers just one direction and is partially excluded. "Yes" renders "No" invisible, the "False" has to be excluded in favor of the "True". Seeking the definitiveness and unambiguity dictated by the omnivorous absoluteness of logic, the signifiers have to be set in an absolute relation to things. Devoid of sense, they have to prove themselves as the origin of speech and meaning. Sense is denied in favor of the possibility of decontextualization, in favor of the invention of universal, abstract signifiers. Signifiers are cemented into this one-sided relation to things. Consequently this formal logic of speech, set as absolute circumstance, thwarts a complete perception of the expressed, lets part of it decline into contradiction and impossibility and therefore become unsayable.

An illustration for this might be found within theories of cognitive development of children. Take for example research on children's ability to operate with quantity and size categories. When asked to reproduce common knowledge, children of a certain age present really absurd answers, entirely wrong, giving evidence of the expected developmental deficit, but revealing the abundance of personal sense. The traditional scientist records the deficit and ignores the confusing subtext. Pedagogy does its best to make those alienating "expressions of primitiveness" disappear. A rich and complex world could be discovered behind those non-categorical, absurd answers. Why not trace these paths of the creation of sense before children have been instructed how to signify things "correctly", and to see through the techniques of rhetorical questioning (which tend to promote the affirmation of facts) and therefore to refuse a "real" answer (Walkerdine, 1988)?

SUBJECTIFICATION AND THE COMMITMENT TO SPEECH

The "overestimation" of logic, which culminates in employing its rules for the relation things-signifiers and produces universal meanings, also affects discursive practices in general. For the speaker within discourses, the following problem ensues: when exposed to the dynamic and drawing in of affinities and desires, each subject positions itself and relates to others. It settles within the sphere of sense. But this settling is mediated by speech, and occurs by means of using words and signifiers. Within discourse, the subject can only make use of the signifiers which are at its disposal. But those signifiers are essentially only capable as universal meanings, they are understood as if referring to things in a definite and unchangeable way, in order to conform to the rules of logic. These rules may vary according to the specificity of a certain language, but in the occidental tradition they generally trust in the basic possibility of logical exclusion. Therefore they offer just one possibility of expression, or better: they provoke one certain way of understanding. One is forced to occupy the same "place" in the discourse over and over again, and meanwhile one unintentionally reproduces and confirms "absolute" signifiers. Within this dynamic one inevitably proves the institutionalized power relations to be true and unchangeable.

Taking a complete view of sense does not mean an inevitable commitment to relativism, or a decline into indifference towards the apparently insoluble problem of "expression". This is the opportunity to focus on utterances which are usually ignored as "abnormal", "wrong", or "impossible". More explicitly: Taking the efficacy of sense seriously means postulating one's "not-understanding", means to trace a kind of personal relevance which is neither definite nor obvious.

"Not-understanding" is not a synonym for egalitarianism, but is the chance to recognize differences. This is difficult to experience through the veil of intelligence, which comforts us with the security of being able to solve rational problems rationally. Because within the efficacy of intelligence, "not understanding" means confessing a personal deficit: What you do not understand is (as it were) what you did not take in when you where taught. Intelligence has no words for the unexpected; like pedagogy it minimizes the risk of creativity and inventiveness. We will come back to this thought later on.

The problem we are discussing is not new. There are numerous attempts to approach it from different theoretical backgrounds, but most of them seem to miss the point or get entangled in its dynamic obscurity. The sublime ideology of categorization, the pretentiously complacent lie of analogy, the circumscribing efficacy of normalization and its tactics – all this has been depicted, analyzed and deconstructed (Broughton, 1987b; Burman, 1994). The decisive question remaining is that of guilt. Who is to be blamed for suppression and normalization, who is responsible for making the subject speechless or obliterating it? A legitimate question, as power is usually thought of as an intentional action with an agent. Furthermore one cannot simply make words responsible for implicit meanings or stigmas. Words are of infinite patience and equability. They may be deconstructed, altered or condemned by "political correctness" without getting rid of their effects (for example the promotion and destruction of "development"; cf. Morss, 1996). The reason for the ineffectiveness of those "wordwars" is again closely connected to the partiality of the understanding of sense.

"Agents" are actually to be found among the "expressing", the speaking people, they are the speaking people. Nevertheless, they cannot be blamed for reproducing and manifesting those powerful signifiers, because they are trapped in the absolute logic of speech and are not free to choose the positions they occupy within discourse. When reflecting on the question of guilt, one ends up suspecting words of having power. They obviously develop animistic features, plan to overwhelm their speakers, force them back into the preformed shapes of identity, and smother them within the endless cycle of the reproduction of meanings (Minh-Ha, 1996, p. 151). In fact this is possible, because the subject cannot just stop speaking. With respect to the dynamic explained above, it has to produce sense and therefore it has to speak. Devoid of a complete perception of sense within the self-fertilizing process of intelligent thinking, disputes rage about "the correct name" for something, discussions slip past each other while seeking a defendant, surreal wrath increases and positions freeze in unreal oppositions. This is a scenario promoted by "rational thinking" and logic, it is made possible by the artificial concealing of one spectrum of sense. Foolhardy, obscure, contradictory questions are not posed, the chance to grasp an idea of the impossible is denied (Deleuze, 1987, p. 25; 141). Logic carries on obliviously, reveals the possible, questions the known, concludes the expected, and proves its own truth (Deleuze, 1987, p. 129).

THE INTACT SUBJECT OF ALTERNATIVE PSYCHOLOGIES

So far we have tried to present our understanding of the notion of sense. Now we would like to examine the consequences this idea might have for theoretical thinking, and to examine the concrete, actual relevance of this project. This is to present the political bias implicit in our application of the concept of sense and to show its historical and social specificity, in other words to move towards a *socio-political exploration* of the notion of sense. We begin this project with a consideration of the nature of the subject in alternative psychologies.

The political changes driven by the reintegration of sense into the processes of subjectification is grounded in our resentment of the ideological connotations of the endless funerals and exhumations of the subject. In the alternative critical psychologies that have gained popularity in the North Atlantic states in the past two decades, the notions of subject and subjectivity seem to play a crucial role. Even if the elaboration of the concepts emerged from completely divergent traditions, there are certain remarkable similarities which deserve attention.

The critical psychological tradition of Marxist origin (Holzkamp, 1983; Tolman and Maiers, 1991) in the final analysis restores the subject as the creator of itself or of its life. The subject with a specific gnostic distance from the world has the chance to choose, and then to win or to lose in the midst of the countless meanings, possibilities and constraints of its societal landscape. The heart of the matter in this critical psychological position is the idea of expansion and extension: Expansion towards possibilities of the context, and extension of the self to a better, omnipotent, generalized self.

By displaying the other side of the "alternative stream", the poststructuralist tradition of argumentation (Hollway, 1984; Parker, 1992) creates the subject as a mere positioning between power relations. Self-legitimating strategies and the claim to power give the subject its name as an abstract subject: The individual as a subject – who has to be understood as the everlasting and thus permanently changing object of discursive practices – controls the possibility to successfully justify its current place in the discourse and of the maximization of its own power. As to critical psychology, the basic idea is that of expansion and extension: expansion of one's own possibilities for dealing in power relations; and extension of the self in order to have a more easily justifiable self in dialogical conditions.

Our question is not whether these ideas are true or false. Their divergence has its origin in the varying organization of the conditions of the visibility of societal space. Our quest is to trace all these small paths which let this variety of ideas appear true; that is to explore the social space and the different perspectives it offers. That is to take the perspective of implicit sense.

Our quest is now to explore the social and scientific space in which these alternative accounts came into being. The generic origin of alternative critical psychologies could be found in doubts about the naturalistic virginity of the so called "psy-complex" (Rose, 1985): that is, all the professional languages for understanding and explaining the other and the self in mainstream psychology. Psychology as a discipline emerges in traditional historiography as an Immaculate Conception in the scientist's mind aiming at an objectivistic reflection of substantial human capacities (Danziger, 1997a; Staeuble, 1991).

As already hinted, our commitment is to engage the same critical stance on alternative psychologies and to trace the conditions of knowledge production in them (Latour, 1987; Knorr-Cetina, 1981). Alternative psychologies should not be excluded from critical scrutiny, because they rely on the productive forces of discourse as much as traditional psychologies do. By no means can they remain outside the dynamic drawing in of sense, and of the production and reproduction of certain species of subjects. The languages of alternative psychologies are made true (real), they creep into our speaking and acting, we reproduce them through our speaking and acting, we make them real and they make us real through their deep dependence on and anchoring in social space – which was supposed to be the target of their critique.

What does that mean exactly? If the definition of the subject in alternative psychologies is not an essential one, then what made and makes this definition so meaningful for us? We have already depicted the lack of concern for sense in alternative psychologies, but what made them so productive? Who finally is the subject of extension and expansion? Is it the "Zeitgeist", or the millions of real, empirical subjects, or maybe some scientists and intellectuals of the West? Is it the subject itself or intellectuals speaking in the name of the subject?

When we seek an answer to these questions we have to look for the image of human beings inherent in alternative psychologies. The subject which constructs itself through extension and expansion either in the discourse or in its own realm of life is an intact, proper subject. The image of human beings in alternative psychologies is as a self-entrepreneurial subject which tends to establish a generic order in its environment by either using power or its potency to act. Here we can observe a striking resemblance between this image and the context in which this image has been fabricated. The intact, self-entrepreneurial subject represents the imperative of the proper functioning of the North Atlantic countries and thus corresponds to a concrete geopolitical order and to an ethical impetus in this specific order (Burchell, 1996). In alternative psychologies, we used to think that implicit truth was an unaccomplished emancipation project. We located the reality of alternative critical psychologies in a desired hereafter. Yet, we want to assert that this truth is something completely different from the ideological preformation of emancipation and liberation. The playground of critical psychologies is aggressive neo-colonial neo-liberalism. And we now recognize that the invisible, excluded other is an inherent part of the articulated (Derrida, 1967). Thus, the constitutive outside of alternative psychologies is post-war neo-liberal rationality.

THE REALITY OF GLOBAL CAPITALISM: Where The Subject Can Also be Mute

What will happen if we accept that the subject is not as intact as critical psychologies suppose? What does the defense of a position which installs a principally mute subject mean? In the net of the hierarchical power relations of the world system which is transnational global capitalism (Altvater and Mahnkopf, 1996), positions actually do exist which produce subjects who remain silent and speechless; or at least have a voice incompatible with ours. This is the uneducated subject searching only for food, the subject of the third world's aggressive nationalisms, the subject of massive rapes in Bosnia and lynching attacks against women in Afghanistan, the subject of rebellion in South Mexico and Colombia and so on. This subject strives for liberation and at the same time reproduces atrocity.

This subject is not intact, morally clean, or "politically correct". But this is not merely an effect of its violent, philistine and unruly character. It is a consequence of the fact that this subject does not fit into the global standards set by North Atlantic countries and transnational organizations. This subject is implicitly defined as "uncivilized" *either* because it has no right to speak in the global language of economic efficacy and information technology (as post-structuralist tradition suggests) *or* because it seems to have no intention to speak with regard to any common respect (as critical psychology suggests). Appearing completely unfit for political discourse this subject has a lack of expressiveness anyway. When this subject *may* articulate itself, it serves as mere example for a footnote in texts on cultural studies or enlivens the travelogue in the feature pages of tomorrow's newspapers.

In neo-liberal societies the right to speak is owned by the person who reflects and acts, who knows the status of surrounding power relations, who has a position which permits him or her to have a voice in the first-world genre. This is the privileged subject of alternative psychologies. These psychologies obliterate the other subject, the morally unclean, ambivalent subject, or at least they see it as a palimpsest inscribed again and again in the eternal return of objectivity.

We have thus not only to challenge the concepts used in mainstream psychology by deconstructing them, as we said earlier, but we must also question the subject of knowledge in general, and open its constructedness to the perspective of sense. In other words, the subject matter of psychology – mainstream or alternative – is only a specific transformation of the North Atlantic, neo-liberal world into a subject. Furthermore we have to recognize that the subject matter of alternative psychologies may be just a specific mode of an indigenous, western psychology (Kim, 1997). In the near future what seemed to be the vanguard positions of alternative psychologies will be inducted into mainstream psychology and will very effectively colonize the discourses of psychologies on the periphery. Postmodern, discursive, cultural, and critical psychologies, activity theories, and their derivatives in western psychology build a new version of North Atlantic psychology.

Taking this into account, we have to reconsider the incapability of speech and the paternalistic structure of languages. We have to counter the logic of subjectivity with its sense. As mentioned before, sense never left – it was always here, implicitly underlying our expression and acting. Reintegrating sense into subjectivity is a political project of rediscovering the partialized subject. Let us explain that further.

SENSE AS POLITICAL REPRESENTATION

The authors of this paper live in a rapidly changing Germany. We are participating in specific ways in reproducing our society. We have to confront our emancipatory visions with melancholic realities, while we contribute to the exclusion and marginalisation of others, and we are still zealous to be concerned about the "voiceless". We desire, and nevertheless fail to remember, arrangements, capitulations, resentments, attempts. These coincidences give us an idea of the fact that the power to colonize thought and lives is not in the hands of an omnipotent colonizer. As mentioned in the preceding analysis of sense, we have to face being a kind of "colonizer" and "decolonizer" at the same time. At the intersection of these two opposite moments, within the deep ambivalences of our existence we search for sense, which reintegrates and legitimates the unthinkable, giving space for the possibility of introducing the political project of reassembling subjectivity and the processes of subjectification. This project aims far beyond imputation, victimization, or the mere shifting of fickle demarcation lines. We want to debunk meanings and signifiers as empty cocoons, as a masquerade of responsibility with no recognizable person behind.

This exchange of priorities between meaning and sense introduces our concept of sense. Admittedly it is not an entirely new way of thinking: Vygotsky claimed that the meaning which is enclosed in words is not a constant and unchangeable magnitude, but an available potency, which materializes — in the literal meaning of the word — through its subjective application (Vygotsky, 1934; Papadopoulos, 1999). He thus defines the possibility of creating the non-identical. Meanings do certainly exist, but they become real only when they are used (Wittgenstein, 1953). And they are subjective because they represent possibilities of expression.

Subjective sense exceeds the possibility of objective theorization because cognitive, volitional and emotional aspects, which cannot be isolated as distinguishable features of subjective experience, converge in it (Vygotsky, 1934; Hildebrand-Nilshon and Kim, 1997). Vygotsky firmly rejects every possibility of an essentialist treatment of the constitution of the subject based on an operationalization of the elements of consciousness. Sense displays the way persons come to terms with themselves and act referring to their subjective, situated perspectives. Sense does not explain the principal themes of psychology such as thought, cognitive processes, emotion, volition etc. Sense produces the condition of individual existence, sense is the presupposition of speech and at the same time is altered or reproduced by speech, it is the implication of cognitive processes, volition, emotions etc.

At this point we see that reintegrating sense into subjectification could serve as an inauguration of political representations in our categories. Sense exceeds the possibilities of an objectivistic generalization because it re-establishes a connection to our lived realities on the one hand and on the other hand reveals the partiality of our existence. This return to a partially concrete perspective of the existence of persons, also means the dismissal of a metapsychology which attempts to acquire ostensible, objectivistic clarity. Reintegrating sense into subjectification not only concerns the realities of people, but also affects the realities of the production of knowledge. Sense has a hard center which lies in the rootedness of its enunciation in concrete social spaces. Sense does not portray an objectivistic representation of some "natural kinds" found in the lives or in the psychic processes of people (Danziger, 1987b). The rootedness of sense challenges the image of psychology, and even disturbs the complacent exceptionality of alternative theories. As Broughton comments: "At risk of hypocrisy, I would argue that to make a career out of criticism would amount to a contradiction in terms. I would go so far as to say that critical developmental psychology can not be contemplated or sustained without a personal, perhaps visceral commitment." (Broughton, 1987a, p. 23) The complete perception of sense does not dispose of the idea of development and logic; on the contrary it raises the question of a fluid, vitalized perspective on the narration of development and logic.

REFERENCES

Altvater, E. & Mahnkopf, B. (1996). *Grenzen der Globalisierung: Ökonomie, Ökologie und Politik in der Weltgesellschaft.* Münster: Westfälisches Dampfboot.

Burchell, G. (1996). Liberal government and techniques of the self. In A. Barry, T. Osborne, & N. Rose, (Eds), *Foucault and political reason. Liberalism, neo-liberalism and rationalities of goverment* (pp. 19-36). London: University College London Press.

Broughton, J.M. (1987a). An introduction to critical developmental psychology. In J.M. Broughton (Ed.) *Critical theories of developmental psychology* (pp. 1-30). New York: Plenum Press.

Broughton, J.M. (Ed.) (1987b). *Critical theories of developmental psychology.* New York: Plenum Press.

Burman, E. (1994). *Deconstructing developmental psychology.* London: Routledge.

Danziger, K. (1997a). *Naming the mind. How psychology found its language.* London: Sage.

Danziger, K. (1997b). Natural kinds, human kinds, and historicity. Vortrag in der 7. Konferenz der *International Society for Theoretical Psychology*, Berlin, 27. April - 2. Mai 1997.

Deleuze, G. (1969). *Die Logik des Sinns.* Frankfurt am Main: Suhrkamp.

Deleuze, G. (1987). *Foucault.* Frankfurt am Main: Suhrkamp.

Derrida, J. (1967). *Of Grammatology.* Übers. v. G. C. Spivak. Baltimore: The Johns Hopkins University Press, 1998.

Foucault, M. (1982). Technologies of the self. In L.H. Martin, H. Gutman, & P.H. Hutton, (Eds.) *Technologies of the self. A seminar with Michel Foucault* (pp. 16-49). Amherst MA: The Universiy of Massachusetts Press, 1988.

Foucault, M. (1984). The ethic of care for the self as a practice of freedom. In J. Bernauer, & D. Rasmussen, (Eds.), *The final Foucault* (pp. 1-20). Cambridge: MIT Press, 1988.

Haraway, D. (1985). Ein Manifest für Cyborgs. Feminismus im Streit mit den Technowissenschaften. In D. Haraway, *Die Neuerfindung der Natur. Primaten, Cyborgs und Frauen* (pp. 33-72). Frankfurt/M.: Campus, 1995.

Hildebrand-Nilshon, M. & Kim, C.-W. (1997). Concerning the compatibility of Vygotsky's concept of semiotic mediation and the cultural psychological challenge of today. Vortrag in der 7. Konferenz der *International Society for Theoretical Psychology*, Berlin, 27. April/May.

Hildebrand-Nilshon, M. & Papadopoulos, D. (1998). Short stories about identity. The tension between self-articulation and the regulation of the self. Paper presented at the 4th Congress of the International Society for Cultural Research and Activity Theory, Aarhus, Denmark, June.

300

Hollway, W. (1984). Gender difference and the production of subjectivity. In J. Henriques et al., *Changing the subject. Psychology, social regulation and subjectivity* (pp. 227-260). London: Methuen.

Holzkamp, K. (1983). *Grundlegung der Psychologie.* Frankfurt/M.: Campus.

Kim, C.-W. (1997). *Baustein für einen kulturpsychologischen Diskurs: Dekonstruktion des unilinearen Entwicklungsgedankens.* Berlin: Dissertation (Fachbereich Erziehungswissenschaft und Psychologie der Freien Universität Berlin).

Knorr-Cetina, K. (1981). *Die Fabrikation von Erkenntnis. Zur Anthropologie der Naturwissenschaft.* Frankfurt/M.: Suhrkamp, 1991.

Latour, B. (1987). *Science in action.* Milton Keynes.

Minh-Ha, Trinh T. (1996). Über zulässige Grenzen: Die Politik der Identität und Differenz. In B. Fuchs, & G. Habinger, (Eds). *Rassismen und Feminismen. Differenzen, Machtverhältniss, und Solidarität zwischen Frauen.* (p.151). Wien: Promedia.

Morss, J. R. (1996). *Growing critical.* London: Routledge.

Papadopoulos, D. (1999). *Lew S. Wygotski – Werk und Wirkung.* Frankfurt/M.: Campus.

Parker, I. (1992). *Discourse dynamics. Critical analysis for social and individual psychology.* London: Routledge.

Rose, N. (1985). *The psychological complex: Psychology, politics, and society in England, 1869-1939.* London: Routledge & Kegan Paul.

Rose, N. (1996). Identity, genealogy, history. In S. Hall & P. du Gay (Eds) *Questions of cultural identity* (pp. 128-150). London: Sage.

Staeuble, I. (1991). Könnte Psychologie auch anders aussehen? Zur historischen Rekonstruktion von Alternativen. In H.E. Lück & R. Miller (Hg.), *Theorien und Methoden psychologiegeschichtlicher Forschung* (pp. 33-42). Göttingen: Hogrefe.

Tolman, C. W. & Maiers,W. (Eds) (1991). *Critical psychology. Contributions to an historical science of the subject.* New York: Cambridge University Press.

Vygotsky, L. S. (1934). Thinking and speech. In L.S. Vygotsky, *The collected works of L.S. Vygotsky. Bd. 1: Problems of general psychology* (pp. 39-285). R.W. Rieber, & A.C. Carton (Eds.). New York: Plenum, 1987.

Walkerdine, V. (1988). *The mastery of reason.* London: Routledge.

Wittgenstein, L. (1953). *Philosophische Untersuchungen.* In L. Wittgenstein, Werkausgabe, Bd. 1 (pp. 225-580). Frankfurt/M.: Suhrkamp, 1993.

FROM LAW TO LIFESTYLE:
"Developmental" Change in the Risk Society

John R. Morss
Dunedin, New Zealand

SUMMARY

Developmentalism, or developmental explanation, has been identified and subjected to critique within psychology by a number of writers over recent years (for example, Bradley, 1989; Broughton, 1987; Burman, 1994; Morss, 1996; Stainton Rogers and Stainton Rogers 1992). The intention of this chapter is to overview this area of the literature, but also to extend the range of issues and resources in potentially significant ways. In order to do so, some materials from literature beyond psychology – from education and from sociology – will be discussed, as well as literature in critical psychology. Consideration is given to the implications of the writings of sociologists Ulrich Beck and Anthony Giddens on the "Risk Society", the impacts of globalisation on personal life, and related concerns. The arguments of Beck and Giddens, and their claims concerning personal life and family dynamics, raise urgent questions about psychology's senses of "developmental" change and possibly help to delineate some of the characteristics of an alternative formulation. Berking's notion of "lifestyle" is considered in this context.

INTRODUCTION

Developmentalism involves assumptions about natural and systematic processes of change over time (eg in children), giving rise to expectations about what can be understood, expressed or manifested by persons of particular age.[1] Sometimes the expectations are fairly specific in terms of chronological age, sometimes they constitute a graded sequence or a trend or "direction" of change postulated across time ("as children get older they become more X or less Y").

Human cultures are replete with such expectations, often very diverse. It may well be the case that some particular sets of such culture-based expectations have given rise to the more systematic and deliberate "theories" of developmental change with which we are familiar. That is to say, articulated theories of human development, which in many ways constitute the best examples of "developmentalism", have not emerged from a void but at least in part from the historically contingent dominance of the normative expectations of some particular cultural communities.

But the phenomena of developmentalism cannot be reduced to the dominance of some particular, narrow set of age-graded expectations (such as those of the canonical able-bodied WASP male). Developmentalism crosses at least some cultural boundaries and it affects our lives in ways that cannot be thought of straightforwardly as (mono-)cultural expression: professionalised ways for example. It does not seem especially helpful to try to locate in some particular culture the expectation that infants are bound to the perceptual here-and-now or that adolescents are unstable – even though these kinds of beliefs must be culturally based in some substantial sense. To attempt to do so seems to court a superficial kind of correspondence theory with respect to specific societal forms and their "psychology".

Fundamentally perhaps, developmental explanation overrides individual diversity by slotting people into categories on the basis of the amount of time they happen to have spent on the planet. Very generally speaking, lawful age-based discrimination is on the decline world-wide (for example, with respect to compulsory retirement ages – despite an unsuccessful rearguard action in New Zealand by the University of Otago). Children's views and judgements are increasingly being recognised in legal process, instead of being simply overlooked. Developmental forms of explanation seem to obstruct this progressive trend, if such it is. At worst, they contribute to the consolidation and legitimation of oppressive practices in ways that science has often done through the centuries.

Perhaps the major problem with developmental thinking of any kind is that it imposes one form of interpretation when there might be alternatives. If one form of interpretation is imposed strongly enough then it becomes difficult or even impossible even to think of alternatives. Looking for alternatives may then appear crazy or subversive, or at best a waste of time. The major purpose of the critique of developmental forms of explanation is to encourage its readers to stop and think that there might be alternatives to the development story (in whatever context they run up against it) and to consider exploring what those alternatives might be. An alternative, if defined, will not necessarily be "better" than the developmental story. That needs a further judgement on the merits of each case. But the insistence on the possibility of alternatives is itself a substantial step, if at times a subversive one.

First, in what follows, are some comments about critical psychology, which has a very important role to play in establishing the functions of developmental thinking and in suggesting alternatives. Next, an attempt is made to indicate the significance of developmentalism in such areas as educational practice. In this context consideration is given to recent proposals and formulations by educationist Kieran Egan (1997). Egan has proposed a scheme of a sequence of kinds of understanding that supposedly develop in children's thinking (namely Somatic; Mythic; Romantic; Philosophic; Ironic). For Egan (rather like Bruner and of course Piaget and many others before him), these quasi-stages of thinking underlie the capacities for response to education in its widest senses.

Moving from educationist writings to sociological writings, some consideration is given next to the implications of the writings of sociologists Ulrich Beck and Anthony Giddens on the "Risk Society", the impacts of globalisation on personal life, and related concerns. The arguments of Beck and Giddens, and to some extent their claims concerning personal life and family dynamics, raise urgent questions about psychology's senses of "developmental" change and possibly help to delineate some of the characteristics of an alternative. In conclusion, some related work of Helmuth Berking (1996) is employed to suggest some of the ways in which the phenomena and the changes which we have been wont to call "developmental" might be reconceptualised. Berking's notion of "lifestyles" is extended and applied to childhood in a conjectural exploration of the late modern experience of "development".

CRITICAL PSYCHOLOGY AND THE CRITIQUE OF DEVELOPMENTALISM

Probably for complex reasons, critical psychology of recent decades has tended to combine interests in psychological theorising with broad-left political agendas (see Sloan, 2000). These agendas have included, or at least have been friendly towards, aspirations toward emancipation and counter-discriminatory projects (as perceived). Age-based discrimination, and consequent oppression (if that is the correct word) may be one of the last forms of discrimination to be fully examined by psychologists, and it has not thus far generated anything like the volume of concern raised by other kinds of discrimination. Theory-sensitised psychologists' interests in childhood and development have tended to be rather technical ones, rather than critical ones as such. Questions concerning the role of biological forms of explanation in developmental psychology, for example, although of undeniably political import, have tended to be studied in fairly technicist ways (eg Morss, 1990). Developmental psychology, taken broadly, has been scrutinised from the position of a fairly generalised social-constructionism much more than from a critical-psychology standpoint (James, Jenks and Prout, 1998). Questions have been asked about theoretical adequacy rather than about the societal consequences of particular ways of defining and dealing with certain sub-sections of the human population. Issues of "children's rights" for example, remain rather peripheral to the discussions on developmental change as perceived in psychology.

However some very significant work has been undertaken on issues of (psychological) development, from within critical psychology. In many ways what this work has demonstrated is that taking psychology's regular notion of "the development of the individual" at face value prevents one from fully recognising the scale of the effects of developmental discourse. Psychology's notion of the reference of the word development – what sort of thing it is that is said to develop – slides around between individuals, species, capacities, anatomical parts, methodologies, and social-historical eras. All of these may from time to time be blithely said by psychologists, sometimes it seems all in the same sentence, to "develop". Critical psychologists interested in developmental change find they cannot ignore the ramifications of the "development complex" and the drawing both of comparisons and contrasts with politically-freighted matters of colonialism, gender, and other broader concerns. The problems with the notion of "development" within psychology, I will suggest, are both broad and narrow (like the streets of Dublin in the old song). They are also both technical and political. And many of the problems bear on matters of the unjust treatment of young people, arguably amounting to oppression or exploitation.

One important task is to indicate some of the recent and contemporary literature that has pressed the critique of development in different contexts. Bradley (1989) has focused on the infancy years, showing how scientific accounts of babies, of their supposed development and of their relationships with adults, reflect those scientists' preconceptions rather than some "reality" about infancy. Thus, psychological accounts of infant development always involve interpretation and the projection of contemporary ideology (for example, about childrearing, gender roles and so on) onto the "data". Broughton (1987) has applied ideas from critical theory to expose the ideological nature of developmental psychology – pointing out the extent to which what we may think of as developmental change is produced through social processes. Burman has scrutinised the issue of naturalness in human development – the persistent claim that a child's development is a natural and hence universal process (Burman, 1994). Rex Stainton Rogers and Wendy Stainton Rogers (1992) have explored the consequences of a "polytextual" approach to developmental discourse, bracketing the kinds of presupposition that are usually unquestioned. Morss (1996) has proposed that developmental change is such a confused and misleading idea that it would be best dispensed with altogether.

A number of very practical issues emerge once our belief in developmental explanation is suspended. Issues about children's needs 'and rights are a good example. Claims about children's "needs" tend to rest on dubious assumptions about developmental change and naturalness (Woodhead, 1990). Discussions about children's rights – for example in the context of the United Nations Convention on the Rights of the Child (Detrick, 1999) – seem to ground those rights in children's needs. And indeed, to define any right as being a *child*'s right – as distinct from a human right – would seem to presuppose some special status or characteristic in children. At least in a literal sense I think such a practice would have to be called discrimination. It would be discrimination on the basis of age, albeit a discrimination benevolently intended (that is, a "protection") – and albeit one quite feasibly positive in its effects. Questions need to be faced about inconsistencies between anti-discriminatory legislation and protectively discriminatory legislation – whether or not both kinds of legislation happen to derive from United Nations initiatives. This kind of public policy issue is clearly adumbrated in Stainton Rogers and Stainton Rogers (1992).

KIERAN EGAN AND "ROMANTIC UNDERSTANDING": A Contemporary Developmental Analysis of Schoolchildren's Thinking

Kieran Egan is an educationist with extensive experience in the curriculum of the early and middle years of school in the English-speaking tradition (and beyond). According to Egan's (1997) *The Educated Mind*, education needs to be thought of as a recapitulationary process (although certainly a flexible one). That is, education is a process "in which the individual recapitulates the kinds of understanding developed in the culture's history" (p. 73). Egan's formulations are lively and thought-provoking and any contribution that generates fresh thinking on the curriculum is to be welcomed. But it may be that a recapitulation framework, however qualified, inevitably sets excessive constraints on the processes being described. A stage theory is a stage theory, and the recapitulation framework seems to set a developmental cage around the concepts of child development and education explored within it (Morss, 1996).

Egan argues that distinguishable steps in "our" cultural history (itself a problematic notion) took place on the road to written alphanumeric practices and gave rise historically to "Romantic understanding", "Philosophic understanding", and finally "Ironic understanding". Romantic understanding itself displaced "Mythic understanding". Romantic understanding (the kind of thinking to which Egan has given most attention, and which has been the most influential of his series of proposals) is a form of thinking exemplified by the writing of Herodotus in ancient times. Correspondingly, modern children of between approximately eight and twelve years or so (the "middle school years") are said to express interests in, and in general to respond well to curriculum focusing on, Romantic themes as Egan comes to define them. For Egan, Romantic understanding is closely tied with literacy. In contrast with the earlier "Mythic" understanding, which it mixes with but does not entirely displace, Romantic understanding is somewhat abstract. It compromises with reality while not accommodating entirely to it.

Acording to Egan, Herodotus' *Histories* were a new kind of writing, and manifest a kind of thinking not possible without writing: a concern with the exotic, with the strange and the great, with the hero role, with transcendent human qualities, but dealt with at the human level and in a somewhat systematic way. Egan compares the Herodotus style to the appeal of the *Guinness Book of Records* with its (highly while peculiarly) organised format and its wonder-provoking while person-centred style. In terms of behavior he compares it to the propensities to "hobbies" such as collecting that supposedly characterise the middle school age-group. Relatedly, Egan suggests with respect to a slightly older age-group that the magazine *Psychology Today* exemplifies a Romantic style.

All the contemporary examples of "Romantic" texts are characterised by explicit claims to be factual, indeed in some respects to be doing away with myth or controlling the unknown. Despite the quantitative aspects of (for example) the *Guinness Book* they take a wholistic kind of approach, impressionistic rather than analytic, and arguably (for Egan) make use of oppositional/binary thinking of a kind that Egan identifies as itself of a Mythic type. Such residual characteristics (Mythic elements in a Romantic specimen) are of course no more embarrassing to Egan than the equivalent residual phenomena in Piaget's theory were for Piaget. The psychology magazine discusses emotions and feelings, topics of less obvious concern for the records book, but it is perhaps in the way those topics are discussed rather in the topics themselves, that the Romantic form of understanding is best displayed. All the contemporary examples (and perhaps Herodotus also) tend to the atheoretical, as indicated by the arbitrary if not bizarre nature of the classification systems that they employ and display.

Remember that for Egan, the characteristics of this kind of cultural product are at the same time in some ways the characteristics of the thinking of an age-stratum of contemporary young person. *The Guinness Book of Records* tells us about "the contents of children's minds" for Egan as did children's propensities for collecting for Stanley Hall a century ago (and Egan now!). For Egan's account continues the Hall tradition and suffers from the general ailments of stage-based, recapitulationary approaches to children's development, even though it entirely outclasses Hall in stylistic ways. However qualified – however much the various kinds of thinking are said to mix and blend, and to vary in their manifestations across individuals or across cultures – the underlying sequence remains firmly in place. And it is a very familiar sequence. Scientific thinking emerges after phenomenonalistic forms, and abstract kinds of thinking emerge out of the scientific. Irony is the highest form of thinking, emerging only in cognitively-mature persons and only in later stages of civilisation. The term "Romantic" is undoubtedly unexpected in the general developmental sequence of kinds of thinking but it turns out to refer in the main to some very familiar aspects of supposedly normative childhood behavior. It is clear that education still awaits a post-developmental consideration of curriculum, and perhaps it becomes ever more clear that such a project is necessary (Cannella, 1997).

ESCAPING FROM DEVELOPMENTAL EXPLANATION?
Suggestions from Risk Theory

Unsurprisingly, developmental thinking in education is connected with broader lines of conceptualisation in the social sciences. Much of sociology for example has in the past adopted evolutionist arguments from the natural sciences, tending to impel it toward naturalistic and functionalist accounts of human activity (much analysed by Giddens). Human development has thus sometimes been seen rather simplistically by sociology as a matter of mere "socialisation" . Among several contemporary movements in sociology and social theory, the extensive lines of work of Anthony Giddens and Ulrich Beck comprise some of the most significantly innovatory contributions to a post-functionalist sociology (postmodern approaches perhaps comprising another). Among other issues, Giddens and Beck have (jointly and severally) discussed family life, personal relationships and intimacy (eg, Beck and Beck-Gernsheim, 1995). One of the most striking notions to emerge from this work has been Beck's notion of the "Risk Society", which serves to focus and to introduce the issues (see Bradley and Morss, in press).

Ulrich Beck's *Risk Society* (1992) was first published in the year of the Chernobyl disaster (also see Beck, 1998; 1999; 2000). Whereas risks have always been present for human society, including risks of people's own making, risks are no longer elements in a larger context: risk has now become total. We can no longer treat technology and technological change as conceptually distinct from the hazardous "side-effects" of such technology. Every technological effect is a side-effect in that sense, combining design and accident in mobile combination. Beck's innovative sense of risk represents a departure from previous senses of the word. Unlike a hurricane or barbarians at the gate, or perhaps even cancer, the "new" or newly significant kind of risk, for Beck, is known by those it affects (at least, known in principle) to be caused by human activity: risk is no longer natural.

Beck's risk is known by those it affects to be identifiable as risk only through the participation of science and other systematised discourses. It tends to be invisible (AIDS, acid rain, toxic waste) and to have its life in the discursive realm. The implied contrast with hurricanes and barbarians serves if anything to heighten the salience of this disembodied kind of risk, which shades into words like "scare" and "panic" more than it does into "probability". Beckian risks are known in terms of international discourses (for example, the risk of picking up a computer virus through the internet) and this kind of globalisation is much more salient for Beck than the mere fact of acid rain (etc) crossing national borders. Hurricanes and barbarians also did the latter. Every aspect of our daily life, whether apparently "natural" or artificial, can now become (literally overnight) a source of risk: any foodstuff, any building material, any child-care practice like bed-sharing, any social trend like increasing incidence of single parents, any comet or virus.

Beck avoids predictions or discerned implications couched in terms of individual dislocation and anxiety (but see Scott, Jackson and Backett-Milburn, 1998). Beck's proposals seem to be at least as much about the changing nature of risk as they are about increased levels of risk as previously defined, and/or increased levels of people's perceptions of risk as previously defined. Very significantly, Beck insists that there is no longer any "nature" "as we knew it". Now we have "the environment" which like "the landscape" is an object defined by human activity. Extrapolating from this position, one could argue that there could not be any such thing as "natural development". Development is replaced by the life project, a work-in-progress ("site under construction"). Developmental change is exposed as mere tradition – or rather (like Giddens' example of the Scots tartan) no more than *ersatz* tradition.

Natural developmental change was perhaps compatible as an idea with the senses of risk predating Beck (that is, with the more familiar senses of "risk"), but is entirely incompatible with a Risk Theory formulation. Actuarial notions of risk fit neatly with a statistical or multi-factorial approach to resilience in a population, predicted risks of school failure or teenage pregnancy and so on. Operating with an orthodox understanding of risk and risks, we can readily agree that any individual life is fragile and at risk of termination; and we can say that any pattern of change deemed (by whomever) to be desirable, is vulnerable to be shifted into another (presumably less desirable) track. Even a vintage model human development theory like Erik Erikson's pays great attention to the risk of "negative" outcomes at each phase, and hence to the fragility of the whole project.

But Risk Theory seems to me to foreground the issue of "the end of the natural" and therefore to support a thoroughgoing social-constructionism of human development. (For example it casts further doubt on any naturalistic account of children's "needs"). It also supplies some slightly more precise ideas about what this might look like. Beck in particular discusses the ways that parents' attitudes to intimacy and to personal relationships, with partners and with children, might change in the Risk Society: a parent's relationship with a child might become the last bastion of a kind of relationship that is disappearing elsewhere in one's life ("partners come and go but the child remains"). There is very much the sense of "the only child" – indeed a literal reality in the West Germany in which Beck was originally writing (cf. Gunter Grass' 1980 novel *The Germans are Dying Out*). One might say that for Beck, every child becomes an only child in the Risk Society.

Children "these days" are treated as special, unique and so on, sometimes radically so, even if they are full siblings: parents (including solo parents) spend their Saturdays driving their different children to different sporting activities and so on. Blended "families" now provide the prototype, for here the differentness of the different children is patent and marked (they may all have different surnames). So the blended-and-extended "family" (a term at which Beck directs some irony) becomes the norm in a serious sense. But even this "new-age" structure as a haven for attachment will die out, Beck implies, since there is no intrinsic reason for parent-child attachment to be indefinitely secure from the threats and instabilities which prevail more generally in our interpersonal environment. Looking ahead in the Risk Society we have to envisage an ever more emotionally fragmented and dynamic lifeworld as if every day should be expected to bring us the kind of scrutiny, re-negotiation and re-affirmation (and pain) that an occasional separation, redundancy, or custody case brings to us these days. Soap opera becomes life.

CONCLUSION: LAW, TRADITION, LIFESTYLE

Critical psychology finds itself in different situations with respect to the education work of Egan, on the one hand, and the social theory work of Giddens and Beck, on the other. Critical psychology has little difficulty highlighting the orthodox developmental presuppositions of Egan's proposals on the curriculum. With respect to contemporary social theory however, critical psychology finds itself somewhat on the back foot. It might even wonder if it is being left behind in some sense. It can perhaps point to some occasional lapses where the social theorists appeal to orthodox expectations on children, such as a suggestion by Beck that attachment is naturally stronger in younger children. More generally the understanding of the role of developmental explanation achieved by critical psychology is corroborated in the work of the social theorists. Postmodernist forms of analysis (Holzman and Morss, 2000) may not be the only possible avenues for critical work at this juncture, as the work of Helmuth Berking illustrates.

Following Beck and Giddens, Berking (1996) has emphasised the "release of individuals from fixed social frames of reference … the erosion of life-contexts stabilised in terms of class-specific cultural aspects, of forms of the family, and of vocational ties", a set of processes which "for the first time in the history of this form of sociation" is not being absorbed and assimilated by the prevailing social structures (p. 191). There is a new kind of individualisation prevailing, as identified by Beck, one which "cannot mean the reinstatement of the old liberal idea of the bourgeois subject, centred on liberty and property" (ibid). Berking describes the individualisation as paradoxical, including

> [A] heightening of the subjective latitudes open to freedom and [at the same time] complete dependence on the market, liberation and [at the same time] standardisation of expression … [I]n short: learning, at all levels of social intercourse, to deal with paradoxical demands on one's behaviour, controlling one's affects without ceasing to be "natural" …
> (Berking, 1996, p 195).

Berking's thought-provoking investigation of the consequences of this situation leads him to focus on "lifestyles and lifestyle coalitions". Lifestyles, he notes, are "post-traditional" entities, and ones which involve at the same time the "aestheticisation of everyday life" and the politicisation of the private. For Berking, the notion of lifestyle makes possible an analysis of the lifeworld of the individual in contemporary late modern society. He contrasts it (again following Beck and Giddens) with the non-reflective "institutionally shaped patterns of life-conduct … centred … on work, profession and family" (p. 191) typical of earlier modern times.

It would seem that normative, law-ful accounts of human developmental change fall squarely within this historically earlier kind of framework. If so, one might now look to the displacement of such institutionally guaranteed norms or laws by "lifestyle" processes. This might involve the ("external") replacing of traditional by "post-traditional" variants, or some more subtle "internal" transformation, leaving only a "shell" of the traditional entity. Developmental *changes*, as we used to understand them, may have in a sense become lifestyle *alternatives*. Put crudely, persons who adopt certain ways of acting and being might have to be thought of as in some valid sense *choosing* to adopt those kinds of "subjective performance" – *even if the persons we are thinking of are children.*

This way of talking may seem outrageous, but surely makes sense at least in the context of adolescence (for example). A young person surely may with a fairly straightforward self-awareness decide to act in certain ways thought of by some as typical (or "traditional") for a "teenager". (A "middle-aged" adult may also choose to act "like a teenager".) We may well think this freedom to be peculiarly recent from a historical perspective. Whether or not a person of similar age living in earlier times – say fifty years ago – must be said to have had significantly less voluntary control on such matters, is of course hard to say. The constraints of tradition can be over-stressed from a distance, either temporal or geographical (this retrospective problem arises in any acccount of tradition). More importantly for our current discussion, if the proposal has some face validity for a "young person" as well as for an adult, how could we set a minimum chronological age below which it could not be held to operate? Why should we not say that babies choose to act like babies? This would be a brave new world indeed.

The argument is not a watertight one but the reconceptualisation of "developmental" change as change of lifestyle may be worth considering further. Those aspects of a child's "developmental" change contributed fairly directly by parents, for example, surely reflect lifestyle as commonly understood, and the scope of this domain surely extends beyond clothes, haircuts and toys. The notion of lifestyle has at least the merit of radically excising the base structure of necessary and universal sequence from accounts of what people do, whatever their chronological age. Not that the "lifestyle" approach should be seen as replacing determinate (developmental) prescription with "free choice". Lifestyles are subject to the intense forces of the global market (and one person's "lifestyle" may be another person's "cliché": see Stephenson, this volume). But thinking in terms of lifestyles at least reminds us that, for any person of any chronological age, there are always alternatives. And that is a kind of emancipation.

Note

1.   My conference attendance was generously supported by the University of Otago.Updating of the conference presentation has been informed by my studies at the Centre for Cultural Risk Research, Charles Sturt University, NSW; thanks to Jane Selby and Ben Bradley for their hospitality. Thanks also to Kieran Egan, to David Fryer and to Judith Duncan.

REFERENCES

Beck, U. (1992). *Risk society: Towards a new modernity.* London: Sage.
Beck, U. (1998). *Democracy without enemies.* Cambridge: Polity Press.
Beck, U. (1999). *World risk society.* Cambridge: Polity Press.
Beck, U. (2000). The cosmopolitan perspective: Sociology of the second age of modernity. *British Journal of Sociology*, 51/1, 75-105.
Beck, U. and Beck-Gernsheim, E. (1995). *The normal chaos of love.* Cambridge: Polity Press.
Berking, H. (1996). Solidary individualism: The moral impact of cultural modernisation in late modernity. In S. Lash, B. Szerszynski and B. Wynne (Eds) *Risk, environment and modernity: Towards a new ecology* (pp 189—202). London: Sage.
Bradley, B. (1989). *Visions of infancy.* Cambridge: Polity Press.

312

Bradley, B. and Morss, J.R. (in press for 2001). Social construction in a world at risk: Toward a psychology of experience. *Theory & Psychology.*

Broughton, J. (Ed.) (1987). *Critical theories of psychological development.* New York: Plenum.

Burman, E. (1994). *Deconstructing developmental psychology.* London: Routledge.

Cannella, G. (1997). *Deconstructing early childhood education.* New York: Plenum.

Detrick, S. (1999). *A commentary on the United Nations Convention on the Rights of the Child.* Boston: M. Nijhoff.

Egan, K. (1997). *The educated mind: How cognitive tools shape our understanding.* Chicago: University of Chicago Press.

Giddens, A. (1994). Living in a post-traditional society. In U. Beck, A. Giddens and S. Lash *Reflexive modernization: Politics, tradition and aesthetics in the modern social order* (pp 56—109). Cambridge: Polity Press.

Grass, G. (1980). *Kopfgeburten oder Die Deutschen sterben aus.* Neuwied: Luchterhand.

Holzman, L. and Morss, J.R. (Eds) (2000). *Postmodern psychologies, societal practice, and political life.* New York: Routledge.

James, A., Jenks, C. and Prout, A. (1998). *Theorizing childhood.* Cambridge: Polity Press.

Morss, J.R. (1990). *The biologising of childhood.* Hove UK: Lawrence Erlbaum Associates.

Morss, J.R. (1996). *Growing critical.* London: Routledge.

Scott, S., Jackson, S. and Backett-Milburn, K. (1998). Swings and roundabouts: Risk anxiety and the everyday worlds of children. *Sociology,* 32/4, 689-705.

Sloan, T. (Ed.) (2000). *Critical psychology: Voices for change.* London: MacMillan.

Stainton Rogers, R. and Stainton Rogers, W. (1992). *Stories of childhood: Shifting agendas of child concern.* Hemel Hempstead UK: Harvester Wheatsheaf.

Woodhead, M. (1990). Psychology and the cultural construction of children's needs. In A. James and A. Prout (Eds) (1990/1997) *Constructing and reconstructing childhood: Contemporary issues in the sociological study of childhood* (2nd Edition) (pp 63—84). London: Falmer Press.

SUBJECTIVITY AND SUBJECTIONING:
Between Determination and Self-Government

Lars Näcke and Eri Park
Free University of Berlin

SUMMARY

The presentation starts with a short summary of Michel Foucault's work, focusing on the three main themes of his research: the three genealogical axes of knowledge, power and subjectivity. Then we concerned with the "end-product" of Foucault's theory, the "concern for self" as a form of self-government, which leads directly into what we shall define as *Identity as the art of life*. This concept will then be further developed, and offered as an alternative means of showing identity in all its different facets, and as a space within which to live and think.

INTRODUCTION

Since Jean-Francois Lyotard announced the end of the "grand narratives" (Lyotard, 1986, p.13) the concept of identity has been experiencing some sort of a renaissance or rather has been subjected to a re-definition. In virtually all of the social sciences attempts have been made to reformulate and rethink this concept of human existence. The predominant motto in Lyotard's eyes seems to be one of the "dissolution of the self" as a freeing from false certainties: "from the chains of fundamentalist thinking, of *one* order, of *one* reason, of *one* truth, from the totalitarianism of their world-conception ... The loss of unity and wholeness, "the decentralisation of the subject" is greeted as the liberation of a multiplicity of independent ways of life, ways of thinking and patterns of behaviour" (Bruder, 1993, p. 139).

Foucault was one of those thinkers who also agreed with this motto. However his form of the concept of identity was considerably different from anything that the scientific market place has to offer by the way of new theories. We argue that the majority of the new theories purporting to follow this motto are caught within the confines and limitations of modern identity theory. They appear to expand the concept of identity by "degrees of freedom", but they do not touch on the foundations of modern thought. Thus for the most part a standardisation of the concept of identity can be found in these theories. Implicitly or explicitly there is always an "external" evaluation point, that defines what is "good" and "right" and what successful identity building could and/or should be.

This approach is unsuitable for Foucault's ideas. He rejects any scientific idea "that prescribes a rigid rule of creation or substantial goal to this creation of people by people" (Foucault, 1996, p. 84).[1]

THE THREE AXES: KNOWLEDGE – POWER – SUBJECTIVITY

Foucault's work deals with three problematic areas: that of knowledge, that of power and that of subjectivity. It appears that he is disregarding the last, but on closer view this is not the case as "it is not [knowledge and] power but rather the subject that is the general subject of my research. But an analysis of [knowledge and] power is unavoidable" (Foucault, 1994b, p. 243).

Foucault maintains that "these three areas of experience can only be understood in their relationship with one another, one cannot understand the one without the other" (Foucault, 1990b, p. 134). Despite this explanation from Foucault himself, if one looks at his works in chronological order, one notices that the earlier and middle periods of his work are linked to the first two areas. This appears to be logically rigorous: "Foucault dissolves the subject, and leaves it behind, in order to find his way to it: ... so that the subject finds and understands itself. Foucault does not question every form of subjectivity, rather he questions the hypostatisation and the imperative of identity" (Rüb, 1990, p. 189).

Knowledge

Foucault takes both of these principles and their conditions of construction in the genealogical analysis of knowledge and power techniques, in order to stress the departure point of his thinking as an alternative to traditional modes of thought. The first genealogical axis is *knowledge*. Thus the hypostatisation of the subject is explored by Foucault in the analysis of the construction of knowledge by the life sciences. Here he tries to explain, through works concerned with knowledge (e.g. Foucault, 1969, 1973), how people "enter into a process of realisation of an object area, and simultaneously construct themselves as a subject with a concrete and determining status" (Foucault, 1996, p. 52). In this analysis Foucault deals with western science and discovers it to be the construction of *a particular* rationality and *a particular* reasoning, that contributes to an estrangement of the subject from itself, construes it as an object, and thereby makes it an epistemological subject, and in the end standardises it.

Thereby Foucault established the historical nature of *this* particular knowledge and truth and exposed this scientific practice as "a particular way of regulating and construing discourses so as to define a particular object area, and at the same time the position of the ideal subject that can and should recognise these objects" (Foucault, 1996, p. 71). The subject therefore "is not an a-historical fact which contains a permanent essence of being, from whose knowledge or liberation determinations about present or future life may be deduced" (Hafiz, 1997, p. 56). This insight would lead Foucault later to perceive exactly these scientific findings in *their* relativity and to postulate *their* changeability through "experience" – "not what people are, but what they could be" (Marti, 1998, p. 2) is what would interest Foucault. Thereby he was not concerned with the formulation of a new "grand narrative" – but rather he would pick out the life courses of individuals as his theme, that is to say, how they organised *and* how they could organise their lives.

Starting from these analyses Foucault came to the analysis of power, since "the use, production, accumulation of knowledge are not separable from the mechanisms of power, with which they have complex relationships that must be analysed" (Foucault, 1996, p. 111).

Power

The second genealogical axis is *power*. As mentioned above the sciences help to give birth to a certain reality in that they "discover". In "discovering" they establish social norms, which are consolidated and stabilised through the mechanisms of power, as is the case with the imperative of identity. Thereby Foucault is not only concerned with the idea of repressive power. "'The power' which is to be analysed here, is marked out in that it concerns relationships between individuals or groups" (Foucault, 1994b, p. 251). For Foucault power is a "relationship of 'partners' " – it is a quality of interactive relationships.

Foucault is using the term "power" (see especially Foucault, 1976, 1977) as a metaphor for the effect of action. "The exercising of power does not simply describe a relationship between individuals or collective partners, but rather the function of certain actions, that change others. There is therefore not anything like *the* power, or *a* thing, power, ... there is only power as something 'exercised by one on another'. Power exists only *in actu*" (Foucault, 1994b, p. 254). Accordingly power is a genuine characteristic of executed action: Power is reproduced and exercised in any interaction. No one of the partners in these relationships possesses something that could be power – power is that other, that is actualised, realised and reproduced *in actu*.

Such a conception of power implies a changeability in relationships, as the exercising of power as actions always provokes an action from the other party and "operates in a field of possibilities, into which the behaviours of the acting subjects has entered" (Foucault, 1994b, p. 255). That means that the "other party", on which the power is being exercised and thereby constituted, has the potential to reply in a way to avoid all that suppresses it. Further, this also means that at the same time they (the other party) are able to construe themselves on their own, in that they discover and realise possibilities by which they can distinguish themselves from others and develop and use their own manner of being. Power is in this sense productive: it creates real entities like the subject and thereby affords them activity, in the sense of the ability to be active.

Accordingly individuals in power relationships become ... "subjects in the double meaning of the word, on the one hand subjects of their actions, and on the other subjects in the eyes of the instances of power. ... Foucault understood this double sided process of constitution as 'subjectivising subjugation', as subject-creation and subjugation in power relationships as one" (Hafiz, 1997, p. 57). That is, the subject through the practice of power is subjugated and at the same time submits actively in order to achieve action possibilities. Thereby, "the subject, created as a moving form of power-processes, indicates a historicity and changeability in the subject-form and identity of the individual" (ibid).

Subjectivity

The third genealogical axis is *subjectivity*. This part of Foucault's work is concerned with those "escape routes" that enable individuals to escape from repression and normalisation. "This autonomy is not grounded in the individual, rather it exists in the choice of subject-form made by the individual in the respective historical connection. That is the way in which the form of the subject takes shape" (Hafiz, 1997, p. 58). In order to elucidate this point Foucault makes a short trip back in history to Greek antiquity and Hellenism. He uses these historical realities as a contrast, to arrive (see especially Foucault, 1976, 1986a) at the forms of subjectivity that build our present reality.

Using this method he comes to what he calls subjectivisation or the "aesthetic of existence". This is expressed in the relationship of the individual with the self. Four perspectives emerge through which the relationship to the self can be analysed (Foucault, 1994a, pp. 275-7). The first concerns ethical *substance*, which describes "the aspect or part of myself or my behaviour that is subject to moral leadership". The second concerns "the way in which people are urged or prodded into their moral duties" and constitutes the mode of *self-subjugation*. The third perspective is ethical *work*, a "self-forming activity or asceticism" related to those means that individuals use "in order to behave ethically" . The fourth perspective, ethical *teleology*, refers to the goal which is behind the mechanisms of subjectivisation. This last perspective is the one which ultimately is capable of influencing and changing the other three aspects of the self relationship. "There is no complete or constant relationship between the techniques and the *telos*" (ibid). Foucault also bases his conception of subjectivity, the "aesthetic of existence" as self relationship, on these perceptions.

The four categories mentioned are used by Foucault to construct an instrument of analysis with which he could recognise the historically created forms of subjectivity, and place them in relation to the other genealogical ontologies, knowledge and power, so as to be able to understand and expose their present day form through the interaction between the dimensions as a historically created fact. From this point of view the self does not appear as a stable core of being but rather as a way of dealing with the historical circumstances, and changeable. Accordingly the subject "is not a substance. It is a form that is neither especially nor always identical with itself" (Foucault, 1985, p. 18).

THE THREEFOLD ONTOLOGY OR THE AESTHETIC OF EXISTENCE

Michel Foucault's historical analysis of knowledge, power and subjectivity can be used to describe the present reality and lead to a different plan of thinking about subjectivity. The three axes are unified in *dispositives*. "We all belong to dispositives and act within them" (Deleuze, 1991, p. 159). In dispositives the axes appear to us as lines of visibility and lines of expression (knowledge), lines of force (power), and as subjectivising lines (subjectivity). By the first two, the dispositive gains the ability "to see and be seen and to speak and be spoken" (ibid, p. 154). Thereby it is determined which knowledge and expressions are possible at a specific point in history. The lines of power provide a guarantee of stability in such a constructed reality: "they manage the coming and going of sight and speech and other things". Finally there are the lines of subjectification. They can build the dimension:

through which the whole area can be reconstructed, so as to stop the lines of power establishing defined contours. The subjectification line is a process, a production of subjectivity, in a dispositive. In the limits of possibility or allowance the subjectification line needs to be implemented. It is a line of escape from all of the other lines. The self is neither knowledge nor power. It is an individualisation process related to persons or to groups, and is removed from the established power relationships and constituted forms of knowledge. (Deleuze, 1991, p. 155-6).

Based on this constellation evidently Michel Foucault is not concerned about a fundamental rejection of subjectivity, as "human beings have in the course of history never stopped ... the construction of an unending and varied series of differing subjectivies. ... Human beings are constantly entering in to processes that constitute them as objects, which at the same time push, form and change them – and which reorganise them as subjects" (Foucault, 1996, p. 85). We are therefore more concerned about recognising the relationships between the three dimensions and about understanding ourselves as subjects within this constellation. "To recognise the insurmountable subjugation and, through his reflected life-art, to construct an 'aesthetic of existence' (Foucault, 1986b, p. 317) and thus to win moments of freedom. Thus a *double subject*, at the same time both free and subjugated" (Rüb, 1990, p. 199).

It is the "aesthetic of existence", as a form of relationship to oneself, that Michel Foucault suggests as a form of subjectivity. It is one which cannot be subjected to any kind of objective measure as "it is a decision concerning existence that the individual makes" (Foucault, 1994a, p. 283), a form of subjectivity "that can no longer be understood as primarily being mediated through differing levels of power and knowledge" (Kögler, 1990. p. 222). This ethical way of thinking about subjectivity also makes contact with the four aspects of the self relationship. Thus Foucault's formulation is without any intent to give any kind of preconditions or instructions for the "good life", as everybody can take part, but nobody must – which also means that everybody must be able to take part when she/he wants to. The "concern for self" (*epimeleia heautou*) is a rule book set by oneself, it is the *telos* of this self relationship. This is a personal decision, that results from personal experience dealing with the determinants and circumstances of the individual life. Thereby personal experience becomes both the starting point of, and motivation for, development.

"Concern for self" represents a form of self-government. "Perhaps the term 'government' is well suited especially through its double meaning, to capture the power relationships. *Government* is at the same time the activity of governing others and a way of self government in a more or less open field of possibilities. The exercise of power exists in the 'governing of governors' and in the creation of possibility" (ibid, p. 222). The "concern for self" includes "concern for the other" (*epimeleia ton allon*) as the individual is not an autonomous structure that lives outside social and societal structures. Only the social surrounding, that allows living within the possibility of action and recognises "the other" as a "free" and autonomous subject, can be the precondition for an "aesthetic of existence" (Foucault, 1994b, p. 225).

Self-determination is a way to make the four dimensions of the self relationship more concrete. Thus the ethical substance is occupied by the individual's body, and thereby the subjugation mode represents the way to follow self given rules (ethical teleology) and to achieve a "good existence" (Kögler, 1990, p. 204). The ethical work consists of "... an autonomous practising and application of the rules. We are concerned with knowing what is the best for oneself in what situation, and at what time. To be able to know and control *oneself* in this way is the precondition for a successful existence" (ibid).

AN IDENTITY, OR THE ART OF LIFE

As already mentioned at the beginning of this paper, the authors want to operate with the Foucaultian way of thinking, so that identity becomes accessible in a different way. "Thereby we are concerned just as much with the destruction of what we are as with the creation of something completely different, a complete innovation" (Foucault, 1996, p. 84). Innovation in this sense is understood as a way of thinking or acting, of questioning oneself or being questioned, of being purposeful or not, aware or unaware, of re-thinking oneself, of understanding identity work as a "creative activity" (Foucault, 1994a, p. 274), to construct another relationship to oneself. Since the basis for the art of life is constructed only by personal experience, identity work is not only understood as a reflexive form of self-relationship, as conscious generation, but also to involve oneself situatively, delivering oneself up to what happens. By the attitude of laissez faire, of neglecting the negation of the self, experience makes innovation possible. Therefore realisation and actualisation of one's system of premises in the unpredictable conditions of life make innovation possible.

We are thereby not concerned about the building of another theory of identity. But the art of life is more concerned about making implementable these possibilities that are produced, created and used everyday. Thus there are many different forms of subjectivity imaginable – but of greater importance is that they do not stay within an abstract status, but are lived as reality by which people re-create themselves every day.

The Material of an Art of Life

With the "material of the art of life" we are aiming at the basic existence, the body, our human being. "Imagining the *bios* as the stuff of a work of art appears fascinating" (Foucault, 1994a, p.272). The central focus is life itself, "...as it is lived, realised through the *acts* of life" (Schmid, 1998, p. 73). Therefore we are concerned with the relationship to oneself, and to one's behaviour, with which one masters life. Accordingly it is a continuous work of "the organisation of life and the self in order to make a work of art out of it" (ibid, p. 74). Therefore we are dealing with a constant questioning of oneself and one's behaviour, that is realised through two forms of dealing with oneself and one's surroundings. On the one hand this "reflection" succeeds when one comes to limits, that confront the individual with its limitation or subjugation. On the other hand it can be realised by the unconscious scrutiny of the premises created by individuals to achieve a "pleasant existence". The *telos* that we are aiming at by the term of the premises, is decisive. There are no abstract criteria according to how the individual has to behave. The evaluation criterion, that forms the foundation of human activity and identity work, arises simply from personal sense. Sense is not created in a vacuum however, but rather in relation to the meanings that are being constantly re-invented in the society and culture. Accordingly a double shift is required by the individual, that is the subject of the aesthetic of existence, in order to be able to find and realise the sense of life. On the one hand there is an intellectual shift, to expose and understand the relationships in which they live and which determine and define them, in order to be able to then deconstruct them; and on the other hand "... an existential reduction, so as to reduce the overwhelming size of the experienced to that which appears to be the essential for oneself" (ibid) so as "to get to the blue-print of one's own existence, the characteristic line that should determine personal style" (p. 73). That is, it is the recognition of "dual existence", as Foucault would describe it, to be aware of, and open to, that which one excludes, in order to be capable of acting. The "doubled subject" is one that finds itself by being suppressed and by self-subjugation, through being constituted and self-constitution, in exclusion through action-relevant reduction and in knowing this. Only from this view does it become possible to influence oneself, to be able to create oneself within the structures – and in using these, another.

Art as a Possibility of the Realisation of the Other

We have already shown that the concept of art refers to the actions of an individual who participates in the "games of life" and constitutes the self by them. Now we are dealing with an "... ability as the art exists in the accessing of possibilities and in the use of techniques" (ibid, p. 74). In most cases actions have the meaning of "*capabilities*, because art consists of the development of possibilities and the use of techniques". Schmid (1998) subdivides one's capabilities into three different levels: creative and inventive; regulated and technical; and the level of shaping and refining.

The capabilities of the first level can be implemented by different techniques of self-referral. For example the idea of "*repetition*" was suggested by Artaud and can be found at the level of "inter-textuality" by Kristeva and others. Other possibilities are the techniques of *caricature*, *persiflage* and *irony*. These techniques help to lead to estrangement and dislocation.

Another technique of the relationship to the self may be *performance*. "To give the other a place in the middle of everyday life, could create the impression of a dissolution of the borders between art and life. But it is only a selective difference in human being and life. The facets of the other are of varied nature" (Schmid, 1998, p. 76). *Performance* in this sense means playing with possibilities, engaging with what is given by knowing how to handle the possibilities playfully and creatively. But this also means to stay open toward the other that appears in those moments one no longer controls. This other therefore can be the power of innovation. That is the reason why the concept of *performance* is related to an experiment. This term is reminiscent of a word Foucault often used: *l'expérience* - experience. By means of the affinity between the word experiment and experience (in French also *l'expérience*) Foucault shows the dimension of chance in every human action. Nevertheless the techniques we described are not the only ones. They are merely an explanation for diversity. Thus every action can potentially become a technique. The only difference is the use in regard to the self.

The second level of capability is the translation of a specific technique into praxis. "I am capable of doing this" is more than expressing a possibility. It implies the realisation of ideas by the help of trained practices, methods and techniques. The meaning of the sentence "I am capable of doing this" does not necessarily include that the given possibilities make an action impossible or that this action will not be re-structured and transformed into another.

The last level refers to the individual shaping and refining of the specific technique. A requirement is to focus on knowledge that is specifically detailed in order to perceive oneself in its relationships, to explore the fine shades of the possibilities for change and to put them into praxis, in order to remain open for these possibilities. Nevertheless these are only examples, numerous other styles of techniques can be used.

322

Final Remarks

Identity in the meaning of the art of life as a system of premises that was set in the past can not only be changed, but can also be transformed in a way that is hardly related to the former premise. Therefore the concept of identity, which is more concrete than a description of shape, needs to be questioned. Although a complete change seems not easy to undergo, the *possibility* exists in every day of one's life. It is in many ways the prerequisite for an existence in a social, economic, and political frame. This change can take place in a linear way like the modernists thought, but it may also be conceptualised in other ways. From another angle it may even be a step backwards. Therefore one cannot predict how development proceeds. The individual identity makes someone capable of handling resources in order to constitute the self and to lead one's life in the "right way".

In our opinion those concepts, that postulate an unity of identity only in mind, but not in action, need to be questioned. "The indissoluble mix of act and result that constantly changes, makes the work of art *a work in progress,* which, in the case of life as a work of art, lasts an entire lifetime. Maybe it stays a fragmentary patchwork up to the end of life. The main point is no longer the exclusion of contradictions. The success or completion is not the primary aim. In principle success or failure are fundamentally equivalent in the art of life" (Schmid, 1998, pp. 75-6).

To sum up, we have attempted to show that these mechanisms and techniques exist in real life. They demand to be recognised and dealt with theoretically. Therefore a psychology that wants to be relevant both for individual living and for living with others, without being oppressed or pre-programmed, needs to invent an implementable synthesis in that sense.

Note

1   Translations of quotations from non-English originals, are by the authors.

REFERENCES

Bruder, K-J. (1993). *Subjektivität und Postmoderne: der Diskurs der Psychologie.* Frankfurt am Main: Suhrkamp.
Deleuze, Gilles (1991). Was ist ein Dispositiv? In F. Ewald & B. Waldenfels (Eds), *Spiele der Wahrheit. Michel Foucaults Denken.* Frankfurt am Main: Suhrkamp.
Foucault, M. (1969). *Die Ordnung der Dinge.* Frankfurt am Main: Suhrkamp.

Foucault, M. (1973). *Archäologie des Wissens.* Frankfurt am Main: Suhrkamp.

Foucault, M. (1976). *Überwachen und Strafen.* Frankfurt am Main: Suhrkamp.

Foucault, M. (1977). *Der Wille zum Wissen.* Frankfurt am Main Suhrkamp.

Foucault, M. (1985). *Freiheit und Selbstsorge.* Frankfurt am Main: Suhrkamp.

Foucault, M. (1986a). *Der Gebrauch der Lüste.* Frankfurt am Main: Suhrkamp.

Foucault, M. (1986b). *Die Sorge um sich.* Frankfurt am Main: Suhrkamp.

Foucault, M. (1990b). Die Rückkehr der Moral. Ein Interview mit Michel Foucault. In E. Erdmann, R. Forst & A. Honneth (Eds), *Ethos der Moderne. Foucaults Kritik der Aufklärung.* Frankfurt am Main/New York: Campus.

Foucault, M. (1994a). Zur Genealogie der Ethik: Ein Überblick über laufende Arbeiten. In H. L. Dreyfus & P. Rabinow (Eds), *Michel Foucault. Jenseits von Strukturalismus und Hermeneutik.* Weinheim: Beltz Athenäum.

Foucault, M. (1994b). Das Subjekt und die Macht. In H. L. Dreyfus & P. Rabinow (Eds), *Michel Foucault. Jenseits von Strukturalismus und Hermeneutik.* Weinheim: Beltz Athenäum.

Foucault, M. (1996). *Der Mensch ist ein Erfahrungstier. Gespräch mit Ducio Trombadori.* Frankfurt am Main: Suhrkamp.

Hafiz, C. H. (1997). *Subjektivierende Unterwerfung oder Ästhetik der Existenz.* Unpublished master's thesis, Free University of Berlin.

Kögler, H.-H. (1990). Fröhliche Subjektivität. Historische Ethik und dreifache Ontologie beim späten Foucault. In E. Erdmann, R. Forst & A. Honneth (Eds), *Ethos der Moderne. Foucaults Kritik der Aufklärung.* Frankfurt am Main/New York: Campus.

Lyotard, J.-F. (1986). *Das Postmoderne Wissen.* Wien/Graz: Böhlau.

Marti, U. (1998). *Michel Foucault.* München: Beck.

Rüb, M. (1990). Das Subjekt und sein Anderes. Zur Konzeption von Subjektivität beim frühen Foucault. In E. Erdmann, R. Forst & A. Honneth (Eds), *Ethos der Moderne. Foucaults Kritik der Aufklärung.* Frankfurt am Main/New York: Campus.

Schmid, W. (1998). Das Leben als Kunstwerk. *Kunstforum, 142,* 72-79.

VI THERAPY AND THE UNCONSCIOUS

FINDING A PLACE TO STAND:

Reflections on Discourse and Intertextuality in Counselling Practice

David Paré
University of Ottawa

SUMMARY

This chapter draws on contemporary theory in discourse and discursive psychology to examine a counsellor education program wholeheartedly devoted to postmodern counselling practices – specifically, narrative and social constructionist approaches. The research focused on what occurs when students, accustomed to drawing on certain established professional and popular discourses, enter into a range of alternative, postmodern discourses that turn many traditional counselling assumptions on their heads. This chapter focuses on one particular issue that emerged from the research dialogue: the challenge, in practice informed by postmodernism's embrace of multiplicity, of not reifying one's theoretical orientation, of not promoting a grand narrative that duplicates the univocal tradition of psychology. A response to this dilemma that emerged from the study involved locating one's practice within an ethical domain, rather that identifying it with any one "pure" theoretical model. One participant called this working from "a place to stand".

INTRODUCTION

This chapter provides an account of research into counsellor education conducted at the University of Waikato in Hamilton, New Zealand. The research drew on contemporary theory in discourse and discursive psychology in examining a counsellor education program devoted to narrative and social constructionist practice. Counselling models or theories were construed as discourses, and the research focused on what occurs when students accustomed to drawing on certain established professional and popular discourses enter into a range of alternative, postmodern discourses that turn many traditional counselling assumptions on their heads. This chapter focuses on one particular issue associated with postmodern practice that emerged from the research dialogue. Specifically, it relates to the challenge, in practice informed by postmodernism's embrace of multiplicity, of not reifying one's theoretical orientation – which, in effect, promotes a grand narrative that duplicates the univocal tradition of psychology. A response to this dilemma that emerged from the study involved locating one's practice within an ethical domain, rather that identifying it with one "pure" theoretical model. One participant called this working from "a place to stand".

DISCOURSE, THEORY AND PRACTICE

When one begins to regard counselling theory and practice as socially constructed discourses, some fascinating vistas open up in the exploration of the counsellor education processes. The study-in-progress I will be discussing in the following pages follows on a series of dialogues with counsellors-in-training informed by this discursive metaphor. Specifically, I will focus here on the manner in which counsellors-in-training may be constrained in the expression of their unique counselling styles by the perception they are "getting it wrong" when not adhering to the textbook version of a particular counselling model.

I will propose a means of engaging with counselling discourses that supports counsellors in expressing their values and creativity amongst the diverse values espoused by the myriad of counselling discourses available to them. In effect, this can be understood as a positioning relative to counselling theory and practice characterized by neither blind allegiance to a unitary counselling discourse, nor an eclecticism which draws on a variety of discourses in an undiscerning manner. One research participant described this as arriving at "a place to stand".

I use the term "discourse" here as a noun, to refer to any more or less coherent body of beliefs, values, and related practices that can be located in cultural and historical context. Discourses describe the world, but as Fairclough (1992) echoing Foucault, points out, the ongoing social process of generating discourses is an act of world-making: a "discourse constitutes the objects of knowledge, social subjects and forms of 'self', social relationships, and conceptual frameworks" (p. 39). Parker and colleagues (Parker, Georgaca, Harper, McLaughlin, & Stowell-Smith, 1996) put it similarly, describing discourses as "systems of statements about the world that create lived realities" (p. 10). Some discourses are clearly identified with institutions, while others have wide popular currency. The discourses of counselling have emerged from a Western context of institutional psychology. But there are many identifiable popular discourses, some of which can be traced to psychology, that speak to counselling practice as well. These may include discourses pertaining to "personal growth" and "self-actualization", the expression of emotion as a vehicle for "healing", and so on.

The curiosity propelling the study described here relates to the ways that various discourses intersect in the lives of counsellors as they formulate their theoretical stances, and indeed as they act from those values with the persons who consult them. The questions informing the study can therefore be traced to my own practice. In my work as a counselling psychologist, I constantly encounter moments in the midst of a therapeutic conversation where I am faced with a choice between responses (sometimes called "interventions' in other contexts) informed by many of these professional and popular discourses. In some cases, the discourses seem to be veritably at odds with each other. For example, when a person consulting me is tearful, I am sometimes aware of one "voice" that advocates "taking charge" and encouraging that person to slow down and stay with the feeling, while another voice suggests making space so they may pursue their own preferred direction, with no preconception on my part of what form that direction might take.

The first option might be understood as associated with discourses of catharsis and therapist-driven process, with the second more closely reflecting postmodern discourses about collaborative, non-hierarchical relationship. As counsellors, we encounter countless decision points like this. Practicing counselling (no less than living a life) involves an unending series of value-laden choices between discursive ideas that inform our actions. In the study I will discuss here, I applied these discursive metaphors to the process of learning counselling. Specifically, I became interested in the experience of counsellors-in-training as they attempted to act from a coherent value stance in the midst of their introduction to a range of challenging discursive ideas and associated practices.

THE DOMAIN OF INQUIRY

I chose the counsellor education program at the University of Waikato in Hamilton, New Zealand for the study. Waikato's program, housed in the Department of Education Studies, is rare among Masters programs of its sort in its almost exclusive emphasis on social constructionist and narrative postmodern counselling practices. The teaching staff has contributed significantly to advancing narrative ideas in the domains of clinical practice and supervision (Monk & Drewery, 1994; Monk, Winslade, Crocket, & Epston, 1997; Winslade, Monk, & Drewery, 1997).

Within the discipline of psychology, narrative theory assumes many guises (cf. Bruner, 1987a, 1987b, 1990; Gergen, 1994; Held, 1995; Polkinghorne, 1988;

Sarbin, 1986; Spence, 1982). The counselling discourses at Waikato are most closely associated with the narrative therapy of Michael White and David Epston (cf. Freedman & Combs, 1996; White & Epston, 1990; White, 1995). They also reflect many of the theoretical assumptions of social constructionism (Burr, 1995; Gergen, 1985; 1994).

Narrative and social constructionism share a deconstructive impulse with regard to much entrenched discourse (both professional and popular) and turn the tables on countless widely held beliefs about human change and therapeutic process. Looking at counsellor education in terms of the meeting of discourses, one might expect some dramatic encounters between discursive ideas and practices in such a program. Consider the following liberal humanist premises versus the narrative and social constructionist premises with which they can be contrasted:

- "Deviance" as indication of pathology (*versus* as resistance to cultural prescriptions)
- Unitary self (*versus* multiplicity of the self)
- Problems located in intrapsychic domain (*versus* interpersonal domain)
- Emphasis on professional knowledge (*versus* emphasis on client knowledge)

Over the course of a year, I resided as a post-doctoral fellow in the University of Waikato's Department of Education Studies, joining counsellors-in-training in an exploration of the meeting of discourses.

Participants in the Dialogue

Participants in the dialogues ranged from beginning counsellors to experienced clinicians returning to school for upgrading and further training. The largest group fell in the latter category, clustering predominantly in an age range from 35 to 50. Most were women, reflecting the demographics of many counselling programs in the 1990's. The vast majority of participants were New Zealanders of European descent. I spoke with some counsellors just two months into the program, while others had completed a full year, and still others had finished two full years of training and were actively applying their learnings as paid service providers in the community. Because the information gathered (see below) involved multiple modalities, the counsellors involved had varying degrees of input into the study, and to supply a simple total of participants would be misleading. All told, I had contact in some fashion with upwards of thirty clinicians. I had one or two in-depth conversations with fifteen counsellors.

Exploring the Topic

The primary vehicle for exploring the topic was one-on one, open ended conversations. In addition, I conducted a series of conversations with counsellors in a group context. This group of six met several times over the course of three months and was structured as a reflecting team (Friedman, 1995). I first spoke with one counsellor while the others witnessed, then the witnessing team reflected on our conversation, following which the initial counsellor and I responded to the reflections. Finally the entire group debriefed on the experience. These conversations and reflecting sessions were audiotaped and transcribed. Additional sources of material for the theorizing that emerged from this study include comments and discussion in classes, students' written assignments, e-mail correspondence, and informal conversations with counsellors over the course of the year.

Because the University of Waikato program is oriented towards a discursive view of counselling, much of the language and concepts I have drawn upon in this chapter were familiar to participants. I opened conversations with a brief summary of the domain of inquiry, and began with open-ended questions designed to elicit dialogue about their experience of the discourses informing their work as counsellors. The material gathered here represents a portion of a substantial body of dialogue, interpretations, and theorizing that has promoted a number of ideas for further investigation. I certainly do not present it as a completed work, but something more akin to a stopping point on an ongoing journey.

CONFLICTING DISCOURSES

At the outset of the research, I assumed counsellors at Waikato would experience what I called a "conflict" or a sense of "dissonance" (Kathie Crocket, personal communication, September, 1998) between the more traditional, liberal humanist counselling discourses most of them had been exposed to through prior training and work experience, and the narrative/social constructionist discourses they encountered through the program. I discovered this was not necessarily the case. Some counsellors were able to maintain a both/and relationship with bodies of discourse I perceived as founded on contradictory premises.

Despite this proclivity by a few to accommodate ostensibly contradictory ideas, most of the participants identified personally valued ideas and related practices associated with liberal humanism that appeared to be called into question by narrative/social constructionism. In some cases the postmodern discourses suggested alternative formulations; in others they appeared to offer an implicit critique by virtue of being mute on the subject. The four most prominently cited themes are listed below:

- Humanistic conceptions of unitary, whole self (*versus* notions of multiplicity and subjectivity)
- Belief in moral foundations (*versus* an anti-foundational, contextually-oriented ethics)
- Spiritual traditions of transcending discourse and perceiving non-constructed truth (*versus* the notion of all experience being an outgrowth of language-based, culturally generated discourse)
- Emphasis on embodiment and materialism (*versus* highlighting the human world as socially constructed)

Most clinicians reported some level of what might be called "conceptual dissonance" associated with embracing narrative/social constructionist values while being unwilling to part with some ideas and practices either critiqued by, or not addressed by, their new learnings. However, it was not immediately evident how this converted to practice or was perceived by persons seeking help. I think it is fair to say there is often a yawning gap between the way counsellors describe their work and what appears to be going on in the consulting room. Argyris and Schon (1992) describe this as the distinction between "espoused theory" and "theory in action". And so I became interested in how this sense of parts not fitting together played out in the counselling process. After all, theory should serve practice: conceptual dissonance is only a problem if it detracts from the helpfulness of therapeutic conversations.

The research therefore turned at this point to the dimension of discourse, not as a mere disembodied idea, but as an idea made manifest through action. As the research dialogue therefore evolved, I began to hear counsellors speak of impaired effectiveness in their work, which they attributed to the conflict of discourses. More specifically, counsellors described having allegiances torn between apparently irreconcilable counselling discourses. I call this predicament "practical dissonance".

PRACTICAL DISSONANCE

When it comes to situating themselves among other models, the dominant counselling discourses do not typically embrace a both/and perspective. Rather, they mimic the competitive impulse of Western capitalism – each making claims for a more accurate representation of the way that things are as they strive for supremacy in an intellectual and economic marketplace. For many of the counsellors I spoke to, this notion that *either* one *or* another theory was correct or appropriate was carried into their learnings at the University of Waikato. The result, when they found themselves drawing from contrasting discourses, was a self critique more debilitating than facilitating in their work.

One counsellor described various discourses she had previously been exposed to but which she did not favor (e.g., Freudian or cognitive therapy ideas) as being mostly "dormant" in her practice. But she said they would "wake up" from time to time in the midst of trying to do narrative work:

> What happens to me is it undermines my belief and my confidence in my work. Because I sort of feel there's more *confusion*, really... It's just dissonance. Whatever it is, it has the effect of me questioning my work.

This self-questioning would cause her to lose her way:

> I think it makes me a bit "muddly". Like I try and grab little bits from everywhere... And also there's also very strong voices (like my supervisor's) saying I should go off and do RET training, and, you know, cognitive behavioral training, all that sort of stuff...

Another counsellor spoke of a similar erosion of confidence, using the term "lostness" to capture the experience of being caught between discourses, feeling the pressure to do a textbook version of one model, in this case narrative: "The more I know, the more I need to know... It has to be the most brilliant piece of work of significant value to the client". This counsellor concluded that lostness encouraged her to get more involved in thinking up the perfect question. The results, she said, were greater distance from and less availability to clients, reduced attention to cues, and a tendency not to check with clients on the progress of the session.

One counsellor indicated that self-judgement was a function of context: she described a sense of "relief" and clear-headedness when on campus which contrasted with her experience at her practicum placement. She portrayed contrasting discourses as "picking away at her" in a workplace peopled by practitioners drawing on alternate, non-narrative models:

> So say that I'm talking to my psychotherapist colleague who gives me an Oedipal analysis of what's going on for a little boy when I say, hey, what do you think's happening here? Then somehow, because I know this stuff, because it resonates with other stuff I've learned in ways that I've had of thinking about the world before... Do I just believe in it totally and think yes she's right, 'cause I have a lot of respect for her and her work, because she's held in a lot of respect. So that is, that's where dissonance happens for me now. It starts happening on the practical level.

While a physical context (such as a workplace) dominated by a paradigm contrary to a counsellor's preferred way of working may exacerbate practical dissonance, we do not escape the influence of other discourses by cloistering ourselves away. In a sense, we all "carry" multiple contexts with us through the discourses we are born into: the immeasurable sweep of ideas and practices, symbols and rituals that inform our work and our daily lives. What seemed evident in my discussions with the participants in this study was the influence of a particularly powerful and ubiquitous discourse: mainstream science. In effect, I would like to argue that when we regard counselling discourses in logico-scientific terms, we are inclined to compartmentalize them – the result being that counselling practice which appears to cross a discourse's boundary may be regarded as "breaking the rules", or worse, *inept*.

Bruner (1987b) contrasts scientific discourse – which tends towards taxonomies of mutually exclusive, universal elements – with narrative meaning-making. Bruner's use of the word "narrative" is not to denote White and Epston's therapeutic approach; rather it depicts a mode of knowing that can be distinguished from traditional scientism. Of course, the narrative therapy associated with White and Epston shares a related epistemological stance. The narrative perspective Bruner writes about is a multivocal, pluralistic view and is less concerned with the logico-scientific tendency to reconcile or reduce elements (Polkinghorne, 1988).

It is interesting to note that even while immersed in a program much aligned epistemologically with this pluralistic view, counsellors judged their performance according to expectations more associated with univocal science. In other words, while being introduced to discourses that promote multiple meanings, participants nevertheless experienced self-criticism for mixing counselling discourses in their work. Put differently, they were subject to self-surveillance and the normalizing "gaze" so richly described by Foucault (cf. 1979) and echoed in the work of White and Epston (1990).

This leads to some interesting speculation about the ways in which counsellors may be constrained in realizing their preferred therapeutic modality and style by the perception that counselling interventions are either "right" or "wrong", with the conclusion dictated by rigidly defined discourses. When we view counselling models according to the parameters of an either/or logic, they appear as self-contained, encapsulated discourses, and work which crosses their boundaries is regarded as "bad" counselling. These admittedly preliminary observations lead me to conclude that it might be helpful to re-cast our view of counselling discourses in order to better represent the manner in which counselling is typically practiced. I will say more about this later; firstly, I would like to clarify the constraints I associate with an encapsulated view of discourses.

ENCAPSULATED DISCOURSES

Learning to throw a pot takes time and patience. At first, the apprentice potter is likely to move too quickly or too slowly, and the pot collapses on the wheel. But with time, the artist learns to keep the clay in balance, and sometimes there emerges a unique pot that defies categorization, but which others find aesthetically pleasing and functional. And so it is with counselling. Sometimes, the pot collapses; at other times a session may exhibit grace and artistry without being easily tied to a specific counselling discourse.

If we ask a painter about her style (i.e., her "discourse") and she says she imitates Picasso, we may well be inclined to admire her skill, but to seek out Picasso's work instead. We expect artists to develop their own unique styles. In the domain of counselling, however, we are less admiring of idiosyncratic practice, unless it bears the title of an identifiable counselling discourse.

Counselling discourses are largely encapsulated. They typically present themselves as mutually exclusive stories, staking out a territory based on what makes them *different* from other discourses. The overlaps are underplayed, the values and commitments shared by theories distinguished by different titles and different "leading figures". As mentioned, this dynamic is consistent with our competitive traditions, but I believe it also reflects psychology's historical alignment with a natural-science paradigm that views "theory" as a truth claim about the "real" world (Howard, 1991). If one theory is "true", then how can another theory *also* be true when it contains contrasting accounts? This positivist perspective is out of step with a discipline primarily concerned with meaning-making.

Staying true to the metaphor of counselling theory as discourse, one might say the *intertextuality* of the discourses is obscured by an emphasis on their mutual exclusivity. Fairclough (1992) defines intertextuality as "the property texts have of being full of snatches of other texts, which may be explicitly demarcated or merged in, and which the text may assimilate, contradict, ironically echo, and so forth" (p. 84). This description aptly captures the interplay between counselling discourses – an interpenetration typically down played by the proponents of any one approach.

This state of affairs leads many counsellors to reject potentially useful interventions or conceptualizations of counselling situations because they are deemed to be situated in a competing "camp". One participant I spoke to guiltily confessed having had a "Gestalt thought" while practicing in a narrative way. And yet there appear to be distinct overlaps between narrative and Gestalt discourses. For instance, narrative therapy promotes the discursive separation of persons and problems, usually known as "externalization". Though theorized very differently, an externalizing conversation is similar to a Gestalt parts dialogue in that it isolates a problematic discourse (a "part" in Gestalt terms) so that a person may experience

336

themselves as separate from and in relation to it. The intertextual dimension of these
discourses is obscured when they are regarded as encapsulated and distinct.

A second example of the possible intertextual application of counselling
practices involves narrative and psychoanalytic practice. For instance, the
psychoanalytic concept of transference is virtually absent from the narrative
postmodern literature, unless in the context of a critique of Freudian theory. And yet,
when translated into narrative discourse, transference might be described as a
process whereby an (externalized) problem is evident in the therapeutic relationship.
Suppose, for example, that a client engages in a competitive relationship with his
male therapist. In Freudian terms, one might construe this as a transference process,
with the therapist substituting for the man's deceased, dominant father. Narrative
ideas might lead us to see this situation as a case of an externalized problem
("machismo", or perhaps "macho discourse") having an influence on the client, and
on the client's relationship with the therapist. While the two counselling discourses
formulate these issues in different ways, there is certainly room within narrative
practice for discussing openly how a problem might be seen as influencing not only
a person's life outside of the consulting room, but impacting on the counselling
relationship as well. Johnella Bird (1999) does this in her narrative practice,
enriching her work in the process.

My conversations with counsellors immersed in narrative/social
constructionist training suggests that even postmodern counselling is prone to the
either/or encapsulating more typical of scientific discourse. True, postmodernism
promotes a both/and perspective, but within a closed system: it does not advocate
postmodernism *and* modernism, for example (Stuart, 1999). For most of the
counsellors I spoke with, this tension between discourses was palpable. It may well
be that the ensuing dissonance promoted useful reflection; however it also seemed to
contribute to a self-monitoring that may have constrained their creativity.

In practice, no counsellor acts from identical discourses. They may share a
label attributed to some identifiable model, but the only practitioner who performs
the model precisely according to specifications is its originator – and readers who
have witnessed prominent practitioners in practice may view even this claim as
questionable. When we distinguish narrative, Gestalt, and psychoanalytic work, we
are certainly pointing to many divergences in conceptualization and practice. But the
formal titles indicate broad domains of values at best, and any impermeable lines
between the theories yield under closer scrutiny.

These issues raise important questions about how to support counsellors in
"storying their professional development" (Winslade, Monk, & Drewery, 1997). If
they are to identify their own unique positioning relative to the work of counselling,
they may well identify concepts or practices that do not sit neatly within any one
demarcated counselling discourse. My sense is that this process may be promoted by
down playing science's univocal view of "theory", and engaging with

counselling models as intertextual discourses. However, I do not mean to advocate a simple eclecticism. Instead, I suggest clinicians in training should strive to identify the values that guide them in their negotiation of many possible counselling ideas and practices. One counsellor characterized this ethical positioning as "a place to stand".

A PLACE TO STAND

The competent artist who does not adhere narrowly to one "school" does not merely draw arbitrarily on any and all techniques and modes of representation. Their work is guided by some form of aesthetic coherence. But counselling is not painting, or potting. A defaced painting or a collapsed pot do not typically harm persons the way incompetent counselling practice may. Counselling is a social endeavor and calls for greater attention to the impact of the "art" on the persons for whom it is intended. It should be guided by an *ethical* coherence.

The counsellors I spoke to provided some useful ideas for escaping the univocality of encapsulated counselling theory without replacing it with an undiscerning eclecticism. One spoke of "moving out from" a set of beliefs and practices generally associated with an established model. But her home base (as it were) was a cluster of core values, a site from which to extend the possibilities, rather than a line which divided competent from incompetent practice.

A second counsellor described seeing her work as *in relation* to various theories, as opposed to an exemplification of any one. But she also was clear that she stood by one. This positioning furnished her with an ethical mooring without constraining her mobility among discourses not commonly associated with her preferred model:

> It gives me a place to stand I guess. That I can take a really, that I can take a stand on something: "These are the ideas that I believe in and that I want to practice". And if I can stand in those ideas, but not shut my eyes, and look out from those ideas, then it becomes an evolving and a growing thing. It doesn't become a closed entity that "This is the way and this is the only way."

The theories and practices of counselling may all be traceable to culturally and historically situated discourses, but the counsellor who authors her own counselling story invariably draws from these in a unique manner. That intertextual narrative is more than "eclecticism" when it discerns between counselling constructs and practices in reference to ethical concerns. For instance, narrative practice eschews the conflating of problems and persons' identities, on the grounds that it pathologizes persons. The view of persons and problems as separate provides an ethically coherent place to stand – both in the sense of coherent as "united by some relation in form or order", and as "clearly articulated and intelligible" (Webster's, 1975, p. 352). From here, one might enact a range of practices not necessarily associated with "narrative therapy", but which share a commitment to the differentiation of persons and problems. As discussed earlier, this could mean working with both a Gestalt parts dialogue, and attention to "transference", in a manner that adheres to ethical assumptions that are wholly congruent with narrative premises. What distinguishes this from eclectic practice is a coherent account of the ethical assumptions undergirding the practice.

To make an idea of practice *ours* is to recruit it to our moral cause in much the same way that Bakhtin describes the process of languaging our experience in the face of a history of language that long precedes us:

> [L]anguage has been completely taken over, shot through with intentions and accents ... All words have the "taste" of a profession, a genre, a tendency, a party, a particular work, a particular person, a generation, an age group, the day and hour. Each word tastes of the contexts in which it has lived its socially charged life... The world in language is half someone else's. It becomes "one's own" when the speaker populates it with his own intention, his own accent ... [this] is a difficult and complicated process. (1981, p. 293)

In the realm of counselling and therapy, that intention or accent should favor the Other: our hard-won "style" should be forged in service to the persons who consult us. The challenge for counsellor education programs is to support this quest for an ethical coherence, a place to stand.

REFERENCES

Argyris, C. and Schon, D. (1992). *Theory in practice: Increasing professional effectiveness*. New York, NY: Jossey-Bass.

Bakhtin, M. M. (1981). *The dialogic imagination: Four essays*. M. Holquist (Ed.). Austin, Texas: University of Texas Press.

Bird, J. (1999). *Working with the effects of abuse*. Workshop conducted at the Family Centre, Auckland, New Zealand, June.

Bruner, J. (1987a). Life as narrative. *Social Research, 54*, 12-32.

Bruner, J. (1987b). *Actual minds, possible worlds*. Cambridge MA: Harvard University Press.

Bruner, J. (1990). *Acts of meaning*. Cambridge MA: Harvard University Press.

Burr, V. (1995). *An introduction to social constructionism*. London and New York: Routledge.

Fairclough, N. (1992). *Discourse and social change*. Cambridge MA: Polity Press.

Foucault, M. (1979). *Discipline and punish: The birth of the prison*. Harmondsworth: Peregrine Books.

Freedman, J., & Combs, G. (1996). *Narrative therapy: The social construction of preferred realities*. New York: W.W. Norton.

Friedman, S. (Ed.) (1995). *The reflecting team in action: Collaborative practice in family therapy*. New York: Guilford.

Gergen, K. J. (1985). The social constructionist movement in modern psychology. *American Psychologist 40*, 266-275.

Gergen, K.J. (1994). *Realities and relationships: Soundings in social construction*. Cambridge MA: Harvard University Press.

Held, B. (1995). *Back to reality: A critique of postmodern theory in psychotherapy*. New York: W.W. Norton.

Howard, G.S. (1991). Culture tales: A narrative approach to thinking, cross-cultural psychology, and psychotherapy. *American Psychologist, 46*, 187-197.

Monk, G. & Drewery, W. (1994). The impact of social constructionist thinking on eclecticism in counsellor education. *New Zealand Journal of Counselling 16*, 5-14.

Monk, G., Winslade, J., Crocket, K., Epston, D. (Eds) (1997*). Narrative therapy in practice: The archaeology of hope*. San Francisco: Jossey-Bass.

Parker, I., Georgaca, E., Harper, D., McLaughlin, T., & Stowell-Smith, M. (1996). *Deconstructing psychopathology*. London: Sage Publications.

Polkinghorne, D. E. (1988). *Narrative knowing and the human sciences*. New York: SUNY Press.

Sarbin, T.R. (1986). The narrative as the root metaphor for psychology. In T.R. Sarbin (Ed.) *Narrative psychology: The storied nature of human conduct* (pp. 3-21). New York: Praeger.

Spence, D. S. (1982). *Narrative truth and historical truth: Meaning and interpretation in psychoanalysis*. New York: W.W. Norton.

Stuart, C. (1999). *Do you have to choose? Exploring the tension between holding two therapy models*. Unpublished Masters thesis, University of Waikato, Hamilton, New Zealand.

Webster, N. (Ed.) (1975). *Webster's new twentieth century dictionary of the English language*. New York, NY: Collins.

White, M. (1995). *Re-authoring lives: Interviews and essays*. Adelaide SA: Dulwich Centre Publications.

White, M. & Epston, D. (1990). *Narrative means to therapeutic ends*. New York: W.W. Norton.

Winslade, J., Monk, G., & Drewery, W. (1997). Sharpening the critical edge: A social constructionist approach to counsellor education. In T.C Sexton & B.C. Griffin (Eds) *Constructivist thinking in counselling practice, research, and training* (pp. 228-245). NY: Teachers College Press.

THE INFLUENCE OF PSYCHOTHERAPEUTIC PRACTICES ON A HERMENEUTICS OF DISCOURSE

Angelina Baydala
University of Calgary

SUMMARY

In laying out principles and practices of psychoanalysis and narrative therapy, this paper clarifies distinct forms of therapy as hermeneutics of discourse. The development of psychoanalytic practice is traced from authoritarian to dialogical access of deep experience. Meaning advances recursively as it is both unmasked and restored. Narrative therapy, by contrast, challenges subjugated, oppressive discourses. Its practices emphasize the generation of new meaning, mutually constructed by therapist and client. Although hermeneutics leaves discourse continually open to re-interpretation, understanding is not held to be constructed, but rather shared in relations of desire. A hermeneutics of discourse highlights psychotherapy as a forum for understanding, emphasizing how it is that the persons involved in therapy specify both the possibility and the limits of understanding. Understanding is radically contextual, dependent not only on the practices of therapy, but on the persons involved in interpreting those practices. The limits involved in shared meaning create the conditions which make understanding possible.

INTRODUCTION

The practice of psychotherapy centers around expressions which patients and therapists exchange in sessions. Psychotherapy as a social, historical, and culturally specific forum for expressing and exchanging ideas has many interests

342

embedded within it, including those of the therapist and patient. Different kinds of therapeutic practices give rise to particular forms of discourse as the expression of ideas is negotiated according to rules of interpretation and understanding. As therapists and patients communicate and interpret ambiguous discursive material according to the tenets of the therapy being practiced, they are engaged in a hermeneutic practice. To explore the confluence of therapeutic practice and theory, some of the technical procedures involved in two distinct forms of psychotherapy, psychoanalysis and narrative therapy, will be described in terms of their implications for a hermeneutics of discourse. Although there are multiple varieties of these practices, perhaps as many as there are therapists, there are general hermeneutical implications for all psychotherapeutic discourses. Rather than position the therapist as the one who identifies or co-constructs meaning, psychotherapeutic practices may be seen to involve a hermeneutics of discourse wherein therapists and patients come to relate to one another and share understanding. From this dialogical perspective, a hermeneutics of discourse resides not in the technique of the practice, but manifests through the people who give life to the interpretative functioning.

HERMENEUTICS OF PSYCHOANALYSIS

Upon reading the original works of Freud, it is possible to recapture certain therapeutic insights of psychoanalytic practice. Beginning with Freud's papers on technique (Freud, 1912/1958a, 1912/1958b, 1912/1958c, 1913/1958d, 1914/1958e, 1915/1958f, 1933/1964a, 1937/1964b, 1937/1964c, 1940/1964d), it is striking how the structural and procedural arrangements of the practice reflect differences in the discourses that emerge. While the patient lies supine on the analyst's couch, a voice is heard from somewhere behind and above their head. The analyst is not visible to the patient but the patient is visible to the analyst, the analyst generates interpretations while the patient generates material for interpretation, the analyst remains as anonymous as possible while the patient reveals as much as possible. Mutual visual contact between analyst and patient occurs briefly upon entering and leaving the session; otherwise, sensory communication is limited to voice and hearing, leaving much space for the workings of the patient's imagination. The arrangements significantly affect who says what.

Differences in the positioning of analyst and patient encourage detached observation and precise, unidirectional statements intended to clarify the meaning of the patient's scattered associations. An orthodox Freudian analysis seems to embody and reinforce the spirit of nineteenth century scientific realism out of which it arose. Analysis is conceived as a scientific method for making the patient's inner world observable. Free associations of the patient are the objective material observed and analyzed to reveal a hidden level of meaning. While the patient's expression taps the symbolic imagination, the analyst's interpretations point to the unthinkable something existing intrapsychically in the patient, causing disturbed, irrational behavior across a variety of situations. What cannot be admitted directly in the patient's discourse and is expressed only in the disguise of symbolism is purported to become meticulously clear to the analyst. The symbolic significance of the patient's discourse is analyzed to determine an understanding true across situations, both within and outside the analytic context. Although authored by the analyst, such a categorical interpretation may secure position and truth for the patient. By disclosing the unspeakable, in dialogue with the analyst, the patient gains greater self-understanding and becomes more aware of what previously only the analyst could discern. This awareness is in itself believed to release the hold of the unconscious and thereby dissipate the symptom. As Freud (1893-1895/1955a) writes, "The patient is, as it were, getting rid of it by turning it into words" (p. 280).

An orthodox reading of psychoanalytic practice tends to hearten the notion that discourse can be given a single, correct interpretation and that doctor knows best. The polysemy of discourse is seen as a problem that can be solved once and for all. Freud writes:

> If one succeeds in arranging the confused heap of fragments, each of which bears upon it an unintelligible piece of drawing, so that the picture acquires a meaning, so that there is no gap anywhere in the design and so that the whole fits into the frame – if all these conditions are fulfilled, then one knows that one has solved the puzzle and that there is no alternative solution. (Freud, 1923/1961, p. 116)

Under the assumption of neutrality, the powerful and privileged position of the analyst, along with the exposed and vulnerable position of the patient, authoritarian notions of interpreting discourse may thwart, instead of help to understand, the worldview of the analysand while affirming the worldview of the analyst. In his early writing, Freud recommends urging the patient to comply with the authority of the analyst's interpretations. In this case, the fluidity of existence is at risk of being rigidly reduced, bottled in an interpretation, and swallowed whole by the patient.

Analysts with positivist pretensions to uninterpreted, unambiguous truth may closely adhere to the psychoanalytic principles of conduct (neutrality, anonymity, evenly suspended attention) to justify the correctness of their interpretation. Instead of analysts and patients moving closer to understanding, these principles may give further authority to posit truth, justified by analytic method, without recognizing the shared nature of understanding. Because of analysts' extensive training and because they can promote themselves as having been analyzed, analysts' interpretations can be privileged on authoritarian grounds as being more true. Psychoanalytically principled interpretations may be advanced as pointing to patients' desires and concerns without pointing to analysts'. As such, orthodox analysts might assume the position of arbiter of reality who can see and point out the analysands' distortions without activating their own. As Merton Gill (1982) comments, there was no name given in classical psychoanalysis for a patient's realistic response to the analyst's counter-transference. The counter-transference was originally considered an obstacle and an intrusion into the analytic process that could be avoided.

While psychoanalytic training and method may be seen to privilege the analyst's interpretation, understanding was also seen to be constituted through agreement. Freud writes:

> After he has succeeded in forcing the repressed event…upon the patient's acceptance in the teeth of all resistances…the patient may say: "Now I feel as though I had known it all the time." With this the work of analysis has been completed. (Freud, 1914/1955b, p. 207)

Belief in the truth of the interpretation develops as the analyst's interpretations are appropriated into the analysand's own understanding. At other times Freud (1910/1966) saw glimpses of psychoanalysis as more explicitly dialogical. In 1910 he writes,

> At its beginning psycho-analytic treatment was inexorable and exhausting. The patient had to say everything himself, and the physician's activity consisted of urging him on incessantly. To-day things have a more friendly air. The treatment is made up of two parts – what the physician infers and tells the patient, and the patient's working-over of what he has heard. (p. 141)

In this instance the practice is seen to be much more of an exchange of positions. By 1937 Freud concedes that interpretations are conjectures, he urges the analyst to claim no authority, but instead to wait and observe the course of future developments (1937/1964c). Understanding begins to be seen more as a process arising out of the eventual convergence of initially different positions rather than merely an excavation of the valid interpretation. In Ricoeur's work, *Freud and Philosophy* (1970), French philosophical thinking makes a complete reading of psychoanalysis as hermeneutical. Emphasis shifts to highlight the productive and not just the reproductive nature of interpretation. Ricoeur proposes that teleology is inherent in the archeological practices and positivistic explanations of psychoanalysis. Innovations in meaning are dialogically produced and confluent with transcendentally deduced causal forces. The intention to propagate meaning cannot be accounted for without positing definitive forces of generation. Ricoeur's hermeneutic reinterpretation of Freudian psychoanalysis demonstrates how it is through a dialectic of teleology and archeology that we can account for the kind of shared meaning which emerges in the actual practice of psychoanalysis.

A central issue in Ricoeur's thesis is the possibility for psychoanalysis to be a practice whereby untold stories are both uncovered and upon reflection understood, where histories are revealed and recognized as meaningful narratives. Psychoanalysis is a discourse that unearths desires hidden in the distorted images and ideas we have of our lives, but when a story is spoken there is meaning inherent in the words used. The speaker is divulging the fact that they are culturally embedded, that their language is part of an inheritance. So not only is the recounting of a personal narrative a discovery of the interpolation of preconscious desires into the text of consciousness, but at the same time it is the transmission of an abundance of culturally pre-constructed mytho-poetic meaning. Understanding is not simply unmasked through the reductive analytic process. Meaning is also restored as the analyst recognizes what the patient is saying. Psychoanalysis is a hermeneutic of discourse because as desires which position us in existence are uncovered, a recursive advancement of meaning is formed in the successive, innovative interpretations of our desires.

HERMENEUTICS OF NARRATIVE THERAPY

The second interpretive framework, that of narrative psychotherapy, makes extreme use of the innovations possible in a hermeneutics of discourse. The arrangements of narrative therapy are more similar to ordinary, daily forms of communication. Therapist and client more equally share space, they are mutually aware of each other, in full eye contact, and reciprocating dialogue. Instead of a one-sided discourse, there are now two people in a room seeming to have a conversation. However, unlike ordinary discussion, there is an attempt to minimize the power differential inherent in the psychotherapeutic setting. In an effort to understand one another, one says something and the other responds either in agreement or disagreement as they search for ways to connect. The psychoanalytic assumption of determinate meaning lying hidden in the discourse is dispelled and replaced with the notion that meaning arises out of the social context. Rather than focusing on how discourse can access deep experience, narrative therapy emphasizes how dialogue generates meaning. In this practice the meaning of discourse is understood as constructed, social, and contextual.

Narrative therapy proposes a post-modern constructivist conception of social life wherein people construct identities from meanings offered by the cultural and historical discourses in which they interact. Although there is not a single narrative approach to therapy, John McLeod (1996) identifies certain commonalities amongst most narrative therapies. Two central practices include working with life-stories and re-authoring narratives. More specifically, in *Narrative Means to Therapeutic Ends*, White and Epston (1990) submit that "we cannot know objective reality, all knowing requires an act of interpretation" (p. 2). The authors then go further in proposing possibilities of unsubjugated reality. They write of unique outcomes or "aspects of lived experience that fall outside the dominant story" (p. 15). The agenda, therapeutically, is to discover lived experiences that are not subjugated by oppressive discourses so that these lived experiences can be used to construct preferred narratives; that is, "for the generation, or re-generation, of alternative stories" (p. 15). In conjunction with their clients, narrative therapists construct preferred narratives by re-authoring life stories based on these unique outcomes.

In order to locate unique outcomes, narrative therapists facilitate by "encouraging", "inviting", or "identifying" the interruption of habits of interpretation or habitual "performances of meaning". Therapists are involved in such processes as

> encouraging persons to map their influence and the influence of their relationships with others, on the life of the problem ... When unique outcomes are identified, persons can be invited to ascribe meaning to them. Success in this ascription of meaning requires that the unique outcomes be plotted into an alternative story. (White & Epston, 1990, p. 16)

Consequently, clients, we are told, "experience a capacity to intervene in their own lives and relationships" (1990, p. 16). In this way, something of the therapists' agency and the principles of narrative therapy become appropriated by the clients. The cultivation of this agency is furthered by the therapeutic prescription to have clients perform their new stories either to an external audience or to themselves. Narrative therapy is, thus, a context which "brings forth new choices for persons regarding the authoring of themselves, others, and their relationships" (White & Epston, 1990, p. 18).

It seems clear that narrative therapy is an expert knowledge with definite suggestions and suppositions. In demarcating strategies for reflecting on and re-interpreting the significance of people's lives, the canonization of narrative therapy has begun. For example, in the tradition of the Dulwich Centre in South

Australia (White, 1997) archives of "solution knowledges" have been accumulated. However, White and Epston (1990) seem to maintain that narrative therapy is neither political nor ideological. They write, "This is not a political activity that involves the proposal of an alternative ideology, but one that challenges the techniques that subjugate persons to a dominant ideology" (p. 29). The practice of challenging subjugation, however, contains its own assumptions and consequences of meaning. Narrative therapy brings to play a number of commitments and tacit values. To be consistent, it must be admitted that the culture of narrative therapy is now the dominant discourse subjugating the client's story and influencing the construction of the preferred realities.

Narrative therapy cannot fully escape its position as therapeutic technique and therefore its participation in a form of domination. In hopes of limiting the relations of power reproduced in therapy, recommendations for making the therapy more egalitarian are suggested. Such practices include (Epston & White, 1992; White, 1997): transparency, wherein therapists deconstruct their own work along with the re-authored preferred realities co-constructed with their clients; accountability, which renders therapists accountable to their clients; and the practice of "taking it back" which involves therapists acknowledging ways they have been influenced by their clients. Therapists may adhere more closely to these principles of practice to justify their conduct, but the assumption that such practices produce better, truer or more egalitarian stories, risks halting the reflective movement of interpretation. Therapists and clients are limited in their ability to willfully escape subjugating discourses when constituting preferable interpretations of life. If every interpretation is tied to a historical cultural context then narrative therapists cannot escape being bound by the culture in which their interpretations and understandings are being made. Although White concedes that narrative practices are not exterior to culture he also writes (1997), "I do not believe that narrative practices are necessarily culture-bound" (p. 231). That "re-authoring" is a practice within a culture and yet not bound by that culture, is an aporia which goes untheorized.

In narrative therapy, the *true* interpretation of orthodox psychoanalysis is replaced by a *preferred* interpretation, but the security of even a preferred interpretation costs in terms of being located in a definite matrix of intertextuality. In theory, narrative therapy seems to belie the full implications of a hermeneutics of discourse. The illusion of inventing meaning puts narrative therapy at risk of collapsing reality into preference. Emphasizing the co-construction of meaning may obscure how one is invested in a hermeneutics. Life stories are infinitely open to re-interpretation, but are subjugate to the limits of the dialogical context in which the interpretations are made. In a hermeneutics of discourse meaning is not assigned, but culturally shared and reflected in a history of desire. In the end, it is not a preferred content that is helpful in understanding life events, preferences are uncertain, it is the hermeneutic process of reflecting and sharing understanding that makes life meaningful.

HERMENEUTICS OF DISCOURSE

A hermeneutics of discourse involves a conflict between multiple possible interpretations. Each interpretation may be equally valid depending on its manifestation in a particular context. But possible interpretations gain their possibility because of the comprehensive limitations inherent in the context. New perspectives may emphasize new meanings, but the new perspective circumscribes an alternative understanding for that perspective. Discourse simultaneously points to meaning, determined by the situation of the discourse, while creating meaning through dialogue and shared understanding. As such, therapists cannot escape personally limiting the understanding of their patients' difficulties. Every understanding invokes assumptions and commitments which introduce unforeseen possibilities while limiting and constraining the range of appropriate interpretations. Hermeneutic constraints thereby potentiate the polysemy of the discourse. The radical contingency of a hermeneutics of discourse is affirmed in recognizing aspects of domination inevitable in sharing any understanding.

In summary, each psychotherapeutic practice involves its own form of discourse and system of interpretation. Perhaps psychoanalysis is more concerned with the intentionality of the patient's discourse and narrative therapy is more focused on intertextuality, but both are engaged in a hermeneutics of discourse. In psychoanalysis, the tendency is for meaning to be understood as revealed by the discourse, interpretation tries to unmask hidden intentions, desires and fears. Analyst and patient are positioned together in the tradition of the session and individually in terms of the systems of knowledge they bring to sessions. The understanding they generate is unique to that situation. In narrative therapy, the tendency is to focus more explicitly on how meaning is co-produced through dialogue. An understanding which is taken for granted is deconstructed to establish alternative interpretations. In both cases, the conditions and the people who constitute the therapeutic practice give life to the discourse, affect what interpretations are made as well as what is understood. Furthermore, what is understood establishes and contributes to the animation and vitality of that way of interpreting. A hermeneutics of discourse is constituted by the convergence of existential meanings and referential truths of those participating in the construction of the discourse.

What is theoretically interesting about psychotherapy is the possibility for discourse to resolve the tension of discrepant positions and through understanding potentiate engagement with life. Psychotherapy, as a hermeneutics of discourse, is a cultural exchange, a merging of discourses, discourses which both reflect knowledge and experience as well as organize knowledge and experience, to render and constitute meaning. Therefore, no matter the technique, meaning will be limited by who the therapists and patients are, the contexts they bring to therapy, how they are situated in terms of their personal histories, values, experiences and knowledge. Therapists' and patients' unique positions in matrices of understanding give life to what the discourse means.

REFERENCES

Epston, D. & White, M. (1992). *Experience, contradiction, narrative & imagination.* Adelaide, South Australia: Dulwich Centre Publications.

Freud, S. (1955a). The psychotherapy of hysteria. In J. Strachey (Ed. and Trans.) *The standard edition of the complete psychological works of Sigmund Freud* (Vol. 2, pp. 253-305). London: Hogarth Press. (Original work published 1893-1895)

Freud, S. (1955b). Fausse Reconnaissance ('Déja Raconté') in psycho-analytic treatment. In J. Strachey (Ed. and Trans.) *The standard edition of the complete psychological works of Sigmund Freud* (Vol. 13, pp. 199-207). London: Hogarth Press. (Original work published 1914)

Freud, S. (1958a). The dynamics of transference. In J. Strachey (Ed. and Trans.) *The standard edition of the complete psychological works of Sigmund Freud* (Vol. 12, pp. 97-108). London: Hogarth Press. (Original work published 1912)

Freud, S. (1958b). On the universal tendency to debasement in the sphere of love. In J. Strachey (Ed. and Trans.) *The standard edition of the complete psychological works of Sigmund Freud* (Vol. 11, pp. 177-190). London: Hogarth Press. (Original work published 1912)

Freud, S. (1958c). Recommendations to physicians practicing psycho-analysis. In J. Strachey (Ed. and Trans.) *The standard edition of the complete psychological works of Sigmund Freud* (Vol. 12, pp. 109-120). London: Hogarth Press. (Original work published 1912)

Freud, S. (1958d). On beginning the treatment. In J. Strachey (Ed. and Trans.) *The standard edition of the complete psychological works of Sigmund Freud* (Vol. 12, pp. 121-144). London: Hogarth Press. (Original work published 1913)

Freud, S. (1958e). Remembering, repeating, and working-through. In J. Strachey (Ed. and Trans.) *The standard edition of the complete psychological works of Sigmund Freud* (Vol. 12, pp. 145-156). London: Hogarth Press. (Original work published 1914)

Freud, S. (1958f). Observations on transference-love. In J. Strachey (Ed. and Trans.) *The standard edition of the complete psychological works of Sigmund Freud* (Vol. 12, pp. 157-171). London: Hogarth Press. (Original work published 1915)

Freud, S. (1961). Remarks on the theory and practice of dream-interpretation as a whole. In J. Strachey (Ed. and Trans.) *The standard edition of the complete psychological works of Sigmund Freud* (Vol. 19, pp. 109-121). London: Hogarth Press. (Original work published 1923)

Freud, S. (1964a). Explanations, applications and orientations. In J. Strachey (Ed. and Trans.) *The standard edition of the complete psychological works of Sigmund Freud* (Vol. 22, pp. 136-157). London: Hogarth Press. (Original work published 1933)

350

Freud, S. (1964b). Analysis terminable and interminable. In J. Strachey (Ed. and Trans.) *The standard edition of the complete psychological works of Sigmund Freud* (Vol. 23, pp. 209-253). London: Hogarth Press. (Original work published 1937)

Freud, S. (1964c). Constructions in analysis. In J. Strachey (Ed. and Trans.) *The standard edition of the complete psychological works of Sigmund Freud* (Vol. 23, pp. 255-269). London: Hogarth Press. (Original work published 1937)

Freud, S. (1964d). The technique of psycho-analysis. In J. Strachey (Ed. and Trans.) *The standard edition of the complete psychological works of Sigmund Freud* (Vol. 23, pp. 172-182). London: Hogarth Press. (Original work published 1940)

Freud, S. (1966). The future prospects of psycho-analytic therapy. In J. Strachey (Ed. and Trans.) *The standard edition of the complete psychological works of Sigmund Freud* (Vol. 1, pp. 139-151). London: Hogarth Press. (Original work published 1910)

Gill, M. (1982). *Analysis of transference: Theory and technique* (Vol. 1). New York, NY: International Universities Press.

McLeod, J. (1996). The emerging narrative approach to counselling and psychotherapy. *British Journal of Guidance and Counselling, 24*, 173-184.

Ricoeur, P. (1970). *Freud and philosophy: An essay on interpretation.* (D. Savage, Trans.). New Haven: Yale University Press.

White, M. (1997). *Narratives of therapists' lives.* Adelaide, SA: Dulwich Centre Publications.

White, M. & Epston, D. (1990). *Narrative means to therapeutic ends.* New York: Norton.

A PROBLEM AIRED:

Radio Therapeutic Discourse and Modes of Subjection

Ian Hodges
University of Westminster

SUMMARY

A theory-driven analysis (cf. Foucault, 1992) of therapeutic discourse which draws upon conversational analytic principles is presented using selected excerpts from a radio phone-in counselling broadcast. It is argued that the discursive techniques identified within the broadcast accomplish a reshaping of the caller's account of their problem at the moment it is told. It is suggested that this reformulation should be conceptualised as a mode of subjection, operating upon callers' self-identity and self-expectations – that is therapeutic discourse should be understood as ethical in operation.

INTRODUCTION

In this paper I interrogate the psychotherapeutic conversation for its ethical operation (cf. Foucault, 1992) in order to move some way towards an understanding of its relation to lines of power or force. I argue that to conceptualise the therapeutic exchange as somehow external to power relations is to miss the key elements of its discursive operation, in particular the ways in which therapeutic discourse might operate as a form of subjection, that is via the constitution of "individuals" as the ethical subject of their own action.

Drawing upon conversation analysis and elements of Foucault's later work I present an analysis of key excerpts from a radio phone-in counselling broadcast[1] and show that radio counselling discourse provides "sanctioned" ways of communicating (and relating to self and others), not only through the provision of expert advice but more importantly through the (re)construction and reorganisation of the language brought by telephone callers to the radio therapeutic exchange.

In methodological terms, I propose that the site of the operation of the therapeutic process is discursive rather than psychologistic. Such an understanding enables a detailed discursive analysis of the operation of power, where "power" is replaced by "regulatory practices of the self" (cf. Miller, 1987). Thus, from a Foucauldian perspective I seek to analyse therapeutic discourse not only through the meanings it conveys, but more importantly, through an analysis of its technical effects, that is through the practical (discursive) operation of counselling techniques. It is important however, to keep in mind the very particular nature and setting of media counselling which requires great caution with respect to linking these findings to other psychotherapeutic settings.

After a brief examination of the dominant model of the operation of language in counselling practice I go on to outline a Foucauldian approach to the examination of therapeutic discourse and then present an analysis of excerpts from a radio phone-in broadcast in which callers speak to counsellors on-air. The discursive techniques identified through the analysis, I suggest, can be conceptualised as a mode of subjection and in this way counselling practices can be understood as ethical in nature.

PRACTITIONER TEXTS AND THE OPERATION OF LANGUAGE IN COUNSELLING PRACTICE

I firstly wish to consider what appears to be a prevailing model of language offered to counsellors through instructions relating to particular counselling techniques. Practitioner textbooks – some of which offer explicitly technical advice – have, in general, very little to say about the operation of language in the therapeutic process (see for example, Egan, 1990; Dryden, 1992; Nelson-Jones, 1992; Dryden and Yankura, 1992; Patterson, 1995). Dryden and Feltham's accessible (1992) *Brief Counselling* is perhaps useful here as it claims to provide – according to the subtitle – "A practical guide for beginning practitioners". At the same time, the guide concerns a model of "brief" counselling which, I suggest, relates – to some extent – to the form of counselling offered during the broadcast conversations analysed here.

Dryden and Feltham suggest that any problems with therapeutic language are the result of a lack of clarity, "when you are explaining it is advisable to avoid jargon altogether" (p. 35); or a lack of fit with the clients style or code, "when working with clients use their language", (p. 57). The model of communication implicit in Dryden and Feltham's technical advice is a familiar one, the transmission of information and ideas (Silverman and Torode, 1980, p. 3). This model belongs to what has been termed the "process school" which Fiske, (1990, p. 6) suggests originates from Shannon and Weaver's (1949) mathematical model. The major concern of these early process theorists was the improvement of the accuracy and efficiency of communication through the reduction of "noise"; successful communication (that is, the successful transmission of content) was deemed more important than the meaning of the message (Fiske, op cit, pp. 7-9).

For Dryden and Feltham therapeutic discourse is something that above all must allow a clear channel of communication, ideally matching the client's individual "style". Summarising their language concerns, they state that it is the client's uniqueness in relation to language-use that is important (p. 58). In other words, it is not the *effects* of the client's language-use with which the beginning practitioner must engage but rather the unique individual expressed *through* it.

Furthermore, when Dryden and Feltham attempt to engage with the dialogical quality of counselling, rather than attending to forms of linguistic operation, they instead segregate counselling practice from everyday conversation via the notion of a special kind of therapeutic listening which they offer as one of the distinguishing features of counselling practice, "One of the features of counselling which distinguishes it from everyday conversation is the quality of listening" (Dryden and Feltham, 1992, p. 43).

This notion of "quality of listening" serves, I suggest, to obfuscate any consideration of the discursive work involved by implicitly constructing the selective nature of this "listening" in terms of accuracy. In other words, I am arguing that by placing an emphasis on the clarity of the supposed "communication channel", Dryden and Feltham's later instructions concerning those elements of the client's account to which the practitioner should attend, or (somewhat more passively) "hear", are shorn of their ethical nature; accuracy obfuscates discursivity. Thus despite their assertion that: "We believe that there is a directive element in counselling and that it is advisable to recognise this and use it to help the client" (Dryden and Feltham, 1992, p. 35), this "directive element" is not explicitly dealt with in relation to the forms of questions practitioners are encouraged to put to their clients. I will show later that during the broadcast considered here, the counsellor's initial questions – often heard as requests for information and clarification – may have a forceful "shaping" effect on the client's account of their problem.

THE ETHICAL OPERATION OF THERAPEUTIC DISCOURSE

For Dryden and Feltham (op cit) then, language provides a potentially corruptible channel of communication and both the linguistic and ethical aspects of the counselling process are absent from these understandings. I will show that such a model of language is wholly inadequate to a proper understanding of the therapeutic process. In particular, I suggest that one key effect of therapeutic discourse is that it offers clients new ways of understanding themselves; new ways of describing their histories, their present experiences and their future goals. These descriptions – offered within therapeutic discourse as objective and factual – provide clients with the possibility of changing their idea of the person they take themselves to be.

Hacking (1995, p. 21) proposes that descriptions of certain kinds of person generate expectations from those in authority – those experts able to offer the description. Such descriptions operate within a feedback loop consisting of the constitutive elements of expert descriptions and the need for these descriptions to respond to changes in patterns of behaviour which they subsequently are unable to capture. Hacking terms this process "the looping effect of human kinds" (p. 21). This "looping effect" refers to more than the linguistic construction of reality but suggests that sense of self is intricately bound up with the production of knowledges and practices concerning it.

Using this model then, therapeutic discourse can be seen to operate on clients' existing sense of self, which will be bound up with their existing everyday practices, in part through altering expectations of conduct; thus I will show in this paper that what makes therapeutic discourse "effective" is its operation upon clients self-expectations. Fundamentally, descriptions of kinds of person open up new avenues for conduct.

In relation to the data analysis which follows we are thus concerned with the shaping effects of therapeutic techniques on the client's self-understanding. This process occurs, I suggest, primarily through the production of *truth*. From a Foucauldian perspective the forms of self found in the therapeutic conversations analysed here are produced through the technical operation of discourse:

> Our conception of the psyche, Foucault contends, has been sculpted by the techniques that we have devised to probe its secrets, to oblige it to give up hidden knowledge that will reveal to us the truth about who we are. Psychoanalysis is from a historical perspective a late addition to that enterprise, born of a long but erratic, lineage of techniques for the care of the self. (Hutton, 1988, p. 121)

Such a perspective raises questions concerning the construction of truth during the therapeutic encounter, as opposed to the mainstream "process" questions which assume that truth is transcendent (cf. Hodges, 1995). How do the techniques available within therapeutic practices enable clients to speak the truth about themselves?

ANALYSIS OF DATA

The data analysis presented incorporates the following three elements from conversation analysis which relate to two of its primary postulates: the sequential structure of conversation and the organisation of turns (Sacks et al., 1974)[2]. Firstly, I employ the concept of "adjacency pairs", in particular the operation of preference organisation (cf. Schegloff and Sacks, 1973; Pomerantz, 1986) which refers to the likelihood of a normative response to the first part of a preferred pair, for example a question and answer. Put another way, a question calls for a normative response in the form of an answer and any other response – termed a dispreferred second part – will invite a special kind of accountability within the interaction. Secondly, I use the term "formulation" to refer to utterances which in some sense represent what the previous speaker is trying to say (or at least claim to do so). Thirdly, I use the term "summation" to indicate a form of words that summarises what the previous speaker is (constituted as) trying to say.

However, in addition to the structural organisation of the talk, I am interested in its operation as discursive practice. In methodological terms this demands attending to the operation of utterances, in part through a close scrutiny of adjacency pairs. In this way the sequential organisation of the talk allows the analyst to begin to understand the effects of each utterance within the unfolding of the conversation; in other words it allows an analysis of the "traffic" of conversation which Antaki (1994, p. 121) has suggested tends to remain absent in primarily content-driven discourse analysis. Note though, that I am ultimately concerned with the discursive operation of these utterances; specifically with their action-orientation (cf. Edwards and Potter 1992). What kinds of discursive processes can be found then, within the transcript data?

RESHAPING THE CALLER'S ACCOUNT: A Mode of Subjection

I consider the *formal* aspects of the discourse in the following three excerpts, where "formal" refers primarily to the effects of the structural organisation of the talk (although there is a sense in which content and structure cannot be considered separately). In the following analyses I refer to the advisor as "A" and the caller as "C". Excerpts from the data are identified by the transcript number followed by the line numbers quoted. Line numbers given in the text for particular utterances, turns or sequences are shown in brackets.

Excerpt 1 (T3: 13-34) (see below)

This segment can be heard as blithe badinage; perhaps the advisor is attempting to put the caller at ease via the continuation of a theme – the "mother-in-law" (15, 17) – from the previous call. However, a closer inspection of this brief

```
13   C: right well my problem is erm it's a grandmother [clicks tongue] I have =
14
15   A: =not a mother-in-law
16
17   C: well I-yes it is a mother-in-law [laughs]
18                                    [
19   A:                             a grandmother-in-law
20
21   C: a grandmother-in-law
22
23   A: and a mother-in-law at the same time
24                                    [
25   C:                             and well it's yes it's whole it's the whole in-law
26   family.hhh or basically [laughs] grandmother
27
28   A: [laughs] so (0.5) not another music hall joke I hope
29                                                    [
30   C:                                          no no no (it's) really quite serious
31   actually                                          [
32                                                    [
33   A:                                          no a serious one (1) yeh
34   sorry Belinda
```

Excerpt 1 (T3: 13-34)

segment of conversation reveals something quite different. At line (15) A produces the following rejoinder to the caller's definition of her problem at (13):

15 A: =not a mother-in-law

and receives some agreement at (17), then interrupts (over-speaks) at (19) with:

19 A: a grandmother-in-law

This term is then mirrored by C at (21) indicating a full agreement. A goes on to provide a summation at (23) and again receives some agreement at (25-26). At (28) A then appears to respond to C's inhalation (26) as signalling the end of her turn, replying with:

28 A: [laughs] so (0.5) not another music hall joke I hope

and pausing for 0.5 seconds, possibly because C continues her turn. C then interrupts, resisting A's humorous frame stating her problem is "...really quite serious actually" (30-31). A then interrupts with an apology in a short utterance which appears to invite C to present her problem (33-34); that is A stops speaking and C begins to detail her problem at (36, see Excerpt 2).

The above segment, I suggest, provides an illustration of the way in which A's turns are actually helping the caller to *shape* her account, that is the precise points at which A interrupts begin – even at this early stage in the interaction – to re-form C's account of her problem; initially offered as "a grandmother" (13), moving through "mother-in-law" (15, 17), "grandmother-in-law" (19, 21), and the "whole in-law family" (25-26) where finally C returns to her original presentation of the "grandmother" (26). A's interruptions and the summation at (23), in this case, help the caller to shape up precisely who is involved in her problem.

Such shaping of the client's account, while obscured by "process" research, has, in fact, always been incorporated into psychoanalytical (technical) theory via Freud's concern with narrative deconstruction. As Maranhão states:

> ...in the psychoanalytic situation preference should be given to those associations that break the flow of the plot spreading the narrative sideways. This usually makes it easier for the therapist to wedge his [sic] interventions in the patient's narrative, retelling it in the psychoanalytic narrative. (1986, pp. 28-29)

For us however, what is important here is not only that the counsellor is (re)constructing the caller's narrative but that in such a brief, time constrained interaction the counsellor is able to very quickly shape the caller's narrative or story at the moment she is telling it.

I now wish to move on to consider the way in which A's turns begin to resemble interpretations. Silverman and Torode usefully – for our purposes – define interpretation as the imposition of neutrality on language:

> In our usage, "interpretation" refers to the practice of treating language as the one "appearance" of an extra-linguistic "reality" pre-supposed by the interpretation. The practice is itself not what it appears to be: It does not do what it says. For it is impossible to formulate an extra-linguistic reality, e.g. "nature", "society", or "grammar" except in language. Thus in pretending to uphold a non-linguistic and so neutral reality the interpretation in practice imposes its own language upon that of the language which it interprets. (1980, p. 7)

I will now explore some of the ways the counsellor achieves this.

Excerpt 2 (T3: 36-74)

36 C: hhh erm [laughs].hh the: I (was) I've been married erm five years to this to the
37 son and erm basically he always got rewarded for his bad behaviour to keep the
38 peace and not to let the child see and all the rest of it .hh he's never accepted the
39 consequences of his actions he's .hh one of these people who's always sat in the
40 chair and criticised an' .hh never did anything with liter- without you standing with
41 a rod over him .hh now erm
42
43 A: sorry who is this Belin-
44   [
45 C: my husband sorry husband=
46
47 A: =he didn't do anything if you didn't (0.5) press him
48
49 C: well I mean he's he's literally he he just is like a spoilt everything is a tantrum
50 .hh erm he would use
51   [
52 A: I see he he the way he exercises power in a marriage is by blowing up
53
54 C: yeh and well and and threatening to wake the child if you don't give him sex and
55   [
56 A: right
57
58 C: blah blah blah and al-all literally totally to the end till it got to the point where erm
59 I had to actually it was getting really violent and I had to actually .hh erm get help to
60 get him away from me
61
62 A: so he actually then became violent towards you
63   [
64 C: Oh: yeh (I   )
65   [
66 A: so it escalated from tantrums and
67 blackmail to to violence
68   [
69 C: well it would have got violent before if I'd never given in
70
71 A: and you are still with this man
72   [
73 C: I used to give in .hhh oh no no I actually had to make myself homeless I've
74 now if it hadn't 've been without friends I would have literally gone (   )

Belinda begins to present her problem at (36) and seems to provide an orientation to a narrative, focused on a description of her husband's conduct who is presented through his relation to the mother-in-law (15, 17) as "...the son" (37). A then interrupts the turn at (43):

> 43 A: Sorry who is this Belin-

and is, in turn, interrupted by C with mitigation (45):

> 45 C: my husband sorry husband=

A's utterance at (43) I suggest is, in part, operating as an instruction, the caller is being shown the correct way to present her case. Thus, in addition to shaping-up C's account, A, by indicating a missing element in the part-narrative (36-41), also indicates the correct way of presenting a problem; in turn available to the over-hearing audience (I consider the audience in more detail elsewhere, Hodges, 1998). We see at (45) that C shows deference to the special, preferred kind of design required by the therapeutic. Then, at (47) A provides a formulation while at the same time inviting agreement from C:

> 47 A: =he didn't do anything if you didn't (0.5) press him

At (49-50) C fails to provide agreement, offering a dispreferred response and introduces a summation regarding her husband's conduct along similar lines to the previous description at (36-41) and A once again interrupts with a second formulation (52):

> 52 A: I see he he the way he exercises power in a marriage is by blowing up

Here A, in addition to inviting agreement, shapes up C's account through the provision of entirely novel words.

The key point here is that during this excerpt A is providing C with a model of the correct way to speak to him. Moreover, concerning the *content* of A's formulation, the exchange of "blowing up" for "tantrum" at (52) appears to remove the implicit notion of childishness offered at (49-50) perhaps making it more aligned with the conduct of a married adult. At the same time however, something entirely novel is introduced – the notion of "the exercise of power" (52). These words have so far not been provided by the caller and, I suggest, begin to turn the formulation into an interpretation. In fact, A's turn at (52) is more than a summation in two respects; (first) it utilises a combination of the use of new words with, (second) the deployment of metaphor which replaces C's deployment of simile at (49-50).

It has been suggested that a metaphor is rhetorically more powerful than a simile (Antaki, 1994, p. 104). I suggest that within this setting the deployment of metaphor lays greater claims to facticity. Furthermore, the notions of summation and formulation seem inadequate to describe the operation of A's utterance (52). Thus, I argue that we must consider this as more than a summary of the immediately previous turn (49-50) in that it shifts the form of vocabulary while at the same time indicating this as the *preferred* form.

At (54) C provides some agreement and indicates that the formulation at (52) seems to have shifted the account of the husband from a passive, almost childlike description to a description of manipulation followed through in the subsequent turn by C:

```
54   C: yeh and well and and threatening to wake the child if you don't give him sex and
55             [
56   A:        right
57
58   C: blah blah blah and al-all literally totally to the end till it got to the point where erm
```

Although C already alluded to this manipulation at (36-38), A's arrangement of words at (47) and (52) in addition to providing the preferred words to say it, introduces a new grammar in a double sense. Firstly, it provides a "standard" rather than colloquial form. And secondly, A's language condenses C's relatively lengthy explanation of the problem into a "singular" utterance. Compare A's version (52) with C's version at (36-41):

```
36   C: hhh erm [laughs].hh the: I (was) I've been married erm five years to this to the
37   son and erm basically he always got rewarded for his bad behaviour to keep the
38   peace and not to let the child  see and all the rest of it .hh he's never accepted the
39   consequences of his actions he's .hh one of these people who's always sat in the
40   chair and criticised an' .hh never did anything with liter- without you standing with
41   a rod over him .hh now erm
```

At (60) A provides a third formulation which once again appears to condense C's presentation of more "facts" in quasi-narrative form (54-60) into a singular utterance, again inviting agreement:

```
62 A: so he actually then became violent towards you
```

Again, A additionally provides C (and the overhearing audience) with a model for how to say the problem. C appears to offer an agreement at (64) and is interrupted by A with a fourth formulation (66-67):

```
66-67 A: so it escalated from tantrums and blackmail to to violence
```

C then responds with partial agreement and more factual information (69).

At this point we can see that C's account is gradually becoming more aligned with A's questions and formulations. At (69) C provides an interrupting response with a single "theme" in a form similar to A's four previous formulations, this time *awaiting* A's reply which does not take the form of an interruption – as with most of A's other turns:

> 69 C: well it would have got violent before if I'd never given in

compared with:

> 47 A: =he didn't do anything if you didn't (0.5) press him

> 52 A: I see he he the way he exercises power in a marriage is by blowing up

> 62 A: so he actually then became violent towards you

> 66-67 A: so it escalated from tantrums and blackmail to to violence

At (73) C begins her turn while A is still speaking, then interrupts herself to respond to the question. We see here – as with the entire excerpt – the way C's account is delivered in relation to A's questions and formulations, so that her responses are becoming more and more aligned in their organisation.

Excerpt 3 (T3: 73-98)

```
73    C:  I used to give in .hhh oh no no I actually had to make myself homeless I've
74    now if it hadn't 've been without friends I would have literally gone (     )
75                                                    [
76    A:                                         so y- you you ran away
77    or you escaped
78          [
79    C:    I literally yeh I (did)
80                        [
81    A:              with your child
82
83    C: with my child (      )
84                  [
85    A:          who is how old
86
87    C: she's three and a half I literally ran away friends were wonderful .hh erm while he
88                      [
89    A:            right
90
```

```
91  C: was at work [laughs] they they lent me a lorry and I got most of my stuff out like
92  and I they  put me up an'
93
94  A: a sort of Thelma and Louise with a difference
95                                              [
96  C:                                          it was wond yeh and I'm now on income support
97  erm housing benefit I've found myself a lovely place (.) wonderful erm but the
98  problem is the grandmother now now I have never
```

A interrupts once more at (76) with a fifth formulation; again providing the preferred words with which to say the problem and continues to shape-up the account through the use of a question/answer adjacency pair (76-79):

```
76  A:                                          so y-you you ran away
77  or you escaped
78          [
79  C:      I literally yeh I (did)
```

That is, if C disagrees with the formulation within A's question at (76) she must produce mitigation in the form of an exonerative account (often marked with a pause or a palliative, see Antaki, 1994, pp. 79-80). At (81) A interrupts appearing to continue his formulation at (76) with "with your child" which is mirrored at (83) by C with "with my child". In the remainder of this excerpt A shapes-up C's account with an interrupting question at (85):

```
83  C: with my child  (      )
84                     [
85  A:      who is how old
```

A offers a formulation at (94) which draws upon a popular film current at the time of the broadcast:

```
94  A: a sort of Thelma and Louise with a difference
```

which gains some form of agreement from C at (96-98):

```
96  C:                                          it was wond- yeh and I'm now on income support
97  erm housing benefit I've found myself a lovely place (.) wonderful erm but the
98  problem is the grandmother now now I have never
```

Within this context then, the deployment of formulations in the form of a question invites the preferred response of agreement where a dispreferred second part will more than likely be produced in relation to the original formulation (in the first part of the pair). The key point here is that in terms of discursive practice A's formulations (and interpretations) exert a powerful force on the caller's discourse which we might understand in relation to subjectification. In other words, the shaping of C's turns by A might be described as a mode of subjection.

The above excerpts then, provide key illustrations of the way in which the advisor shapes the form (and to some extent the content, I consider this in more detail elsewhere, Hodges, 1998) of the caller's account of her problem. Far from providing straightforward clarification of the details of C's account, A provides both organisational models for how to say the problem and the preferred words to say it. Thus, the "therapeutic" process of the transformation of the account begins before A offers any advice and occurs through the very way C is brought to present her problem to the counsellor (and the overhearing audience).

CONCLUSION

The theory-driven analysis presented here indicates that A's discourse has a powerful shaping effect upon that of C, during the excerpts analysed C's utterances and account gradually became more aligned with A's. A provided novel words for C to express the problem, condensed C's sometimes long and complex turns into singular utterances and thus reworked the overall organisation of C's account. In addition, A – at the same time – provided models for C (and the overhearing audience) for how to execute a call. The (discursive) processes identified here should, I argue, be considered as techniques which operate in relation to the production of truth, thus the shaping-up of C's account can be understood as a forceful mode of subjection. In other words, these discursive processes entail the constitution of truth and falsity through which the caller is enjoined to recognise her troubles within the therapeutic problematisation (cf. Foucault, 1988).

These findings are somewhat at odds with the transmission model of the operation of language we met earlier (cf. Dryden and Feltham, op cit). We have seen that C's original problem is reshaped discursively rather than simply through perceptive listening. Moreover, this reshaping appears to alter the ethical relations (for example with respect to exactly who is the accountable/culpable party within this story, the "grandmother" or the "son") already present in the problem C brings to the exchange. In this sense therapeutic discourse must be considered far from disinterested or value-free.

It is important however, not to ask too much of the brief exchanges analysed here, a relatively short phone-call to a counselling broadcast may or may not

364

constitute a therapeutic/transformative event in the everyday life of the caller. However, we can see that the mode of subjection operating within this exchange opens up alternative possibilities for conduct via the provision of different understandings of oneself and one's relations to others (cf. Hacking op cit).

Finally, we may now return to our question offered earlier in the paper: how do the techniques available within therapeutic practices enable clients to speak the truth about themselves? The therapeutic mode of subjection identified here operates through discursive techniques which reshape the caller's words at the moment she utters them, enabling the caller to bear witness to her own (truth-telling) role in the production of a therapeutic account of her troubles. In this sense, the discursive techniques examined in this paper are all the more forceful because they function not simply to construct the truth about the caller's problem but to enable callers to tell the truth about *themselves* – and this is the sense in which the processes identified here can properly be termed subjection.

Notes

1. Three complete broadcasts of the LBC (London Broadcasting Corporation) "counselling hour" were recorded off-air between August 1991 and May 1992. From these broadcasts ten complete telephone exchanges were selected in order to provide: a) as broad as possible a range of problems/topics; b) a balance of gender (five women and five men); c) a range of three different advisors; d) inclusion of the two different days/times of the broadcast (as the counselling hour went out weekly on Mondays from 9.00-10.00 p.m. and Wednesdays from 12.00 – 1.00 a.m.). The exchanges were transcribed to the quality required by conversation analytic research using accepted transcription notation conventions (cf. Atkinson and Heritage, 1984).

2. However, the approach adopted here remains in opposition to the notion of structure-in-talk (cf. Boden and Zimmerman 1991).

REFERENCES

Antaki, C. (1994). *Explaining and arguing: The social organisation of accounts*. London: Sage.
Atkinson, J. M., and Heritage, J. (Eds). (1984). *Structures of social action: Studies in conversation analysis*. Cambridge: Cambridge University Press.
Boden, D., and Zimmerman, D. (Eds). (1991). *Talk and social structure*. Cambridge: Polity.
Dryden, W. (1992). *Rational-emotive counselling in action*. London: Sage.

Dryden, W., and Feltham, C. (1992). *Brief counselling: A practical guide for beginning practitioners*. Buckingham: Open University Press.Dryden, W., and Yankura, J. (1992). *Daring to be myself: A case study in rational-emotive therapy*. Milton Keynes: Open University Press.

Edwards, D., and Potter, J. (1992). *Discursive psychology*. London: Sage.

Egan, G. (1990). *The skilled helper: A systematic approach to effective helping* (4th ed.). CA: Brooks/Cole.

Fiske, J. (1990). *Introduction to communication studies* (2nd ed.). London: Routledge.

Foucault, M. (1988). On problematisation. *History of the Present, 4*, 16-17.

Foucault, M. (1992). *The use of pleasure: The history of sexuality, Volume Two*. London: Penguin.

Hacking, I. (1995). *Rewriting the soul: Multiple personality and the sciences of memory*. New Jersey: Princeton University Press.

Hodges, I. (1995). Changing your mind: Therapeutic discourse and Foucault's ethics. In I. Lubek, R. van-Hezewijk, G. Pheterson, and C. Tolman (Eds), *Trends and issues in theoretical psychology* (pp. 301-305). New York: Springer.

Hodges, I. (1998) *A problem aired: Exploring radio therapeutic discourse and ethical self-formation*. Unpublished PhD thesis. University of London, UK.

Hutton, P. H. (1988). Foucault, Freud and the technologies of the self. In L. H. Martin, H. Gutman, and P. H. Hutton (Eds), *Technologies of the self: A seminar with Michel Foucault* (pp. 121-144). London: Tavistock.

Maranhão, T. (1986). *Therapeutic discourse and Socratic dialogue: A cultural critique*. Wisconsin: University of Wisconsin Press.

Miller, P. (1987). *Domination and power*. London: Routledge & Kegan Paul

Nelson-Jones, R. (1992). *The theory and practice of counselling psychology*. London: Cassell.

Patterson, C. H. (1995). *Theories of counselling and psychotherapy*. New York: Harper Collins.

Pomerantz, A. (1986). Extreme case formulations: A way of legitimising claims. *Human Studies, 9*, 219-230.

Sacks, H., Schegloff, A. E., and Jefferson, G. (1974). A simplest systematics for the organisation of turn-taking for conversation. *Language, 50*, 696-735.

Schegloff, A. E., and Sacks, H. (1973). Opening up closings. *Semiotica, 8*, 289-327.

Silverman, D., and Torode, B. (1980). *The material word: Some theories of language and its limits*. London: Routledge.

PSYCHOLOGY IN THE TWENTY-FIRST CENTURY:
Closing the Gap between Science and the Symbol

Agnes Petocz
University of Western Sydney, Macarthur

SUMMARY

Contemporary psychology remains hampered by its failure to resolve its identity problem *vis-à-vis* its status as a science, its neglect of the human being as *animal symbolicum*, and its continued acceptance of an impassable gulf between "science" and "meaning". This gulf has become particularly prominent as a result of the impact of various postmodernist movements and their critique of the empiricist foundationalism of traditional scientific psychology. Unfortunately, however, many of these movements have succeeded in further entrenching scientific psychology's own pre-existing misconceptions both of "science" and of "meaning", misconceptions which have received scattered attention but which are now in need of more extensive scrutiny. Such scrutiny opens the way for a rigorous and systematic elucidation of the concept of "meaning" from the perspective of the logical and psychological requirements by which that concept is demonstrably constrained, thus re-locating the symbol appropriately within scientific psychology.

INTRODUCTION

As psychology moves into the twenty-first century, it remains hampered by three disturbing facts about its present state. Firstly, psychology as a discipline has still not succeeded in resolving its identity problem. No matter how old we claim psychology to be – whether we point to the relatively recent opening of Wundt's experimental laboratory, or focus on Ancient Greek speculations about mind and reality – we have to concede that psychology remains today as Kuhn (1962) characterised it, "pre-paradigmatic": fragmented and uncoordinated, with little attempt at synthesis or cross-domain generality, torn apart by theoretical and ideological schisms, and still bearing the logophobic marks of its desperate attempt to extricate itself from its parent philosophy. These internal divisions do little to help our already shaky external image, with the result that we are criticised and scorned (occasionally even offered redundancy packages) by just about every other physical and social science.

The second disturbing fact is the complete neglect by mainstream psychology of something which is central to us – symbolism (along with the related concept of "meaning"). The ancients characterised the human being as *animal politicum* (a community-living creature) and as *animal rationale* (a creature endowed with the ability to reason). Almost sixty years ago, Cassirer (1944) proposed another characterisation: *animal symbolicum*. We are symbol-producing, symbol-using, and, often, symbol-dominated beings. Symbolic activity of all kinds is central and distinctive in our behavior and in our mental life. And yet, as Bertalanffy (1981) observes, "In spite of the fact that symbolic activity is one of the most fundamental manifestations of the human mind, scientific psychology has in no way given the problem the attention it deserves" (p. 42). Certainly, there is an enormous amount of literature on this topic, but it is all outside mainstream psychology, and there is little sign of its being brought within the mainstream domain.

The third disturbing fact about psychology's present state brings the first two problems together. Many would agree that the core of psychology's ongoing identity crisis lies in the question of its scientific status. For at least the last century, psychology has been struggling to extricate itself from its philosophical roots and become a respectable science. And part of this scientific respectability, it is felt, involves ruling out of court anything which is not amenable to rigorous scientific investigation. Hence the neglect of symbolism. In the vast extra-psychological literature on meaning and the symbolic, the message is loud and clear: symbolism or meaning in all its forms is much too elusive; the complex, multifaceted nature of the symbol rules out the possibility of any coherent scientific treatment. Thus we have a continued acceptance of an impassable gulf between "science" and "meaning". I say "continued" because this distinction is by no means new, having emerged from the gradual appropriation of hermeneutics by philosophical movements, and being given a boost by Dilthey's treatment of the distinction between the *Geisteswissenschaften* and the *Naturwissenschaften*. Thus, for most of the last century psychologists accepted the formulation that "an approach which stresses *meaning* is the exact opposite of the natural science approach which stresses the study of *behavior*" (Eysenck, 1985, p. 194), and they have felt obliged to choose which side of the science/meaning gap to set up camp.

Those in the "science" camp, mainly academic experimental psychologists, committed to the rigorous empirical methods of science, typically deny or ignore the concept of meaning (and all that is encompassed within its domain - interpretation, hemeneutics, symbolism, intentionality, significance, etc.). They either locate these topics beyond psychology in other social science areas, or they relegate them to those areas of psychology (the so-called "non-experimental" areas) which are regarded as somewhat lacking in scientific respectability. Those on the opposite side of the science/meaning gap argue that, since psychology unquestionably deals with meanings, it must abandon its misguided scientism, and must embrace instead hermeneutics as the correct approach to studying human behavior. Since human action is "semantic or textual rather than abstract or causal" (Packer, 1985, p. 1086), it is hardly surprising that "the need to focus on subjective meaning, anathema to the behaviorist and problematic for any scientist, has been increasingly realised in psychology" (Valentine, 1982, p. 157)

Despite the considerable influence of the science camp, the meaning camp has lately been receiving reinforcements from a most powerful ally, one whose major target is science as a whole, and whose weapons are all to do with language and with meaning - postmodernism. The literature which has appeared in the last several decades on new directions in psychology, and in the social sciences generally, reflects the wave of postmodernist movements in the philosophy of the social sciences (social constructionism, hermeneutics, post-structuralism, ideology critique, rhetorical analysis, etc.), movements which have been described by Gergen (1991) as "traditions marginalised by the empiricist hegemony, metatheories of longstanding intellectual currency removed from common consciousness by the prevailing practices" (p. 16), and now poised to become "successor projects" to empiricist science.

What I wish to argue here is that the gulf between science and meaning, which has seriously disabled psychology in its quest to understand and explain human behavior, and which has done untold damage to psychology's identity, is actually misguided, that it is fuelled by misconceptions both of "science" and of "meaning", and that these misconceptions are held by psychologists on both sides of the divide. Thus, "science" is misunderstood and misrepresented not just by its detractors, but also by its supporters within mainstream scientific psychology. And the same can be said, *mutatis mutandis*, about "meaning" or about "symbolism". Furthermore, while the recent postmodernist reinforcements are not responsible for creating the original misconceptions, they have certainly played their part in further entrenching them, and in thus effectively widening the science/meaning gap.

CONTEMPORARY MISCONCEPTIONS OF SCIENCE AND OF MEANING

In his survey of myths of science in contemporary psychology, Bickhard (1992) points out that many psychologists appear to share with anti-scientists the belief that science is co-extensive with positivism and behaviorism, and so they operate with a number of mistaken beliefs, such as: that empiricism is equivalent to experimentalism; that experiment is the only valid way to test causal models or the only legitimate form of research; that testing a theory is a purely empirical, practical enterprise; that only what is directly observable can be allowed into scientific discourse; and that measurability is the criterion *par excellence* for scientific study. As Bickhard notes, "The damaging effects of these mythologies on the process of the science of psychology are multiple and serious. They result in an enormous waste of resources in the pursuit of fallacious notions of how to do 'good science' and in the avoidance of and ignorance of scientifically more fruitful alternatives" (1992, p. 322). Others have elaborated on, and added to, this list. For example, Greenwood (1992) has argued that scientific realism is too often equated with what is thought of as "traditional empiricism". Green (1992) has shown how psychology's continued obsession with "operationalising" variables of interest has the unfortunate result that the desperate attempt to "strip pre-theoretic social knowledge away from the experimental situation through the process of operationalization simply allows the critic to bring it back as criticism of the experimental outcome" (Green, 1992, p. 311). Greenwood (1992), Friedman (1998) and Hibberd (in press, a,b) have demonstrated that the version of logical positivist instrumentalism favoured by many "scientific" psychologists, and attacked by the postmodernist, anti-scientific movement, is actually extremely close to the Kantian-derived social constructionism to which both sides think it is antithetical, and that what it is really antithetical to is scientific empirical realism. Michell (1999) has exposed the "particularly pernicious form of Pythagoreanism" (p. xiv) which has led armies of "scientific" psychologists into the widespread, blatantly *un*scientific, practice of treating many variables of interest as if they were quantitative, without first doing the scientific job of testing the hypothesis that they are; in that respect, mainstream psychology's treatment of the concept of measurement evidences a systematic breakdown in its application of scientific method. In short, today's experimental scientific psychology is littered with examples of what Chomsky (1959), in his criticisms of Skinner, identified as a "kind of play acting at science" (p. 559).

These misconceptions leave scientific psychology vulnerable to attack from many quarters, and it is the postmodernist who has been particularly willing to move in, for it seems only a small step from the criticisms of empiricism to a wholesale rejection of science. Specifically, the critic points to the "waning of empiricist foundationalism" (Gergen, 1991, p. 13), to the failure of scientific observation to guarantee truth and indubitability, to the distortions of its "ideology of objectivity", and the sterility of the outmoded "Rhetoric of Scientific Truth" (Ibañez, 1991, p. 187). Science claims that it can *discover* truths, but it fails to acknowledge that what we really do is *create* or *construct* truths; it is a question, therefore, of "exploring our growing propensity towards making truth, and our decreasing obligation to *find* it" (Corradi-Fiumara, 1992, p. 1). Consequently, by focusing on the ideological underpinnings of the rhetorical and discursive practices of theorising itself, including scientific theorising, we are led to move away from traditional science, and embrace instead phenomenology, relativism, historicism, contextualism, constructivism, and so on. The heyday of realism has receded into the past, and science, unless it is radically to re-invent itself, must follow.

Although the misconceptions of science in contemporary psychology have received a certain amount of (albeit scattered) attention, there has not been the same kind of attention directed at possible misconceptions of the concept of "meaning" (aside from the occasional reminder that, contrary to the belief of many mainstream psychologists, hermeneutic and causal explanation need not be incompatible). Yet a similar case can be made that this notion, too, is much misunderstood and misrepresented, not only by its opponents, but also by its advocates. To begin with, both groups regard "meaning" as fundamentally intractable from a scientific point of view. Mainstream psychology has continued to neglect, or at least marginalise, the concept of meaning and all questions relating to symbolism; not only are these concepts patently not quantitative, but it is difficult to imagine how they might be "operationalised" at all. Those on the opposite side of the divide regard the symbol as, if not vehicle of the ineffable, then infinitely complex, intrinsically elusive, perpetually shifting, necessarily subjective and relativist; meaning has to do with values rather than with facts (whose ontological status is in any case highly suspect); meaning is "plurivocal" and requires a dialectical perspective; therefore, "meaning" simply cannot be adequately handled by the categories and methods of science.

However, a reconsideration both of science and of meaning suggests that there are good reasons to abandon the view that there is an impassable gulf between the two. Once a satisfactory conception of science is embraced, it becomes possible to see why symbolism and meaning lie within the domain of scientific psychology, and how a scientific investigation of these fundamental aspects of human behavior might fruitfully proceed.

TOWARD A SATISFACTORY CONCEPTION OF SCIENCE

To begin with, even the briefest survey of the history and philosophy of science reveals facts about science which give the lie to some of psychology's misconceptions. A broader, historically more accurate and enlightened, picture reveals the fundamental basis of science to be the careful and systematic search for knowledge. Amongst its aims are to discover, describe, understand, explain, and predict, although obviously not all of these on every occasion. Of course, it may be used for all kinds of other human purpose, such as control, manipulation, and distortion, but the account of science which I am concerned to present here is not a sociological one, but a logical/epistemological one (see e.g. Friedman, 1998, for an excellent discussion of the differences between these two). Science, then, treats empirical investigation (i.e. observation – for by "empirical" is meant "available to the senses" and hence it is not co-extensive with experimentation) as typically the best available method, but it acknowledges that the senses are fallible and that none of its discoveries is indubitable. Indeed, the recognised fallibility of the senses is what underlies science's concern with publicly accessible methods of observation and potential replication. But, as Crombie (1994) points out in his recent three-volume work *Styles of Scientific Thinking in the European Tradition*, experimentation is not the only valid form of investigation: in the history of science and the scientific method, the experimental strategy sits alongside five other styles of scientific thinking: postulation, hypothetical modelling, taxonomy, probabilistic and statistical analysis, and historical derivation. Hence, science does not regard experimentation as co-extensive with research. Further, the testing of theories is not a purely empirical, practical enterprise; it is a mixture of theory and practice, of logical and empirical scrutiny, the former involving such processes as clarification, establishing coherence, and identifying implications and assumptions, the latter involving such processes as identifying existing support or making new observations. Above all, these processes must all be open to scrutiny by others. As Cohen and Nagel (1934) put it:

> In virtue of its method, the enterprise of science is a self-corrective process. It appeals to no special revelation or authority whose deliverances are indubitable and final. It claims no infallibility, but relies upon the methods of developing and testing hypotheses for assured conclusions. The canons of inquiry are themselves discovered in the process of reflection, and may themselves become modified in the course of study. The method makes possible the noting and correction of errors by continued application of itself (Cohen and Nagel, 1934, pp. 395-6).

Since science is not a subject matter, but a method, it cannot exclude a priori any subject matter from its focus of inquiry – not even itself and the potential biases of its proponents. Nor can it privilege one kind of variable (e.g. quantitative) over another kind of variable (e.g. qualitative). In Michell's (1999) words: "There are many things in human life which may not be quantitative . . . If nonquantitative they can be investigated in terms of their own 'categories' and such investigation is no less scientific than measurement. Quantitative structure is but one (important) kind amongst many and it holds no franchise over scientific method in its entirety" (p. xiv). In sum, then, science is a method whose tools are, on the one hand logic, argument and critical analysis, and, on the other hand, systematic, careful (though admittedly fallible) observation.

So, then, if we adopt this broader, more enlightened (and, as I am claiming, more historically accurate) conception of scientific activity, how might we begin to show that the concept of meaning is not beyond its grasp - that perhaps it is one of those variables which Michell suggests may be investigated scientifically in terms of their own "categories"?

TOWARD A SCIENTIFIC INVESTIGATION OF MEANING: "Linguistic/symbolic" and "experiential" meaning

In any kind of scientific research, the investigation must begin with logical tests - with attempting to define and clarify the subject. As Lévi-Strauss (1978) pointed out, this is no easy task in the case of meaning: "There is something very curious in semantics, that the word 'meaning' is, probably, in the whole language, the word the meaning of which is the most difficult to define" (p. 12). Anyone who takes a close look at the literature which deals with meaning will discover a field which is disorganised, confusing, and riddled with disagreements. As a first step in formulating a general theory of meaning, however, it is possible to identify two kinds of meaning: "linguistic or symbolic" meaning, and "experiential" meaning.

In the case of the first category, linguistic or symbolic meaning is generally described as "referring to", "signifying", "standing for", "indicating", "substituting for" or "representing". This category is further divisible into two kinds, although the terminology used for the two groups is not consistent. On the one hand are the "conventional symbols" such as those which occur in language, mathematical and logical symbols, and even social rituals such as a handshake - all of which are, as the label indicates, decided by convention and learned by the individual in a social setting. On the other hand are the "nonconventional symbols" - those which occur in dreams, symptoms, rituals, myths, art, folklore, etc., whose meanings are not agreed on by convention, but are controversial and have been discussed and disputed for centuries. Despite very important differences between these two groups (notably the greater difficulty, in the case of nonconventional symbols, in identifying what it is that the symbol stands for), there is one significant similarity: in all cases, "meaning" is actually a three-term relation between the signifier/symbol, the signified/symbolised, and the person for whom the signifier stands for the signified. Each of these three terms is necessary for any instance of meaning. This fact, that meaning is a relation, is an important point about the logic of meaning. Any full account of meaning, therefore, will need to meet a number of logical constraints which are entailed by the ontological status of meaning as a relation. Given that it is a relation, meaning cannot be a thing, cannot be intrinsic, cannot be a property, cannot be reduced to just one of the terms, cannot be converted into a binary relation, and so on.

There are countless confusions in the literature on meaning which can be traced back to a failure to appreciate this point about meaning as a tripartite relation, and a consequent failure to meet the logical constraints which follow from it; witness, for example, the elusiveness of a "semantic theory" for mental representations, with which Fodor (1985) and others have struggled in their attempt to capture, in the information-processing representationist model of mind, the "intentionality" of mental states; or, to take another example, the collapsing of the signifier and signified, and the obliteration of the signifying subject, in much semiotic and hermeneutic theory. Perhaps the most damaging confusion has been the relativisation of the concept of meaning itself. The fact that, in the meaning relation, each term is related to the other, does not imply that there is anything relative about the existence either of the entities so related, or of the meaning relation itself. Signification is a relation into which pre-existing entities enter, and the fact that x means y to person p (within such-and-such an environment) – this fact is not itself relative - it is a fact as objective as any other. Hence, there is nothing inherently mysterious or metaphysical about relations. We have spatial relations, temporal relations, causal relations. Meanings belong to the category of relations, and relations are facts, states of affairs located in the spatio-temporal realm of real events. Furthermore, the most important logical constraint of all, particularly from the psychologist's point of view, is that meaning is that particular kind of relation which requires as one of its terms a cognising organism.

It is this last point which brings the field of meaning inextricably into the subject matter of psychology: put in a slightly different way, it is a point of logic about symbolism that every theory of the symbol must be a psychological theory, because a person (a cognising organism) is a necessary part of the three-term relation. From this logical point, a number of psychological requirements follow, requirements which any general theory of meaning and symbolism would be expected to meet. Thus, a complete psychological theory of symbolism would be required to explain: (i) the ontogenesis of symbols – how and why they occur; (ii) the selection of the symbolised – why certain meanings arise instead of others; (iii) the differences between individual symbolism and universal symbolism, and how these two may nevertheless be related; (iv) variations in the *tertium comparationis* (what connects the symbol with the symbolised, why this varies from one symbol to another, why it changes over time, etc.); and (v) the relationship between putative conscious and unconscious elements in symbolism. In sum, it would be the task of psychology, of scientific psychology, to systematically meet these requirements in any discussion of meaning, or in any theory of symbolism. Of course, the above account is perforce sketchy and incomplete, for there is not room here to develop these arguments in the detail required. I have done so elsewhere (Petocz, 1999), suggesting that one of the most promising psychological frameworks for demonstrating the illusory nature of the gap between science and meaning is psychoanalytic theory. The point I wish to make here is that, when these lines of argument are pursued, it soon becomes clear that the question of meaning is a perfectly respectable, scientifically amenable one, even though it might sometimes, especially in the case of nonconventional symbolism, be an extremely difficult one.

But this analysis has considered only the first category of meaning – what I have labelled the "linguistic/symbolic" kind. While some may be prepared to concede that scientific psychology can handle this first kind, there appears to be greater consensus that in psychology a second kind of meaning – "experiential" or "existential" meaning, sometimes identified as "personal significance", captured partly in the existentialist literature by the term *Erlebnis* – is scientifically intractable. Once again, however, closer scrutiny of the literature reveals otherwise, for there are many examples suggesting that the traditional treatment of this kind of meaning involves unnecessary and misleading mystification – that "experiential meaning" can be clarified, and, in a sense, demystified. This demystification involves showing that, while there is still, loosely speaking, the three terms: person, event, and what that event "means" to that person, nevertheless, what is at the heart of experiential meaning (for example, the "meaning" of my mother's recent death) is the set of a person's beliefs, feelings, etc. about a particular event or experience, together with his or her motivational states. Now these, of course, are good old-fashioned psychological states (viz. the belief-desire model), and they are perfectly acceptable to scientific psychologists, unless the latter are of the radical behaviorist kind, which hardly anyone is these days, or eliminative materialists (in which case they will eventually, if successful, rob themselves of meaningful discourse, and be silenced forever). Nobody would want to suggest that studying ordinary psychological states like beliefs, desires and emotions is easy, but the point is that very few scientific psychologists exclude them from their field of inquiry. Thus, it is simply not true to claim that experiential meaning is unanalysable by science. Rather, if we wish to continue to use the term "meaning" here, we should recognise that it is no more special or mysterious than the linguistic/symbolic kind, being, rather, a blanket term to cover a combination of straightforward, comprehensible, standard psychological factors, and drawing, to some extent, on the logical and psychological aspects which

376

constrain the linguistic/symbolic meaning relationship. This is not to suggest that the investigation of experiential meaning is not an extremely difficult and complex enterprise – it is only to emphasise that it does not involve any special, mysterious, non-natural processes outside of those covered by the ordinary categories of psychological science.

CONCLUSIONS

To return to the three disturbing facts about psychology's present state with which I began - the failure to resolve its identity problems, the complete neglect in mainstream psychology of the topic of symbolism, and the continued acceptance of a gulf between science and meaning – I conclude with the following. To deny the existence of phenomena which manifestly do exist, or to acknowledge them but put them into the "too hard" basket, is to retreat from science. In this respect, therefore, mainstream scientific psychology is retreating from science, just as it has retreated from science in a number of additional ways. The first step for mainstream psychology, if it is to make proper use of science in the investigation of human behavior, is to shake off its misconceptions about science. This would lead inevitably to exposing psychology's equally debilitating misconceptions about "meaning". Relations are real, and meanings are a special kind of relation, in which one of the terms is a cognising organism, a person. Thus, the concept of meaning is part of the fabric of the human world and, as such, a legitimate subject for scientific inquiry. An investigation of meanings must be a psychological enterprise, one which adheres to the logical constraints upon any general theory of the symbolic, and one which addresses the psychological requirements which, as I have argued, follow from them. The time has come for mainstream psychology finally to lay to rest the myth of the science/meaning gap, and thus to avoid spending another century struggling in vain with pseudo-problems derived from a long-sustained pseudo-dichotomy.

REFERENCES

Bertalanffy, L. von (1981). *A systems view of man*. Colorado: Westview Press.
Bickhard, M.H. (1992). Myths of science. *Theory & Psychology, 2* (3), 321-37.
Cassirer, E. (1944). *An essay on man*. New Haven CT: Yale University Press.
Chomsky, N. (1959). A Review of B.F. Skinner's *Verbal behavior*. Reprinted in J.A. Fodor & J.J. Katz (1964). *The structure of language*. New Jersey: Prentice-Hall.

Cohen, M.R. & Nagel, E. (1934). *An introduction to logic and scientific method.* London: Routledge & Kegan Paul.

Corradi-Fiumara, G. (1992). *The symbolic function.* Oxford: Blackwell.

Crombie, A.C. (1994). *Styles of scientific thinking in the european tradition.* London: Duckworth.

Eysenck, H.J. (1985). *Decline and fall of the Freudian empire.* Middlesex: Viking.

Fodor, J.A. (1985). Fodor's guide to mental representation: the intelligent auntie's *Vade-Mecum. Mind, 90,* 76-100.

Friedman, M. (1998). On the sociology of scientific knowledge and its philosophical agenda. *Studies in the History & Philosophy of Science, 29,* (2) 239-71.

Gergen, K.J. (1991). Emerging challenges for theory and psychology. *Theory & Psychology, 1* (1), 13-35.

Green, C.D. (1992). Of immortal mythological beasts. *Theory & Psychology, 2* (3), 291-320.

Greenwood, J.D. (1992). Realism, empiricism and social constructionism. *Theory & Psychology, 2* (2), 131-51.

Hibberd, F. J. (in press, a). Gergen's social constructionism, logical positivism, and the continuity of error. Part 1: Conventionalism. *Theory & Psychology.*

Hibberd, F. J. (in press, b). Gergen's social constructionism, logical positivism, and the continuity of error. Part 2: Meaning as use. *Theory & Psychology.*

Ibañez, T. (1991). Social psychology and the rhetoric of truth. *Theory & Psychology, 1* (2), 187-201.

Kristeva, J. (1973). The system and the speaking subject. In The tell-tale sign: a survey of semiotics II. *Times Literary Supplement, 12 October,* 1249-50.

Kuhn, T.S. (1962). *The structure of scientific revolutions.* Chicago: University of Chicago Press.

Lévi-Strauss, C. (1978). *Myth and meaning.* London: Routledge & Kegan Paul.

Michell, J. (1999). *Measurement in psychology.* Cambridge: Cambridge University press.

Packer, M.J. (1985). Hermeneutic inquiry in the study of human conduct. *American Psychologist, 40,* 1081-93.

Petocz, A. (1999). *Freud, psychoanalysis and symbolism.* Cambridge: Cambridge University Press.

Valentine, E.R. (1982). *Conceptual issues in psychology.* London: George Allen & Unwin.

THE DYNAMIC UNCONSCIOUS REVISITED:

The Role of Motivation, Affect, Embodiment and Intersubjectivity in Catching Ourselves Unawares

Doris McIlwain
Macquarie University

SUMMARY

Bringing to light a strand of Freud's thought not acknowledged in contemporary debate establishes a single epistemic view of unconscious processes which blurs the current sharp distinction between a cognitive unconscious and a dynamic unconscious. The difference is one of degree (of affective and motivational influences) rather than a difference in kind. In the laboratory there is no question as to why material is processed at an unconscious level, because fleeting presentation or "masking" ensures its unconscious status. The question is what plays this role in real-life? Affective and motivational influences are implicated both in rendering material dynamically unconscious and in the means by which the mind grasps at its own activity, in how the habitual becomes open to the possible. These concerns bring to the fore the role of embodiment and intersubjectivity as means by which we become consciously aware, they are discussed within a psychoanalytic theory of mind with implications for a comprehensive theoretical and empirical psychology.

INTRODUCTION

But what part is there left to be played in our scheme by consciousness, which was once so omnipotent and hid all else from view?
(Freud, 1900/1976, p. 776)

Consciousness has been both hailed as marker of our humanity and dismissed as epiphenomenon. Therapeutic evidence claims conscious awareness as one avenue of rendering explicit previously automatic processes that may have been efficient in past circumstances, but which now have less than optimal outcomes. Unconscious processes have had a similarly troubled history, and while their existence is now accepted in the laboratory and the clinic, there is currently a lack of theoretical clarity concerning the unconscious/conscious divide. Too sharp a distinction between a cognitive unconscious and a dynamic unconscious, renders mysterious the further evidence required for material being dynamically unconscious. Or, having created two "systems", work must then be done to integrate them, (Epstein, 1994; Westen, 1992). There is a viable "epistemic" view of unconscious processes (Petocz, 1999), a strand of Freud's thought not acknowledged in contemporary debate whereby unconscious processes differ from conscious processes only as a result of their being unavailable to consciousness, which is not an ontological difference in kind. "This approach to unconscious mentality is consistent with the view of mentality (conscious or unconscious) which regards mental processes (knowing, believing, perceiving, remembering, etc.) as *relations* between a cognising subject and a state of affairs cognised" (Petocz, 1999, p. 162). The epistemic view of unconscious processes, I argue, encompasses phenomena currently attributed to both the cognitive unconscious and the dynamic unconscious.

Additional affective and motivational contingencies need to be addressed to show why (without postulating two separate systems) material might become unconscious in a dynamic sense. While this would require a philosophical reworking of the Freudian concept of repression (thankfully beyond the scope of this chapter), affects and drives are theoretically positioned in such a way that they are likely to afford us insights into the processes of material becoming conscious or unconscious. Both affects and drives are liminal between the bodily and the mental. They are physically underpinned, impel us into expressive action and towards others, and are intentional in that they point us towards the world. As such, they are of central importance to the means by which we become consciously aware. This chapter addresses how the mind grasps at its own activity, and what the consequences of this are for the system as a whole: the human subject. I consider the role that embodiment and intersubjectivity play in this process. The issues raised are discussed within a psychoanalytic theory of mind with implications for a comprehensive theoretical and empirical psychology.

Defending the Epistemic Over the Systemic Account of Unconscious Processes

Different effects arise as a result of accessing material that has been rendered unconscious for different reasons. Preconscious material is unconscious only as a result of inattention (e.g., you are not currently attending to your telephone number). There is no anxiety attendant on accessing this material. Motivational conflicts or affectively laden experiences (e.g., memories of past actions or impulses which conflict with current convictions) are candidate cases for material that is unconscious in a more dynamic sense. It is this latter sense of dynamically unconscious material that is my focus.

If we accept that not being epistemically available to awareness is a feature of any material that is unconscious, then important questions concern the different processes involved in making the material unavailable, and different effects consequent on momentary access to it. These processes concern motivational and affective contingencies which are implicated in the process of material becoming or remaining unconscious, but are additional to the ontological status of unconscious mental processes. They are contingencies that arise from our cultural experiences and socialization history. Thus a dichotomous picture of a cognitive unconscious and a dynamic unconscious gives way to concern with processes and effects differentially instantiated and to differing degrees. Particular *contents* are not automatically relegated to one system or another, their status depends on the affective charge, or motivational conflict involved. For example, when a desired but forbidden person asks for your phone number, that innocent fact may become dynamically unconscious.

The Prehistory of the "New" Cognitive Unconscious

Although an epistemic view of unconscious processes was part of Freud's thinking from the very start, he increasingly favoured a "systemic" view of the unconscious which assumes essential, intrinsic differences between conscious and unconscious mental processes. The observation of a number of peculiar characteristics (exemption from mutual contradiction, timelessness, replacement of external reality with thought reality) led Freud (1915/1984) to consider them as characteristics of a separate system. But the peculiarities of mechanism, characteristics and contents ascribed by Freud only to the system unconscious have been shown to be "on the contrary, just as familiar in conscious mentality" (Petocz, 1999, p. 155).[1]

Listing the attributes of the system unconscious leads Epstein (1994) to suggest that such a system might be able to generate dreams and psychotic aberrations, but makes little sense from an evolutionary perspective.[2] He poses the puzzle as to how a theory of the unconscious with such a critical flaw could have endured for so long. Epstein then outlines a "new unconscious, sometimes referred to as the *cognitive unconscious*" (1994, p. 710, emphasis in original). This is "a fundamentally adaptive system that automatically, effortlessly and intuitively organizes experience and directs behaviour" (p. 710). This view he contrasts with the one he ascribes to Freud:

> Unlike the thinking of Freud, who assumed that all information (other than that acquired during a preverbal period) would be conscious in the absence of repression, the new concept holds that most information processing occurs automatically and effortlessly outside of awareness because that is its natural mode of operation, a mode that is far more efficient than conscious, deliberative thinking. (1994, p. 710)

Invoking but not quoting Freud, Epstein says, "all information would be conscious bar repression" (p. 710). In contrast, I argue that one could read Freud as saying that everything would be (epistemically) unconscious were it not for the further occurrence of conscious awareness. Everything conscious has an unconscious preliminary stage ("...every mental process...exists to begin with in an unconscious stage or phase": Freud, 1916-17/1976, p. 336). What is unconscious may remain at that stage and nevertheless claim to be regarded as having the full causal role of a psychical process. Freud notes, "every psychical act begins as an unconscious one, and it may either remain so, or go on developing into consciousness, according as it meets with resistance or not" (1916-17/1976, p. 55). This underpins his famous commitment to a concept of mind wider than that of consciousness.

By attributing automatic information processing only to the new conception of the unconscious, Epstein (1994) robs Freud of that very (epistemic) conception of the unconscious that is a major part of his original writings.[3] Epstein's (1994) cognitive-experiential self-theory aims to reconceptualize the cognitive unconscious "in a way that could account for the behaviour of full-blooded, emotionally driven and conflicted people" (1994, p. 710). He distinguishes between the "mode of the experiential system which is assumed to be intimately associated with affect" and "processing in the mode of the rational system which is assumed to be relatively affect free" (p. 711). That the two modes do not entail differences in kind, is captured in the phrase "relatively affect free".

Beyond Hot Cognition: Motivation and Affect

The term cognitive unconscious is overly restrictive in so far as it seems to exclude affective and motivational influences. These processes are central to fleshing out how material might become dynamically unconscious, since this entails (among other things) that a subject is motivated not to know something.

But these processes might also be the real life reasons for the fleeting or masked experience of stimuli that the tachistoscope produces in the cognitive unconscious experimental paradigm.

One cannot get round the issue of motivation merely by talking about "hot cognition". One cannot say with Westen (1992), that wishes are mismatches between desired and cognized states of affairs, since they are desires *to get rid of* the mismatch. To focus on the discrepancy (the cognitive representation), says Baumeister (1992), is to lose the essence of motivation. We are not just "knowers" we are "wanters" (Baumeister, 1992; Maze, 1983). Affective processes and motivation are central to accounts of unconscious processes (Westen, 1998).

From a Freudian perspective, all knowing is motivated knowing; what is salient, what is taken for granted depends not merely on our cognitive mental apparel, it hinges on motives, urges, affects and drives. Memories are repressed not because of the events they concern, but because of the unacceptability of the impulses expressed in those events (Wollheim, 1971). That material can become in some sense dynamically unconscious is central to psychoanalysis. But not all evidence supporting the causal effects of mental events of which we know nothing supports a *motivated* forgetting, or forgetting due to anxiety. Concern with material that is dynamically unconscious broadens the scope of inquiry to include reasons why material has become epistemically unavailable. These issues do not hinge on the epistemic relations alone. Westen (1998) notes that cognitive scientists may be wary of extending the concept of unconscious processes to affect and motivation, may baulk at the concept of defense which entails exploring whether "affective considerations can bias the way thought is assembled outside of awareness" (p. 336). Evidence already supports more than a completely pared back cognitive notion of unconscious processes. We need a framework to understand what forms of unconscious processes experimental evidence supports, before we can point to research gaps that implicating affective and motivational processes might entail.

Beyond the Simple and Irrational: Unconscious Complexity, Feelings and Acquired Constructs

Experimental support for the existence of unconscious processing has been reviewed elsewhere (Epstein, 1994; Westen, 1998). Support is not restricted to cognitive effects such as priming, masking and implicit memory. Affective and motivational themes are increasingly present in experimental work on unconscious processes. There is evidence for unconscious influences on our feelings and attitudes towards others (Lewicki, 1985). Subliminal exposure to ghastly pictures led subjects to rate another's personality portrait more negatively. This has implications for stereotyping in that it is based on affective conditioning that is unconscious and automatic and therefore highly resistant to change. While Woody and Phillips (1995) suggest that the dynamic unconscious must not be confused with "the relatively simple and low-level processing characteristic of the cognitive unconscious" (p. 127), Bargh (1997) contends all is not simple and irrational just because it is unconscious. Rather he contends that "the history of a person's learning in a given situation in embodied in habitual and automatic motives" (cited in Westen, 1998, p. 343). Unique personal history is implicated since acquired constructs can function in a highly automatic way. Less attention is required to process self-relevant information than information irrelevant to the self, suggesting such chronically accessible constructs have some qualities of automatic cognitive processes – they are unintentional, efficient, lacking in control and lacking in awareness (Bargh, 1992). There is evidence of complexity; effects generalize to associatively connected ideas. Susan Andersen (1992) demonstrated that subliminal activation spreads to related thoughts with measurable consequences for perception and judgement. Westen (1998, p. 339) notes that the meta-analysis of over one hundred studies supports the existence of subliminal psychodynamic activation effects. Subliminal messages addressing material likely to evoke inner conflict or defensive reactions have more effect than neutral messages on subsequent information processing.

Experimental paradigms addressing unconscious processes use the most fleeting of stimuli to tease apart the subjective threshold of detection from the objective. Like the clinical use of free association they show that just because you think you are guessing, doesn't mean you are. One intriguing possibility is that repression in ordinary life may mimic the laboratory: affective or motivational processes may render certain cognitions so fleeting as to preclude conscious cognitive awareness. Exploring the different causal profiles for experience on which we can report, and for embodied experience upon which we may act, may not merely mean bringing affect and motivation into the laboratory. We may also wish to explore ecological versions of the laboratory parameters of transience and masking.

Advantages of this Framework

Putting dynamically unconscious phenomena in this framework renders them more plausible ontologically and empirically than in the systemic account of unconscious processes. Further, this framework is in conformity with evidence in according unconscious processes causal efficacy. It still allows a case to be made for repression and defense, separate from the issue of the ontological status of unconscious material.

There is also much to lose in abandoning any notion of the causal efficacy of unconscious processes in a uniquely hermeneutical treatment of the concept such as that promoted by Woody and Phillips (1995). They assert, "the psychodynamic unconscious is an artefact of the processes of interpretation and self-interpretation whereby human beings knit their experiences together into networks of meaning" (p. 127). They suggest that "the dynamics of meaning-relations revealed in psychotherapy must not be confused with … the causal relations to be sought in neurophysiology" (p. 127). While such networks of meaning are of undoubted significance, meanings and causes are indivisible features of Freud's whole endeavour: namely that causal, bodily processes are involved in the production of meanings. The relation of the signifier to the signified is a hermeneutic consideration. Psychoanalysis concerns more than this in so far as it addresses motivated meanings: signifier, signified and motivated knowing subject. Some oppose an identity theory of mind without realizing how much hinges on it. An identity thesis suggests that the question is not how the gap between body and mind is overcome, but what are the consequences of recognizing that there is no gap. That there is no gap is central to any psychosomatic nuance to understanding illness, and to any theory that allows conversion symptoms, that is the bodily expression of psychic conflicts. How can we recognize the mental in something so physical as (say) vomiting, to use Lear's (1990) example? Depending on one's theoretical commitments this bodily expression of unconscious processes may extend to the sedimented form of a symptom. Not all identity theories of mind assume that there can be psychosomatic effects and conversion symptoms (since these positions entail many more assumptions), but an identity thesis does underpin such phenomena. You cannot give up on the causal efficacy of unconscious processes if you want all this, though one's level of causal description may differ from that of neuropsychology.

Catching Ourselves Unawares: Detecting Unconscious Processes

Some of Freud's most famous clinically vital distinctions (such as remembering, repeating and working through) hinge on his supposition that information can causally influence our actions without reaching the level of conscious awareness. It is now widely accepted (even outside psychoanalysis) that introspection is not incorrigible. We sometimes act upon beliefs which escape our capacities for introspection and self report (Tversky and Kahneman, 1974). We have a capacity for property discrimination where our capacity for articulation runs out. It seems there is a motoric primacy of response in that we can act on the basis of information or stimuli that we cannot speak about. As Epstein (1994) notes, Pavlov spoke about a primary and a secondary signalling system; non-verbal conditioning and verbally mediated processes respectively, and the distinction between procedural and declarative knowledge is well known. Our conscious awareness may occur contemporarily at a level that is nonetheless inaccessible to linguistic expression (Epstein's [1994] "experiential awareness"). Some therapists suggest that those who attempt to modify people's cognitive schemas may well be leaving this level untouched.

Conscious Awareness: The Limits of Language and the Periphery of the Body

These points suggest there are drawbacks in placing too much emphasis on linguistic accessibility as the dividing line of conscious/unconscious, since this is not the only means by which we can become consciously aware. Through our bodily awareness, proprioception and kinaesthesia, we can apprehend that we are about to act upon an impulse, and only at this moment become aware that we have the impulse. It might literally be the motor program already starting to run off which makes us aware of an impulse to act (Maze, 1983). This may conflict with other urges or moral convictions, resulting in a touch or a blow being arrested mid-air. We do not need an autocerebroscope to become consciously aware, since thoughts, drives and affects have bodily effects.

The essence of consciousness is that perceiving or remembering a state of affairs is taken as object of a second act of awareness. Nothing is added to the first moment of knowing, but something is added to us as system. Consciousness can occur via many processes, and if the usual brain links are gone, we use the periphery of our body to work out what (for instance) the other hemisphere has been visually exposed to. But we cannot assume that we do not use as an additional source of information the peripheral stimulation of our body even if brain links are there. In this non-visual way we may consciously observe our own unconscious mentality. We can reflect on a state of affairs (as it is happening, or in the past), or we can reflect on we who are the knowers (self-reflection) and tease out the relevant attributes (we were wiser then, or happier, ignorant and wild).

Intersubjectivity and the Permeable Subject

If we sometimes act upon and give bodily and facial expression to beliefs and affects of which we are not consciously aware, others may pick up on them. Others may, at times, have privileged access to our unconscious mental states. Others may, at times, perceive more clearly than we do ourselves when we are motivated by urges or influenced by facts outside of our own awareness. This is a radical form of intersubjectivity.

There is a sense in which "your" unconscious is "in you-out-there". Unconscious processes are not fully contained or housed by a subject. At the level of unconscious processes, there can be a blurring of the boundaries of self and other, something that is implicated in affective contagion and other forms of collective effervescence. It may occur as pressure placed upon another to act in ways that confirm our expectations, or fulfil earlier patterns of interaction of affective engagement. The notion of projective identification describes a vanishing point as to where one person ends and another begins. It is the limit case of intersubjectivity and identity, and is not accepted by all clinicians of a dynamic persuasion. It entails one person's attempts to manipulate another into playing a part in their fantasy (Bion, 1959, cited in Ogden, 1979, p. 365). The fantasy may involve the repetition of old relationship patterns, repetition which may be avoided if the recipient recognizes the pressure to act a part, sees what the requirements for doing that would be, but does not fulfil the fantasy. This entails neither merely unconscious to unconscious communication in the first instance, nor merely the mirroring back of unconscious processes, but their reception and transformation. Many see this process as a powerful pathway for psychological change (Ogden, 1979).

Suggesting that unconscious to unconscious communication can occur is not to suggest that others have privileged or complete access to every aspect of our mental experience. Some contemporary philosophers of mind suggest that conscious awareness is accompanied by phenomenal experience; a non-discursive consciousness, that is inevitably private, available to no one but oneself. From this perspective these quale, the "what it is like to" experience (say) the juiciness of a particular peach in a unique state of thirst for you on just such a morning, are not able to be shared. This plausible position forms a limit case to the scope of empathy.[4] It does not mean that the mental is private.

What Does Consciousness Add?

The acceptance of unconscious perception and information processing within the last two decades in mainstream psychological research and the demonstrated efficiency of such processes leaves us wondering why we would ever need anything else? What does consciousness add?

In his earliest writings, Freud asks, in what does consciousness consist? "But what part is there left to be played in our scheme by consciousness, which was once so omnipotent and hid all else from view?" (Freud, 1900/1976, p. 776). He wonders whether he is constrained to accept the position put forward by the philosophers of his day that consciousness is an acausal epiphenomenon. No, he

388

says, we are rescued from this embarrassing position. But rescued by what? I'm embarrassed to say, by an analogy:

> Those philosophers who have become aware that rational and highly complex thought-structures are possible without consciousness playing any part in them have found difficulty in assigning any function to consciousness; it has seemed to them that it can be no more than a superfluous reflected picture of the completed psychical process. We, on the other hand, are rescued from this embarrassment by an analogy between our Conscious system and the perceptual systems.
> (Freud, 1900/1976, p. 777)

The psychical apparatus, itself turned towards the external world, is in itself the external world in its relation to the "sense-organ of consciousness". Consciousness is likened to a sense organ that perceives psychic facts. For Freud, in the first instance the direction of attention automatically occurs with the activation of sensory pathways, directed to the incoming spread of excitation. The real control comes from conscious awareness however, where there is a more discriminating regulation of attention. In his view, consciousness enables us "to work over even what is associated with the release of unpleasure" (1900/1976, p. 778). Consciousness thus perfects the efficiency of the apparatus permitting a new process of regulation, which for Freud constitutes "the superiority of men over animals" (1900/1976, p. 778). If we act with awareness, we can weigh our options differently. We can weigh up our urges, needs and knowledge, we can balance what we want now with what the present and future contingencies are likely to be. That is no guarantee whatsoever that we will act like good citizens, just that a different process will underlie the action.

Freud's historical position thus offers satisfactory perspectives on certain features of consciousness, which, Paul Churchland (1998) has recently argued, are consciousness' defining features. It involves directable attention and does not require new sensory input, affords us some control in terms of inhibition, and reflection. This might underpin the flexible intelligent behaviour philosophers characterize as deriving from conscious awareness (Graham, 1998). For philosophy and cognitive science what matters is the ontological status of conscious processes, whether they have causal efficacy and consequences of such processes for one's metaphysical commitments in a theory of mind. The emphasis is different if one takes a more psychotherapeutic perspective on consciousness.

Consciousness Undoes Automaticity

That we can efficiently process information without awareness is well established. But the very efficiency of those automatic processes might pose a problem at another level. For thoughts, emotions and experiences of the past merely to be running off within us is not sufficient for consciousness. Melanie Greenberg (1995) suggests in her review article on Post-traumatic Stress Disorder that rumination can itself become the problem if no fresh perspective is gained. Rumination, an unbidden reliving of trauma, rather than bringing relief, may play a role in moving a person from having an acute stress reaction to Post-traumatic Stress Disorder. Intersubjectivity may not be just a mode of access to unconscious processes, but also a key mode for transformation.

Automatic processing in terms of socially acquired constructs or schemata may narrow our perception of reality over the life span, making it more selective and more culturally congruent. While the encounter with reality is likely to be influenced by what is personally and culturally salient, what is schematized does not exhaust what is perceptible. In the case of perception it is vital for an organism to be able to accept data contradicting its most centrally held beliefs. If perception is an entirely top-down process, then the perception of novelty is impossible (Griffiths, 1997, p. 95). To argue that we are selective in our perception of reality is not also to argue that therefore we construct reality. One can retain the individual uniqueness of phenomenological experience and the relativity of cultural and subcultural perspectives that come with acknowledging that when someone perceives or remembers it is always from a particular vantage point without departing from a realist ontology.

What gets laid down in memory may be schematized, and increasingly so with passage of time (as we develop personal narratives, and self-defining memories). For example, writing an autobiography in no way guarantees fresh insights or a transformed understanding of the past. Bruner (1993) likens this special form of self-recollection to a form of "legal pleading", noting that "both depend on the achievement of a convincing reality" (p. 46). Discussing autobiography, Phillips (1994) says that there is no personal history without psychoanalysis, only its concealment. He suggests we should ask of an autobiography, "who is its implied, ideal reader and what is the catastrophic reading it is trying to avert" (p. 71).

Our self-constructs may be or become less than optimal, but because the processing occurs at an unconscious level, we do not notice the selectivity they result in, and cannot change the constructs or schemata, or assess their optimality. This outcome is possible whether or not one accepts evidence for the existence of material that is rendered unconscious for reasons of psychic defense. If this latter point is accepted, different patterns of selectivity may occur depending on the specific material causing anxiety, or resisting the full acknowledgment of personal meaning and significance via various defenses. Most therapeutic interventions rely on the unhinging of habits (of thought, action or emotional relationship) whether or not they explicitly suggest that one needs to become conscious of those habits or of the environmental stimuli that maintain them, or the way they preclude possible disconfirming evidence. Narrative therapists, such as those inspired by the work of Michael White (1997) have an ear for the unusual outcome that disconfirms the main narrative. They listen for a counterplot, for alternative narratives that draw in as central, capacities disregarded by the dominant narrative (which may have become disabling). The habitual becomes open to the possible.

Available cultural discourses also influence how we position ourselves in the present and in reflection. This selectivity regarding individual memory is true also of social memory. What is recorded in archives and public records is likely to concern verbal, literate, socially visible groups. Attwood's (1989) case study of the historical disenfranchisement of an Aboriginal woman is possible only because she had such a civic presence via her letters. The past is a scarce resource. What remains is not merely indicative of what was, but indicative of what has been retained and what has been allowed to perish. History (personal or social) entails what can be said of what was from where we are now.

As conscious awareness permits us to explore the origins and optimality of unconscious constructs (categories, schemas, and scripts) for present life placement, a critical perspective plays a comparable role in the history of a science. Both render "visible" processes, concepts and assumptions that have structured exploration of the world while escaping critical theoretical appraisal. The putative systemic difference between a dynamic unconscious and a cognitive unconscious is just such an assumption that has structured contemporary debate in unhelpful ways. I argue that viewing a dynamic unconscious and a cognitive unconscious as fundamentally different kinds of unconscious process rests on an illusory ontological distinction. Recognizing this, or even entertaining it as a possibility opens up theoretical and research avenues.

Notes

1. For a convincing series of arguments showing that attributes supposedly unique to the system unconscious are "demonstrably not distinctive of unconscious processes", see Petocz (1999, pp. 154-156).

2. For a contrary argument as to the evolutionary advantageousness of such a system see Edelman (1992, p. 145

3.   Petocz (1999) gives an excellent account of the complexity of Freud's shifting and at times confused positions, and a rigorous theoretical synthesis showing the pitfalls of a systemic view of unconscious processes and the aligned structural view of repression

4.   I do not see quale as epiphenomenal, nor a threat to materialist conceptions of mind. Quale have behavioural influence in that the sweetness of the peach may determine whether I buy more from the same orchard or change my supplier. Further, they may have behavioural influence by preserving phenomenal attributes of the source of information. I may pause before acting on something seen in the evening (because I doubt the accuracy of visual information perceived under conditions of scotopic adaptation), but not before acting on auditory information gained at the same time

REFERENCES

Andersen, S. (1992). Toward a psychodynamically relevant empirical science. *Psychological Inquiry, 3*, 14-21.

Attwood, B. (1989). *The making of the Aborigines*. Sydney, NSW: Allen & Unwin.

Bargh, J. A. (1992). Does subliminality matter to social psychology? In R. F. Bornstein & T. S. Pittam (Eds), *Perception without awareness* (pp. 236-255). New York: Guilford.

Bargh, J. A. (1997). The automaticity of everyday life. In R. S. Wyver Jnr. (Ed.), *The automaticity of everyday life: Advances in social cognition, 10* (pp. 1-61). Mahwah NJ: Erlbaum.

Baumeister, R. F. (1992). Neglected aspects of self theory: Motivation, interpersonal aspects, culture, escape and existential value. *Psychological Inquiry, 3*, 21-29.

Bruner, J. (1993). The autobiographical process. In Robert Folkenflik (Ed.) *The Culture of autobiography: Constructions of self-representation* (pp. 38-56). California: Stanford University Press.

Churchland, P. M. and Churchland, P. S. (Eds) (1998). *On the contrary: Critical essays, 1987-1997*. Cambridge: MIT Press.

Edelman, G. (1992). *Bright air, brilliant fire*. New York: Basic Books.

Epstein, S. (1994). Integration of the cognitive and psychodynamic unconscious. *American Psychologist, 49*, 709-724.

Freud, S. (1900/1976). The interpretation of dreams. *Standard edition, I,* London: Hogarth.

Freud, S. (1915/1984). The unconscious. *Standard edition, XIV,* London: Hogarth.

Freud, S. (1916-17/1976). *Pelican Freud Library,* Volume 1. Harmondsworth: Penguin.

Graham, G. (1998). *Philosophy of mind: An introduction.* (2nd ed.) London: Blackwell.

Greenberg, M. A. (1995). Cognitive processing of traumas: the role of intrusive thoughts and reappraisals. *Journal of Applied Social Psychology, 25*, 1262-1296.

Griffiths, P. E. (1997). *What emotions really are*. Chicago : The University of Chicago Press.

Lear, J (1990). *Love and its place in nature: A philosophical interpretation of Freudian psychoanalysis*. New York: Farrar, Straus and Giroux.

Lewicki, P. (1985). Nonconscious biasing effects of single instances on subsequent judgements. *Journal of Personality and Social Psychology, 48*, 463-474.

Maze, J. (1983). *The meaning of behaviour*. London: Allen & Unwin.

Ogden, T. H. (1979). On projective identification. *International Journal of Psychoanalysis, 60,* 357-373.

Petocz, A. (1999). *Freud, psychoanalysis and symbolism.* Cambridge: Cambridge University Press.

Phillips, A. (1994). *On flirtation.* Cambridge MA: Harvard University Press.

Tversky, A. & Kahneman, D. (1974). Judgement under uncertainty: Heuristics and biases. *Science, 185,* 1124-1131.

Westen, D. (1992). The cognitive self and the psychoanalytic self: Can we put our selves together? *Psychological Inquiry, 3,* 1-13.

Westen, D. (1998). The scientific legacy of Sigmund Freud: Toward a psychodynamically informed psychological science. *Psychological Bulletin, 124,* 333-371.

White, M. (1997). *Narratives of therapists' lives.* Adelaide SA: Dulwich Centre Publications.

Wollheim, R. (1971). *Freud.* London: Fontana.

Woody, J.M. & Phillips, J. (1995). Freud's "Project for a scientific psychology" after 100 years: The unconscious mind in the era of cognitive neuroscience. *Philosophy, Psychiatry and Psychology, 2,* 123-134.

SYMBOLISM OF THE TOWER AS ABJECTION[1]

Inna Semetsky
Teachers College, Columbia University

SUMMARY

One of the most dramatic, horrifying and powerful images in the Tarot deck is the image of the Tower – trump # XVI – which in some decks is called The Tower of Destruction. This paper, employing the method of interpretive analytics, attempts to decipher the symbolism inscribed in the imagery of this card. What emerges as a result of interpretation is a two-fold hybrid of Kristeva's (1982) theory of abjection and the Jungian and post-Jungian archetypal psychology. The paper also, focusing on both symbolic and semiotic features of the image, explores the conditions for the construction of subjectivity within a double process of negation and identification thus implicitly addressing the therapeutic implications of this card's reading. The paper concludes, continuing the two-fold investigative approach, by expanding on the individual reading of the Tower and illustrating its meaning on the collective level as presented in a feminist tradition.

IMAGERY

The picture on "The Tower" card – one of twenty two major cards in a deck – shows two human figures apparently being thrown out of a tower struck by lightning (see Figure 1)[2]. It is a fall, but not a free fall; it is a violent ejection. The figures' mouths are gaping in horror, but the lump in their throats stops any sound from coming out. Their eyes look and see nothing. They are cast far into the deep. Will they still be alive when they reach the ground – or will their hearts be ruptured before landing? And, if they remain alive, will their minds endure? Or, rather, under the almost unbearable lightness of the fall, will their psyches break down?

394

The tower stands erect – it is only its crown that has been knocked down by the blazing flames caused by lightning. The two beings on the card have built the tower – and sealed it at the top: there is no entry or exit. They have imprisoned themselves in their own creation – the rigid, phallic, mental structure – and the only way out is through the agency of a threatening, violent breaking force that would necessarily bring along a traumatic experience.

The two figures are neither subjects nor objects. In the midst of a crisis, they are in-between two categories – pictured as literally positioned between symbolic sky and symbolic ground – they are, in fact, abjects, "beset by abjection" (Kristeva, 1982, p.1). The sky above is pierced by lightning, and the ground below is ruined by earthquake. Or there is no ground at all: some decks portray a tempestuous sea.

It may be suggested that in a futuristic deck with postmodern denotations the Tower trump will have been identified with a key word *abjection*. The imagery of the card indeed transmits, in a mode of graphic communication, the meaning of abjection described as

> one of those violent, dark revolts of being, directed against a threat that seems to emanate from an exorbitant outside or inside, ejected beyond the scope of the possible, the tolerable, the thinkable. (Kristeva,1982, p. 1)

The violent fall from the tower, the feeling of the catastrophe amidst thunder and lightning, brings two figures to the "border of [the] condition as a living being" (Kristeva,1982, p. 3) barely withstanding the effect of a rapid and shocking change.

ABJECTION ACCORDING TO KRISTEVA

Kristeva, describing abjection, uses the infinitive "to fall", *cadere* in French, hence cadaver, the corpse, finding vocabulary that appears curiously – perhaps synchronistically – close to a possible interpretation of the meaning of this card's imagery:

> [M]y body extricates itself, as being alive, from that border. Such wastes drop so that I might live, until, from loss to loss, nothing remains in me and my entire body falls beyond the limit – *cadere*, cadaver. If dung signifies the other side of the border, the place where I am not and which permits me to be, the corpse, the most sickening of wastes, is a border that has encroached upon everything. ... "I" is expelled. (Kristeva, 1982, pp. 3-4).

The falling bodies approach the limits of human endurance; they seem in their suffering to exist between life and death because in this fall "death [is] infecting life" (Kristeva, 1982, p. 4). The symbolic fall is infinite and feels like eternity -- signified by two figures caught up in a state of perpetual suspension, indeed within "the utmost of abjection" (Kristeva, 1982, p.4).

The mood of this card ("is mood a language?", asks Kristeva [1997, p.192]) is permeated with uncertainty and fear, confirming the claim that "abjection is above all ambiguity" (Kristeva, 1982, p.9). The sense of "perpetual danger" (1982, p.9) and an unconscious anticipation of a shock, when 'I' – "the twisted braid of affects and thoughts" (1982, p.1) – will eventually have to hit the ground, makes the existence of the still alive "I" unbearable. This part of self that is "I" is so desperate and feels overwhelmed to such an extent that it becomes greater than the self: an autonomous heavy body "which is dissociated, shattered into painful territories, parts larger than the whole" (Kristeva, 1998, p.152).

In the psychoanalytic tradition, abjection is linked to the image of the splitting mother, thus to one's "desire for separation, for becoming autonomous and also the feeling of an impossibility of doing so" (Kristeva in Baruch & Serrano, 1980/1988, p. 136). The mother-image, however, is symbolic and in no way limited to the actual mother in the mother-infant relationship. The notion of splitting accords, for example, with Jung's defining, in a framework of analytical psychology, complex as a split-off fragment of the psyche and emphasizing the psychological transition as occuring in mid-life; significantly, Jung is considered as a forerunner of of contemporary field of adult development. In this respect, the attempt to release the hold of the symbolic umbilical cord, as if guided by the notion of rejection embedded in bodily structure, by means of the violent breaking away from the womb, may take place at any time along the developmental continuum. But this body is the only and immediate life-world "I" knows, thus by the fact of falling down, by subjectivity becoming in the process "the jettisoned object ..., it is no longer I who expel, [but] 'I' is expelled." (Kristeva, 1982, pp.2-4).

The violent force, symbolized by the image of a sudden lightning, acts in and upon the unconscious, both coming from without and appearing from within. It "draws me toward the place where meaning collapses" (Kristeva, 1982, p.2). This force becomes a sign of "the breaking down of a world that has erased its borders" (1982, p. 4). The visible presence of this sign on the card, the affect expressed in the imagery, makes reading move beyond techniques employed in the traditional psychoanalysis. The reading process tends toward Jungian analytical, or depth, psychology (cf. Semetsky 1994, 1998) by means of incorporating "the paradigm of the *active, interventionist therapist*" (Samuels, 1986/1994, p. 197) who is engaged in what Samuels calles a "supportive" (1986/1994, p.197) session in accordance with Jung's analytical *ethos*. Jung, elaborating on the subject of psychoanalysis, has pointed the limitations of the Freudian practice and indicated that Freud was blind towards the ambiguous and paradoxical contents inscribed in the unconscious as well as to its collective character; according to Jung, Freud "did not know that everything which arises out of the unconscious has ... an inside and outside." (Jung 1963, p. 153).

ARCHETYPAL SYMBOLISM

In a framework of Jungian psychology abjection may be considered linking to the archetypal *temenos* (cf. Samuels et al., 1986/1996) in one's psychic structure. The original meaning of *temenos* in Greek is a sacred precinct like a temple; a synonym for it is a hermetically sealed vessel or, for that matter, the Tower. *Temenos,* as employed in Jungian analysis, has acquired psychological connotations as the psychically charged area surrounding a complex, and may be experienced sometimes through the symbolism of any closed container such as a womb or a prison.

A complex is defined as a sum total of affects derived from the archetypal core and actual experiences. The notion of a complex rejects the idea of a single identity and implies the existence of multiple selves characterized by "splinter psyches" (Jung CW 8, p. 202). Because "complexes behave like independent beings" (CW 8, p. 253), each possible self is relatively autonomous. A complex implies an assemblage of archetypal patterns of behavior that contains both personal and impersonal, or collective, aspects. The affects inscribed in the complex are derived from the ego being positioned within the contextual dynamic of conflicting interactions. Jung asserted that complexes may cluster around the archetype and acquire a common emotional, or feeling, tone. Constellation of complexes profoundly affects behavior and emotions even in the absence of any conscious awareness on behalf of the defensive ego. The complexes, however, may carry positive connotations as well as negative ones: they are the "necessary ingridients of psychic life. Provided the ego can establish a viable relationship with a complex, a richer and more variegated personality emerges" (Samuels, Shorter, and Plaut, 1986/1996, p. 34).

The complexes constellated round the archetypal core of the Tower create the content that may be described by Kristeva's notion of deject:

> The one by whom the abject exists is thus a *deject*, who places (himself), *separates* (himself), situates (himself), and therefore *strays* instead of getting his bearings, desiring, belonging or refusing. ... Instead of sounding himself as to his 'being,' he does so concerning his place: "*Where* am I?" instead of "*Who* am I?" For the space that engrosses the deject, the excluded, is never *one,* nor *homogeneous,* nor *totalizable,* but

essentially divisible, foldable and catastrophic. (Kristeva,1982, p. 8)

The archetypal *temenos* – or the psychically charged area – is symbolized by the imagery of bright sparks surrounding the Tower on the picture. Thunder and lightning saturate the air with energy, creating the aforementioned catastrophic space, and the effect of pure difference between having been sealed in a closed container and suddenly breaking out of it, is experienced by the figures-dejects as an electric, even more, psychic shock acting upon a precarious and already fragmented psyche and making it especially fragile. Because the vessel – the womb, the prison, the Tower – is sealed hermetically, the force looking for its way out will be ultimately felt as acting from within in an erratic and unpredictable manner.

The deject, situated in space specified as divisible, foldable and catastrophic, becomes

> a divisor of territories, languages, works, [it] never stops demarcating the universe whose fluid confines – for they are constituted of a non-object, the abject – constantly question his solidity and impel him to start afresh. The deject ... has a sense of danger, of the loss that the pseudo-object attracting him represents for him. (Kristeva, 1982, p. 8)

A sense of danger grows into the horror experienced by deject-abject whose psyche is threatened by the lightning aiming at the self-erected structure. Furthermore, the structural stability is endangered by the dynamic force of the thunderbolt that is just about to hit. Hence the ego undergoes extreme humiliation and the loss of any defenses; it is driven to

> a downfall that carries [it] along into the invisible and unnamable... Never is the ambivalence of drive more fearsome than in this beginning of otherness (Kristeva 1997: 188)

– that may lead the ego in its vulnerability to the borderline of a psychotic breakdown.

In other words, the complex may become dissociated from the ego, while the latter unconsciously identifies with the complex. Jung asserted that complexes indicate fragmented personality and act as autonomous beings; in Kristeva's terms, ego becomes non-object, "no longer seen in [its] own right but forfeited, abject" (Kristeva, 1982, p. 5). Worse, the figures on the picture are unable to see the flash of lightning; the ego in its ultimate denial gave up, turned against itself, re-jected itself. But the lightning strikes nonetheless even if "I", the subject of the reading, is as yet unaware of that, because "the impossible constitutes its very being"

(Kristeva, 1982, p. 5) or, in Jung's words, "an intense inner contradiction" (CW 6, p.390), and "a brutish suffering that 'I' puts up with." (Kristeva, 1982, p.2).

The feminist philosopher of education Nel Noddings, addressing the problem of suffering in an abusive situation, has pointed out that a

> large part of human suffering derives from separation and helplessness and the fear of those states. ... When we set aside propositions about God, sin and science, we find at the bottom of each suffering event pain that cries for relief, a threat of separation that triggers an increased need for connection, and a dread of helplessness that begs for empowerment. (Noddings, 1989, pp. 128-129)

The unconscious, projected into the artifact of the image, represents such a cry for help and signifies its timely appearance in the reading.

The Tower image is an embodiment of ambivalence: hidden pain that wants to be relieved, attempts to connect because of the approaching separation, the reality of powerlessness and the appearance of the omnipotence, or "depression ... concealed by a feverish activity" (Kristeva, 1987, p. 387). Jung too used the notion of contradiction with regard to the meaning of the tower which he, at a symbolic level, identified with the Tower of Babel (Jung 1963), that is, symbol of false omnipotence and mistaken certainty, a priori condemned to destruction during the most powerful and confusing instance of the contradiction (see Figure 2) – signifying the aforementioned division of "territories, languages, works."

Kristeva (1998), speaking of contradiction, has stressed that its very conditions were

> always to be understood as heterogeneity... when the loss of unity, the anchor of the process cuts in...[and] the subject in process discovers itself as separated. (Kristeva, 1998, p. 149).

And sure enough, sometimes the Tower trump appears in a reading session as a signifier of a sudden end of the status quo in a relationship, especially a marital or spousal relationship based on "the fragile equilibrium" (Kristeva, 1998, p.152) of compromise, submission or codependency, fatal attraction or, worse, the partners' unconscious playing of sado-masochistic roles.

Quite significant is the fact that the trump #XV, immediately preceding "The Tower" in a deck and called "The Devil," is traditionally interpreted in terms of bondage, sexual submissiveness or material dependency, and may indicate, very much in Nietzschean sense, the ultimate slave morality in the relationship between oppressor and oppressed, even if the interplay of forces involved in this interaction persists at the unconscious level only. It is only when a set of relations becomes totally unbearable for the psyche, infusing it with fears and phobias, then the next archetype, Tower, comes forward. Or, rather vice versa, when "The Tower" archetype is activated, the breaking down of the current psychic state becomes unavoidable. Consequently, the polyvalence of the next major card #XVII, "The Star", connotes the field of meanings which include healing, hope and inspiration, thus semiotically transmitting the message that no destruction is final. Analogously, Kristeva points to the possibility "of rebirth with and against abjection" (Kristeva, 1982, p. 31) following catharsis.

DOUBLE SIGNIFICATION

Signification, according to Kristeva, always functions as a fluctuation between stability and instability, or static quality and negation of a stasis. Symbolic lightning from above, by breaking the order of things and so negating the stasis of one's identity within the existing order, simultaneously illuminates the way to the new order and new identity, albeit through abjection, an abject becoming an ambiguous sign, a deject, "a tireless...stray" (Kristeva, 1982, p. 8).

In Jungian terms, lightning has been identified with a symbol of a sudden and totally overpowering change in one's psychic state (Nichols 1980/1990) leading to a potentially overwhelming numinous alteration in consciousness. "A flash of lightning ... is discharged like thunder", says Kristeva, as if herself peculiarly narrating the Tower picture, and

> the time of abjection is double: a time of oblivion and thunder, of veiled infinity and the moment when revelation bursts forth. (Kristeva, 1982, p.9).

During a Tarot reading the Tower card may appear as an indication of an abreaction, taking the form of catharsis, that is, a dramatic and forceful replay of the unconscious material in one's consciousness, when indeed one's "fortified castle begins to see its walls crumble" (Kristeva, 1982, p. 48). However, the enforced evacuation, breaking all defenses, frees one from being incarcerated in the symbolic tower of one's own making, whether it be psychological, ideological, cultural, or any other belief system. Any unforeseen cataclysmic event that suddenly brings people down to earth by disturbing the existing norm and order of things, simultaneously raising the level of consciousness, is expressed through the Tower.

The change in one's consciousness – via abjection – represents the movement between "negation of identity and constitution of identity" (Oliver, 1998). Negation is characterized by a temporary interruption in the periodic dynamic process, a pause – appearing, as claimed by Kristeva, in a form of a surplus of negativity which would ultimately destroy the balance of opposites. That is why "the deject is in short a *stray*. ... And the more he strays, the more he is saved" (Kristeva, 1982, p. 8), that is, constitution takes place via negation, ultimately contributing to the organization of reality at a new level that would take place in one's subjectivity.

Thus both rejection and stasis, or negation and identification, considered by Kristeva as the essential elements of subjectivity, indeed "precede Lacan's mirror stage" (Oliver 1998) – if the Lacanian mirror is taken metaphorically and not as solely predicated upon a preoedipal infant – that is, they exist in their semiotic reality prior to recognition, in a form of the iconic sign of the card. The function of the sign thus becomes to amplify (am-*pli*-fy, or unfold, where *le pli* means the fold) the unconscious content, so as to permit "recognition of the want on which any being, meaning, language or desire is founded" (Kristeva, 1982, p. 5). The amplifying function also constitutes the basis of Jungian *synthetic* method which implies that it is what *emerges* from the starting point that carries the most significance in analysis. Synthetic method thus encompasses both the present and the future and may be said to indeed amplify psychoanalysis, which was considered by Jung as reductive because of its orientation solely to the past:

> Psychological fact ... as a living phenomenon, ... is always indissolubly bound up with the continuity of the vital process, so that it is not only something evolved but also continually evolving and creative.
> (Jung, CW 6, p. 717).

SEMIOTIC *CHORA*

Kristeva emphasized "the working of imagination [in] the experience of the want" (Kristeva, 1982, p. 5), that is, the realm which is virtual, non-visible and "logically preliminary to being and object" (1982, p.5), that would find its signification in nothing but the spoken language. In a Tarot reading, however, signification appears before articulation in a semiotic, iconic and indexical mode and through the working of not imagination but imagery. Both are incorporeal, yet imagery in the Tarot assumes corporeality and visibility in the modality of the cards. Consequently, it is a signification of the higher order, or a metasignification founded upon interpretation: signs are translated into words thus assigning meaning to the image of bodies falling down.

Thus the semiotic significance of the card as an iconic sign is justified by its representing the site of the subject in process – "a strange place, ... a *chora*, a receptacle" (Kristeva, 1982, p.14) always already constituted by conflicting desires and perverse "drives, which are 'energy' charges as well as 'psychical' marks."

(Kristeva, 1984, p. 25) – a field of archetypal forces *in actu.*

The term borrowed from Plato, *chora's* original meaning is a connective link between realms of the intelligible and the sensible, implying a quality of transition or passage, a bridge – albeit invisible and in itself formless – between the two. Structure-less, *chora* can be designated solely by its function which is explicitly feminine: to engender, to provide conditions – or rather, in its (her!) relational economy, to be *the* condition, the symbolic home – for the genesis of forms.

For this reason *chora* is a site saturated by forces, itself "a moving force" (Casey, 1997, p. 324). By means of it being a space surrounding the Tower, the place where abject is to stray, *chora* indicates the polyvalence of the Tower image. This card represents a container that is sealed yet open and having "an oxymoronic structure: it is an open/enclosure." (Casey, 1997, p. 325).

Kristeva, acknowledging the dynamic and even organizing character of *chora*, "a ... totality formed by the drives and their states in a motility that is as full of movement as it is regulated" (1984, p. 25), stresses its provisional and nonexpressive quality within the limits of verbal discourse. In the Tarot, however, *chora* becomes expressive as the discursive boundaries expand to incorporate the non-verbal, translinguistic mode of expression in its "semiotic articulation" (Kristeva, 1998, p. 142). Specifically, *chora,* or space occupied by the subject in process signified by the Tower trump, functions "as a multiplicity of ex-pulsions" (1998, p. 134), an expulsion being "the mode of ... permanent aggressivity" (1998, p.144) the primary function of which is self-destruction or the death drive.

One's sealed world was initially created due to the presence of the primary, out of awareness, masochistic desire to imprison oneself in the Tower. The image of expulsion from the Tower indeed seems to be

> the logical mode of this permanent aggressivity, and the possibility of its being positioned and thus renewed. Though destructive, a "death drive", expulsion is also the mechanism of relaunching, of tension, of life (Kristeva, 1998, p. 144).

That is, its function doubles to play a creative role in one's construction of subjectivity.

The heterogeneity of meanings inscribed in the semiotic *chora* constitutes the dynamic character of the subject in process, who in fact is not a subject, but abject. During a Tarot reading, however, when the unconscious contents become narrated and interpreted, the subject, in a process of identifying with the meaning of the Tower image, is able to recognize its own shifting identity as abject. The subject – functioning in its capacity of the abjective self – becomes animated by expulsion, by abjecting the abject:

Such an identification facilitates control, on the part of the subject, a certain knowledge of the process, a certain relative arrest of its movement, all of which are the conditions for its renewal and are factors which prevent it from deteriorating into a pure void (Kristeva, 1998, p. 149).

Thus, although the reading of the card when indeed "revelation bursts forth" (Kristeva, 1982, p.9), seems in itself to be a violent act, in a sense of its shattering one's set of privileged beliefs – such a violence of expulsion, a sort of negation of negation, experienced by the subject, "rejects the effects of delay" (Kristeva, 1998, p. 153) and hence makes the subject rather than breaking it.

Ultimately, *chora* fulfills its caring function. For this reason, covertly, the Tower card sometimes appears in a reading as a sign not of a breakdown but a breakthrough, albeit in both cases necessarily indicating the abruptly terminated current psychological state.

AFFECTS AND SIGNS

Kristeva (1995), acknowledging the presence of a gap that exists between verbal expressions and her analysands' affects, points to the loss of meaning in contemporary life due to dissociation between affects and language: the words are meaningless because the soul is empty. But the unconscious contents projected in the cards' imagery indicate that the soul, or psyche, is never really empty: it is filled with signs[1] which, albeit not directly observable and existing prior to articulation, are semiotically real and indeed, according to Charles Sanders Peirce, perfuse the whole universe. The pragmatic function of a Tarot reading, then, is to bring those symbols to the level of cognitive awareness thus filling the gap with significance and returning meaning to its bearer.

The affective world was considered by Kristeva as enigmatic precisely because of it not being reducible to the verbal mode of expression. All affects exist only through signs that stand for the

> psychic representations of energy displacements.... [whose] exact status ...remains, in the present state of psychoanalytic and semiological theories, very vague. No conceptual framework in the relevant sciences... has proven adequate to account for this apparently very rudimentary representation, presign and prelanguage. (Kristeva, 1997, p. 192)

As a mode of pictorial semiotics, Tarot cards (cf. Sebeok, 1994) laid out in a specific reading, enable the shift of a subject-position from the infamous abstract view from nowhere to the contextual and concrete view from the here-and-now. A layout functions in the capacity of "a modality of significance" (Kristeva, 1997, p.193) for affects, moods and thoughts, which are indeed inscriptions [or] energy disruptions... [that] become the communicable imprints of affective reality, perceptible to the reader. (Kristeva, 1997, p. 193).

Typos, as a composite of the archetype, means imprint, stamp or pattern. Irrepresentable by themselves, archetypes of the collective unconscious[2] literally become a mode of communication when acquiring content in a form of tarots while having found their expression by arousing affect and manifesting in outer behaviors above and over one's will solely. Not limited to biological drives, they are particularly recognizable when clustered around those fundamental life experiences as "birth, marriage, motherhood, death and separation" (Samuels et al, 1986/1996, p. 26) – the latter partaking on the imagery of the Tower.

SOCIAL REALITY

The symbolic Tower of Destruction may be erected not only on an individual level but also on the collective one. In the feminist interpretation (Gearhart & Rennie, 1981), this card signifies radical intervention bordering on revolution when any false consciousness is overthrown, violent social conflict and change, destruction of the old order along many levels, and liberation from having been imprisoned in the patriarchal structure during its demolition.

However, the collapse of symbolic Panopticon that was founded on the meticulous organization of space, generates chaos out of the former order: the abjection in this case loses its phobic quality, becoming not the power of *horror*, but power of *terror*. It turns instead into the unleashed rage of violence against violence when the long repressed emotions, deprived of expression, explode and "spill out from their … container." (Casey, 1997, p. 323). No longer projected inward, the released violence becomes directed into the space where the abject "does not respect borders, positions, rules" (Kristeva, 1982, p. 4) and "abjection allows us to move beyond the Law of the Father." (Bogue & Cornis-Pope, 1996, p. 10). In a sense there is jouissance in a process: Kristeva points out that subjects as "victims of the abject are its fascinated victims." (1982, p. 9).

Revolt *against* may turn into revolt *for*: ambiguity leads to appropriation of the other, that "Other who precedes and possesses me, and through such possession causes me to be" (Kristeva, 1982, p.10). Jouissance? Perhaps, but one that borders on a violent passion. The joy is highly problematic indeed: it is only jouissance for as long as the power is distributed properly. The joy of destruction, if overdetermined, may contribute to erecting yet another tower, to replacing one Symbolic Order with another. The historicity is in the place and "in place": it is so inscribed in the genealogy of space[3] that any tower attracts lightning and is destined, sooner or later, to be blasted by a thunderbolt. The subject, if *not* in process, is spaced-out and, respectively, is out of place both symbolically and literally:

> the space of the subject collapses in on itself and the subject without psychic space is prey to aggressive drives and paranoid projections of the kind exhibited in misogyny, nationalism, racism and war. (Kirkby, 1998, p. 111)

To conclude, let us recall the eternal words: *He who exalts himself will be abased.* (Luke, xiv, 11). Such is the essence of this card's communicative action: those who, by whatever means, exalt themselves will be abased, and those who humble themselves will be exalted. The image does create its own pictorial text, the articulation and interpretation of which create those "other means, symbolic or imaginary" (Kristeva, 1987, p. 391) that contribute to the pragmatic, transformative and therapeutic, role of the reading.

Notes

1. This paper was first published in *Parallax* 6:2 (2000) pp. 110-122. The author and editors are grateful to publishers Taylor & Francis Ltd, PO Box 25, Abingdon, Oxfordshire, OX14 3UE (http://www.tandf.co.uk/journals) for their kind permission to reproduce the paper.

2. For Figures, see below.

REFERENCES

Bion W. (1977). *Seven servants.* New York: Jason Aronson
Bogue, R. & Cornis-Pope M. (Eds). (1996). *Violence and mediation in contemporary culture.* Albany: State University of New York Press.
Casey, Edward S. (1997). *The fate of place: A philosophical history.* Berkeley and Los Angeles: University of California Press.
Gearhart, S. & S. Rennie (1981). *A feminist Tarot.* Persephone Press.
Jung, C. G. (1953-1979). *The Collected Works.* Vol. I-XX, (Trans. R.Hull, ed. H.Read, M.Fordham., G.Adler, and Wm.McGuire). Bollingen Series XX. Princeton, NJ: Princeton University Press.
Jung, C.G. (1963). *Memories, dreams, reflections.* A. Jaffe (Ed.), New York: Pantheon Books.
Kirkby, J. (1998). Julia Kristeva: A politics of the inner life? In J. Lechte & M. Zournazi (Eds), *After the revolution: On Kristeva* (pp. 109-123). Australia: Artspace Visual Arts Center.
Kristeva, J. (1980). Interview with Julia Kristeva. In E. Baruch & L. Serrano (Eds) *Women analyze women: In France, England and the United States.* New York: New York University Press.

Kristeva J. (1982). *Powers of horror: An essay on abjection.* (L. S. Roudiez, Trans.). New York: Columbia University Press.

Kristeva, J. (1984). *Revolution in poetic language* (M. Waller, Trans.). New York: Columbia University Press.

Kristeva J. (1995). *New maladies of the soul* (R. Guberman, Trans.). New York:Columbia University Press.

Kristeva, J. (1997) Black sun. In K.Oliver (Ed.), *The portable Kristeva* (pp. 180-202). New York: Columbia University Press.

Kristeva J., (1998). The subject in process. In P. ffrench and R.-F. Lack (Eds), *The Tel Quel reader* (pp. 133-178). London and New York: Routledge.

Nichols, S. (1980/1990). *Jung and Tarot: An archetypal journey.* York Beach, Maine: Samuel Weiser, Inc.

Noddings, N. (1998). *Women and evil.* Berkeley CA: University of California Press.

Oliver, K. (1998). Tracing the signifier behind the scenes of desire: Kristeva's challenge to Lacan's analysis. In H. Silverman (Ed.) *Cultural semiosis: Tracing the signifier* (pp. 83-101). London: Routledge.

Samuels A. (1986/1994). *Jung and the post-Jungians.* London and New York: Routledge.

Samuels A., Shorter, B., and Plaut, F. (1986/1996). *A critical dictionary of Jungian analysis.* London and New York: Routledge.

Sebeok, T., (Ed.) (1994). *Encyclopedic dictionary of semiotics.* (Approaches to Semiotics; 73). Berlin, New York: Mouton de Gruyter.

Semetsky I. (1994). *Introduction of Tarot readings into clinical psychotherapy: Naturalistic inquiry,* Unpublished MA thesis, Pacific Oaks College, Pasadena, California.

Semetsky I. (1998). On the nature of Tarot. *Frontier Perspectives,* 7(1), 58-66. The Center for Frontier Sciences, Temple University, Philadelphia, PA.

Stevens, A. (1999). *Ariadne's clue: A guide to the symbols of humankind.* Princeton, NJ: Princeton University Press.

Figure 1. Illustrations from the Rider-Waite Tarot Deck, known also as the Rider Tarot and the Waite Tarot, reproduced by permission of U.S. Games Systems, Inc., Stamford, CT 06902 USA. Copyright © 1971 <<u>mailto:Copyright©1971</u>> by U.S. Games Systems, Inc. Further reproduction prohibited.

Figure 2. The Lovers' Tarot by Jane Lyle (illustrated by Oliver Burston). The pack is published by Connections (January 2000) in the UK and St. Martin's Press in the US.

INDEX